808   17⁰⁰

T3-BGL-954

CHILDREN AND YOUTH
Social Problems and Social Policy

CHILDREN AND YOUTH
Social Problems and Social Policy

Advisory Editor

ROBERT H. BREMNER

Editorial Board

Sanford N. Katz

Rachel B. Marks

William M. Schmidt

THE
JUVENILE
COURT

Introduction by

Robert M. Mennel

ARNO PRESS
A New York Times Company
New York — 1974

Reprint Edition 1974 by Arno Press Inc.

The Child, The Family and The Court was
reprinted from a copy in The University
of Illinois Library

CHILDREN AND YOUTH
Social Problems and Social Policy
ISBN for complete set: 0-405-05940-X
See last pages of this volume for titles.

Manufactured in the United States of America

Library of Congress Cataloging in Publication Data
Main entry under title:

The Juvenile court.

(Children and youth: social problems and social
policy)
Reprint of the Chicago Juvenile Court, by H. R.
Jeter, first published in 1922; of The child, the
family, and the court, by B. Flexner, R. Oppenheimer,
and K. F. Lenroot, first published in 1939, and of 3
other previously published articles: In re Gault and
the future of juvenile law, by N. Dorsen and D. A.
Rezneck; The Gault case: its practical impact on the
philosophy of juvenile court, by J. W. Polier; and the
Dilemma of the post-Gault juvenile court, by J. G.
Miller.
Includes bibliographical references.
1. Juvenile courts--United States--Addresses,
essays, lectures. I. Series.
HV9091.J88   345'.73'08   74-1688
ISBN 0-405-05965-5

HV
9091
.J88

CONTENTS

Jeter, Helen Rankin
THE CHICAGO JUVENILE COURT (Reprinted from *U. S. Children's Bureau Publication No. 104),* Washington, D. C., 1922

Flexner, Bernard, Reuben Oppenheimer, and Katharine F. Lenroot
THE CHILD, THE FAMILY AND THE COURT: A study of the Administration of Justice in the Field of Domestic Relations (Reprinted from *U. S. Children's Bureau Publication No. 193),* Washington, D. C., 1939

Dorsen, Norman and Daniel A. Rezneck
IN RE GAULT AND THE FUTURE OF JUVENILE LAW (Reprinted from *Family Law Quarterly,* Vol. I), Chicago, 1967

Polier, Justine Wise
THE GAULT CASE: Its Practical Impact on the Philosophy and Objectives of the Juvenile Court (Reprinted from *Family Law Quarterly,* Vol. I), Chicago, 1967

Miller, Jerome G.
THE DILEMMA OF THE POST-GAULT JUVENILE COURT (Reprinted from *Family Law Quarterly,* Vol. III), Chicago, 1969

ALMA COLLEGE
MONTEITH LIBRARY
ALMA, MICHIGAN

Introduction

In the 1820s, three institutions for juvenile delinquents were founded by established citizens in New York, Boston, and Philadelphia. These houses of refuge and the state and municipal reform schools which succeeded them beginning in the mid-nineteenth century were developed in order to provide systematic means of confining children apart from adult criminals. The larger dilemma of the criminal justice system, which institutions sought to address, was the quandary of judges and juries faced with the alternatives of releasing younger children and thus supposedly encouraging their disrespect toward the law or of sending them to jail where they learned to admire and copy the habits of mature felons.

Reform schools have fallen into such disrepute today, that it is difficult for us to conceive of a time when they were well thought of. Before the Civil War, however, accounts such as Joseph Allen's memoir of Westboro (Mass.), the first state reform school, reflected a widespread hope that institutional confinement built around a workshop routine would provide boys with regular habits which would enable them to prosper or at least to behave as farmers or tradesmen. Similar expectations were not entertained for girls whose delinquencies often included prostitution thus making their reformation unlikely from the moral point of view of the time. Overall, however, advocates and officials of early reformatory institutions boasted great successes, not only in individual cases but also in establishing the parental power of the state *(parens patriae)* as superior to the claims of the inmate's parents who were often poor immigrants. In 1838, for example, the Pennsylvania Supreme Court denied a writ of habeas corpus of an inmate's father whose child had been confined on a minor charge of vagrancy with the observation, "The infant has been snatched from a course which must have ended in confirmed depravity."

Armed with a broad legal definition of delinquency, institutions for delinquent children proliferated in number and kind in the later nineteenth century. In addition to the standard boys' reform school, a number of states added separate schools for girls and reformatories for older youths who were first time offenders. However, the increased demand for various reform schools brought severe problems. Often underfunded, the institutions relied upon contract labor for operational revenue. Contractors often insisted upon total control of inmates during the long working day and enforced a severe discipline on their young labor force. Small wonder that by the late nineteenth century, incindiarism and even murder increasingly characterized institutional routines. Confidence in the benevolent purposes of the institution eroded accordingly as indicated by the increasing number of legal decisions which sided with parents seeking release of their children from minor sentences. "Why should minors be imprisoned for misfortune?" asked an Illinois court of Chicago Reform School officials in 1870, "Destitution of proper parental care, ignorance, idleness and vice, are misfortunes, not crimes."

By the early twentieth century, the shortcomings of the reform schools were increasingly recognized but the institutions themselves remained in operation because they continued to serve functional roles in the new system of juvenile justice which was developed around the juvenile court. The court emphasized treatment of delinquents in their own homes and neighborhoods through probationary supervision and yet court officials still required institutions for children who disputed their authority. Significantly, the popularity of the juvenile court's probation function revived state parental power by successfully claiming it for the entire legal process as it touched the delinquent even though that process could and often did include commitment to an institution. In Commonwealth v. Fisher, a 1905 Pennsylvania decision, the court concluded, "the legislature may surely provide for the salvation of . . . a child, if its parents or guardians be unable or unwilling to do so, by bringing it into one of the courts of the state without any process at all, for the purpose of subjecting it to the state's guardianship and protection."

The Fisher decision became a bulwark of the legal defense of juvenile court and thus continued to rationalize the existence of reform schools and other custodial institutions which served the court. Ironically, the juvenile court's popularity and public support led to increases in the number of incarcerated children. Detention homes where children were confined prior to court appearance were often filled to overflowing and, in localities where these facilities were absent, children often awaited their hearings in jail. And, until the 1930s, delinquents who violated federal laws received no juvenile court hearing at all but were remanded directly to federally subsidized state reformatories. Efforts to improve institutional treatment, whether through cottage plans or farm schools or half way houses such as Miriam Van Waters' El Retiro school in Los Angeles in the 1920s were notable for their humanity but fragile and exceptional for the same reason. Exploitation, drudgery and debasement continued to be the rule as several of the studies in this anthology indicate.

In the past decade several developments have restricted the channels through which children have traditionally been confined. Popular exposés of reformatory institutions such as Howard James' *Children in Trouble* (1970) combined with successful legal challenges of the benevolent purposes of the juvenile court itself have been important deterrents but non-institutional delinquency prevention programs have also played a role. In California, local youth community service programs are subsidized by the state so that at least some children will not have to be sent to reform schools. Jerome Miller, when he was Massachusetts Commissioner of Youth Services, closed down state reform schools in favor of a variety of community programs and surrogate homes located in or near the child's own neighborhood. Whether these programmatic trends indicate a broad popular willingness to deal with juvenile delinquency on the basis of community resources is an open question. Miller's reforms, for example, never received full funding and hence have not been completely implemented. It can only be said that in the years ahead, reform schools and the detention homes will become less important only to the degree that responsibility for preventing juvenile delinquency is seen as a significant duty of local communities and supported accordingly.

March, 1974
Durham, New Hampshire

Robert M. Mennel
University of New Hampshire

U. S. DEPARTMENT OF LABOR

JAMES J. DAVIS, Secretary

CHILDREN'S BUREAU

GRACE ABBOTT, Chief

THE
CHICAGO JUVENILE COURT

By

HELEN RANKIN JETER

Bureau Publication No. 104

WASHINGTON
GOVERNMENT PRINTING OFFICE
1922

CONTENTS.

	Page.
Letter of transmittal	v
Editor's note	VII
Origin and development of the Cook County juvenile court	1
The jurisdiction of the court	11–16
Character of the court and area covered	11
Classes of cases	11
Jurisdiction over children accused of committing serious offenses	14
Age groups	15
Jurisdiction over adults	16
The administrative problems of the court	17–25
Number of children brought into court	17
Problems relating to the delinquent child	18
Problems relating to the dependent child	21
Organization of the court	26–34
The judge	26
Woman assistant to the judge to hear cases of delinquent girls	27
The probation department	28–33
Appointment and discharge	28
Number	29
Salaries	30
Organization	30
Police probation officers	32
Records and reports	33–34
Annual reports	33
Case records	33
Other records and forms	34
Preliminary procedure	35–48
Complaint and petition	35
Investigation	35–42
Dependent children	36
Delinquent girls	39
Delinquent boys	39
Police probation officers' investigation	40
Other investigations	41
Adjustment of cases without court action	42
Physical and mental examinations	46
Detention	49–56
Detention policy	49
Number of children cared for in detention home	50
Overcrowding	51
Equipment of the juvenile detention home	53
Reception of children	54
The daily routine	55
Dietary	56
Clothing	56

Page.

Hearings _____ 57–62
    Summons_____ 57
    Time and place_____ 58
    Procedure_____ 59
    Cases of dependent children_____ 60
    Cases of delinquent girls_____ 61
    Cases of feeble-minded children_____ 62
    Aid to mothers cases_____ 62
The court order_____ 63–90
    Dismissal and continuance_____ 63–68
        Dismissed and continued generally_____ 63
        Continued for a definite period_____ 65
    The final order_____ 68–90
        Probation _____ 71
        Appointment of guardian_____ 78
        Commitment to child-placing societies_____ 84
        Commitment to hospitals and schools for defectives_____ 85
        Deportation_____ 85
        Commitment to institutions _____ 85–88
            Dependent children _____ 86
            Delinquent boys_____ 87
            Delinquent girls_____ 88
        Transfer to the criminal court_____ 88
        Other procedure in cases of delinquent children_____ 90
Subsequent relationship of the court, the child, and the custodial agency_ 91–99
    The court and the guardian_____ 92
    The court and the institution_____ 93–97
        Institutions for delinquent children_____ 93
        Institutions for dependent children_____ 94
    Recovery of children who escape from institutions_____ 97
    Following up the dependent child and his family_____ 98
Cooperation with other agencies_____ 100–107
    Social agencies_____ 100
    Relationship to other courts_____ 103
List of references to Illinois statutory sources_____ 109
Index _____ 111

LETTER OF TRANSMITTAL.

U. S. DEPARTMENT OF LABOR,
CHILDREN'S BUREAU,
Washintgon, May 1, 1922.

SIR: There is transmitted herewith a report on the Chicago Juvenile Court by Helen R. Jeter, one of a series of studies now being made by the Children's Bureau.

It is believed that this description of the organization and methods of operation of the oldest and one of the largest juvenile courts in the country will be of special value to all students of juvenile delinquency.

In planning the investigation and writing the report Miss Jeter had the assistance and counsel of Prof. S. P. Breckinridge, of the University of Chicago who also edited the report.

Respectfully submitted.

GRACE ABBOTT, *Chief.*

Hon. JAMES J. DAVIS,
Secretary of Labor.

EDITOR'S NOTE.

The following study of the Cook County, Ill., juvenile court, the oldest of the juvenile courts organized under express statutory authority, was made during the period between January 1, 1920, and June 30, 1921.

Miss Helen R. Jeter, now assistant in the graduate school of social service administration of the University of Chicago, formerly of the Chicago School of Civics and Philanthropy, with the assistance of various investigators, collected the material and wrote the report.

The sources drawn upon for the study were the records of many cases covering the whole history of the court, selected at random; the careful summarizing of 95 cases heard by the court during the first two weeks of January, 1920; a study of the statutes under which the court has developed; the annual reports of the court, of the chief probation officer, and of other county officials, ordinarily contained in the "Charity Service Reports, Cook County, Ill."; and interviews with the officers of the court, of the Juvenile Detention Home, and of the Institute for Juvenile Research. To all of these grateful acknowledgments are made. The report, of course, could not have been prepared without the consent of Judge Victor P. Arnold or the helpful and sympathetic cooperation of the chief probation officer, Mr. Joseph L. Moss.

The Illinois Legislature met in the winter of 1921. In preparation for that session the director of the department of public welfare of Illinois appointed a committee of persons interested in child welfare work for the purpose of "setting forth a program of adequate child care, of correlating efforts of existing boards and departments in the interests of children, of codifying the laws relating to children, and establishing throughout the State minimum standards of child welfare."[1] Judge Arnold was an active and helpful member of that committee, and during the session of the legislature he gave effective support to a revision of the aid-to-mothers law,[2] granting to the court more ample powers in the matter of making allowances under

---

[1] Report of the Department of Public Welfare of Illinois, Children's Committee, December, 1920, p. 3.

[2] Laws of Illinois, 1921, p. 162.

that act and providing for an increase in the fund now known as the mothers' pension fund.

On June 6, 1921, Judge Arnold, for five years judge of the juvenile court, was reelected by a substantial majority, thus assuring the court of community confidence and support in the development of a program which will make possible the elimination of some of the administrative difficulties which. as this report indicates, have reduced the efficiency of the court in the past.

S. P. BRECKINRIDGE.

THE CHICAGO JUVENILE COURT.

ORIGIN AND DEVELOPMENT OF THE COOK COUNTY JUVENILE COURT.

Before the enactment of the juvenile-court law in Illinois children who had violated the law were dealt with exactly as adult persons charged with crime with respect to arrest, detention, and trial. Illinois had been admitted to the Union as a common-law State in 1818. The age of criminal responsibility was therefore 7 years, until the enactment of the criminal code in 1827,[1] which raised the age to 10. The child of 10 or more might, however, still be considered a criminal, and this provision[2] remains unchanged to the present time, though its importance has been considerably affected by other enactments.

Judge Merritt W. Pinckney, formerly judge of the juvenile court, described the situation of the child of 10 or more prior to July 1, 1899, in the following language:

> When a law of the State was violated the State demanded vindication, the same vindication from a lad of 12 as from an adult of 25. Punishment, not reformation, was the first fundamental thought of our criminal jurisprudence; punishment as an expiation for the wrong and as a warning to other possible wrongdoers. The lad of 12 years was arrested, put in jail, indicted by the grand jury, tried by a petit jury, with all the formality of the criminal law, and if 12 men, tried and true, found that he had violated some law, then the great Commonwealth of Illinois, through the judgment of the court, visited its punishment upon him.[3]

The only point at which the treatment of the juvenile criminal differed from that of the adult was the form that such punishment might take. As early as 1831 certain exceptions are found in the method of punishing minors. An act[4] of that year providing for the establishment of a State penitentiary stated that persons under 18 were not included in the terms of that law, but were still to be dealt with under the criminal code of 1827.[5]

---

[1] "An infant under the age of 10 years shall not be found guilty of any crime or misdemeanor." Revised Laws of Illinois 1827, p. 124, sec. 4.

[2] Hurd's Illinois Revised Statutes 1919, ch. 38, sec. 283.

[3] Charity Service Reports, Cook County, Ill., 1913, p. 216.

[4] Laws of Illinois 1830-31, p. 103, sec. 43.

[5] This meant considerably lighter sentences for persons under 18. The act of 1831 imposed sentences varying from 7 years to life imprisonment in the penitentiary, while the criminal code of 1827, which was still to remain in operation for young persons, imposed sentences of whipping, fines, and imprisonment, usually not over 3 years, for the same offenses. (Revised Laws of Illinois 1827, p. 124, secs. 29, 46, 47, 48, 50.)

In 1833 the criminal code included for the first time the provision that " persons under 18 shall not be punished by confinement in the penitentiary for any offense except robbery, burglary, or arson; in all other cases where a penitentiary punishment is or shall be provided, such person under the age of 18 shall be punished by imprisonment in the county jail for any term not exceeding 18 months at the discretion of the court." [6]

This provision remained the only statute modifying the treatment of minors until 1867, when provision was made for the establishment of the first State reform school.[7]   This act provided [8] that " All courts of competent jurisdiction are hereby authorized to exercise their discretion, in sending juvenile offenders to the county jails, in accordance with the laws made and provided, or in sending them to the reform school." The school was established for boys under 18, while girls of that age throughout the State, as well as boys in Cook County, were committed to the reformatory already established in Chicago. Persons under 18 could no longer be committed to the penitentiary for arson, burglary, or robbery, but commitment to county jails for these and other offenses was left to the discretion of the courts.

In 1874 the law concerning jails and jailers was amended by the addition of a provision [9] requiring that minors should be " kept separate from notorious offenders and those convicted of a felony or other infamous crime."

In 1891 the State reformatory was divided into two departments, one for boys between 10 and 16, the other for boys between 16 and 21.[10]   The act passed at this time required that boys under 16 convicted of an offense punishable by imprisonment in a county jail or penitentiary be committed to the reformatory, although those guilty of minor offenses might still be punished in county jails.

The statute authorizing the establishment of the Illinois Home for Juvenile Offenders was enacted in 1893 and provided for commitment to the home, at the discretion of the court, of girls between the ages of 10 and 16 who were convicted of offenses punishable by imprisonment in a county jail or house of correction.[11]   In 1895 this law was amended to include offenses punishable by imprisonment in the penitentiary.[12]

Thus, until the enactment of the juvenile court law in 1899, the delinquent child between 10 and 16 was subject to all the criminal

[6] Revised Laws of Illinois, 1833, p. 209, sec. 158.
[7] Ibid., 1867, p. 42.
[8] Ibid., sec. 16.
[9] Hurd's Illinois Revised Statutes 1874, ch. 75, sec. 11.
[10] Laws of Illinois 1891, p. 52, sec. 9.
[11] Ibid., 1893, p. 23, secs. 16 and 17.
[12] Ibid., 1895, p. 295.

processes applicable to adults so far as arrest, detention, and trial were concerned and could still be committed to a house of correction or to a county jail at the discretion of the court, except for more serious offenses, for which he was committed to a State reformatory.[13]

For the care of dependent children, provision had been made by " An act to provide industrial schools for girls " in 1879 [14] and "An act to provide for and aid training schools for boys " in 1883.[15] These acts provided for the incorporation of industrial and training schools to receive dependent children under 18 who were committed to their care by the county court and for whose support the county might pay a certain amount. The schools were subject to State supervision but received no State appropriations. Cases were brought to the attention of the court by petition, and a jury of six was required to pass upon the question of dependency.

The validity of the earlier of these two acts was attacked in 1882, on the following grounds: (1) That the institutions created under the act were really penal institutions, and, therefore, that commitment was a punishment resulting in the restraint of liberty, and that the procedure, therefore, violated various constitutional safeguards such as trial by a jury of 12; (2) that the institutions might be sectarian within the meaning of the constitutional prohibition against payment of public funds to sectarian institutions; (3) that the liability for the support of dependent female children could not be placed upon the county. None of these objections was, however, sustained by the court. The second of these arguments was the basis for an action brought in 1917, but its validity was again denied.[16] Thus the earlier law was upheld.[17] The validity of the second act has never been attacked.

These acts still remain in operation and were not affected by the passage of the juvenile court law except that jurisdiction in dependent cases was bestowed upon the circuit as well as the county courts in other counties than Cook, in Cook County being restricted to the circuit court.

The so-called juvenile court act of 1899, under which the juvenile court of Cook County was established, was the culmination of nearly 10 years' discussion and experiment on the part of social agencies and of persons interested in child welfare. As early as 1891 the

---

[13] Hurd's Illinois Revised Statutes, 1897, ch. 118.
[14] Laws of Illinois 1879, p. 309.
[15] Ibid., 1883, p. 168.
[16] Dunn v. Chicago Industrial School, 280 Ill. 613.
[17] Petition of Ferrier, 103 Ill. 367, and County of McLean v. Humphreys, 104 Ill. 378. Art. VIII, sec. 3, of the State constitution provides that " neither the general assembly nor any county, city, town, township, school district, or other public corporation shall ever make any appropriation or pay from any public fund whatever anything in aid of any church or sectarian purpose, or to help sustain or support any school controlled by any church or sectarian denomination whatever."

Visitation and Aid Society of Chicago[18] introduced into the legislature a bill designed to give an authoritative basis for the work of that society by providing for the commitment of children to the care of organizations of the same general character. The bill, however, failed of passage.[19] It dealt only with dependent and neglected children and, had it been passed, would have solved only part of the problem.

One of the first efforts in behalf of delinquent children was made about 1893, when a school for the boys in the county jail was started by a private citizen and was later taken over, supported, and established on a fairly permanent basis by the Chicago Woman's Club.[20] Not the least important of the results of this experiment was the public interest aroused in the number of children confined in the county jail and in the condition of these children. An effort soon developed to secure a special law dealing with the treatment of delinquent children; and in 1895, after a study of the probation system established in 1878 in Massachusetts for both adults and children,[20a] a bill was drafted at the instance of the Chicago Woman's Club, containing provisions for a separate court and for a probation staff. The question of its constitutionality was raised, however, and the bill was abandoned without being introduced in the legislature. During the next few years the Chicago Woman's Club continued to support the school in the county jail, established manual training in the house of correction, and secured separate housing for boys committed to that institution. Considerable discussion of the various problems connected with the care and treatment of the young offender in Cook County was carried on in the press and in public meetings during this period.

In 1898 the questions of the reform of court procedure and of a probation system were among the subjects discussed by the Illinois State Conference of Charities, and at that time Dr. Frederick W. Wines, the veteran prisoner reformer, formerly secretary of the Illinois State Board of Charities, declared:

We make criminals out of children who are not criminals by treating them as if they were criminals. That ought to be stopped. What we should have in our system of criminal jurisprudence is an entirely separate system of courts for children in large cities who commit offenses which would be criminal in adults. We ought to have a "children's court" in Chicago, and we ought to have a "children's judge," who should attend to no other business. We want some place of detention for those children other than a prison (reference made

---

[18] Hurley, T. D.: "Development of the juvenile court idea," in Charities, Vol. XI. p. 423 (Nov. 7, 1903).

[19] For draft of bill, see Hurley, T. D.: Juvenile Courts and What They Have Accomplished. The Visitation and Aid Society, Chicago, 1904.

[20] Most of these facts regarding the early history of the Illinois juvenile court movement are drawn from Lathrop, Julia C.: "Development of the probation system in a large city," in Charities, Vol. XIII. p. 344 ff. (Jan. 7, 1905).

[20a] Massachusetts Acts and Resolves, 1878, ch. 178, p. 146.

to the New York system of detention). A thing we want to borrow from the State of Massachusetts is its system of probation. No child ought to be tried unless he has a friend in court to look after his real interests * * * In such cases in Massachusetts the judge sends a probation lawyer to investigate the conditions of the home and all the circumstances-surrounding the case.[21]

The Illinois State Board of Public Charities, the Illinois Federation of Women's Clubs, the Chicago Bar Association, the Chicago Board of Education, and the Illinois State Conference of Charities, all interested themselves in the passage of the act entitled "An act to regulate the treatment and control of dependent, neglected, and delinquent children,"[22] which was signed April 21 and went into effect July 1, 1899.

This law contained the essential features of later juvenile-court legislation. In it were provisions (1) for the separate hearing[23] of children's cases in a court having chancery rather than criminal jurisdiction; (2) for the detention of children apart from adult offenders; and (3) for a probation system. It was, however, weak at many points, and its administration had often to be supplemented by private effort. A number of amendments[24] intended to cure the various weaknesses of the original law have been adopted, and the present organization and practice of courts acting under the statute are the result of a gradual development that is probably not yet complete. The present study deals with only one of those courts, namely, the Cook County court sitting in Chicago. That court operates under such provisions of the act as are of general application and under other provisions applying to counties of more than 500,000 population—that is, to Cook County.

The first session of the Cook County court was held on July 1, 1899, and at that session, Mrs. Alzena P. Stevens, a resident of Hull House, volunteered to serve as probation officer.[25] The act had authorized the creation of a probation staff for the probationary care of delinquent children, but it was also specified that such officers should not be paid from public funds.[26] The framers of the act had acquiesced in this program for two reasons:[25] First, because they feared lest the prospective cost involved in the payment of probation officers might defeat the bill; and, second, because probation officers if paid from public funds might be selected on a political basis. The salaries of Mrs. Stevens and four or five other volunteer officers were raised for the first few years by private subscription.

[21] Fifteenth Biennial Report of the Board of State Commissioners of Public Charities of the State of Illinois (1898), p. 336.

[22] Laws of Illinois 1899, p. 131.

[23] Section 3 required a special court room in Chicago.

[24] The law of 1899 was amended: 1901, p. 141; 1905, pp. 151 and 152; 1907, p. 70; and 1911, p. 126.

[25] Lathrop, Julia C.: "Development of the probation system in a large city," in Charities, Vol. XIII, p. 345 (Jan. 7, 1905).

[26] Laws of Illinois 1899, p. 131, sec. 6.

In 1904 those interested in the support of these probation officers incorporated as the Juvenile Court Committee,[27] and by that time the number of officers had increased to 15, of whom 4 were men and 11 were women.

Besides these officers, representatives of various social agencies, such as the Illinois Children's Home and Aid Society (nonsectarian Protestant), the Visitation and Aid Society (Roman Catholic), and the Bureau of Personal Service (Jewish), were commissioned as probation officers. Individuals interested in particular cases were also appointed as volunteer probation officers. Moreover, in 1899 the mayor of Chicago at the request of the judge of the juvenile court directed that two police officers from each station be detailed as probation officers.[28]

In 1905, 15 probation officers were being paid by the Juvenile Court Committee, and about 20 police officers were assigned to work with the juvenile court.[29] In that year an amendment was adopted [30] providing that in counties of more than 500,000 population (i. e., Cook County) the judges of the circuit court might determine how many probation officers were necessary, such officers to be appointed in the same manner and under the same rules and regulations as other officers of the county and paid under authorization of the board of county commissioners.

The legal status of the probation staff, however, was not even then determined. The amendment of 1905 had placed payment in the hands of the board of county commissioners, and appointment " in the same manner as other county officers " was understood to mean certification by the county civil service commission. For six years the law was interpreted in this manner, and the number of probation officers paid by the county was increased from 23 in 1905 to 37 in 1911. In that year a newly elected county administration attempted to bring political pressure to bear upon the probation staff. A campaign of abuse was waged in the public press—attention was called to cases which, it was claimed, had resulted disastrously; probation officers were pictured as " child snatchers;" and the work of the juvenile court was rendered extremely difficult. The county civil service commission joined in the attack through a pretended

[27] Among the early officers of this committee were Mrs. Joseph T. Bowen, the Very Rev. Dean Summer, Father Andrew Spetz, Dr. Rabbi Joseph Stoltz, Mrs. Charles M. Walker, Mrs. George R. Dean, and Mrs. Wm. Thomas. In 1909 the name was changed to the Juvenile Protective Association of Chicago. The association continued its financial assistance to the court until 1908. Since that time it has been concerned exclusively with community problems affecting delinquency.

[28] Testimony of Judge Pinckney in Breckinridge and Abbott: The Delinquent Child and the Home, Charities Publication Committee, New York, 1912, p. 240.

[29] The number was at first about 20 and was increased to 30 in 1908. See Charity Service Reports, Cook County, Ill., 1903–1911.

[30] Laws of Illinois 1905, p. 151.

investigation of the court. These attacks failed to command public confidence, however, and finally the board of commissioners of Cook County was prevailed upon to appoint a committee of five citizens to make an impartial investigation.[31] On September 28, 1911, before the report of the committee had been completed, however, the president of the county board of commissioners suspended the chief probation officer and filed with the county civil service commission charges against him, alleging "incompetency, lack of executive ability, and neglect of duty." The hearing on these charges extended over a period of three months and included an investigation of the work of the probation department, of the detention home, and of the industrial schools to which dependent children were committed by the court. On January 6, 1912, the civil service commission decided adversely to the chief probation officer and dismissed him. He appealed the case, with the result that that portion of the act providing for the selection of probation officers by the county commissioners was held unconstitutional[32] as a violation of the principle of separation of powers laid down in Article III of the Illinois constitution. The right of the court to be free from interference in the selection of its officers was thus recognized. Probation officers were declared to be assistants to the court, performing judicial functions, and as such to be chosen only by popular vote or appointed by the court itself.[32a] The selection of probation officers was thus left in the hands of the judges of the circuit court; they agreed to delegate that selection to the judge of the juvenile court, who had suffered greatly from the political attack on the work of the court. He devised at this time a substitute for the civil service test that has worked admirably and is still in use. Since that time probation officers have been appointed by the judge on the basis of competitive examinations, held from time to time under the direction of a committee of citizens[33] chosen by the judge because of their unquestioned special fitness for the task and their public spirit. Since 1912 five such examinations have been held, two for chief probation officer, one in 1913 and another in 1918, and three for assistant probation officer, in 1913, 1916, and 1919.[33a] This

[31] The members of this committee were Willard E. Hotchkiss (chairman), Saul Drucker, Rev. C. J. Quille, Rev. August Schlechte, and Mrs. James E. Quan. The committee reported in January, 1912. The report is entitled " The Juvenile Court of Cook County, Ill. Report of a Committee Appointed under Resolution of the Board of Commissioners of Cook County, Aug. 8, 1912."

[32] Witter v. Cook County Commissioners, 256 Illinois, 616. See also People v. C., B. & Q. R. R. Co., 273 Illinois, 110. The report of the citizens' committee shortly after showed no grounds for this decision of the civil service commission.

[32a] This decision did not affect the position of clerical assistants, who are still appointed under civil service regulations.

[33] The first committee was composed of members of the Juvenile Court Committee that had chosen and paid probation officers before the amendment of 1905.

[33a] A fourth examination for assistant probation officer was given in 1922.

device has served to protect the judge from political pressure and to maintain the quality of the probation service.

Again, in 1917, the status of the probation officers was attacked through a bill to enjoin the county treasurer from paying the salaries of any of the probation staff. The bill was dismissed for want of equity by the superior court of Cook County, but appeal was allowed to the appellate court of Illinois, and for more than a year, pending decision, the payment of salaries by the county treasurer was made possible only by the guaranty of funds by private citizens and by a special act of the legislature.[34] Finally, on June 14, 1918, the appellate court of Illinois[35] confirmed the decision of the lower court, and the status of probation officers was once more assured.[36]

The constitutionality of the juvenile court law itself was attacked in 1912 by an appeal[37] from a judgment of the Cook County court declaring a child to be dependent and appointing a guardian under the act. The supreme court, though it reversed the decision of the court in the particular case, upheld the law at every point at which it was attacked.[38]

The law of 1899 had contained no provision for the detention of children except one prohibiting commitment of children under 12 to a jail or police station and giving authority to place a child awaiting trial in "some suitable place provided by the city or county."[39] Since neither the city nor the county had at first a suitable place, the task of providing one, like that of paying probation officers, was undertaken by private initiative. The Illinois Industrial Association assumed the care of boys awaiting hearing on delinquent petitions, the city and the county each paying half the board of the children.[40] Dependent children were detained, when necessary, in a room of the Cook County Detention Hospital. In 1903 the Juvenile Court Committee took over the care of all children and established a detention home at 625 West Adams Street. The expenses were paid in part by this committee, but the larger share was borne by the city and the county.[40]

The establishment consisted of an old residence in which dependent children were housed and a remodeled barn for delinquent boys. The delinquent girls were detained in an annex to one of the police stations, where older women were also confined. At first the detention home was placed under the care of a police officer, and little

[34] Laws of Illinois 1917. p. 536. This law safeguards a public officer from personal liability for the disbursement of funds in emergencies of this kind.
[35] Gilbert et al. v. Sweitzer. 211 Illinois App. 438.
[36] See p. 30 of this report for discussion of salaries of probation officers.
[37] By a writ of error, Hurd's Illinois Revised Statutes 1919. ch. 23. sec. 190d.
[38] Lindsay v. Lindsay. 257 Ill. 328.
[39] Laws of Illinois 1899. p. 131. secs. 5 and 11.
[40] Lathrop, Julia C.: "Development of the probation system." in Charities. Vol. XIII, p. 346 (Jan. 7, 1905).

amusement and no schooling were provided. In 1906, however, the city board of education assigned a teacher for the instruction of delinquent boys.[41]

In 1907 a law was passed [42] authorizing the establishment of a detention home by county authorities on vote of the people of the county; but without awaiting a popular vote, the county and the city entered into a cooperative undertaking to erect a juvenile court building on Ewing Street, accommodating both the detention home and the juvenile court rooms.[43] This building is still occupied as a detention home, but in 1913 its crowded condition led to the removal of the court to the county building, where other courts are held.[44]

A third important development in the Chicago juvenile court resulted from the enactment of the funds to parents and aid to mothers laws,[45] which added to the earlier work of the court a class of cases involving principles of public relief and requiring a complicated administrative machinery. The first of these acts, the funds to parents act,[46] was a brief amendment to the juvenile court law authorizing in certain dependent cases the granting of relief by the court. That amendment read as follows:

If the parent or parents of such dependent or neglected child are poor and unable to properly care for the said child, but are otherwise proper guardians and it is for the welfare of such child to remain at home, the court may enter an order finding such facts and fixing the amount of money necessary to enable the parent or parents to properly care for such child, and thereupon it shall be the duty of the county board, through its county agent or otherwise, to pay to such parent or parents, at such times as said order may designate, the amount so specified for the care of such dependent or neglected child until the further order of the court.[47]

In 1913 a more elaborately drawn aid to mothers law superseded the amendment of 1911. This law not only defined the group of eligible families to whom grants might be made and fixed conditions under which those grants might be enjoyed but also provided for a special tax to be set aside as a special fund for mothers' pensions.[48]

---

[41] Thurston, H. W.: "Ten years of the juvenile court of Chicago," in The Survey, Vol. XXIII, pp. 656, 662, and 663 (Feb. 5, 1910).

[42] Laws of Illinois 1907, p. 59. Hurd's Illinois Revised Statutes 1919, ch. 23, sec. 271.

[43] First Annual Message of William Busse, president of the board of commissioners of Cook County, in Charity Service Reports, Cook County, Ill., 1907, p. 29.

[44] The building at 202 Ewing Street (now 771 Gilpin Place) has now become inadequate for the detention home and is soon to be replaced. See p. 53.

[45] Hurd's Illinois Revised Statutes 1919, ch. 23, sec. 298

[46] Laws of Illinois 1911, p. 126. See also Hurd's Revised Statutes 1919, ch. 23, sec. 175.

[47] Laws of Illinois 1911, p. 126. Hurd's Illinois Revised Statutes 1919, ch. 23, sec. 175. The administration of the mothers' pension law has been quite fully discussed. See Abbott, Edith, and Breckinridge, S. P.: The Administration of the Aid-to-Mothers Law in Illinois. Children's Bureau Publication No. 82, Washington, 1921.

[48] Three-tenths of 1 mill on the dollar to be levied on all taxable property of the county. Laws of Illinois, 1913, p. 127; Hurd's Illinois Revised Statutes, 1919, ch. 23, sec. 298 fol. The 1911 act had proved inadequate in many respects other than the financial provisions.

The courts held in 1915, however, that this act did not increase the total amount of the county taxes the county was authorized to spend but merely reduced the amount available for other county expenditures.[49] The county board therefore appropriated annually for mothers' pensions less than the actual amount of the special tax fund. In June, 1919, however, the law was amended so as to authorize an increase in the total volume of county expenditures and to provide an adequate fund that should be available exclusively for mothers' pensions.[50]

Various aspects of the practice of the court, chiefly those of an administrative nature, will be discussed in the following chapters. It has perhaps been made clear that at no time during the court's existence have the conditions under which it functioned been entirely satisfactory. It has suffered from open political attack, from legislative caution and legislative blundering, from the hostility of other administrative bodies, and from public indifference. These difficulties should be kept in mind throughout the following discussion.

---

[49] People v. Chicago, Lake Shore & Eastern R. R. Co., 270 Ill. 477.

[50] The law was amended June 21, 1919, to provide for a tax of four-tenths of 1 mill on the dollar in counties of over 300,000 population and was further amended nine days later to provide for a tax of four-fifteenths of 1 mill to correspond with a change in the assessed valuation from one-third to one-half the cash value of the property. (See Laws of Illinois 1919, pp. 780–781, and pp. 781–782, and Hurd's Illinois Revised Statutes, 1919, ch. 23, sec. 313.)

THE JURISDICTION OF THE COURT.

CHARACTER OF THE COURT AND AREA COVERED.

The juvenile court law of Illinois created no new or special courts, but in all portions of the State except Cook County conferred jurisdiction in cases arising under the law upon circuit and county courts. In Cook County, which constitutes an entire and single judicial circuit, original and exclusive jurisdiction was conferred upon the circuit court alone.[1] The juvenile court sitting in Chicago is thus technically the juvenile court of Cook County, and is a division or branch of the circuit court of the county. As such its territorial jurisdiction covers besides the city of Chicago a considerable outlying territory that is both suburban and rural in character. In this outlying district are 5 incorporated cities from 2,000 to nearly 25,000 in population, and about 70 villages of from a few hundred to 19,000 population.[2] The suburban district covers an area of about 733 square miles and contained in 1910 a population, urban and rural, of 219,950.[2] From the point of view of administration such territorial jurisdiction presents many difficult problems.[3]

CLASSES OF CASES.

The jurisdiction exercised by the juvenile court includes three classes of cases. The first is composed of those over which the jurisdiction is original and exclusive under the juvenile court law. These are cases of delinquent children, dependent or neglected children, and mothers' pension cases.

A delinquent child, as defined by the statute,[4] is a boy under 17 or a girl under 18 who violates any law of the State; is incorrigible, knowingly associates with thieves, vicious or immoral persons; without just cause and without the consent of its parents, guardian, or custodian absents itself from its home or place of abode, is growing up in idleness or crime; knowingly frequents a house of ill repute; knowingly frequents any public shop or place where any gaming device is operated; frequents any saloon or dram shop where intoxicating

---

[1] Hurd's Illinois Revised Statutes 1919, ch. 23, sec. 171.
[2] Thirteenth Census of the United States, 1910, Vol. II, Population, p. 445.
[3] See p. 32 of this report for organization of work in outlying districts.
[4] Hurd's Illinois Revised Statutes, 1919, ch. 23, secs. 170, 298.

11

liquors are sold; patronizes or visits any public pool room or bucket shop; wanders about the streets at night; habitually wanders about railroad yards or tracks or jumps on any moving train, or enters any car or engine without authority; uses vile, obscene, vulgar, profane, or indecent language, or is guilty of indecent or lascivious conduct.

A dependent or neglected child[5] is a boy under 17 or a girl under 18 who, for any reason, is destitute, homeless, abandoned, or dependent upon the public for support; has not proper parental care or guardianship, habitually begs or receives alms; is found living in any house of ill fame or with any vicious or disreputable person; or has a home which by reason of neglect, cruelty, or depravity on the part of the parents, guardian, or any other person in whose care it may be, is an unfit place for such child; and any child under 10 who is found begging, peddling, or selling any articles or singing or playing any musical instrument for gain upon the street, or giving public entertainments or accompanying any person so doing.

In these cases and in aid to mothers cases as well,[6] the jurisdiction is technically exercised over the child. Actually, however, the entire family is brought under supervision.

The second class of cases is that in which the juvenile court exercises jurisdiction as a branch of the circuit court. The jurisdiction is therefore not exclusive. These are cases of truants under the parental schools act, feeble-minded children, children given in adoption, and illegitimate children.

Under the parental schools act,[7] providing for commitment of habitual truants to such schools, jurisdiction is conferred upon the county and circuit courts of the State. In Cook County, under an agreement of the circuit judges with the county judge, this jurisdiction is exercised by the juvenile court alone. Truant officers are, however, appointed by the board of education and subject to that authority, and the only real contact of the juvenile court with the truant child is the hearing in court.

Jurisdiction under the adoption law[8] may likewise be exercised by the county or circuit courts of the State. All such cases filed in the circuit court of Cook County are, by agreement, heard by the judge of the juvenile court. With the exception of the judge, then, no officers of the juvenile court have any legal authority over cases involving only adoption. In the case of a delinquent or dependent child, however, a petition may be filed under the juvenile court law praying the appointment of a guardian authorized to consent to legal adoption,

---

[5] Hurd's Illinois Revised Statutes 1919, ch. 23, sec. 169. The 1899 law defined as delinquent only one who violated a law of the State or a local ordinance. The amendment of 1905, p. 152, included the present definition.

[6] Hurd's Illinois Revised Statutes, 1919, ch. 23, sec. 298.

[7] Ibid., ch. 122, sec. 144.

[8] Ibid., ch. 4, sec. 1. The county judge has entered into no agreement on this subject.

and the court in which adoption proceedings are pending may accept the consent of the guardian appointed without further notice to parents or relatives.[9] This amounts to the juvenile court's hearing all the evidence in the case, the court before which the case is pending entering the formal decree. Investigations are conducted by probation officers. but adoption proceedings are not included in the legal records of the juvenile court.

The act to provide for the care and detention of feeble-minded persons places jurisdiction in the circuit, county, and municipal courts of the State.[10] When, therefore, a delinquent or dependent child brought before the juvenile court appears to be feeble-minded, the judge may adjourn the proceedings under the juvenile court law and conduct the hearing on a petition under the act for the care and detention of feeble-minded persons.[11] This means that the juvenile court has jurisdiction over feeble-minded children only incidental to their being brought into court as dependent or delinquent children. For the sake of securing prompt action, the investigation department brings into court on a " feeble-minded " petition children called to their attention whom they think not only dependent or delinquent but feeble-minded as well, and children in a situation involving dependency are brought by the same process by social agencies before the court. No agreement has been made by the circuit, county, and municipal courts to concentrate these cases in the court of the juvenile court judge, and cases of feeble-minded children who are not dependent or delinquent are heard by other courts.

A recent amendment to the bastardy law provides that the juvenile court shall " with other courts of competent jurisdiction " have jurisdiction over all cases arising under the act.[12] The State's attorney has, however, refused to prosecute such cases before the juvenile court, and the court has not then exercised jurisdiction over this class of cases.[13] Bastardy cases are tried before the domestic-relations branch of the municipal court under authority of the law which created that court.[14] Juvenile court officers, however, investigate and present in the court of domestic relations bastardy cases in which the mother is under 18 years of age or in which the court has already obtained

[9] Hurd's Illinois Revised Statutes, 1919, ch. 23, sec. 183.

[10] Ibid.. ch. 23. sec. 324.

[11] Ibid.. sec. 341.

[12] The amendment was passed in 1919. Hurd's Illinois Revised Statutes 1919, ch. 17, sec. 4.

[13] Since the election of June 6, 1921, this opposition seems no longer an obstacle. The judge has up to the present writing (Dec. 1, 1921) taken no action to claim this jurisdiction, possibly arguing that unless additional resources are placed at the service of the court, the additional burden would be too heavy.

[14] Hurd's Illinois Revised Statutes 1919, ch. 37, sec. 265. " All suits of every kind and nature, whether civil or criminal, or whether at law or in equity, which may be transferred to it, by a change of venue or otherwise by the circuit court of Cook County, the superior court of Cook County or the criminal court of Cook County." But see Hosking r. So. Pac. Co. 243 Ill., 320, and P. r. Olson, 245 Ill., 288.

jurisdiction over the family through other elements of dependency or delinquency.

JURISDICTION OVER CHILDREN ACCUSED OF COMMITTING SERIOUS OFFENSES.

Under a provision of the juvenile court law defining a delinquent child as a boy under 17 or a girl under 18 who "violates any law of this State," [15] the juvenile court is apparently given jurisdiction in all cases of children within those ages, however serious the offense with which the child may be charged. The law provides, moreover, that if a child is taken before a justice of the peace or police magistrate, "it shall be the duty" of such justice or magistrate to transfer the case to the juvenile court. [16] This jurisdiction has, however, never been acknowledged by the prosecuting authorities, and a concurrent jurisdiction is exercised by the criminal court of Cook County in the trial of children charged with serious offenses. The chief probation officer, in his annual report for 1920, made the following statement: [17]

During the past year there have been a number of cases in which, following the filing of a petition in the juvenile court and while the case was still pending, an indictment has been voted by the grand jury, followed by a hearing in the criminal court. The interesting thing is that after weeks and months of delay, during which time the child was held in the county jail, the criminal court has in each of the cases either referred the case to the juvenile court for disposition or has entered an order placing the child under probation to the adult probation department. The probation orders could have been arrived at with quite as much force and by a much simpler process under the juvenile-court law.

The attitude of State's attorneys in the past has usually been that juvenile-court action in cases in which crimes were committed has been only through the suffrance of the State's attorney; that in any cases which he chooses to characterize as "serious," he might take action in the criminal court. This situation is one which it is hoped may be settled at an early date by a ruling of the criminal court or by a supreme-court decision.

In the case of a 16-year-old boy, for example, who, early in 1921, was charged with the theft from a bank of $700,000 worth of bonds, a petition was filed in the juvenile court. The State's attorney, however, is reported to have said in answer to a proposal that the case be heard in the juvenile court, "This is a criminal case, and the boy will be tried in the criminal court, regardless of his age. And I believe in speedy trials, too." [17a] The grand jury was therefore directed to take up the case, and two indictments were voted, one charging embezzlement, and the other larceny. The result of the

[15] Hurd's Illinois Revised Statutes 1919, ch. 23, sec. 169.
[16] Ibid., sec. 178.
[17] Charity Service Reports, Cook County, Ill., 1920, p. 243.
[17a] Chicago Daily Tribune, Feb. 20, 1921.

trial in the criminal court was a failure of the jury to agree, and a motion was granted for a new trial.[17a] The judge made no claim to exclusive jurisdiction either in this or in other cases to which the chief probation officer refers. This inactivity on the part of the judge is due undoubtedly to a doubt on his part as to the interpretation the supreme court would put upon the law should the issue be squarely raised and to a hesitation to sacrifice a young person to the confusing and demoralizing experience of being handled by two sets of authorities. His view of what the law should clearly state is expressed in a report made by a committee appointed in 1920 by the director of the department of public welfare and signed by the judge with other members of the committee [18] to the effect that "the circuit, county, and juvenile courts be given original and *exclusive* jurisdiction in all cases coming within the act entitled 'An act to regulate the treatment and control of dependent, neglected. and delinquent children.' "

AGE GROUPS.

The juvenile court law provides that all persons under the age of 21 shall be considered wards of the State and shall be subject to the care, guardianship, and control of the juvenile court.[19] The law then proceeds in its definition of the dependent and delinquent child to include any boy under 17 and any girl under 18. Thus jurisdiction attaches only to the earlier ages, but once obtained may be exercised until the child becomes 21.[20]

As a matter of fact, it is not the policy of the court to exercise this jurisdiction in the cases of boys between 17 and 21. That is, whenever a boy of 17 or 18 already on probation commits a new offense, it is the policy of the court to allow him to be proceeded against in the criminal court [21] rather than to attempt again to deal with him. The officers of the court are of the opinion that if probation under juvenile-court officers has not been effective when the boy was younger, it is not likely to be effective as the boy grows older.

[17a] The second trial came to an end May 19, 1922. with a second failure of a jury to agree. Chicago Daily Tribune, May 20, 1922.

[18] Report of the Illinois Department of Public Welfare Children's Committee (December, 1920, p. 10.)

[19] Hurd's Illinois Revised Statutes 1919, ch. 23, sec. 169.

[20] The Hotchkiss committee in 1912 apparently supported this interpretation and urged that the age of obtaining jurisdiction be raised to 21: "The committee feels that the provisions of the juvenile-court law should be amended so that any person under the age of 21 years, regardless of previous contact with the court, may be brought into the juvenile. rather than the police court. At present we have the anomalous situation of a boy of 19, who has never been brought before the juvenile court, arrested and forced to associate in the police court with the worst criminals in the community, while a boy with a long record in the juvenile court, evades police jurisdiction by virtue of this court record. In other words a premium is placed on getting a juvenile court record."-- (Juvenile Court of Cook County. Illinois--Report of a Committee appointed under Resolution of the Board of Commissioners of Cook County, p. 25.)

[21] This may be the boys' court—a branch of the municipal court—a lower court dealing with misdemeanants if the offense be committed outside Chicago, or the criminal court of Cook County.

JURISDICTION OVER ADULTS.

The juvenile court has no jurisdiction over adults except in so far as an order may be entered requiring a parent to contribute to the support of a dependent child committed to an institution. In such cases the court may enforce its order by requiring deductions from wages and by punishment for contempt of court. This lack of jurisdiction over adults will be discussed at a later point.[22]

---

[22] See p. 103.

THE ADMINISTRATIVE PROBLEMS OF THE COURT.

In order that the administrative problems of the juvenile court may be understood it is necessary to supplement the definitions of the various types of cases placed under its jurisdiction and to know the number of children brought into court, the relative numbers in the various groups, the conditions in the home and in the community making it necessary for them to be brought into court, and the differences among the various groups that demand differences in the method and treatment. It is difficult, for various reasons, to discover these facts, but certain data have been assembled for the purpose of illustrating the nature of the court's problems and the weight of its burden.

NUMBER OF CHILDREN BROUGHT INTO COURT.

During the first 21 years of the court's existence—that is, prior to July 1, 1920—79,000 children were brought into court.[1] It is impossible, however, to determine without laborious tabulation the number of children who have been handled by the court in each of these years. The total number during the period is the only information that can be given regarding children as distinguished from cases, since the statistics published by the court deal with cases rather than with children. A child may be brought before the judge several times in the same year and may be counted three, four, five, or possibly six times as a case, the number of repetitions varying considerably with the class of case. Thus, it must be remembered that whenever figures from the annual reports of the court are quoted in the following pages they represent cases, not children. From a social point of view this is unfortunate, since it would be desirable to know the facts in their relationship to child life in general. From an administrative viewpoint, however, the case is perhaps more significant, since it represents a certain amount of machinery set in motion each time a child is before the court.

Table I shows the numerical importance of the various types of cases heard by the court during the five-year period from December 1, 1914, to November 30, 1919.

---

[1] This figure was obtained from the docket numbers. It is customary to give the same number to a child even if he is brought into court again after a release.

TABLE I.—*Class of case; cases heard by the juvenile court, 1915–1919.*[1]

Class of case.	Cases heard by the court.	
	Number.	Per cent distribution.
Total..........	37,881	100.0
Delinquency..........	15,143	40.0
Dependency..........	10,631	28.1
Truancy..........	2,327	6.1
Aid to mothers..........	9,470	25.0
Feeble-minded..........	310	0.8

[1] Compiled from figures for fiscal years ending Nov. 30. Charity Service Reports, Cook County, Ill., 1915–1919. For 1920 the figures are as follows: Delinquency, 2,550; dependency, 1,262; truancy, 556; aid to mothers, 3,245; feeble-minded, 58. For 1921 they are: Delinquency, 2,415; dependency, 1,292; truancy, 648; aid to mothers, 1,429; feeble-minded, 69.

As to the problems especially characteristic of these separate groups, the annual reports of the court give little information other than the ages of children, the disposition of cases, and the offenses of delinquent children.

No attempt will be made here to describe the children included in the groups of cases under the acts covering aid-to-mothers, truant, and feeble-minded jurisdiction.[2]

PROBLEMS RELATING TO THE DELINQUENT CHILD.

With regard to the delinquent children, a study of the delinquent wards of the court during the first 10 years of the court's existence found that the problems of the delinquent child were primarily problems of immigrant adjustment, of poverty, of the broken, the degraded, and the crowded home, of school and neighborhood neglect, and only secondarily and to a very slight extent, of the unmanageable child in the midst of favorable circumstances.[3]

Among the cases of delinquent children by far the greater number are boys. Table II shows for the five-year period, 1915–1919, 11,799 cases of delinquent boys and 3,344 cases of delinquent girls. The greater number of boys is in part the result of different methods of investigation which will be discussed at a later point, and in part due to the method of reporting cases rather than children, since the boys tend to repeat oftener than girls. It is, also, a matter of difference in character of offense, as the girls are seldom brought to

[2] For mothers' pension cases, see Abbott, Edith, and Breckinridge, S. P.: Administration of the Aid-to-Mothers Law in Illinois. Children's Bureau, Publication No. 82, Washington, 1921.

For cases of truant children, see Abbott, Edith, and Breckinridge, S. P.: Truancy and Nonattendance in Chicago Schools. University of Chicago Press, Chicago, 1917.

For mental defectives, see Healy, William: The Individual Delinquent. Little, Brown & Co., Boston, 1915; and Mental Conflicts and Misconduct. Little, Brown & Co., Boston, 1917.

[3] Breckinridge, S. P., and Abbott, Edith: The Delinquent Child and the Home, Chapters III–X, Charities Publication Committee, New York, 1912.

court for childish pranks or gang depredations but nearly always for serious immorality, which necessitates immediate and vigorous action.

While the law names no lower age limits for juvenile-court jurisdiction, the State schools for delinquent boys and girls can receive no children under 10 years of age. All children under that age are therefore treated as dependent rather than delinquent, unless the child's experience has been such that he can not be placed with dependent children. For this reason Table II, which presents the ages of delinquent children, shows only one case of a delinquent child under 10 years of age.[4]

TABLE II.—*Age, by sex of child; delinquency cases heard by the juvenile court, 1915–1919.*[a]

Age of child.	Delinquency cases heard by the court.			
	Number.		Per cent distribution.	
	Boys.	Girls.	Boys.	Girls.
Total	11,799	3,344	100.0	100.
9		1		(b)
10	350	36	3.0	1.1
11	697	55	5.9	1.7
12	1,104	120	9.3	3.6
13	1,517	236	12.9	7.1
14	2,415	501	20.5	15.0
15	2,683	787	22.7	23.5
16	2,973	855	.25.2	25.6
17	c 59	730	0.5	21.8
18	c 1	c 21	(b)	0.6
19		c 2		(b)

[a] Compiled from figures for fiscal years ending Nov. 30. Charity Service Reports, Cook County, Ill., 1915–1919. For 1920 the figures are: Boys, 1,912; girls, 638. For 1921 they are: Boys, 1,754; girls, 661.
[b] Less than one-tenth of 1 per cent.
[c] Jurisdiction obtained at prior hearing before juvenile-court age limit was reached.

A difference in grouping of boys' and girls' cases might be expected from the difference in age limitation defined by the law—16 for boys and 17 for girls. The wider range exhibited by the girls' cases is therefore of no significance. There is, however, more concentration toward the upper age limit than in the case of the boys. Table II shows, for example, that 31.1 per cent of the boys were under 14, while only 13.5 per cent of the girls were so young. This again is in part the result of the differences in the character of offense, as shown by Table III.

---

[4] It is not possible to say definitely, but for this child it is probable that a dependent petition was substituted at a later date for the delinquent petition.

TABLE III.—*Offense, by sex of child; delinquency cases heard by the juvenile court, 1915–1919.*[a]

Offense.	Delinquency cases heard by the court.			
	Number		Per cent distribution.	
	Boys.	Girls.	Boys.	Girls.
Total	11,799	3,344	100.0	100.0
Stealing	8,067	397	68.4	11.9
Incorrigibility	1,900	1,387	16.1	41.4
Malicious mischief	605	5	5.1	0.1
Assault	509	19	4.3	0.6
Immorality	234	1,467	2.0	43.9
Miscellaneous offenses	484	69	4.1	2.1

[a] Compiled from figures for fiscal years ending Nov. 30. Charity Service Reports, Cook County, Ill., 1915–1919. For 1920 the figures are: Boys, 1,912; girls, 638. For 1921 they are: Boys, 1,754; girls, 661.

The offense, as given in this table, is never stated in the records as a formal charge against the child; but, as pointed out in the report of the chief probation officer, "is the conclusion of the statistical clerk after reading the complaint in the history sheet for each case."[5] The results shown in the table are therefore open to question because of the vagueness of the terms, the possible variation in classification, the method of classifying when there are two or more offenses, and the inadequacy of the history sheet itself. Nevertheless, the general results compare fairly closely with those presented in "The Delinquent Child and the Home,"[6] in which the classification was based on a careful reading of the whole case record and in which attention was given to a child accused of two or more offenses. The differences in the results, moreover, may be largely due to the classification by children in one table and by cases in the other.

Stated in general terms as they are, the list includes offenses of varying degrees of delinquency. Under the head of stealing have been grouped all the offenses that the court has separated into larceny, burglary, and robbery, as well as particular kinds of theft, such as the taking of automobiles or mail or stealing from railroad cars. Burglary, larceny, and robbery, however, may be used to describe a great many offenses connected with the taking of property, from the theft of a newspaper at the door to taking merchandise worth several hundred dollars from a store. This group of offenses against property is the most important class of offenses among the boys and contains 68.4 per cent of the cases.

The list of the girls' offenses presents a marked contrast to that of the boys: Nearly 44 per cent of the girls were brought into court for

[5] Charity Service Reports, Cook County, Ill., 1919, p. 263.
[6] Breckinridge, S. P., and Abbott, Edith: The Delinquent Child and the Home, p. 39, Charities Publications Committee, New York, 1912 (see special discussion pp. 27–30).

" immorality," meaning always questions of sex experience. Another 41.4 per cent were brought in for " incorrigibility," a term used whenever possible in girls' cases to avoid accusation of immorality, but very often indicating either suspected immorality or the danger of its development.

PROBLEMS RELATING TO THE DEPENDENT CHILD.

Very little information regarding the problems of the dependent child is available, except for age, number of times in court, and disposition of cases. The annual reports of the court give only an inadequate classification of home conditions. The problem is often a complicated one; and yet only one circumstance, such as a " drunken father " or " feeble-minded mother," is set down for each child. It is, however, entirely possible to have in the same family a combination of factors, such as both a drunken father and feeble-minded mother. Moreover, no extensive study of case records of dependent children has ever been made. It is, therefore, impossible to state with assurance what children constitute the group termed " dependent."

The ages of dependent children are shown in Table IV. Among these children no appreciable differences are found between the age distributions of the girls and of the boys. The table is therefore presented for both sexes combined.

TABLE IV.—*Age of child; dependency cases heard by the juvenile court, 1915–1919.*[a]

Age of child.	Dependent cases heard by the court.	
	Number.	Per cent. distribution.
Total	10,631	100.0
Under 7 years	4,137	38.9
7 years, under 14	5,661	53.2
14 years, under 16	699	6.6
16 years and over	134	1.3

[a] Compiled from figures for fiscal years ending Nov. 30. Charity Service Reports, Cook County, Ill., 1915–1919. For 1920 the figures are: Dependency cases, 1,262. For 1921 they are: Dependency cases, 1,292.

It appears that during the five-year period 1915–1919 more than one-third, 38.9 per cent of the dependent children, were under 7 years of age; more than one-half, 53.2 per cent, were 7 and under 14; and very few, only 7.9 per cent, were 14 and over. This is in marked contrast to the group of delinquent children, none of whom were under 9 and a large majority of whom were 14 and over—68.9 per cent of the boys and 86.5 per cent of the girls.[7]

[7] See Table II, p. 19.

The juvenile court law uses the two terms "dependent" and "neglected" as applicable to the same group of children. It might have been possible to assign certain clauses in the definition implying destitution to a "dependency" classification and others implying the presence of degrading influence to "neglect." Had this been done, a study of the records might more easily have revealed the relative numbers of the two groups. Such a classification has not been made, however, and it has been the custom of the court to call all the children brought in under this section "dependent."

How far the court is concerned with cases involving poverty only, it is therefore impossible to say. The group of children of widowed mothers who formerly might have formed a large part of the group of dependents are now, of course, cared for by the aid-to-mothers division [6] of the court. It was never the policy of the court, however, to break up a family on account of poverty only; such examination of the records as has been made indicates that the pension group is a group of children different from those treated under the dependency clause, the only type of case involving destitution alone handled under the dependency definition being that of the child both of whose parents are dead or permanently incapacitated and whose relatives are too poor to assume the responsibility for his care. And this seems to be a rare type of case, for the situation is usually complicated by the incompetence or the neglect of the relatives or of the neighbors who assume the care of children left alone by the death or incapacity of their parents.

Such a case of neglect, for example, was that of four children, three girls and a boy, aged 16, 14, 10, and 6, all the victims of active tuberculosis. The parents were both dead, and the children lived with a young married sister. But her husband worked irregularly, and she was careless about their illness and failed to see that they went regularly to the free dispensary for treatment.

Another case illustrating the fact that with destitution are often found elements of degradation is that of two girls, 15 and 8 years old, and a boy of 13, whose parents were both in a State hospital for the insane. An older sister assumed responsibility for them, but she was only 24 years of age, was divorced, and was suspected of being a prostitute. The 15-year-old girl, lacking the control and help needed, became delinquent before the court's attention was again called to the family.

In some cases illness combines with poverty to prevent the parents from fulfilling their responsibilities to their children.

Such a case was that of four children, all under 13. The mother had died of tuberculosis, and the father, though himself able to work only irregularly because of tuberculosis, was trying to keep the family together. In the end it was necessary for him to go to a sanatorium and to allow the court to make provision for the children.

---

[6] "Mothers' pension division" since enactment of amending law, June 29, 1921. Illinois Laws, 1921, p. 162.

When both parents are living, it is often some neglect on their part that brings the child into court. The neglect, however, may be quite unintentional and the result of ignorance or of sheer inability to meet the situation.

For example, in the case of two Lithuanian children, a girl of 11 and a boy of 8, the mother was a paralytic and had been in the county hospital for months. The father worked in the steel mills 12 hours a day. The children had not been in school all year and were alone all day, doing whatever housework was done.

Perhaps the commonest form of neglect is the desertion of the children by one or by both parents. Neither the deserted wife nor the unmarried mother is eligible to aid under the aid to mothers law. A mother whose husband deserts, leaving her to support several small children, may be able for a time to hold the family together, but if sickness comes or a time of unusual strain, the only course open to her may be to place the children in an institution, and for this purpose she appeals to the court. The child of the unmarried mother frequently becomes " dependent " in the same way.

If the mother is dead, the father finds it even more difficult than the mother to take the place of both parents. Leaving the children with relatives often seems the easiest solution of the problem, but it is not always a satisfactory solution.

Such a case was that of a 12-year-old dependent girl found living with her maternal grandmother and aunt in a house of prostitution. Her mother was dead; her father had married again and had other children. He had allowed the grandmother to keep the little girl. He seldom saw her, and he knew nothing of the conditions in the home.

When the mother has died, the father sometimes attempts to meet the needs of the family by employing a housekeeper. This often leads to friction with the older children and sometimes to irregular sex relationships. It is not then surprising that many fathers who are not very vigorous, despair of finding a way out and, lacking a keen sense of responsibility, desert the home and abandon the children to the mercy of the community. The burden in these cases may fall on older children who are still too young to be expected to assume the cares of a large family, or who already have families of their own. The court is often called upon to assist in the adjustments necessary in situations of this kind.

One father, for instance, deserted six children a few years after the mother's death. He had a housekeeper for a time, who lived with him as his wife, but the children objected, and he finally left home. The 22-year-old married son, who had tuberculosis, was trying to care for a sister of 15 and three brothers of 12, 10, and 8; but his wife's illness made it necessary for him to ask the court to find homes for the children.

Desertion on the part of the mother is probably less common than on the part of the father. There is, however, no reason to believe that if left alone the mother assumes the double burden more willingly than the father whose wife has left him. The mother who deserts is usually one who runs away with another man, leaving the children with their father. The situation that the father must meet is more difficult than that caused by a mother's death, for his sense of responsibility is naturally weakened by her defection and by the feeling that he is after all not entirely to blame for what may happen to the children.

In the case of five children under 14 whose mother deserted, nothing seemed possible but to distribute the children among relatives and institutions.

So far the cases cited have illustrated a comparatively simple form of neglect, that caused by the desertion of one or both parents. More difficult to handle are those cases in which the parents are either incompetent through physical or mental defect or are actually so degraded as to be a menace to the well-being of the children. The presence of mental defect and of tuberculosis is frequently the dominating factor in the situation.

A mother of nine children was found to have a mental age of 11 years. Two of the younger children had glandular tuberculosis, but all the social agencies who had been interested in the family had found it impossible to impress upon her the necessity for sending the children to the dispensary. An 18-year-old daughter was mentally subnormal and became delinquent. The 17-year-old son was in court several times for stealing and was finally committed to the house of correction for burglary. The 13-year-old boy was a truant and stole property from the school. The home was dirty and disorderly. The father seemed no more competent to manage the family than the mother.

It is often particularly difficult in the absence of vigorous control by the health authorities to enforce parental responsibility for the health of the children.

A deserted mother who had pulmonary tuberculosis in such an advanced stage as to be a menace to the health of her three children, aged 7, 5, and 1, finally consented to go to a county sanatorium, where the children were also to be treated for glandular tuberculosis; but when the ambulance arrived she managed to escape, taking the baby and deserting the other two children.

Somewhat special cases are those in which parents try to dispose of their children in return for money.

In one case, an Italian mother was deserted by her husband just before the birth of her second child. The first child was only 14 months old, and she allowed the doctor to give the second baby away. Complaint was made to the court that the baby had been given to a colored woman who kept a disorderly house. The baby was placed for a time in an institution, then given back to the mother. Later, however, the mother gave the child to the same woman on her promise to pay $500. Needless to say the mother never received the $500; but the baby had been removed from the court's jurisdiction, and months of effort on the part of the court failed to locate the child.

From the citation of these cases it will be seen that the problem of the dependent child is a problem into which enter a number of complicating and interrelated factors—destitution, sickness, mental defect, moral degradation, desertion, ignorance, incompetence, and neglect. It is the problem of the juvenile court to break the vicious circle of poor inheritance, lack of training, and social neglect that often characterize the experience of the parents and to lift the dependent children out of circumstances that cause suffering and deprivation or that may lead to delinquency.

ORGANIZATION OF THE COURT.

THE JUDGE.

The judge of the juvenile court is one of the 20 judges of the circuit court of Cook County. As such, he is elected by popular vote for a term of six years and is selected as a judge of the juvenile court by vote of all the circuit court judges of the county. He receives a salary of $12,000 a year, paid half by the State and half by the county. The selection may, by law, be made " at such times as they shall determine,"[1] but it has been the practice of the circuit court judges in Chicago to continue to select the same person as judge of the juvenile court as long as he remains in office or as long as he can be persuaded to serve. During the 20 years of its existence only four judges have presided regularly over the juvenile court.[2]

A number of other judges, however, have presided over the court temporarily. When the judge of the juvenile court is on vacation, ill, or necessarily absent from the bench for some other reason one of the other judges of the circuit court hears juvenile cases. Since 1919, moreover, when the work became too heavy for one judge, the judge of the juvenile court has devoted one week in each month to the hearing of contested cases and to special administrative work and during that week another judge sits in his place. That judge is from another circuit and was designated by the supreme court, and so far as possible he acts in all cases in which the judge of the juvenile court can not be present. When he is unable to sit, other judges have to be called in, and they are designated by the circuit court. The hearings, naturally, are noticeably different when one of the judges less experienced in juvenile court work is on the bench. In general, however, the presiding judge is disposed to recognize that he is sitting only as a substitute and to rely upon the probation department for guidance or to continue the more difficult cases until the judge of the juvenile court returns.

---

[1] Hurd's Illinois Revised Statutes, 1919, ch. 23, sec. 171.

[2] Hon. Richard S. Tuthill, who served from July 1, 1899, to June 30, 1905, and from July 1, 1907, to June 30, 1908; Hon. Julian W. Mack, from July 1, 1905, to June 30, 1907; Hon. Merritt W. Pinckney, from July 1, 1908, to June 30, 1916; and Hon. Victor P. Arnold, from June 30, 1916, to the present time.

The duties of the judge are both administrative and judicial, but whether or not he takes an active part in the administrative affairs of the court depends somewhat upon his own inclination, for he is given power by law to intrust to the probation department all administrative duties. That it is possible for him to retain the direction of general policies is shown by the testimony of Judge Pinckney [3] before the county civil service commission. When, however, the judge is called upon to hear more than 8,000 cases in a year, an average of 30 cases a day, 5 days in the week, it is obviously impossible for him to attend to administrative details. In practice, then, the judge is responsible for the formulation of important general rules of administration, and the actual carrying out of policies is left to the probation staff.

The personality and the high qualifications necessary for a judge of the juvenile court have often been stressed. Judge Mack, formerly judge of the Chicago court, in speaking of the training necessary for the judge, says:

The public at large, sympathetic with the work, and even the probation officers who are not lawyers, regard him (the judge) as one having almost autocratic power. Because of the extent of his jurisdiction and the tremendous responsibility that it entails, it is, in my judgment, absolutely essential that he be a trained lawyer, thoroughly imbued with the doctrine that ours is 'a government of laws, not of men.' He must, however, be more than this. He must be a student of and deeply interested in the problems of philanthropy and child life as well as a lover of children. He must be able to understand a boy's point of view and ideas of justice; he must be patient and willing to search out the underlying causes of the trouble and to formulate the plan by which, through the cooperation, ofttimes of many agencies, the cure may be effected." [4]

The Chicago court has been particularly fortunate in its judges, who have been remarkably free from political influence and have fulfilled as nearly as can be expected the conditions mentioned above. The judge now sitting is said to have an extraordinary patience, sympathy, and capacity for inspiring confidence. It is said that his decisions are rendered after a hearing so fair, gentle, courteous, and firm that they seem to all parties inevitable and conclusive.

WOMAN ASSISTANT TO THE JUDGE TO HEAR CASES OF DELINQUENT GIRLS.

The juvenile court law makes no provision for the appointment of a woman to hear cases of delinquent girls. The difficulties of hearing

[3] Breckinridge, S. P., and Abbott, Edith: The Delinquent Child and the Home, Appendix II, Charities Publication Committee, New York, 1912.
[4] Mack, J. W., "Legal problems involved in the establishment of the juvenile court," *in* Breckinridge, S. P., and Abbott, E.: The Delinquent Child and the Home, Charities Publication Committee, New York, 1912, p. 198.

girls' cases in open court, however, led the judge in 1913 to recommend to the county board the creation of a probation officer's position which might serve such a need. The judge was given authority to appoint a woman, who is known as assistant to the judge but has the legal status of a probation officer. The woman appointed was a lawyer who had been for a number of years public guardian. She has served as assistant to the judge from 1913 until the present time. As probation officer she has no power to render a decision in any case, but issues an opinion in the form of a recommendation to the judge, which in practice is rarely reversed.

The adoption of this policy gave rise to certain criticism, however, and in 1915 complaint was made to the grand jury that cases were decided by the assistant, who was sitting "without warrant of law" and holding a "mock court." The result was, nevertheless, a cordial indorsement of the plan, for after hearing many witnesses and after an investigation of the administration of the court by a committee of its members, the grand jury reported to the criminal court of Cook County [5] that, while it was incompetent to pass upon the legality of the work of the assistant to the judge, it felt that "it would be highly desirable to amend the juvenile court act so as to remove all doubt as to the powers and duties of the woman assistant to the presiding judge. * * * It desires, however, to commend in the strongest terms the idea that cases of delinquent girls should be held, as at present, as privately as possible before a competent court."

THE PROBATION DEPARTMENT.

Appointment and discharge.

Probation officers, as before stated, are appointed by the judge of the juvenile court on the basis of competitive examination. In general no minimum educational requirements are specified, but the committee in charge of the examination may refuse to recommend anyone who fails in the particular examination to give evidence of a certain educational standard.

While this method of selection and appointment has been strictly adhered to, there had, until October 4, 1921, been no similar provision for facilitating the discharge of officers who eventually prove to be unfit for service. It is, of course, a defect of many civil-service systems that the provision for the discharge of incompetent persons is ineffective. The civil service law usually contains a provision for dismissal after a formal hearing on a specific charge of misconduct or incompetency. The Chicago court has established no substitute for this civil-service method. Hence, the exercise of his unquestioned power of dismissal brings upon the judge the entire odium result-

---

[5] Charity Service Reports, Cook County, Ill., 1915, p. 224.

ing from the dismissal, and he may hesitate, for various reasons, to dismiss incompetent persons.[6] As a matter of fact, only one dismissal and one suspension upon a charge of incompetency have occurred since the dismissal of the chief probation officer in 1911.

Number.

The number of probation officers is determined each year by the circuit judges. At the present time [7] the staff numbers 145 persons— 17 civil-service appointees, 26 police probation officers paid by the city of Chicago, and 102 probation officers paid by the county. Among those designated as probation officers are the woman who acts as assistant to the judge, hearing cases of delinquent girls, and the chief probation officer, who is responsible for the direction of the entire staff. Under him are a deputy chief probation officer and 5 assistant probation officers who act as heads of the investigation division, the family supervision division, the delinquent boys' division, the child-placing division, and the aid to mothers' division. Eighty-three assistant probation officers are assigned to these various divisions. Eleven others are assigned to special work and would not ordinarily be considered probation officers. They include a psychologist working with the Institute for Juvenile Research, the secretaries to the judge and to the assistant to the judge, a nurse connected with the court dispensary, four court reporters, two interpreters, and an officer whose function is to see that orders of the court for payment of support are enforced. The 17 civil-service employees are clerical assistants.

Of the 90 officers who carry on the work usually regarded as probation work, 75 are women and 15 are men. Twenty-six were appointed before 1913 and were reappointed without further examination when the portion of the law under which they had been ap-

---

[6] On Oct. 4, 1921, however, the following actions on the part of the chief probation officer were authorized:

Suspensions.—The chief probation officer to have authority to suspend any assistant probation officer for a definite period without pay, not to exceed 30 days, by notifying the officer of his suspension either verbally or in writing, and at the same time submitting to the judge of the juvenile court a written statement reciting the name of the employee, the date of suspension, the period thereof and the cause therefor, and in case the suspension is to be followed by charges, a request for discharge or removal. The officer shall have the right to appeal to the judge within 5 days of the date of the suspension.

Removal and discharge.—In case request is made for removal or discharge of any assistant probation officer, written notice of the filing of charges against the officer shall be given to him stating specifically the facts alleged to constitute the cause for removal. A written reply to the charges may be made by the officer to the judge within 5 days.

Causes for removal or discharge.—(1) Has violated a lawful and reasonable departmental order publicly posted in the department.

(2) Has failed to obey a lawful and reasonable direction made and given him by his superior officer where such failure amounts to an act of insubordination or serious breach of proper discipline, or resulted or might reasonably have been expected to result in loss or injury to a child.

(3) That he fails to perform properly the duties of his position.

[7] The fiscal year ending Nov. 30, 1921.

pointed was declared unconstitutional; the other 64 have obtained their positions by passing one of the competitive examinations held by the court itself.

Salaries.

The juvenile court law provides for the payment of the salaries of the probation staff by the county board of commissioners. This means that the amount of the salary is determined by the county board, although the number of officers is determined by the circuit judges and appointment is in the hands of the juvenile court judge. The payment of all salaries depends, of course, upon appropriations of the county board of commissioners. Thus, as in the case of funds for mothers' pensions, the juvenile court is dependent upon a separate and at times hostile department of the government for the provision of funds to establish a competent and sufficient force of probation officers. The complaint is frequently made that the court can not get better trained officers, particularly men, because the salaries paid do not measure up to those in allied professions, nor in some cases to those having a more political character. The salary of the assistant to the judge is at present [8] $5.500 a year; that of the chief probation officer, $3,300; of the deputy chief probation officer, $2,400; of heads of divisions, $2,196; of district officers, $1,788, out of which "field expenses" are paid.[9] To be sure, the salaries of heads of divisions and district officers compare favorably with the salaries of private case-work agencies doing similar work. For example, the district superintendents of the United Charities receive from $1,680 to $2,000 and visitors from $1,080 to $1,680. But these positions are largely held by women; the positions are notoriously underpaid, and those organizations, too, suffer from excessive "labor turnover."

Organization.

The organization of the probation department is necessarily somewhat complicated. The chief probation officer is the administrative head of the department responsible for carrying out such policies of the organization as have been agreed upon with the judge for the general supervision of the entire staff, for securing cooperative relations with other agencies, etc. The deputy chief probation officer assists the chief probation officer in the discharge of his administrative duties and in the general supervision of the work of the probation officers. In addition, the deputy chief probation officer acts as chairman of the committee that investigates all cases of dependent

---

[8] Fiscal year ending Nov. 30, 1921.
[9] Two of the officers who have charge of farm placements receive $19 per month extra for field expenses. Tickets to outlying districts are furnished to any of the officers and paid for as office expenses. Ordinary carfare is, however, paid by the officers.

and neglected children before they are brought into court receives all applications for the release of delinquent children who have been committed to institutions, and handles the correspondence in the cases of nonresident children who are brought to the court's attention.

ORGANIZATION OF THE PROBATION DEPARTMENT.

Judge.

Assistant to Judge—Woman lawyer.	Chief probation officer. Deputy chief probation officer.

Police probation officers' division: 26 officers (paid by city of Chicago).	Investigation division: 14 officers.	Family supervision division: 30 officers.	Probation for delinquent boys' division: 15 officers.	Child-placing division: 8 officers.	Aid to mothers division: 21 officers.	Probation officers on special work: 11 officers.	Clerical assistants, including 7 stenographers, 5 typists, and 5 clerks.

The assignment of the probation officers to the various divisions is generally based upon the principle of specialization of function, although as will be seen from the later discussion there are many points at which this principle can not be applied. The investigation division with 14 officers has charge of the investigation of all complaints made directly to the court. The family supervision division includes 30 officers who supervise dependent children and delinquent girls placed on probation in their own homes. The delinquent boys' division with 15 officers is responsible for the probation of delinquent boys; the child-placing division with 8 officers secures family homes for dependent children and delinquent girls removed from their own homes but not committed to institutions; and the aid to mothers division with 21 officers investigates and supervises all mothers' pension cases. The accompanying chart indicates the organization of the probation department.[10]

Within the divisions the work is organized in the main along territorial lines, with each officer responsible for the cases in a given district. This system, however, is not uniformly followed. In the investigation division, for example, one officer has developed such skill in handling cases in which delicate moral situations are involved that all such cases are now assigned to her; in the family supervision division two officers devote all their time to follow-up work with the families of children committed to manual-training and industrial schools; and in the delinquent boys' division two officers have entire charge of farm placements.

---

[10] Chart from Charity Service Reports, Cook County, Illinois, 1918, p. 206 (figures brought up to date).

In addition to the two interpreters mentioned, whose work is in the courtroom, the probation staff includes officers speaking Polish, Hungarian, Italian, German, Lithuanian, and most of the Slavic dialects. Under the district system a foreign-speaking officer is assigned to a district in which his language is prevalent. This does not mean, however, that all foreign-speaking officers supervise only foreign-speaking families or that all foreign families are assigned to officers of their own nationality. Of the five negro officers, however, four work exclusively with negro families.

All the territory in the county outside the limits of the city of Chicago is included in the regular probation districts with the exception of four towns lying to the north. In one of these the secretary of the associated charities acts as truant officer and also takes charge of all dependent and delinquent cases. She is paid by the town and is commissioned as a volunteer probation officer by the juvenile court. The truant officer in another town and the township supervisor of the poor in each of the other two act as volunteer probation officers. All these officers take charge of all police cases, bring children to the detention home, and perform all the functions of the regular county probation officers.

Except in these towns, cases outside the city of Chicago which are reported to the court by police officers are investigated by officers of the investigation division. Most such cases, however, have already been dealt with by justices of the peace and are formally transferred by them to the juvenile court. Children in these districts are placed on probation to the regular probation officers of the juvenile court.

Police probation officers.

The police probation officers form a distinct division of the probation staff. The chief of police has assigned 26 of these officers paid by the city to the juvenile court. They work under the immediate direction of one of their number; but inasmuch as they receive commissions as probation officers from the juvenile court, they are also brought under the supervision of the chief probation officer. In 1899, when the judge of the juvenile court requested the assignment of police officers, such officers met a very real need that could not have been met otherwise. Whether or not it is wise to retain them now that higher standards of work have been developed and better trained officers have been secured by the court is open to question. Two reasons, however, for perpetuating the system are: First, the volume of work which is very great in proportion to the size of the staff; second, the fact that complaints, particularly of delinquent boys, will probably always be made at police stations, and it is well to have a certain officer from each station assigned to handle juvenile cases so that he will receive some supervision from the probation office and become familiar with juvenile court procedure.

The police probation officers are assigned to police districts and within those districts perform some of the functions of the regular juvenile court probation officers. Their duties, however, are now narrowly restricted. They receive complaints filed at police stations, investigate the cases involved, file petitions and appear in court with the children to present the case. They are not allowed to do any probation work, and cases continued under supervision are always assigned to the regular probation officers. The police probation officers wear citizen's clothes and are not to be confused with the uniformed police force of the city, although they are under the authority of the chief of police. The principal importance of their work lies in the more intelligent handling of juvenile cases in the police stations and in the elimination of the uniformed police officer from the juvenile court room. Their work will be described at greater length in the section dealing with methods of investigation.[11]

RECORDS AND REPORTS.

Annual reports.

The chief probation officer and the matron of the juvenile detention home report annually to the board of commissioners of Cook County. These reports are published each year with the reports of other departments of the county government in the Cook County Charity Service Reports and separate reprints are issued as well.

The annual report of the chief probation officer contains a brief summary of the progress made during the year, the plans for the future, numerous statistical tables, and in some years a history of the court. In 1919, 38 of the 70 pages of the report were devoted to statistical tables. The character of this statistical information has improved within the last few years, at least from the point of view of accuracy, though errors are still not uncommon. The material selected for presentation is not, however, always that of the greatest value to persons interested in the condition of the children who become wards of the court. Tables such as those showing home conditions and offenses are compiled by statistical clerks after hasty reading of parts of the case records. These tables fail by their simplicity to give a picture of the very complicated conditions existing and are, therefore, likely to be misleading. The summary tables of children placed on probation and committed to institutions for each year since 1904 fail to agree with the figures given in other tables presented and seem to be of little value. Finally, the tables present information only for cases, never for children.

Case records.

The records of the juvenile court include not only legal papers but social records giving as completely as possible the information

[11] See p. 40.

that the court has obtained with regard to the child and the family. The legal papers, including the petition, the summons, the stenographic report of the hearing, and the judge's order regarding disposition, are in charge of the clerk of the circuit court and are filed in the vaults of the county building. They are public records open to any interested citizen.

The records of the probation department, however, the social records, are private records for the use of the court and are open to outsiders only upon the order of the chief probation officer. This order is usually granted to a representative of a recognized social agency interested in a particular case.

Case records for all the children in one family are kept in folder form, and filed alphabetically—delinquents and dependents in one file, mothers' pension cases separately. Formerly a separate record was kept for each child in court, but the duplication of reports and the cross references involved made the system too complicated for convenience.

These records, dealing sometimes with three or four children of the family and covering considerable periods of time, become very bulky and difficult to read. They are arranged by sections. One part, for example, may contain all the hearings for all the children at various times, while another part contains the probation officer's reports of the progress of the case. They are difficult to disentangle for any one child or for any one period of time.

Active case records of dependent and delinquent children are filed together in a room devoted entirely to clerical work. Closed cases, pension records, and supervised-complaint records are kept in separate files in this room. Another file contains records of runaway children picked up in Chicago whose cases are investigated by the juvenile court.

Other records and forms.

In addition to the case records, the court keeps two card-index systems—one recording the name and disposition of every child who has ever been in court, the other a record of every case investigated but not brought into court. Besides these, a ledger is kept, in which are recorded the cases assigned each probation officer, the charge, the disposition, and the number of visits the officer makes to each child each month. From this ledger a monthly report is prepared for the chief probation officer and for the heads of divisions. showing for each officer the number of families under care. the total visits made by that officer in the month, and the number of families not visited. These reports are used as a check upon the officers to see that the mini mum requirement of one visit per month to each family is fulfilled so far as possible.

PRELIMINARY PROCEDURE.

For the ordinary criminal procedure that might include, according to the seriousness of the offense, arrest by warrant, examination by a magistrate, holding to bail, possibly indictment, and finally trial by jury, the juvenile court process has substituted the less rigorous sequence of complaint, investigation, petition, summons, and an informal hearing. At any point in this process the child may be removed to a special place of detention or may be left at home without bail.

COMPLAINT AND PETITION.

The juvenile court law provides that a case may be brought to the attention of the court by a petition filed by any reputable citizen.[1] This applies to all classes of cases; and when a petition has been filed the case must be heard by the court, no matter what the result of the investigation. In order, then, to eliminate from the docket cases that really have no basis of fact or that could be easily adjusted without court action, the "complaint" system has been devised. That is, whenever "any reputable citizen" reports to the court a condition that, in his opinion, needs investigation, unless he insists upon filing a petition, he is encouraged to state the difficulty in an informal complaint. This gives the court an opportunity to make a preliminary investigation, and a petition is then filed by an officer of the court only if conditions found seem to warrant court action. It may be said that while this seems to place in the hands of the investigation division wide powers of discretion which the law contemplated bestowing upon the judge of the juvenile court, any person who feels aggrieved can insist upon filing a petition. Investigation is, moreover, one of the crucial points of juvenile court procedure; and if a child can be saved even from so informal an experience as a juvenile court hearing and record, the use of this device is highly desirable. The court has been hearing an average of 30 cases a day during the last few years; the immediate filing of a petition for every complaint would lay upon the judge an impossible burden.

INVESTIGATION.

It is the function of the investigation division to receive complaints and to make investigations. The division is theoretically

---

[1] Hurd's Illinois Revised Statutes, 1919, ch. 23, sec. 172.

responsible for all investigations; in actual practice, however, only cases of dependent children are handled exclusively by its officers. Some cases of delinquent girls are investigated by officers of the family-supervision division under the direction of the head of the investigation division. Cases of delinquent boys reported directly to the court are investigated by officers of the delinquent boys' division, also under the direction of the head of the investigation division; and cases of delinquent boys reported to the police, by far the greater number of delinquent boys' cases, are investigated and brought to court by the police probation officers with no report to the investigation division. Applications for mothers' pensions are investigated by the aid to mothers division, and truancy cases are investigated by the truant officers of the compulsory education department of the city board of education.

When cases are brought to the court by cooperating social agencies, the investigation by the agency is usually accepted by the court. This is particularly true of agencies whose representatives are commissioned as volunteer probation officers, such as the Juvenile Protective Association and the group of Jewish social agencies—including the Bureau of Personal Service and the Jewish Home Finding Society, of Chicago, now organized as the Jewish Social Service Bureau. The court records in such cases are often quite scanty, and it is difficult to say how adequate the investigations have been, particularly when the same agency is given the supervision of the case and when the only contact of the court officers with the case is the hearing.

Dependent children.

It is in the investigation of cases of dependent children that the court most nearly realizes its standards of work. These cases, as it has been said, are handled entirely by the investigation division. The first task of the division is the receipt of complaints and the elimination of all that are too trivial for attention and of those that do not belong to the juvenile court. Anonymous complaints are not received but are turned over to a voluntary organization, the Juvenile Protective Association. Except in the case of well-recognized social agencies complaints are not received by telephone but must be made in person at court, where they are received by a trained investigator, usually the head of the division, who can can tell whether the difficulty complained of is properly a matter for juvenile court concern, or whether it should be handled by some other court or agency. To pass judgment on the complaints as they are made requires a nice sense of discrimination, a knowledge of the resources of the community, both public and private, and a familiarity with juvenile court procedure. Approximately one-half of the complaints received at the desk are disposed of without further attention by the division. Complaints received by mail are carefully studied by the head of the division and eliminated, referred to some other agency, or investigated, as the circumstances require. As a result of this preliminary scrutiny of complaints, the number of investigations undertaken is greatly reduced, and the time and energy of officers are saved for the most important work.

The complaints accepted are first "cleared" at the confidential exchange, known as the bureau of social registration, and a record made of all the social agencies that have known the family. The case, with the list of agencies already registered, is then assigned to an officer for investigation.

Upon receipt of the complaint slip the officer assigned to the case makes the kind of investigation that is made by any good case-work agency. The court is concerned not only with learing the truth or falsity of the allegations of the complainant but also with understanding the whole family situation. The names, ages, occupations, and earnings, or school and grade, of every member of the family are obtained so far as possible, and inquiries are made as to the names of relatives, the date of the parents' marriage, length of time in Chicago, housing conditions, and the family's moral status. The technique is that of a case-work agency, and the investigation must necessarily vary from case to case. The complainant, if he has not been interviewed in the office, is always consulted first and the family itself is always visited. Information is secured from the usual sources: The school, the employer, the church, relatives, and official and social-agency records. A school record must be obtained if the case is to be heard by the court; otherwise, the officer uses her own discretion about obtaining information from the school.

The head of the investigation division keeps in close touch with the progress of the investigation, reads the reports submitted in connection with all visits made, and is at all times accessible to the officer for informal conferences on difficult questions. No complaint can be dropped or otherwise disposed of without her approval.[2]

Dependent cases are not, however, brought into court on the judgment of the investigation division alone. A committee, known as the dependent-case-conference committee, acts as a board of final review. This committee is composed of the deputy chief probation officer, the head of the investigation division, the head of the family-supervision division, the officer in charge of the work with children committed to institutions, and an assistant from the State's attorney's office. Cases presented to the committee by the investigating officer, with the consent of the head of the investigating division, are subjected to

---

[2] The number of complaints adjusted without court action will be discussed at a later point. See p. 42.

a searching analysis by the case conference committee. The committee passes only upon cases for which the investigation division thinks court action is needed and upon cases which the Juvenile Protective Association or the Jewish agencies wish to bring into court. It is not concerned with the large number of cases that the investigation division, on its own authority, decides should not be brought into court. In this respect the work of the committee differs from that of a similar committee of the aid-to-mothers department,[3] which passes judgment on all cases investigated by that department. After assuring itself that the investigation has been thorough—that is, that all necessary facts have been secured and that they are in convincing form—the committee proceeds to consider whether the case necessitates court action. One principle is always kept in mind, namely, that children are to remain in their homes if possible. A strong reason for removal must exist if the committee is to recommend placing children in institutions or in homes other than their own.

Cases necessitating removal of children from their homes tend to fall into two classes: (1) Those in which the parent or guardian is unable or unwilling to provide maintenance and care for the child; (2) those in which the parents or guardians are mentally or morally unfit to provide proper care. In considering cases of the first type the committee goes carefully into the income and resources of the family. There is no disposition to make it easy for the parent or guardian to shift the burden of support to the county and, ordinarily, even when there seems no alternative to institutional care for the children, the case will not be brought into court if the committee considers the family able to pay for that care. Sometimes, however, even if a parent is able to pay for a child in an institution, the case has to be brought into court because the institutions prefer the security of an order for payment made through the court to the uncertainty of a private agreement. If court action is recommended because of the parents' neglect, the committee makes sure that the neglect is of an obvious and unmistakable kind. For instance, the committee refused to recommend filing a petition in the case of a family complained of because the 11-year-old girl was overworked and undernourished. It was decided, however, to carry the case as a supervised complaint so that the committee might be assured that the parents were living up to the promises they made with regard to the girl's diet. If the moral character of the parents is in question, the evidence must be of a kind that would be admitted in a regular criminal court, and not mere opinion or hearsay.

Whenever the filing of a petition is decided upon, a recommendation for disposition of the case is also prepared, so that the case

---

[3] See p. 42 of this report.

usually comes to the judge with a specific suggestion for action. If commitment to an institution is recommended, the officer in charge of the work with institutions makes sure by preliminary inquiry that there is a vacancy in the selected institution. Usually the judge accepts these recommendations and takes advantage of these arrangements.

Delinquent girls.

Cases of delinquent girls come to the attention of the court either through some " reputable citizen " who makes a complaint to the court, as in the case of dependent children, or through the police to whom complaints are frequently made· or who arrest girls under various circumstances. In any case the investigation is made by the investigation division with the difference that in cases reported directly to the court the investigation is made before the petition is filed and an attempt is made to adjust the case without court action; whereas in the cases reported to the police the police probation officer files the petition, and the real investigation is made often after the first. hearing. This means that it is impossible to spare the girl the necessity of appearing in court or the stigma of a delinquency record.[4]

The investigation is usually made by the officer in the family-supervision division in whose district the girl lives. The officer reports to the head of the investigation division and is under her supervision. The type of investigation made is similar to that in the cases of dependent children. It is concerned primarily with the circumstances of the offense and the character of the girl herself, but also covers the family situation. The methods used, with some minor exceptions, are the same as those used in dependency cases. The rule that school records are to be obtained when the girl is in school is more rigidly enforced than in dependency cases. The petition may be filed with the sanction of the head of the investigation division without consultation with any committee corresponding to the dependent-case-conference committee.

Delinquent boys.

Cases of delinquent boys come to the attention of the court in the same way as cases of delinquent girls—that is, either by direct complaint to the court or through the police; but by far the larger number come through the police. If the case is reported to the court, the

---

[4] This system of investigating cases of delinquent girls is of recent origin. Prior to 1919 all cases reported to the police were investigated by the police probation officers. In 1919 three policewomen were assigned to the court to investigate these cases. They worked under double supervision, that of the police department and of the head of the investigation division. In 1920 the policewomen were removed and the present method adopted.

investigation is made by an officer in the delinquent boys' division under the direct supervision of the head of the investigation division. The reason for having this work done by the officers in the delinquent boys' division is not only that the officers in the investigation division have not time to investigate all cases, but also that the officers in the delinquent boys' division are men, and the advantages of having men for the work with delinquent boys is thought to compensate for the disadvantages coming from divided authority and lack of specialization in the one field.[5] This investigation, too, follows the lines described in connection with investigation of dependency. It is an investigation of the family situation by the methods familiar to case-work agencies, as well as an investigation of the truth of the particular complaint.

Police probation officers' investigation.

Most of the delinquent boys' cases, however, as already stated, are reported to the police; and in these cases the police probation officers make their own investigations and file their own petitions without consulting any other department of the court. The police officers work under the direction of one of their own number, designated as the officer in charge of the police probation officers. Except in those cases in which the boy is held in custody in the detention home, they are not required to report to this officer the steps taken in the investigation or the decision reached as to treatment. In these cases a report of the reason for detention and of the plan for action is required. The officer in charge of police probation officers makes a monthly report to the chief probation officer, giving the number of cases handled by each officer and their disposition. He does not report on individual cases. There are no rules governing the process of investigation, and each officer is free to carry on the investigation of each case as he sees fit. He may secure the information he desires by visiting the home or by calling the boy or his parents into the police station. In general, there is no attempt to make a social investigation such as that made by the investigating division, but the inquiry is limited to ascertaining the truth or falsity of the complaint. Many of the officers, however, have worked for several years in their districts, know many of the families, and take cognizance of particularly bad family situations.

The police probation officers do not clear cases with the confidential exchange and make no effort to secure previous social records of the family. Each officer, it is true, keeps a record of all com-

---

[5] At one time a man officer was assigned to the investigation division for full-time work and was given the more difficult boys' cases to investigate. This arrangement was very satisfactory to the head of the division, but because of difficulty in securing efficient men for the delinquent boys' division, he was transferred to that division.

plaints that he has handled, from which it is possible to discover whether a complaint has been previously made concerning a particular boy, but in practice the officer usually relies on his memory rather than on his record. No attempt is made, moreover, to use the files of the court for purposes of clearing. A minor offense of a child already on probation is frequently dealt with by police probation officers without consulting the officer of the delinquent boys' division who has the boy under his care and is responsible for his conduct while on probation. After the complaint has been disposed of in such a case the police officer usually reports the facts informally to the head of the delinquent boys' division, who makes a memorandum of the matter and gives it to the officer on the case.

Even when the police probation officer decides to bring into court for rehearing a case already on probation, he makes no special effort to notify the boy's probation officer, and it is sometimes quite by chance that the officer learns of the difficulty.[6]

The aim of the police probation officers, as of the juvenile-court probation officers, is to settle cases out of court if possible; and the great majority of cases are so settled—14,500 out of 16,995 complaints received by police probation officers in 1919.[7] While there are no rigid rules determining which cases should be settled without court action and which are to be brought before the court, in general the officers try to settle the less serious complaints, and particularly those involving first offenders.

No established method of adjusting cases out of court has been developed, but in some precincts the custom has grown up of holding a conference with boys, parents, and complainant at the police station in the precinct. Because of the desire not to interfere with the boys' school work the conferences are usually held on Saturday mornings, and in some precincts a number of cases are settled at this time. It is obvious that these hearings may be the source of very real confusion on the part of both boy and parents as to where the authority over children has been lodged.

Other investigations.

The investigation of applications for pensions under the aid-to-mothers law is conducted by the officers of the aid-to-mothers division. The process has been described in a study of mothers' pensions in Illinois.[8] It is in general the investigation of a relief society, with more rigid rules than are common as to verification from official records of facts relating to the death or incapacity of the father,

---

[6] See p. 75, case Edward O.
[7] Charity Service Reports, Cook County, Ill., 1919, p. 287.
[8] Abbott, Edith, and Breckinridge, S. P.: "Administration of the Aid-to-Mothers Law in Illinois." Children's Bureau, Publication No. 82, Washington, 1921.

the amount and expenditure of insurance, the marriage of the parents, and the ages of the children. All applications are passed upon by a conference committee consisting of the chief probation officer, the head of the aid to mothers division, and the county agent or his representative. Only those cases which the committee recommends for a pension go before the court, unless the applicant is dissatisfied with the action of the division and gets some reputable citizen other than herself to file another petition.

The investigations of cases of truant children are made by the compulsory-education department of the city of Chicago, and petitions are filed by officers of that department. The juvenile court has no other connection with this work and no other control over it than to determine whether or not the child shall be committed to an appropriate parental school.

Feeble-minded children over whom the court has jurisdiction are brought to its attention because they are dependent or delinquent children. In cases investigated by the court officers the fact of feeble-mindedness is usually discovered in the process of investigation by means of the mental examination described below, and a " petition in the matter of a feeble-minded person " is filed as the original petition. In cases investigated by the police officers or in those cases in which the petition is filed before investigation the original petition has to be dismissed and the case continued for a petition in the matter of a feeble-minded person.

Although adoption cases are outside the jurisdiction of the juvenile court as such, investigations are made by the investigation division of the court, and its recommendations are reported to the appropriate court.

ADJUSTMENT OF CASES WITHOUT COURT ACTION.

Frequent reference has been made to the efforts of the officers to reduce the number of cases brought to court—that is, to settle as many cases as possible without formal court action. Questions arise as to why this is desirable and what happens to the children in such cases. It is argued that if a condition exists that warrants complaint by a " reputable citizen " it is surely the duty of the court to make the adjustment, no matter how slight the trouble, and to see to it that there is no cause for further complaint. The officers of the court reply that court action should be avoided for a number of reasons. First and foremost is the wish to spare the child a court record, for the trial of dependent and delinquent cases in the same court has resulted in attaching a stigma even to dependency proceedings. In the second place, the moral effect of a voluntary arrangement is thought to be happier than that produced by the order of the judge, and even if that order is with the consent of the parents, the flexibility of an informal disposition is often to be preferred to the rigidity of a court order. In the third place, it is imperative that the overburdened judge shall not waste his time and energy on unnecessary cases. A fourth consideration is the saving of taxpayers' money; every case heard in court involves a certain expense. Adequate investigation of complaints of dependent cases, moreover, often uncovers several possible sources of aid and support that can be resorted to without court action.

The number of complaints adjusted out of court by the investigation division and the police probation officers is shown in Tables V and VI. The statistics presented by the investigation division are for family complaints, and, as stated in the report, the figures must be multiplied by three or four to give the number of cases represented. The police probation officers' figures, on the other hand, are for children or individual cases, and therefore appear to be very much more numerous. The proportion adjusted without court action is somewhat larger in the case of the police probation officers than of the investigation division.

TABLE V.—*Disposition; complaints investigated by police probation officers, year ending Dec. 31, 1919.*[1]

Disposition.	Complaints.	
	Number.	Per cent distribution.
Total	16,995	100.0
Brought into court	2,495	14.7
Adjusted without court action	14,500	85.3

[1] Charity Service Reports, Cook County, Ill., 1919. p. 287. Figures for 1920 are: Brought into court, 2,132; adjusted without court action, 14,316. Figures for 1921: Brought into court, 1,960; adjusted without court action, 13,641.

TABLE VI.—*Disposition; complaints investigated by the investigation division, year ending Nov. 30, 1919.*[1]

Disposition	Complaints.	
	Number.	Per cent distribution.
Total	2,914	100.0
Brought into court	679	23.3
Adjusted satisfactorily without court action	1,075	36.9
Adjusted but not wholly satisfactorily	254	8.7
Found not to come under juvenile court jurisdiction	649	22.3
Pending at close of year	257	8.8

[1] Charity Service Reports, Cook County, Ill., 1919. p. 287. In 1920 there were 2,556 complaints; in 1921, 3,280.

The annual report from which these tables were compiled gives no explanation of the categories used by the investigation division in classifying its disposition of cases. The terms are difficult to define, for one group is not clearly distinguished from another. Furthermore, the classification of cases under them will always be a matter of individual judgment. The head of the division explains the classification as follows: Cases "not under the court's jurisdiction" are those which, after slight investigation, prove to belong to other agencies. They can not be eliminated without some investigation because either the complainant is not in possession of all the facts in the case or he is not candid in his statements. Cases "satisfactorily adjusted" are those in which after more or less effort the officer has been able to remedy the difficulty complained of; and "cases adjusted, but not satisfactorily" are those in which a difficulty is felt to be latent, although a slight temporary improvement has been effected in the situation, and court action is at any rate postponed. It should be noted that 254 cases, or about 9 per cent of those investigated by the officers of the investigation division in 1919, were considered to be of this nature.

In the case of delinquent boys brought before the police probation officers in the precinct police stations, although a large number of adjustments are made without court action, no attempt is made to follow up the case with any supervision. In cases handled by the investigation division, however, not only is a more prolonged effort made to discover what can be done in the case, but in some cases what amounts to probation work without formal court order is done. Cases treated in this way are known as "supervised complaints."

No statistical study of the treatment of cases by the investigation division has ever been made and a detailed study would be beyond the scope of this inquiry. A reading of some 25 cases at random, however, reveals certain common types of service that the officers of the investigation division often render. One of the most frequent complaints comes from a man who through the death or illness of his wife is left with a family of small children for whom he is unable to care, but for whose support he can afford to pay. He needs expert advice, and this he receives from the probation officer. Perhaps she merely assists him in placing his children with relatives, or she may consult a child-placing agency that makes a specialty of such work. In the course of the investigation as to whether the case lies within the court's jurisdiction a permanent settlement may be reached. In making arrangements with relatives, the home is investigated chiefly with reference to the financial status and moral character of the relatives. The investigation is not as searching as that made by regular child-placing agencies. In general, where the situation is one of dependency due to poverty alone without the elements of neglect or degradation, the officers make the adjustment without court action, provided county support is not needed and the child has a legal guardian to assume responsibility for the arrangement.

Cases involving neglect or unfitness on the part of the parents or custodians of the child are more difficult than those presenting the problem of destitution. Here the effort of the officer must be to effect some permanent change in the conduct of those in charge of the child. Her weapon is moral suasion, backed by the potential authority of the court.

A successful example of this kind of activity occurred in the case of an unmarried mother, who, after her confinement, wished to place her baby out for adoption and be free. The officer gained her confidence, persuaded her to take a week to think matters over, adjusted difficulties with former employers, induced her to keep the child, helped her to recover a sum of money from the father in the court of domestic relations, and left her in the care of an agency that specializes in finding work for women in her situation.

Usually the adjustment does not come so quickly and easily. Where prolonged effort on the part of the officer is required, the case is carried as a "supervised complaint." Here the work is similar to that of the probation officers of the family supervision division, the only difference being that the authority of the court is potential, not actual, and that the rules for work are more flexible. While no regulations exist governing the length of time during which a complaint may be carried, the division does not intend to allow an unsatisfactory situation to drag on for a long time. If improvement is not evident, steps are taken toward court action.

The following case is an example of a supervised complaint:

An 8-year-old child was reported as being cruelly treated by a stepmother. The officer verified the facts by careful investigation, brought the case into the court of domestic relations, and secured a verdict placing the parents on probation under an adult probation officer. The action of that court, supplemented by frequent visits from the juvenile probation officer, during which good advice about diet and sleeping arrangements were given, effected a change in the conduct of the stepmother.

Another type of supervised complaint occurs when some relief agency feels that it must cease giving relief unless a woman whom it has been helping dismisses a boarder with whom she is suspected of having immoral relations. The relief organization has no authority to force her to comply with the request. The juvenile court officer, however, by threatening to remove the children by court action, can sometimes improve the conditions and will continue to supervise the family, the relief society agreeing to continue its assistance.

The supervised complaint ends sometimes, however, in formal court action. If the treatment under the investigation division has been all that might have been accomplished under court order, nothing has been lost, but occasionally it seems to be a matter for regret that action was not taken sooner.

Such was the case, for instance, of a 15-year-old boy who had got beyond his mother's control and was continually running away from home. His case was carried for six months as a supervised complaint with no apparent improvement. Then the family moved without notifying the officer and could not be located until the mother, seven months later, reported that the boy had run away taking all the money she had in the house. After several trials in a county institution and on parole, it was necessary to commit the boy to the State school for boys.

Another such case was that of a dependent girl of 14, whose mother had been dead a number of years. The case had once been in court, and the petition dismissed when an aunt in California took charge of her. Several months later, however, she was returned to Chicago, and complaint was made to the court that the relatives could not be responsible for her care. For a year the case was handled as a complaint. From October until April the girl lived with an aunt, who complained of her unruliness. From April until August she was left in the home that her father established with a mentally deficient grandmother as housekeeper, the father working at night. Then the father gave up the attempt to keep a home, and from August until October the girl wandered about from one home to another, staying with friends and becoming more untruthful and dishonest. Part of the time she was working in a department store, and later on as a telephone operator. Finally she became definitely immoral and was brought into court on a delinquent petition.

The above, of course, are isolated cases, and it is not intended to imply that the supervised complaint always or frequently ends in court action. Nor is it certain that court action at first would have been any more successful than informal supervision. The possibility always exists, however, that it might have been more effective if applied promptly. The moral effect of bringing a delinquent boy before the judge is often marked, but, on the other hand, a distracted mother who appeals to the court to control an unruly child may be discouraged by the long-drawn-out process of the supervised complaint.

PHYSICAL AND MENTAL EXAMINATIONS.

For the examination of the child's physical and mental condition by persons competent to pass judgment, special organization is of course necessary.

The law gives the court no specific power to require such examinations. The court may, however, commit a child in need of medical care to a hospital[9] or may adjourn proceedings for the filing of a feeble-minded petition,[10] and presumably it has authority to inquire into the facts in such cases.

As in the case of payment of probation officers and the provision for a detention home, the machinery necessary for medical and

[9] Hurd's Illinois Revised Statutes, 1919, ch. 23, sec. 177b.
[10] Ibid., sec. 341.

psychological examinations was first provided by private philanthropy. Medical examination was begun in 1902, when the Children's Hospital Society furnished a trained nurse who was present at each session of the court and secured hospital and medical care for every child committed to her by the court. In 1907 this service was extended by the society, and all children in the detention home, as well as all others whose parents would consent, were given a general medical examination.[11] The work thus begun by private funds was taken over by the county commissioners in 1909.[12]

At the present time a physician and dentist working part time and three nurses working full time are paid by the county and employed at the detention home. In addition a woman physician employed by the city examines delinquent girls at the dispensary maintained in the juvenile court rooms.

All children brought in for hearing, with the exception of cases investigated by police probation officers, are given medical examinations. Children placed in the detention home are examined there by the attending physician. Children who are not placed in the detention home are examined at the court by the same physician.

The examination at the court includes the condition of the skin, glands, eyes, ears, nose, throat, teeth, and lungs. In the case of a delinquent girl, when immorality is suspected and if the parents consent, a vaginal examination is also made by the woman physician employed by the city.

Children received at the detention home are immediately taken to the dispensary, where a graduate nurse records temperature, pulse, and respiration, and takes throat cultures and vaginal smears. The children are then isolated until the next morning, when the attending physician makes a thorough physical examination. The report of this examination and any recommendation for treatment are sent to the court before the hearing.

Psychological and psychopathic examinations were first given in 1909, when the Juvenile Psychopathic Institute was established through the generosity of a public-spirited citizen. The institute was organized for five years as a private association directed by Dr. William Healy and was maintained by private endowment, though all of its services were given to the work of the juvenile court. In 1914 the institute was taken over by an appropriation of the board of county commissioners as a regular department of the court. It was continued under county auspices until 1917, when the director [13]

---

[11] Charity Service Reports, Cook County, Illinois, 1907, p. 112.

[12] Thurston, H. W.: " Ten years of the juvenile court of Chicago," in The Survey, Vol. XXIII. p. 663 (Feb. 5, 1910).

[13] Dr. Healy resigned in 1917 and was succeeded by Dr. Herman M. Adler, the present director.

was appointed State criminologist under the Illinois Department of Public Welfare. Opportunity thus being given to extend the work throughout the State, the Juvenile Psychopathic Institute became a State organization under the authority of this department and immediately under the direction of the State criminologist. Under this plan an arrangement for cooperation between the State and the county has been made, the county continuing to contribute to the expenses [14] of the institute in return for the services rendered in examining children brought before the juvenile court. In 1920. after considerable reorganization, the name was changed to the Institute for Juvenile Research.

Cases are referred to the institute by individuals and by social agencies, as well as by officers of the juvenile court, and the court has ceased to have any control over its work.

It has never been possible to have all the children examined, and the problem of selecting those who need examination has not been an easy one for persons untrained in psychiatric and psychological work. At one time an attempt was made to have a psychologist at court to give elimination tests to all children brought in for hearing; but the children were found to be abnormally nervous and excited by the court hearing, and the practice was abandoned. At present all the children who are placed in the detention home even for a day are given brief tests designed to eliminate those who are definitely not feeble-minded. These tests are given by the teachers in the detention-home school and are graded by the two psychologists employed by the Institute for Juvenile Research and stationed at the detention home. A child found by this test to be defective is given a thorough examination by the psychologist; and if any abnormality of behavior is observed he is also given a psychiatric examination by a psychiatrist either at the detention home or at the office of the Institute for Juvenile Research. A diagnosis of the case, together with a recommendation for treatment, is reported to the court at the hearing.

---

[14] The county pays the salary of one psychologist and one stenographer. The work of these persons is not, however, confined strictly to the county.

DETENTION.

DETENTION POLICY.

The juvenile court law provides that "No court or magistrate shall commit a child under 12 years of age to a jail or police station; but if such child is unable to give bail, it may be committed to the care of the sheriff, police officer, or probation officer who shall keep such child in some suitable place provided by the city or county outside of the enclosure of any jail or police station."[1] The building erected, as before stated,[2] under the amendment of 1907 still serves as a detention home. While children of 12 or more do not come within the prohibition, it has become customary for both the juvenile court and the police to use the detention home for children between 12 and 17 or 18 as well as for the younger children.[3]

Many children awaiting hearing are left in their own homes. Unless the home is detrimental to the child or unless there is reason to fear that the child or the family will disappear before the hearing, it is the policy of the juvenile court to leave the child in his own home without bond, relying upon the promise of the parent or guardian to produce the child at the specified time.

In practice it has been difficult to maintain a consistent policy of detention, especially with regard to children brought into court by the police probation officers. It is difficult to obtain the figures necessary to determine the proportion of cases held in the detention home among all those brought before the court. The chief probation officer in his annual report for 1918 stated that not more than 15 per cent of the children whose cases were investigated by county probation officers were ever taken into custody.[4] Cases investigated in this way, however, form a small part of all the cases before the court;[5] hence, it is the practice of the police probation officers that is more important in this respect, but no statistics are available showing what proportion of children brought in by these officers are placed in the detention home.

---

[1] Hurd's Illinois Revised Statutes 1919, ch. 23, sec. 179.
[2] See p. 9.
[3] See p. 8 of this report.
[4] Charity Service Reports, Cook County, Ill., 1918, p. 208.
[5] In 1919 police probation officers filed 2,495 petitions; the investigation division only 679.

NUMBER OF CHILDREN CARED FOR IN DETENTION HOME.

The total number of children cared for in the detention home in each year for the two years 1918 and 1919 is shown in Table VII.

TABLE VII.—*Source, by years; cases cared for in the juvenile detention home, 1918–1919.*[1]

Source.	Cases cared for in the juvenile detention home.	
	1918	1919
Total...	4,636	5,104
In detention home at beginning of year............	139	124
Juvenile probation officers........................	626	694
Police probation officers..........................	2,648	3,024
Sheriff and Federal officers.......................	40	11
Truant officers....................................	53	88
Juvenile court.....................................	944	995
Officers of institutions...........................	84	60
Children returned from hospital....................	77	97
Children asking shelter............................	25	11

[1] Figures are for fiscal years ending Nov. 30. Charity Service Reports, Cook County, Ill., 1918 and 1919. For 1920, 4,861 cases were reported as cared for in the juvenile detention home.

It appears from Table VII, which presents the number of entrances to the home rather than the number of children cared for, that children are received from a number of different sources besides the police probation officers who bring in more than one-half and the county probation officers who bring in less than one-sixth of the children. One important source is the juvenile court itself. That is, children are not only brought into the detention home by probation officers to await hearing but are returned there by court order after hearing. This may come about for either of two reasons: The case may be continued and conditions may be unfavorable for the return of the child to his own home, or a delay may occur in carrying out some order of the court. The order may be for the commitment of the child to an institution in which there is no vacancy. Feeble-minded children form only a small part of the detention-home population, but such children are frequently detained for months because of the crowded condition of the State school for the feeble-minded. Or the order may be that the child be placed in a family home, and it may require considerable time to complete the necessary arrangements.

Children are received from officers of institutions either after escape from the institution, or when, for some other reason, the institution finds it impossible to keep them. Children returned from the hospital are those whose examination on entrance to the home showed the need of special treatment or those who became seriously ill while detained.[6]

[6] Thus a child returned by the court or by a hospital may be counted two or three times during a short period of detention.

The average length of stay for children of all classes was 8 days in 1917,[7] but in individual cases the period might extend to 25 or 30 days. The average daily population of the home for the last five years has ranged from 105 to 123.

The number of delinquent children detained in 1919 was 4,185; of dependent children, 919.[8] The number of delinquent cases heard by the court in that year was 3,402; of dependent cases, 1,836.

OVERCROWDING.

More important than the total number of children detained during the year is the number of children in the home at any one time in relation to the facilities for caring for them. This problem has been before the officers of the court frequently during the last few years when the home has been often overcrowded, and it has been necessary to leave children in unsatisfactory surroundings or to take them to police stations.

The legal relationship between the court and the detention home is noteworthy in this connection. The court itself has no authority over the detention home, which was established under a separate act giving the board of county commissioners the authority to establish and maintain a place where children could be kept instead of being sent to jail. The institution is therefore controlled by rules and regulations laid down by the board of county commissioners, and neither the judge nor the probation department has any control over its management.

That this division of authority is wasteful has been recognized since 1912, when the Hotchkiss committee after its investigation both of the court and the home reported:

The real supervision over the home as over the probation department should rest with the court and the cooperation between court, probation department, and home should at all times be full and complete.[9]

No change was made, however, in the control of the home, and in 1918 the situation became urgent. The boys' quarters were particularly crowded. Boys constitute 70 per cent of the population of the home. The two larger wards, for delinquent boys, accommodate 60; but they often housed 70 boys, so that a number of boys were without beds and some slept on mattresses on the floor, others on beds without mattresses. The same overcrowding occurred in the dependent boys' quarters, which were intended for 32 children and often housed from 45 to 60 boys.

In order to learn how much the court could help in relieving the congestion of the home, the judge, in September, 1918, assigned an as-

---

[7] Charity Service Reports, Cook County, Ill., 1917, p. 357.

[8] Ibid., 1919, p. 292.

[9] Juvenile Court of Cook County, Ill. Report of a Committee Appointed under Resolution of the Board of Commissioners of Cook County, Chicago, 1912, p. 45.

sistant probation officer to work with the officers of the detention home in investigating the causes of overcrowding, and the following analysis was submitted to the court,[10] attributing the conditions of the home to the following causes:

1. Delay in getting cases before the court for hearing because of overcrowded calendar. This delay is ordinarily about 7 days, but during the past year has been as much as 25 or 30 days.

2. Lack of room in both public and private institutions which would enable them to accept children, both dependent and delinquent, who have been committed by the court. Children committed to institutions are usually held at the juvenile detention home until they can be accepted at the institution.

3. The detention of children who have normal homes in which they might remain pending a hearing in the juvenile court. A constant effort is made to keep children in the custody of their parents pending hearing. There is a surprisingly large number of children who will not agree to stay at home until their cases are reached and a larger number of children whose parents refuse to accept responsibility for the child's appearance in court.

4. Unusual cases, including lost children, children who have run away from their homes in other States and in whose cases correspondence is necessary, and children whose cases are continued at the juvenile court for sufficient reason and who must be detained.

So far as the congestion in the home was due to a crowded court calendar or to overfilled institutions, the juvenile court was powerless to effect a remedy. Other aspects of the problem could, however, be dealt with, and as a result of this report certain restrictions were placed upon the freedom of probation officers to place children in the home. A rule was made that no child should be admitted to the home without the approval of the chief probation officer or of the officer in charge of police probation officers. An officer is thus no longer free to take any child to the home on his own responsibility, but must first show his supervising officer why it is not safe for the child to stay in his own home. In practice it has been necessary to modify this rule somewhat, owing to the fact that children are sometimes picked up at night and that emergencies arise making it necessary to act without waiting to secure approval. At present it is, therefore, customary for the police probation officer to take the children to the home and to report the matter at once to their supervising officer, who looks into the facts and releases the child if such action seems advisable.

This new ruling, it seems, has had the desired result, for in his report for 1919 the chief probation officer said:

One of the outstanding things of the year is the successful operation of a plan by which the judge places in the chief probation officer and the officer in charge of police probation officers the responsibility for the detention or release of any child held in the juvenile detention home pending a hearing.

Parents are encouraged to take children home pending investigation and hearing, when, in the judgment of the chief probation officer and the aforementioned

---

[10] Charity Service Reports, Cook County, Ill., 1918, p. 209.

officer in charge, the public welfare will not be jeopardized by the child's release. All idea of using the juvenile detention home as a place where the child may be held by way of punishment while awaiting trial is done away with. The net result has been a quicker movement of the population of the home, so that at no time during the year was it necessary to refuse to admit children because of overcrowding. This condition is in striking contrast to the three previous years during which the juvenile detention home was crowded practically all the time and children were held in police stations because of lack of room in the home.[11]

The reduction in overcrowding has meant that it is no longer necessary to hold children in police stations because they can not be admitted to the detention home, a condition to which the chief probation officer had called attention in his reports for 1916, 1917, and 1918. It has not entirely eliminated detention at police stations, however, since a police probation officer, with the consent of his supervising officers, occasionally detains a boy in the police station if the detention home refuses to receive him because he has previously escaped or proved unmanageable.[12] More rarely the police officer keeps a boy in the police station if from his knowledge of the boy he thinks there is danger that he will escape from the home. No figures are available giving the number of children held in police stations in 1919. The chief probation officer, however, estimates the number at approximately 25.

EQUIPMENT OF THE JUVENILE DETENTION HOME.

The present equipment of the juvenile detention home is not of great significance in view of the fact that the voters of Cook County in November, 1919, approved a bond issue of $1,000,000 for the erection of a new juvenile-court and detention-home building. The erection of this building has not yet begun, however, and meantime the present equipment must suffice.

The present detention home is a three-story brick building, erected in 1907. It occupies three sides of a hollow square with a central quadrangular court and an annex housing the detention-home school. The juvenile detention home belongs to the county; the school belongs to the city and is under the authority of the board of education and under the direction of the principal of the public school nearest the home.

The central part of the first floor of the main building is occupied by offices, the branch office of the Institute for Juvenile Research, and a large reception room in which the children see their parents. The remainder of the first floor is devoted to the boys' and girls' receiving wards and isolation rooms. On the second and third floors are the dormitories, playrooms, dining rooms, kitchen, and pantries.

---

[11] Charity Service Reports, Cook County, Ill., 1919, p. 225.
[12] The authority of the officers of the detention home to refuse any child admittance remains absolute.

The dormitories and receiving and isolation rooms are equipped with toilets and with hot and cold shower baths.

The school was completed in 1915. It is a two-story brick building connected with the main building by two bridges, one leading to the girls' section, the other to the boys' section. On the first floor are five classrooms, a manual-training room, and a gymnasium, and on the second floor, two large dormitories, a manual-training room, a classroom, a sewing room, and a hospital.

The children are divided into five groups, each with a separate dormitory and playroom. In general, the dependents and delinquents are separated, but the smaller boys from 5 to 14 years of age are kept together. This group includes "little dependents, truants, runaways, and trivial first offenders," who have a dormitory of their own with 20 beds, a separate playroom, individual lockers, toilets, and 2 shower baths. This is thought to be very much better than keeping the younger delinquents with the older ones, as was formerly done. In the girls' wing one dormitory is set aside for dependents and another for delinquents, but girls of all degrees of delinquency are kept in the delinquent department.

A graduate nurse is on duty in the home at all times except between midnight and 8 a. m. In addition, a woman is in attendance day and night in the delinquent-girls ward, a man and two women in the dormitories for delinquent boys, and two women in the dependent sections.

RECEPTION OF CHILDREN.

When a child is admitted to the home, important facts regarding the case are recorded. The child is then taken to the graduate nurse, who records temperature, pulse, and respiration, takes a throat culture, swabs the throat with an antiseptic solution, and administers a grain of calomel, followed by magnesium sulphate. If the child is a girl, an examination for gonorrhea is made as a protection to the other inmates. A shampoo and antiseptic bath are given, and the child is dressed in detention-home clothes, so that its own may be sent to the fumigator

The house physician is on duty every morning except Sunday and examines each child who has been admitted during the previous 24 hours. The doctor's findings and recommendations are recorded on a card which accompanies the child to court and is given to the judge, who advises the parents if the child needs medical care and obtains their signature if they consent to carry out the recommendations.

As a precaution against the spread of disease all children are kept in the receiving wards after admission to the home until the result of the doctor's examination and the throat and vaginal cultures is known. This period of isolation is usually from 24 to 48 hours. Most medical and surgical cases, including all gonorrheal infections and cases of ringworm of the scalp, are sent to the county hospital for treatment. Certain contagious diseases and some kinds of eye, ear, nose, and throat trouble are treated in the isolation rooms of the home.

As a precaution against the spread of contagion the one or two days that the children are kept under observation in the receiving wards are inadequate. The incubation period of acute contagious disease is from one day to three weeks, but owing to cramped quarters, particularly downstairs in the receiving wards, the children are allowed to go upstairs as soon as their cultures are reported on, providing there is no evidence of disease.

The attending physicians have repeatedly stressed the fact that better isolation facilities should be provided for sick children. In 1917 the home had within its walls 190 cases of acute tonsilitis, 42 of pharyngitis, 45 of impetigo, 68 of venereal disease, 22 of ringworm, 24 of scabies, 3 of trachoma, as well as a few very severe cases of pediculosis and 141 diphtheria carriers, all demanding rigid quarantine.[13] In 1918, cases of sickness among its inmates numbered 1,650.[14] Thus the request for a separate small hospital building does not seem unreasonable.

The teeth of all children kept in the home over 48 hours are examined, except in the cases of positive throat cultures. A record is made of conditions found and of all work done. So far as possible in the limited time children are under detention, defects are remedied, and the children are taught to care for their teeth. The dentist's services are provided only 18 hours a week, and a great deal more work is needed than can be accomplished in that short time.

THE DAILY ROUTINE.

Much of the work in their own sections is done by the children themselves, thus:

The delinquent children do practically all of the work in their own departments. They rise at 5 a. m., turn back their bedding, throw the windows open, and begin their daily duties. They scrub almost their entire department before breakfast, which is at 6.45 a. m. Immediately after breakfast they clear their tables, wash the dishes, and tea towels, scrub the dining room and make their beds. At 9 a. m., when the work is usually completed, they wash, comb their hair, and change their clothes, ready for school at 9.30 a. m. The girls, besides doing the work in their own section, assist in the preparation of the vegetables and wash the employees' dishes. They also scrub the dormitories of the dependent section and assist in making the beds of that department. The boys scrub the main hall of the dependent section and the kitchen. If at any time the girls are under quarantine, the boys are detailed to the kitchen work.[15]

[13] Charity Service Reports, Cook County, Ill., 1917, p. 319.
[14] Ibid., 1918, p. 269.
[15] Charity Service Reports, Cook County, Ill., 1915, p. 267.

After these strenuous hours the children spend from 9.30 to 12 and from 1.20 to 4 in school. Children under 10 years of age are cared for in a group by themselves, and their work is informal and social. The kindergarten room for little dependents is particularly attractive. Visiting and recreation hours are from 4 to 5 p. m. and from 7 to 8 p. m. Parents may visit the children during these hours five days a week. The boys play outdoors in the court under supervision, but the girls have no outdoor recreation. Time hangs heavy on the hands of the children under observation in the receiving rooms, inasmuch as they can neither go to school nor play outdoors and have no one to direct their play in the house.

The children are entertained every Friday evening with music, lectures, stereopticon views, and aesthetic dancing, and a special entertainment is always provided on holidays. Occasionally the downtown theaters present the home with tickets for some suitable play. Religious instruction is furnished for both Catholic and Protestant children by outside religious organizations.

Discipline is usually left to the nurses in charge. Under no circumstances is corporal punishment resorted to, but occasionally when special severity seems needed, children are put on a bread-and-milk diet and sometimes they are placed in solitary confinement for an hour or two " to think it over."

DIETARY.

A study of the diet made in 1917 under the direction of a member of the home economics department of the University of Chicago, showed the diet to be unsatisfactory. It was monotonous, to some extent poorly cooked, some foods were served too frequently, and the evening meal in particular was not sufficiently satisfying. A new diet was then agreed upon by the superintendent and the dietitian making the study.

CLOTHING.

During working and recreation hours the girls wear blue gingham dresses and the boys overalls and jumpers; during school hours the girls wear blue, brown, tan, and white middies, and the boys khaki suits. The children are put into home uniforms so that their own clothes may be disinfected and cleaned, or possibly destroyed. A majority of the delinquent boys and girls enter the home so dirty that their clothing has to be destroyed at once; almost all the dependent children have to be given new clothing also. Supplying a sufficient number of new outfits has always been one of the problems of the home.

HEARINGS.

SUMMONS.

When the investigation has been completed and a date set for the hearing, a summons is served by the probation officer, requiring the parent or guardian to be in court with the child on the appointed day. Summons, less formal than a warrant, does not constitute arrest, but failure to obey constitutes contempt of court.[1] For most cases such informal procedure is sufficient to bring all the needed persons into court. In some instances, however, it is necessary to issue a warrant for arrest served by the sheriff. Occasionally the hearing of a case may drag on for a considerable period of time because of failure to compel attendance.

A social agency complained to the court that two brothers, 8 and 9 years of age, had glandular tuberculosis, that the home was neglected and dirty, and that the mother was mentally defective and refused to take the children to the dispensary for treatment. The court had already had five years' experience with the family because of one delinquent girl and one delinquent boy and had removed three other children from the home as dependents. Four children, all under 10, had been left in the home. It is somewhat surprising, therefore, that the case of these two children who had never been in court before was allowed to drag on for six months before there was a real hearing, being continued six times because no one was present. No mention is made of any effort to secure the cooperation of the father. The following brief statements indicate the difficulties encountered.

November 24, 1919: First hearing. Mother refused to come. Case continued.

December 2, 1919: Second hearing. Mother refused to come. Probation officer asked for a warrant. Case continued.

December 16, 1919: Case in court. No hearing. Continued.

January 6, 1920: Case in court. No hearing. Warrant never served. Case continued.

January 19, 1920: Case in court. Probation officer reported family had moved and could not be located. Case continued generally.

May 28, 1920: Probation officer located family and called to serve summons. Mother denied that children were living with her.

May 11, 1920: Case in court. No one present. Warrants issued. Case continued.

July 6, 1920: Seventh hearing. Children and brother-in-law present. Mother still refused to come. Case continued.

July 13, 1920: Eighth hearing. Probation officer reported that married sister and her husband now in the home were assuming responsibility for the children and conditions were improved.

July 26, 1920: Case continued under supervision.

---

[1] Hurd's Illinois Revised Statutes, 1919, ch. 23, sec. 173.

September 28, 1920: Conditions greatly improved. Placed on probation.

That is, although the court had the power of the State back of it, it found itself unable for 10 months to secure the presence of a subnormal mother. It is true that the continued effort brought the married sister into the situation; the burden, however, was certainly not one that could be borne wholly by her and her husband, but rather was one that required the aid of the community agency organized supposedly to deal with such situations.

If a parent or guardian is believed to have left the State or if, after reasonable effort he can not be located, the law provides for publication of the case " once " in " some newspaper of general circulation," requiring appearance within 20 days.[2] Delay is, of course, often the result of conforming with this futile requirement of the statute, incident to such publication, especially since the publication often does not occur until after the case has already been brought into court for hearing.

TIME AND PLACE.

The general equipment of the court has slowly expanded as the number of cases has increased. During the early days of the court, hearings were held only two afternoons a week in the circuit court room of the old courthouse. By 1905 hearings were held two days a week—dependent children in the morning and delinquent children in the afternoon.[3] From 60 to 80 cases were heard each day, and as all cases were set for the same hour, many persons were kept waiting for the hearing in which they were interested. In that year the old courthouse was torn down, and the juvenile court was established in a room over a store on a busy street. In 1907, when the juvenile court building was erected, a small court room and several waiting rooms were provided, and five half-day sessions were held.[4] It was not until September, 1910, however, when the judge began to give his full time to the juvenile court, that more frequent sessions were possible.[5] Since that time sessions have been held both morning and afternoon, five days a week.

To insure the complete separation of dependent and delinquent children different classes of cases are heard at different sessions of the court. The schedule of the court at the time the investigation was made was as follows: Three mornings a week, cases of dependent children; four afternoons, cases of delinquent boys; one morning, pension cases and cases of feeble-minded children; and one morning, truant cases. Conferences on cases of delinquent girls were heard four mornings a week in a separate room. Facts are pre-

[2] Hurd's Illinois Revised Statutes 1919, ch. 23, sec. 173. The publication is often inserted in the " Calumet," a paper of 5,000 circulation.

[3] Thurston, H. W.: " Ten years of the juvenile court," in the Survey, Vol. XVIII (Feb. 5, 1910), p. 661.

[4] Charity Service Reports, Cook County, Ill., 1907, p. 111.

[5] Ibid., 1910, p. 145.

sented by a woman officer to the judge in the regular court room, who satisfies himself as to the wisdom of the recommendation formulated by the woman assistant to the judge, and renders a decision in the case.

Since 1913, when the juvenile court building became too crowded for both the court rooms and the detention home, hearings have been conducted in a building erected jointly by the city and county, containing all municipal and county courts as well as administrative departments. It is located in the midst of a busy downtown district and, except for its central location, has little advantage to offer as a children's court building. The juvenile court occupies a part of one floor and consists of a court room, a small room in which girls' cases are heard, a waiting room, a large room containing desks for probation officers, the dispensary, a record room, and the offices of the judge, the chief probation officer, the investigation division, the family-supervision and the aid-to-mothers division, the delinquent boys', the child-placing, and the police probation divisions. The new building which is to be erected for the detention home will also contain all juvenile court rooms and offices.

Hearings, except those of cases of delinquent girls, are public; but the benches on which both witnesses and outsiders sit are arranged at the back of the room, leaving considerable unoccupied space between them and the judge, and the hearings are conducted in such a way that little can be heard except by persons interested in the case or officially connected with the court.

The judge's desk is not on a raised platform but is, with the reporter's desk and the benches for the jury, separated from the rest of the room by a low railing. Only the width of the desk, placed directly behind the railing, separates the judge from the child whose case is being heard.

PROCEDURE.

When the judge comes into the room, court is opened in a formal manner by the bailiff. The clerk then calls each case in order, and the officer who has made the investigation comes forward with the child, his parents if present, and witnesses. They group themselves around the judge's desk, facing him. The probation officer who has made the investigation or filed the petition, the police probation officer in most of the delinquent boys' cases, or the truant officer in truancy cases, makes a brief statement to the judge, outlining the main facts in the case, and then stands aside. He is, of course, ready to give further information and to help in any way that the occasion demands. In general, the attitude of the officer, and this is especially true of the county probation officers, is that of an impartial friend of the child and the family and distinctly not that of a prosecuting officer.

After the probation officer's statement the judge, with the case record of the family before him, begins his questioning. When the case is that of a delinquent or truant boy, he usually begins with the child, sometimes starting with the concrete charge and asking him what his story is, what his reasons were, and working back to his age, his work, what he does with his leisure time, and questions of a more general nature. In other instances he works up to the charge more gradually. If the boy has been in court before, the judge always reminds him of it and of what happened at that time. Perhaps the most striking thing about the questioning of the boy compared with the examination of the accused in criminal courts is that no attempt is made to induce the child to incriminate himself, none of the questions are designed to trap him, none are asked whose bearing he will not see. The judge's manner is friendly but never to the point of seeming to condone the offense, and when the occasion calls for it, he may become very stern and severe. Usually the questioning of the child is followed by questioning of the parents. After this, anyone else who is present is given an opportunity to make such statement as he may desire. The time devoted to a case varies from a few minutes in simple cases to possibly half an hour in cases in which the truth is difficult to establish. In general each case is so dealt with that there is no impression of perfunctoriness or of haste in dispatching the day's work.

Occasionally the boy or the complainant is represented by an attorney, and this usually complicates the proceedings. If a contest over the court's action arises, the case is postponed and heard in the one week of the month devoted to contested cases. Frequently, however, even with an attorney present no contest is involved, and the case is heard in the regular session. Proceedings in contested cases are somewhat more formal; witnesses are sworn, and the attorney does the greater part of the questioning which in other cases is done by the judge. As great care, however, is taken to discover all the facts and to do what is best for the child in those cases in which neither the child nor the complainant is represented by an attorney as when one or both are so represented.

CASES OF DEPENDENT CHILDREN.

The procedure in cases of dependent children differs slightly from that in delinquency cases. In the first place a jury of six is required by the laws providing for commitments to manual-training and industrial schools.[6] Their service in the Cook County court seems to be largely perfunctory, as the decision is arrived at by the judge and submitted to the jury for their approval, which is seldom withheld. The social value that accrues from acquainting six men who sit in

---

[6] Hurd's Illinois Revised Statutes 1919, ch. 122, secs. 323 and 337.

,court for two weeks with the problems that confront the youth of the city and with the policies of the juvenile court is, however, very great.

A second difference in the proceedings is caused by the fact that while it is the child over whom the court has jurisdiction, it is the parents who are directly responsible for his presence in court,· and it is really the parents who are on trial, although the court has no jurisdiction over them. It is natural, therefore, that the judge should begin his questions in these cases with the parents and should devote most of his time to them. Frequently the child is not questioned at all except to establish his identity. At times also, when the facts to be brought out are not such as a child should hear, the judge directs the officer to take the children to the rear of the room.

CASES OF DELINQUENT GIRLS.

The real, as distinguished from the technical, hearings in delinquent girls' cases are held in a private room before the woman assistant to the judge. This room is in appearance a small and attractive office, having no suggestion of a court room. No one is admitted to this room except the persons directly concerned with the case and the officers of the court. Ordinarily, no one is present but the assistant to the judge, the girl, her mother, her father whenever possible, the probation officer, a court stenographer who is a woman, and the police probation officer who filed the petition in those cases in which the complaint was made to the police. This officer is usually the only man present aside from the girl's father. The proceedings are even less formal than those in open court; the hearing is in reality a helpful, friendly conference of all concerned. If the petition has been filed by a police officer he gives his information relating to the case; the probation officer who has made the social investigation then presents the facts she has learned and describes the conditions as she sees them. The girl is encouraged to state her side of the case and to express her feelings and point of view. The difficulty is discussed with the parents and the probation officer, and they are consulted with regard to the wisest plan to pursue. Every effort is made by the judge's assistant to establish confidential relations with the girl and to make her feel that here she has a real friend genuinely interested in her welfare. She and her parents stand close to the desk during proceedings, no strangers are present before whom she hesitates to tell her story, and it is seldom that she fails to be more or less won by the evident friendliness of the atmosphere. After the facts have been brought out, the assistant tries to persuade the parents to agree to what seems to her the best course of action and in any event makes a recommendation as to the disposition of the case. The probation officer then takes the girl and her parents, with the legal papers, before the judge and reports to him the facts of the case with the recommendations of the assistant to the judge. The judge acquaints himself quickly but adequately with the problems; but if there are no objections on the part of the parent, he generally concurs in the recommendation of his assistant. Neither the girl nor the witnesses are questioned, nor is any statement of the case made in open court. Any parent or his representative may however, object and demand that the judge himself hear all the facts in the case. If that is done, the case is heard in open court in the week devoted to contested cases. That means, of course, that the privacy with which the court has tried to shield the girl can no longer be maintained. It is very rarely, however, that an open hearing is insisted upon, for in general the parents and friends of the girl are impressed with the fairness of the private hearing and appreciate what the court is trying to do.

CASES OF FEEBLE-MINDED CHILDREN.

Hearings in cases of feeble-minded children are conducted by the judge and a commission appointed by him as required by law.[7] In practice this commission always consists of two representatives of the Institute for Juvenile Research. Since an examination of the child must be made by an expert before the case is brought into court, the hearing is merely a report of the result of this examination, followed by a formal order for disposition.

AID TO MOTHERS CASES.

Mothers who are to receive pensions under the aid to mothers law must appear with their children before the judge to have their applications granted. The hearings in these cases are usually brief, as in most instances it is necessary only to ratify the action of the committee composed of the chief probation officer, the head of the aid to mothers division, and the county agent or his representative.

---

[7] Hurd's Illinois Revised Statutes, 1919, ch. 23, sec. 328.

THE COURT ORDER.

The real test of the value of the juvenile court as an enduring social institution lies perhaps in the character of treatment that is provided for the child after the hearing of the facts of the case. It is a comparatively simple task for the legislature to do away with the forms of the criminal procedure, to say that the child is not a criminal but a delinquent " misdirected and misguided and needing aid, encouragement, help, and assistance,"[1] and as such that he shall not be punished but shall be placed in such surroundings and under such influences that he will cease to be even delinquent. But it is not so easy for the judge and probation officers of the juvenile court to determine in each case what method of treatment is most likely to bring about definite improvement, nor for the probation officer who is intrusted with the supervision of the child to embody in concrete results whatever ideals of probation work he may have. In the case of the neglected child the task is even more difficult, for it then involves reorganizing a whole family and helpful cooperation often secured from the parents of a delinquent child may be lacking.

DISMISSAL AND CONTINUANCE.

Dismissed and continued generally.

The form that the court order may take varies with the class of case, the legal restrictions, and the public provision for the care of each group of children. There are, however, two broad lines of action that the court may take in all classes of cases. It may assume responsibility for the child or it may refuse to assume that responsibility. In the Chicago juvenile court practice a child is never " discharged " or " acquitted," for these terms imply that he was formally accused of a specific offense. If the facts brought out in the investigation or in the hearing do not reveal conditions that warrant the court's assuming control over the child the case may be either " dismissed " or " continued generally." A case is dismissed when the facts seem to indicate that there is no need for court action. " Continued generally " amounts to continued indefinitely in contrast with continued for a definite period of time or to a specified date. A case is " continued generally " when conditions do not seem to warrant the supervision of a probation officer and yet

---

[1] Colorado Revised Statutes, 1908, sec. 597.

the judge is unwilling to dismiss the case. The orders of "dismissed" and "continued generally" are alike in that neither provides for further work on the case. They differ in the fact that if a "dismissed" case is to be again brought into court a new petition must be filed, while a case "continued generally" remains nominally under the court's jurisdiction and a new petition is unnecessary. In neither case does the child receive supervision.

The "continued generally" order may also be used as a temporary expedient when (before a case has reached the stage of a definite order) the family moves without notifying the probation officer. In such cases, instead of entering an order of continuance for a definite period, the judge continues the case "generally" to allow the probation officer to locate the family and to bring in the case whenever it is possible to do so. The purpose here, of course, is quite different from that first mentioned. In Table VIII the numbers of cases of the various types dismissed and continued generally are shown for the three-year period 1917–1919.

TABLE VIII.—*Dismissal and general continuance, by class of case; cases heard by the juvenile court, 1917–1919.*[1]

Class of case.	All cases.	Cases heard by the court			
		Dismissed.		Continued generally.	
		Number.	Per cent of total.	Number.	Per cent of total.
Total	23,270	1,439	6.2	2,060	8.9
Delinquency:					
Boys	7,281	683	9.4	1,575	21.6
Girls	2,164	279	12.9	93	4.3
Dependency	5,992	381	6.4	309	5.2
Truancy	1,614	27	1.5	69	4.3
Feeble-minded	192	11	5.8	14	7.3
Aid to mothers	6,027	58	1.0		

[1] Compiled from figures for fiscal years ending Nov. 30. Charity Service Reports, Cook County, Ill., 1917–1919. Figures for 1920 are : Dismissed, 521 ; continued generally, 544

Among 23,270 cases heard by the court in the three-year period 1917–1919 only 1,439, or 6.2 per cent, were dismissed and only 2,060, or 8.9 per cent, were continued generally. The use of these orders varies somewhat with the type of case. Aid to mothers cases are never continued generally and are rarely dismissed, because the investigation is necessarily very complete and the pension must be recommended by the conference committee before a petition is filed. Among the feeble-minded children the fact that even 14 cases were continued generally is explained by the court as meaning "that the whole situation of the child was not serious enough for the court to order a commitment as feeble-minded, but that it was bad enough so that it might later become necessary to make a commitment. Under this order the court retains jurisdiction, so that the child can be brought into court without filing a new petition."[2]

Continued for a definite period.

Before the court definitely dismisses the case or by some other final order assumes the care of the child, cases are frequently continued for a definite period. This order may be used for two reasons: First, because the child or its custodian fails to appear in court, sometimes even necessitating delay for publication; and, second, in the hope that the child may improve in conduct or the home conditions may be so changed as to render a final order unnecessary. Under such circumstances the case may be dismissed, and the child saved from whatever stigma may be attached to a juvenile court record.

The essential difference between continuing a case generally and continuing it for a definite period is in the supervision provided in the latter case. As long as the judge orders the continuance of a case with the definite intention of having it brought into court at a later time, the officer who has made the investigation, unless some other officer is designated, is responsible not only for the child's ultimate appearance in court, but for whatever developments may take place in the meantime. Children brought to court by police probation officers are never left under the supervision of these officers but are placed, by special order, under the supervision of some other officer, usually the probation officer for the district in which the child lives.

The effect, then, of the order for definite continuance, usually stated in the case record as "continued under supervision," seems to be practically that of probation. Certain administrative differences exist, however. Many of the supervising officers, especially in the cases of children brought in on dependent petitions, are officers of the investigation division. In such cases the children receive adequate care. The work of the division may, however, be seriously disorganized by the necessity of caring for a great number of supervised cases, and the practice is recognized by the chief probation officer as a violation of the principle of specialization of function maintained in the organization of the staff to which he credits a considerable part of its successful work.

The relation of the court to the problem of the child during these periods of continuance is one that has been very little discussed. As has been said, neither the annual reports of the court nor of the chief probation officer contain data with reference to it. It is, how-

---

[2] Charity Service Reports, Cook County, Ill., 1919, p. 285.

ever, evidently a relationship of sufficient importance to be of interest to the student of the court. The following cases, while few in number, illustrate situations that are typical of many situations with which the court deals through this device:

Virginia D., aged 15, was brought into court by her mother. She had been keeping late hours in bad company, and one night stayed out until 2 a. m. The case was continued for seven months under the supervision of the district officer.

October 27, 1919: First hearing. Virginia working without a certificate. Disobedient and defiant. To live at home under supervision.

November 7, 1919: Probation officer visited. Virginia had obtained a work certificate. Was doing office work and going to night school.

November 26, 1919: Case in court. Virginia had stayed away from home all night. Found in park next morning. Said she had ridden round on street cars all night. Given another chance at home.

December 2, 1919: Probation officer reports home conditions poor, but Virginia behaving better.

January 19, 1920: Virginia left home. Family learned that she was staying with a family in Geneva, Ill., who were at first willing to keep her, but a month later sent her home, as they did not wish to be responsible for her.

March 29, 1920: Case in court. Virginia working and causing no trouble. Continued to April 23, 1920.

April 2, 1920: Probation officer visited. Virginia working.

April 16, 1920: Virginia admits she has not been working for a week. Mother can not manage her.

April 23, 1920: Case in court. Virginia again working. Has lied about her age to employer and is not going to night school. Case continued.

May 20, 1920: Virginia ran away from home. Picked up by the police and taken to the detention home.

June 2, 1920: Case in court. Virginia had been unmanageable in detention home. Placed under supervision of child-placing division to live at M. E. Club.

June 30, 1920: Case in court. Virginia had run away from club and had been immoral. Probation officer on case stated that she had never seen the girl. Committed to the House of the Good Shepherd.

Harriet L., a colored girl, aged 17. Mother dead, father married again. Stepmother complained that girl had stolen money from her father and had torn up her stepmother's clothing. Case continued five months.

December 30, 1919: First hearing. Evidences of mental defect, but father and probation officer have been unable to get her to the psychopathic institute for an examination. Case continued to January 6, 1920.

January 6, 1920: Case in court. Continued for a warrant, as girl refuses to come to court or to have psychopathic examination.

January 21, 1920: Case in court. Continued for report of examination.

January 28, 1920: Case in court. Psychopathic institute reports that Harriet is neither feeble-minded nor insane, but has very peculiar reactions. Girl complains of stepmother's treatment. Willing to try working in a private home. Continued under supervision of district officer. To be placed in private home.

February 2, 1920: Case set for hearing before Judge Arnold to confirm assistant's recommendation. No one present. Continued.

February 21, 1920: Placed in working girls' home. Matron refused to keep her because she was so slovenly. Discharged from laundry because too slow.

March 11, 1920: Placed in another family. Probation officer visited once. Found that Harriet was doing day work and was dirty and untidy. Her father had given her money for clothes. A friend of hers was interviewed a month later, but the girl was not seen.

June 4, 1920: Case in court. No one but probation officer present. Girl was then 18. No improvement was reported, but the case was continued generally.

Irene T., aged 13. Neighbors complained of her conduct and case was brought to court by police probation officer. Continued eight months.

June 10, 1919: First hearing. Girl had been out of school. Neighbors had complained that she was often alone in the house with a man who, according to her mother, was a friend of her brother's. Mother refused to allow a medical examination, but had a satisfactory statement from her own doctor. Case continued, with no order for supervision.

June 27, 1919: Case in court. Truant officer testifies that absence from school accounted for by illness. Mother objects to suggestion of sending her to a convalescent home. Case continued.

Case in court four times between June 27, 1919, and January 6, 1920. Each time mother failed to appear, and the case was continued.

January 6, 1920: Case in court. Irene had given birth to a child on Christmas day. A few weeks before this the mother had had her married at the city hall by giving her age as 16. She had paid a doctor $2 to give her the statement presented to the court at the first hearing. Case continued.

January 20, 1920: Case in court. Irene complains that she was forced to give the child to her sister-in-law for adoption. Continuance one week to investigate the matter.

January 27, 1920: Case in court. Irene to live at home. Child to remain with aunt. Marriage has been annulled. Irene's brother undertakes to see that she does not live with the man again until she is 16 and can be legally married. Case dismissed.

Richard R. was a dependent boy 9 years old. His parents were divorced, and his mother worked as a housemaid in a private family. He had been under the court's jurisdiction since 1918 and had been placed in several homes. In 1919 his custodian complained of his bad habits and stealing and refused to keep him any longer. The case was brought to court for rehearing in February, 1919, and was continued seven times during a period of nine months, ending in dismissal.

February 24, 1919: Case in court. Probation officer requests continuance to see what she can do with child.

March 12, 1919: Case in court. Temporary home found by Illinois Children's Home and Aid Society. Continued.

March 12, 1919: Case in court. Probation officer has found home. Continued.

March 31, 1919: Case in court. Report that child is provided for until September. Continued.

July 2, 1919: Case in court. Report that child is provided for until September. Continued.

September 8, 1919: Case in court. No one present. Continued.

September 17, 1919: Case in court. Boy so attached to custodian that arrangement prolonged until January.

January 6, 1920: Case in court. No one present. Continued.

January 19, 1920: Case in court. Custodian wishes to keep child. Case dismissed.

The record contains no report of any visit to this family or of the conditions in the home. It is probable that the home was approved by the Illinois Children's Home and Aid Society.

John C., a delinquent boy, 13 years old, in company with another boy had been involved in six different burglaries.

October 31, 1919: Case in court. Good home. Parents want to give boy another chance. Continued under supervision of district probation officer.

January 29, 1920: Case in court. John placed in a farm school by probation officer and his father. Judge approves arrangement. Case continued.

May 12, 1920: Probation officer learns that John had taken a large sum of money from his father and had run away from the school with several other boys. School refused to take him back.

June 4, 1920: John working in his uncle's cigarette factory. Reports favorable.

June 23, 1920: Case in court. John registered for a summer camp. Case dismissed.

A brief summary does not wholly reveal the work of the court, as it is impossible to note all the work done in each case. The difficulty is due, however, not only to the method of presentation but also to the inadequacy of the court record in these cases. It is often difficult to ascertain what work the probation officer has done. Each hearing, however, has been included, and all other steps that seemed to have an important bearing on the case. The reader of these cases is struck in some instances by a somewhat hasty dropping of the case by a " dismissed " or " continued generally " at the first indication of improvement, especially when the boy or girl is near the upper age limit, so that if the jurisdiction of the court be lost it can not again be obtained.

The published reports of the court do not include the number of continuances, since they are not final orders. An idea of the extent to which this order is used, however, was gained by reading a number of selected records of cases heard by the court during the first two weeks of January, 1920. Among 86 records of delinquent and dependent children, 66 cases had been continued at least once. As many as 35 of these continuances had lasted from 1 to 3 months, 20 from 4 to 10 months, and only 11 had been continued for less than 1 month. Continuances of less than one month were for the most part necessary for technical reasons, such as changing the petition from delinquent to dependent, feeble-minded or truant, or in order to bring into court persons interested in the case. Sometimes these arrangements cause long continuances that are very difficult to bring to an end.

THE FINAL ORDER.

The final order of the court does not always result in treatment that differs from the treatment under an order for continuance for a definite period. It creates a different status, however. It is more definite. The case is no longer frequently brought before the judge but can be reopened only by a new petition or a notice of rehearing. In cases of feeble-minded and truant children and under the mothers' pension law the possible methods of disposition are limited by the special character of these cases. The methods of disposition in such cases will be briefly indicated, and the remainder of the chapter will be devoted to the more complicated methods of handling cases of delinquent and dependent children.

Table IX shows the disposition of feeble-minded cases for each year, beginning with 1915, that is, with the first year that the court was given jurisdiction in cases of feeble-minded children.

TABLE IX.—*Disposition of cases, by year; cases of feeble-minded children heard by the juvenile court, 1915–1919.*[1]

Disposition.	Cases of feeble-minded children heard by the court.				
	1915	1916	1917	1918	1919
Total	([2])	79	60	58	74
Dismissed	([2])	4	4	1	6
Continued generally	([2])	4	4	6	4
Committed to State school for the feeble-minded	39	71	52	51	64

[1] Figures for fiscal years ending Nov. 30. Charity Service Reports, Cook County, Ill. 1915–1919. Figures for 1920 are: Dismissed, 3; continued generally, 14; committed to State school for the feeble-minded, 41.
[2] Figures not available.

As might be expected, by far the greater number of such cases are committed to the State school for the feeble-minded at Lincoln, since a feeble-minded petition is never filed until after an examination by the Institute for Juvenile Research and a recommendation for institutional care. The capacity of the State school is inadequate to care for all the feeble-minded needing institutional care and as a result the court is obliged to commit only those children whose need is most pressing. Even so, the school can not receive all the children committed by the court, and the detention home is frequently obliged to care for these children for months pending their transfer to the institution.

Table X shows the disposition of truant cases in 1919, the first year since the establishment of the Chicago Parental School for Girls. The school for boys has been in existence since 1902.

TABLE X.—*Disposition of cases, by sex of child; truancy cases heard by the juvenile court, year ending Nov. 30, 1919.*[1]

Disposition.	Truancy cases heard by the court.			
	Total.		Boys.	Girls.[2]
	Number.	Per cent distribution.		
Total	623	100.0	570	53
Dismissed	15	2.4	11	4
Continued generally	47	7.6	40	7
Placed on probation to truant officer	63	10.1	61	2
Committed to Chicago Parental Schools	498	79.9	458	40

[1] Charity Service Reports, Cook County, Ill., 1919. Figures for 1920 are: Dismissed. 24; continued generally, 49; placed on probation, 30; committed to parental school, 453.
[2] The Parental School for Boys was established in 1902; that for girls in June, 1919 Figures for girls are, therefore, for five months only.

Nearly 80 per cent of these truant children are committed to the parental schools. Children are in fact generally brought into court by the compulsory-education department of the city board of education for the express purpose of commitment to the parental school. The compulsory-education department, through its truant officers, has itself the authority to visit and supervise truant children. Thus no real need for court action exists unless the child has proved too unmanageable to be left at home and must be placed in the parental school. As previously stated the only contact of the juvenile court or its officers with the truant child is through the hearing in the court. The work of supervision as well as that of investigation is performed by the compulsory-education department.

The order in a mother's pension case may take the form of " dismissed," " granted," " increased," " reduced," or " stayed," that is, discontinued.

In dealing with delinquent children the court is acting under the law to which it owes its existence and attacking the problem for which is was primarily created.

Table XI gives the final orders of the court in cases of delinquent children during the five-year period, 1915–1919.

TABLE XI.—*Disposition of case, by sex of child; delinquency cases heard by the juvenile court, 1915–1919.*[1]

Disposition.	Cases of delinquent children.			
	Boys.		Girls.	
	Number.	Per cent distribution.	Number.	Per cent distribution.
Total.........	11,799	100.0	3,344	100.0
Dismissed.........	1,020	8.6	425	12.7
Continued generally.........	2,751	23.3	111	3.3
Placed on probation.........	4,113	34.9	1,039	31.1
Committed to institutions.........	2,603	22.1	1,333	39.9
Guardian appointed.........	621	5.2	330	9.8
Placed in hospitals and in schools for defectives.........	16	0.1	7	0.2
Deported.........	6	0.1	2	0.1
Held to the grand jury.........	70	0.6	....	....
No change of order in rehearings [2].........	599	5.1	97	2.9

[1] Compiled from figures for fiscal years ending Nov. 30. Charity Service Reports, Cook County, Ill., 1915–1919. For 1920 the figures are: Boys, 1,912; girls, 638. For 1921 they are: Boys, 1,754; girls, 661.
[2] A rehearing is counted as a new case.

For both boys and girls probation and commitment to institutions are the most important orders, including 57 per cent of the boys' cases and 71 per cent of the girls' cases. A comparatively small number are placed under the care of a guardian, committed to hospitals or schools for defectives, deported, or held to the grand jury for indictment on criminal charges. " No change of order " indicates merely that a case has been reheard but that the disposition of the child remains the same as before.

Before discussing the various methods of treatment set forth in Table XI it is well to consider a similar table dealing with dependent children: for at certain points the treatment of dependent and delinquent children overlap, and the machinery of the court set up for one group serves also the other group. In Table XII is presented the disposition of cases of dependent children during the period 1915–1919.

TABLE XII.—*Disposition; dependency cases heard by the juvenile court, 1915–1919.*[1]

Disposition.	Cases of dependent children.	
	Number.	Per cent distribution.
Total	10,631	100.0
Dismissed	635	6.0
Continued generally	584	5.5
Placed on probation	2,805	26.4
Committed to institutions	4,330	40.7
Committed to child-placing societies	491	4.6
Guardian appointed	1,341	12.6
Placed in hospitals and schools for defectives	63	0.6
Deported	46	0.4
No change of order in rehearings	336	3.2

[1] Compiled from figures for fiscal years ending Nov. 30. Charity Service Reports, Cook County, Ill., 1915–1919. In 1920 there were 1,262 cases of dependent children; in 1921, 1,292.

In 26.4 per cent of the cases of dependent children, the child was placed on probation, and in 40.7 per cent committed to institutions. Commitment to child-placing societies, appointment of a guardian, placing in hospitals, and deportation provided for the remainder of the group.

Probation.

Cases placed on probation, as shown in Tables XI and XII, include 34.9 per cent of the delinquent boys, 31.1 per cent of the delinquent girls, and 26.4 per cent of the dependent children. The probation order means that the child may live in his own home or in the home of relatives or close friends designated by the court, subject to the supervision of the district probation officer. The policy of the court is to use this order whenever the circumstances are not such as to render it obviously imprudent. The court prefers to make its errors on the side of too frequent rather than too slight use of probation.

The number of cases in which children were placed on probation in their own homes and in family homes other than their own is shown in Table XIII.

TABLE XIII.—*Probation, by class of case; delinquency and dependency cases heard by the juvenile court, 1915–1919.*[1]

Class of case.	Dependency and delinquency cases.			
	Total.	Placed on probation.		
		Total.	To live at home.	To live in other homes.
Total	25,774	7,957	6,686	1,271
Delinquency:				
Boys	11,799	4,113	3,965	148
Girls	3,344	1,039	878	161
Dependency	10,631	2,805	1,843	962

[1] Compiled from figures for fiscal years ending Nov. 30. Charity Service Reports, Cook County, Ill., 1915–1919. For 1920 the figures are: Probation at home, 806; in other homes, 125. For 1921 they are: Probation at home, 763; in other homes, 90.

In more than one-third of the cases of dependent children placed on probation the child is placed in a home other than his own. The home in which the dependent child is placed on probation is usually that of a friend or relative, not one that the court finds for him. The distinction should be made here between the technique of placing a child on probation in a home other than his own and what is known as " child placing." The former work is under the direction of the family-supervision division, the latter under the direction of the child-placing division, whose chief officer is appointed guardian of the child with the right to place and sometimes the right to consent to adopton. The probation order is generally used to meet problems more temporary than those met by child-placing.

Probation is handled by two separate departments of the court— the family-supervision division and the delinquent boys' division. The work of supervising dependent children and delinquent girls falls to the officers of the family-supervision department and is described as follows in the annual report of the court for 1918:

The task of reconstructing homes which have been found by the court to be unfit is one that can only be successfully performed by experts. It is a task in which organization and system play a considerable part, but which would fail entirely without the personal appeal of the probation officer. Only women probation officers are assigned to this division. Visits to the home are employed largely to establish the necessary personal contact which makes possible many helpful relations. The work here is friendly supervision and sympathetic help as contrasted with surveillance. Some of the things in the way of special help which the probation officers of this division are able to do are the following:

Finding new quarters for the family.

Teaching mothers how to care for their children.

Showing mothers how to buy to advantage, etc.

Securing legal advice.

Securing medical aid.

Securing employment for different members of the family.

Sending children and mothers to the country for vacations.

Making outside contacts for the family with individuals and associations, such as settlements, recreation centers, etc.

The average number of families assigned to a probation officer of this division is 54.[3]

This statement of kinds of service rendered represents an ideal toward which the probation department is striving rather than an actual accomplishment, inasmuch as with the large number of cases assigned each officer it is quite impossible to secure such detailed supervision in all instances. The court recognizes the value of supervision; and the work of the officers is directed by the head of the division, who reads all reports of visits made by the officers, makes suggestions about matters needing attention, and confers with the officers about families who present special difficulties. In addition to this an attempt was made in 1919 to secure more efficient work by the adoption of a set of rules intended to serve as minimum standards for probation work. These rules were drafted by a committee of the heads of the divisions and are as follows:

1. Read record before going out on case.
2. First visit within one week; report of first-visit should include—
    (a) Tentative plan.
    (b) Definite statement of reason for court action and what should be accomplished by probation.
    (c) Environment sheet must be completely filled out if same was not done at time case was brought into court.
    (d) Definite information must be gotten as to the name and address of employers of the working members of the family as well as amount of wages.
    (e) First report must be plainly and definitely marked "first report" so that same can be margined by typists.
3. Division head to specify minimum number of visits on each case per month and how frequently child itself should be seen.
    (a) Division head will notify officer on receipt of first report as to this.
    (b) Division head will also make such notation on the record.
4. Report of child's progress in school should be made once a month; if same is unsatisfactory, matter should be taken up at once.
    (a) School reports will give information as to deportment, attendance, application, appearance, and any other information gleaned from teacher and principal.
    (b) School report should be plainly marked "school report" so that same can be margined by the typist.
5. Every member of the family and household should be seen at least once during the probation period.
6. At the end of a six months' probation a summary should be made showing what was accomplished, and if the cause for court action has not been remedied, why.

---

[3] Charity Service Reports, Cook County, Ill., 1918, p. 217.

It is the intention of the present head of the family supervision division that cases which show no improvement after they have been on probation for a year or more shall again be brought into court.

In addition to the rules quoted, which apply to all officers having charge of children on probation, officers having supervision over delinquent girls are required to visit employers, when the girls change jobs, to verify the girls' statements about their work and earnings and to visit the girls themselves, as well as their families, at least once a month. In cases of dependent children it is considered sufficient if the family with whom the child is living is interviewed periodically at longer intervals. Occasionally, if circumstances seem to warrant it, delinquent girls are directed to report to their officers at a settlement or at some similar convenient place.

Delinquent boys placed on probation are under the supervision of the officers in the delinquent boys' division, all of whom are men. These officers are under the supervision of the head of that division, who directs their work in much the same way as that described above. The rules already cited apply to them as well as to the officers in the family supervision division. The work is primarily with the offending boys, but the officers recognize the importance of family conditions and, so far as possible, adjust any difficulties they may observe or call in the service of an agency better adapted to deal with the problem.

The rule is that boys be visited in their own homes at least once a month. Some of the officers supplement their visits to the boys by having the boys report to them at stated times, usually at a settlement house in the district. The head of the division does not object to this practice if the individual officers think it successful, but he does not encourage officers to adopt it, as he is convinced that the difficulties connected with the practice are likely to outweigh its advantages. In no case are the reports to the officer allowed to take the place of visits to the boys in their homes, but are always used to supplement the regular visits. Aside from the rules quoted above there are few regulations governing the work of the officers, but each case is dealt with as the situation seems to demand. School reports must be obtained if the boy is still in school; employers, however, are seldom seen unless the position was obtained with the assistance of the probation officer, as it has been found that attempts to cooperate with the employer occasionally lead to the discharge of the boy, and in more cases cause fear of discharge on the part of the boy and irritation on the part of the boy's parents. Special attention is paid to boys during the early part of the probation period, as this is recognized as the crucial period.

Depending as it does upon the varying conditions in the individual cases, it is difficult to make any general statement about the actual work of probation. In reading a number of cases selected at random it has been apparent that the rules of the department are not slavishly followed. They are, if these cases are typical, often overlooked, sometimes with good reason, sometimes apparently through carelessness. The following summaries of cases of children placed on probation for a considerable period of time will present a better picture of the situation than any general statements could convey. Despite the inadequacy of the records, some idea may be gained from these cases of the difficulties both of the child and the probation officer.

Edward O., a fatherless delinquent boy 14 years old, had been on probation for nine months when the case was read. He was one of eight children. Three older boys were living at home and supporting the family. He was brought into court first in 1917, when he was accused of throwing a stone and breaking a church window. He denied the charge, and as no evidence was produced in support of the charge, the court was satisfied with his denial and the case was " continued generally."

Edward was next brought to court more than a year later after stabbing and wounding another boy. His mother was working. An older brother offered to pay the costs and promised to look after the boy, but the court ordered Edward to pay $3 a week for three weeks to pay the doctor's bill. (He was at that time earning $10 a week, but the record does not give his occupation.) The case was continued under the supervision of a probation officer who received payments from the boy but reported no other supervision or visits. When the required payments had been made in April, 1919, Edward was placed on probation. The probation officer reported his first visit one month later. Edward was then working at " some steel company " as an errand boy, earning $9 a week. Three more visits to the home were reported during the next five months, but the boy himself was not seen until October 25, when he was out of work. The probation officer sent him to the vocational bureau to get a job, but received no report and did not see him again until he was again brought into court on December 1. A few days before this the officer had visited Edward's mother and happened to learn that the boy had stolen $5 from his mother, had run away from home, and finally had been arrested for stealing some flashlights from an automobile. A police probation officer had filed a petition. The case was continued under supervision. The subsequent history may be summarized as follows:

The next day after the hearing Edward reported to probation officer and was sent to the vocational bureau to get a work certificate. Got a job as errand boy at $10 a week.

Three weeks later: Visit of probation officer to mother. Report favorable.

Two weeks later: Case in court on continuance. Probation officer had not seen boy since day after hearing, but reported his conduct satisfactory and recommended probation. Court ordered probation.

Three weeks later: Probation officer visited mother. Report favorable.

Two weeks later: Vocational bureau notified probation officer that boy had been discharged for unsatisfactory work. Probation officer promised to visit but did not do so.

Five days later: Vocational bureau requested probation officer to call at office, as boy had stolen $2 from doctor's office while waiting to be examined. Advised court action, but probation officer decided to have a psychopathic examination first, which showed a mental age of 12 years; that is, some retardation.

A physical examination showed incipient pyorrhea. The vocational bureau refused a new work certificate until the boy's teeth were in good condition, and he was sent to a dentist. When the probation officer next visited, Edward was away on a vacation, and a month later was working. This was the last record when the case was read two months later.

Anna G., a 15-year-old girl, was brought into court for immorality. She had left home and with two other girls rented a room in a hotel. She admitted having had immoral relations with one man previous to this time, and her mother was willing that she should marry him, but as she was only 15, under the law of Illinois she could not be married. The case was continued during the time the man's case was pending in the morals court, and Anna was kept for more than a month in the detention home. At the end of this time she was placed on probation, and the whole family was thoroughly impressed with the fact that the marriage could not take place for five months. The probation officer made four visits during this time, but saw Anna only once. She had not passed the fifth grade and could not get a working certificate, but apparently no attempt was made to keep her in school. About the time she was 16 she began to work. The man was allowed to call, but the family were quite anxious to cooperate with the officer in looking after Anna, and there was no further trouble. She was married as soon as she was 16 and was released from probation.

Mary B., a 15-year-old colored girl, was reported to the court by a school principal for writing indecent notes and for immorality. She was one of eight children, and the home was poor and neglected. Commitment to the State school for girls was recommended by the assistant to the judge, and Mary was sent to the detention home to await the judge's confirmation of this recommendation. Meantime Mrs. W., for whom Mary had worked after school, asked the court to allow Mary to work at her house every day from 9 until 7 instead of sending her to Geneva. The arrangement seemed satisfactory to the probation officer, and the judge placed Mary on probation to live at home.

When the probation officer visited less than two weeks later, Mary wanted to work in a factory because she could earn more. The family had moved, and conditions were improved.

A week later when the officer called the family had decided that Mary should go back to school and graduate, as she was too young to work.

A month after this the probation officer called and found that Mary was in school and was working for Mrs. W. after school. For two months Mary remained in school, and the reports of her conduct were good. The probation officer enlisted the cooperation of a social agency working with colored families, and this agency persuaded Mary and her sister to join the Y. W. C. A. and a community club. After school was out in July the officer visited and found that Mary was staying at home during the day with younger brothers and sisters while her mother worked. She seemed dissatisfied with this arrangement, however, and wanted herself to go out to work. For four months after this the family was not visited, and in November when the officer finally called the family had moved. Two weeks later when the record was read they had not been located.

Frances L., a colored girl of 16, had been brought to court in 1917, after she had run away from an institution for dependent girls. She had stolen money from one of the girls there and had been immoral. Both her parents were dead, and she was committed to the State training school for girls. In 1919 an aunt of the girl's asked for her release from the institution. The institution reported that the girl was mentally defective, had congenital syphilis, and was losing her eyesight. The court therefore continued the case for three months. At the end of this time the report as to the girl's condition was still unfavorable, but a probation officer reported favorably upon the aunt's home, and the judge released Frances on probation on condition that she be given close supervision.

For two months Frances remained in her aunt's home helping with the housework. The probation officer visited twice during this time. When the officer visited the aunt the next month, Frances was in the county hospital for eye treatment. She remained in the hospital for three months and the officer visited her aunt twice. For nearly three months more conditions remained about the same, Frances staying with her aunt and doing very well. Then the aunt reported to the probation officer that Frances was having immoral relations with one of her lodgers. (Up to this time there has been no mention of lodgers in the home.) The court physician reported that Frances was pregnant. Nearly two months later the probation officer visited and found that Frances had been away from home for two weeks. After several weeks it was discovered that she had been living with a man and working to support him.

The case was then brought into court for hearing. Frances's statements seemed to point to the fact that her aunt was keeping a disorderly house. When the home was first visited a man was present, but the aunt had told the probation officer that he was not living there and that she had no lodgers. She admitted in this hearing that she had had lodgers at that time. The case was continued for a week for further investigation, but when brought in again, the aunt was ill. Since Frances had no other place to go and the aunt needed her help, the court made no change of order. The record was read a few days after this hearing.

Mrs. M. asked the court to place her four children—three girls and a boy, all under 14. Her husband's whereabouts was unknown, and she was working as a waitress earning $10 a week. During the investigation the mother was arrested for shoplifting. She was sent to the county jail for 10 days, and meantime the children were placed in the detention home. While in jail the mother was given a mental examination and was reported to be feeble-minded and "almost committable."

November 26, 1919: First hearing. The mother's statements seemed quite contradictory and unreliable. The case was continued for publication for the father, who, according to Mrs. M., had died in France. The mother and children were placed in a charity lodging house.

December 20, 1919: Mrs. M. left the lodging house and applied at a police station for lodging, saying she had no money.

December 23, 1919: Case in court. Mrs. M. still unreliable. Case continued under supervision of child-placing division.

December 31, 1919: Mother placed by the adult probation officer of the municipal court in the psychopathic hospital for observation. All the children taken to a rescue mission in a suburb.

January 6 and 12, 1920: Case in court. Mother still in hospital and case continued.

January 16, 1920: Mother called at court asking for children. Had been discharged from hospital diagnosed as psychopathically unfit to care for the children.

January 19, 1920: Case in court. Leona, aged 13, and Ione, aged 11, committed to an industrial school for dependent girls; Jack, aged 4, and Mazy, aged 2, to an orphanage. Adult probation officer is to be responsible for the mother.

At this time information was received from a social agency in another city that the two younger children were illegitimate and that the mother had taken the two older ones from a home in which they had been placed.

May 3, 1920: Mother asked for release of children. Was working in a hotel, earning $20 a week.

May 7, 1920: Mother called with a man for whom she was to keep house. Probation officer consulted with sisters of a convent who recommended the man, and probation officer approved the plan. The man had four children.

May 28, 1920: Children released and placed on probation to live with mother.

June 5, 1920: Probation officer visited. Home dirty. Children away. Mrs. M. sullen and resentful.

June 26, 1920: Mrs. M. took her children and left her place of employment, going to the charity boarding home.

July 7, 1920: Probation officer visited family at boarding home. Mrs. M. working in a hotel. Children well cared for in the nursery.

September 17, 1920: Probation officer visited. Mrs. M. not seen, but matron gave good report.

October 14, 1920: Mrs. M. called at office. Raved incoherently. Wanted court to leave her alone.

October 15, 1920: Probation officer consulted matron of home, who reported that Mrs. M. had left with her children and did not say where she was going, although she had told some one she was leaving the city.

Two months later, when the record was read, the family had not been located.

These cases reveal the paucity of community resources for meeting many of the needs revealed by the court hearing. The ease with which families move from one city to another renders the task of supervision extremely difficult; there is the difficulty of seeing the older children if they have gone to work; making an investigation on which to base a plan of permanent care takes time. These few cases illustrate the way in which officers cooperate with the vocational bureau, with the organization intended to deal especially with problems among colored people, with the settlement, the Y. W. C. A., and with the members of the adult probation department. They illustrate, too, the kind of situation in which the authority of the court constitutes an important factor in the exercise of parental or filial responsibility.

Appointment of guardian.

Another order that the court may enter in cases both of delinquent and of dependent children is the appointment of a guardian. For delinquent children the provision of the juvenile court law reads as follows:

The court may appoint some proper person or probation officer guardian over the person of such child and permit it to remain in its own home, or order such guardian to cause such child to be placed in a suitable family home.[4]

The provision for dependent children is as follows:

If the parent, parents, guardian or custodian consent thereto, or if the court shall further find that the parent, parents, guardian or custodian are unfit or

---

[4] Hurd's Illinois Revised Statutes, 1919, ch. 23, sec. 177.

improper guardians or are unable or unwilling to care for, protect, train, educate or discipline such child, and that it is for the interest of such child and the people of this State that such child be taken from the custody of its parents, custodian or guardian, the court may make an order appointing as guardian some reputable citizen of good moral character to place such child in some family home or other suitable place which such guardian may provide for such child.[5]

This order is used in general in those cases in which it appears that the arrangement made must be of relatively long duration; that is, when the home is unfit and no possibility of its improvement appears to be likely in the near future, when both parents are dead and no relatives are found to care for the child, and when the mother is dead and the father is unable to provide care for the child and prefers placing in a family home to commitment to an institution. In cases of delinquent children special consideration is given to the possibility of the child's making good in new surroundings.

The order appointing a guardian may be stated in either of two forms, " with the right to place " or " with the right to consent to adoption." The second of these two orders was authorized by an amendment to the juvenile court law passed in 1907 and providing that—

the court may in its order appointing such guardian empower him to appear in court where any proceedings for the adoption of such child may be pending, and to consent to such adoption; and such consent shall be sufficient to authorize the court where the adoption proceedings are pending to enter a proper order or decree of adoption without further notice to or consent by the parents or relatives of such child.[6]

The order giving the guardian the right to consent to adoption, a stronger order than the one merely giving the right to place in a home, is used only in those cases in which it is desired to effect a permanent separation of the child from its parents or from those who have the custody of the child. This order, it should be noted, gives the guardian only the right to consent to adoption; no child can be adopted until a proper petition has been filed in a court of competent jurisdiction and the fact established that the state of affairs justifies adoption. The effect of this order is that the parents from whom the child has been taken by court order need not be made defendants in the adoption proceedings as would otherwise be required.

The comparative infrequency with which the order appointing a guardian is used is indicated in Tables XI and XII. Only 5.2 per cent of the cases of delinquent boys, 9.8 per cent of the cases of delinquent girls, and 12.6 per cent of the cases of dependent children have been disposed of in this manner, in contrast with 34.9 per cent, 31.1 per cent, and 26.4 per cent, respectively, placed on probation, and 22.1 per cent, 39.9 per cent, and 40.7 per cent committed to institutions. It is,

---

[5] Hurd's Illinois Revised Statutes, 1919, sec. 175.
[6] Ibid., ch. 23, sec. 183.

however, an important authority for the court to possess. Such an authority would be an essential factor in a policy of child-placing were the court ever given the resources to develop the field of placing in family homes as a substitute for the institutional care on which it must at present so largely rely.

The "reputable citizens" appointed as guardians are either persons known to the parent, though such persons are rarely appointed, or officers of the court. In the cases of both delinquent and dependent girls and a few of the younger dependent boys the officer appointed as guardian is the head of the child-placing division. This division was organized about 1914 in order to provide private boarding homes for semidelinquent girls, for whom a change of environment was considered advisable and who were not delinquent enough to be sent to an institution for delinquent girls. The work soon proved so useful that the division extended its activities to dependent children also. The annual report of the juvenile court for 1918 gives the following account of the work of this division:

Officers of the child-placing division place in family homes or in private institutions children who have been committed to their care by the judge of the juvenile court. During the past year 704 children, approximately one-third of whom were delinquent girls and the other two-thirds dependent boys and dependent girls, were so placed. No public money is paid for the support of these children. In some cases the parents pay the child's board. The older schoolgirls and girls of working age, who are placed in family homes, receive compensation ranging from $1.50 to $6 per week for services which they render in these homes. On December 1, 1918, 423 children were in the care of officers of this division.[7]

Most of the girls placed are 15 or 16 years old. An effort is usually made in the case of dependent girls to secure for them positions as mothers' helpers, a type of work chosen because it brings the girl into intimate relationship with the family life and puts her under the close supervision of her employer. Delinquents and semidelinquents are more likely to be employed as maids in private families. Children under 12 years of age are generally placed in institutions, though sometimes in free private homes where they may be given the opportunity to go to school.

Applications from women who wish to take wards of the court into their homes are investigated by a special officer of the division. She is expected to visit the home and to talk with the mistress, to learn the composition of the family and the number and condition of the rooms, and to assure herself that the girl will have a bedroom of her own which is provided with a key. No effort is made to see other members of the family, and the woman's word is taken as to the absence of boarders. At least two persons, not relatives.

7 Charity Service Reports, Cook County, Ill., 1918, p. 219.

given as references by the family, are also visited. Any woman who wishes to take a girl must agree to the following conditions:

1. That the girl be allowed to attend night school if she chooses.

2. That she report twice a month alone in person to her probation officer at the Mary B Home.

3. That she shall not be required to do any washing.

4. That she is to be in the house by 9 o'clock at night.

5. That she is not to go out in the evening with anyone of whom the mistress of the house does not approve.

The extent to which these instructions are carried out by the officer can not be judged from the records of the division, as those records are very slight. The results of the carefully outlined investigation of homes are not recorded in detail. The only report of conditions in a foster home selected by the division, aside from remarks entered in the case records of an individual child, is that recorded on a four by six card which contains the name and address and the number of persons in the home.[7a]

One of the great difficulties with which the child-placing department was formerly confronted was that of finding working homes for girls fresh from the court room. They are likely at first to appear too friendless and woe-begone to be attractive to strangers. Thus a pleasant temporary home where the girls might rest and recover self-possession and a little courage was greatly needed. This need was met by equipping from private funds two small clubs to which girls could be sent directly from the court. One, known as the Mary B, is for dependents; and the other, the Mary A, is for semidelinquents. The board of directors publishes a circular in which the clubs are described as follows:

In 1914 money was raised to furnish a six-room flat, which later grew into a two-story-and-attic house. Here the girl remains for a day, a week or perhaps longer, as the case requires, the thought back of the home being to acquaint her with the requirements, responsibilities, and joys of real home conditions. She is helped to wash and mend her clothing and takes part in the pleasures as well as the work of the household. If frail and undernourished, she remains until able to take a place where she may earn her livelihood or perhaps work her way through school. If adenoids or tonsils should be removed, she is cared for at the club while convalescing from these minor operations. While her physical wants are thus cared for, the moral and spiritual help she receives from the knowledge that somebody really cares about her welfare and that there is a place she may always call home, brings to her self-confidence and courage to take her place in life.

The need of the girl whom we might term a semidelinquent was quite as urgent as that of the dependent girl, and friends came forward again in 1916 and established a second home.

The Mary B club for dependents accommodates 18 girls; the Mary A cares for 8.

[7a] Since this writing a new system of records for the child-placing department has been established and complete reports of investigations of foster homes are now kept on file.

Many of these girls are entirely destitute except for the clothes they are wearing, and before leaving the club for a new home each girl is given a small suit case containing a change of underwear, a night dress, a comb and brush, and various other articles necessary for care of the person and helpful in properly starting a new career.

No girl committed by the court to the head of the child-placing division may be released, without special application to the court, before she has reached the age of 18. During this period the girl is under the close supervision of some officer in the division who must make monthly written reports to the head of the division. Every two weeks, as has been stated, the girl reports to the officer, and she is visited once a month in her home. When the girl has shopping to do, she brings her wages and is assisted by the officer in making her purchases. The division handles savings accumulated by the girls that range from $5 to $450. The social life of these girls has received special attention during the last two years. On Sundays they may entertain their callers in the Mary B home. Outings, concerts, and entertainments are arranged for by societies interested in the recreation of young girls. In general, girls under 17 are not allowed to receive callers in their homes, though exceptions are made in special cases.

Until recently the officers of the child-placing division worked only with children who were to be placed in homes and had no contact with the child's own home. These officers are now required to keep in touch with the home as well, and to make an effort to deal with the entire family situation.

It frequently happens that when a girl reaches the age of 16 and is free to select an occupation she prefers an occupation other than domestic work, such as, for example, that of telephone operator or office work. In that case the department finds for her another home where she can pay board. Although wards of the division are released from guardianship at the age of 18, they frequently avail themselves of the help and advice of the officers for a few years longer.

The following case supervised by the child-placing division illustrates the difficulties of finding satisfactory homes, the danger of delinquency developing in uncongenial surroundings, and the methods employed by the division:

Victoria J., aged 17. Father and mother both dead. Under the court's care as a dependent since 1910. She had been at first on probation, later placed in an institution for dependents, and since October, 1915, had been under the care of the child-placing division. During this time she had remained for three years in one family home which proved to be very satisfactory. Then her custodian died, and during the next nine months she was placed in four different homes. She was not contented in any of these, complained of being ill, and upon examination was found to be pregnant. She was then sent to a maternity home, but the matron found her unruly and refused to keep her. On October 8, 1919, she was brought into court on a delinquent petition. A mental examination two days before this showed her mental age to be 12 years. The case was continued five months under the supervision of the child-placing division.

October 8, 1919: In court. Continued to January 5, 1920. Maternity home willing to give another trial.

October 14, 1919: Sent with probation officer's approval to work in the kitchen of a large hospital until her confinement.

January 5, 1920: Confinement. Arrangements made for Victoria and baby to go to an infant's home until bastardy case against the man responsible is heard.

March 1, 1920: Baby died. Victoria in family home. Man paid burial expenses, and bastardy charge dismissed.

March 19, 1920: In court. Delinquent petition dismissed.

April 8, 1920: Victoria complains of loneliness in private home.

June 10, 1920: Custodian reports Victoria keeping late hours.

July 5, 1920: Continues to keep late hours. Custodian suspects immorality.

July 9, 1920: Victoria admits immoral relations. Taken to detention home.

July 12, 1920: Case in court on delinquent petition. Victoria committed to the House of the Good Shepherd.

In the cases of delinquent boys and dependent boys over 12 years of age, the guardian appointed is the head of the delinquent boys' division, who assigns the care of these boys to three officers of the division, two handling cases of Catholic boys, the third those of Protestant boys. The two Catholic officers have 180 boys under their care, and the Protestant officer has had as many as 90, but in 1920 he reported about 50. Although the boy may be placed in any situation that the officer deems suitable, and some boys are allowed to enlist in the Army or Navy, a farmer's home is generally selected. It has been the experience of the officers that the farm with its outdoor life, contact with animals, and opportunities for hunting and swimming, makes a strong appeal even to the city-bred boy and often proves so attractive to him that he remains on the farm after his period of supervision by the court is over. This terminates by law at his twenty-first birthday, and may be ended before that time.

No specific regulations governing the activities of these officers exist. Each one is given great latitude in working out his own method of procedure. Farms within a radius of 50 miles of Chicago are usually investigated personally by the officer who has been assigned the case. Farms at a considerable distance from Chicago are not personally investigated, but references from prominent citizens in the town near which the farmer lives are taken instead. Until about 1920 boys were widely scattered over Illinois and adjoining States, but since that time an effort has been made to place them on farms within convenient distance of Chicago. Each officer has his own standards of conditions which make a farm a suitable place for a boy. Moreover, these standards vary according to the individual needs of the boy concerned. **Comfortable quarters, arrangements** for bathing, and wages of at least $10 a month to cover the cost of clothing are some of the requirements. No stipulation about conditions of work is made, but farmers with a reputation for overworking their employees are avoided. The officer is not in a position to make too precise demands because the farmer feels that it is a favor to take the boy at all. In selecting a farm, the character of the boy is always kept in mind. For instance, a home with young children would not be selected for a boy who had immoral tendencies, nor one with unusual opportunities for stealing for a dishonest boy. Although the officer states the truth when asked, he avoids going into detail about the boy's past record.

If a boy is not satisfied with the first home in which he is placed, he is given a chance to try others. Rarely an officer brings a boy back to court. He prefers changing him about many times to giving up the plan of placing him on a farm.

As in the child-placing division, the officers make a monthly report with regard to each child under their care. The boys make no regular reports to the officers. Those at a distance write letters, while those near Chicago are frequently conferred with by telephone and visited approximately every six weeks. As many of the boys as possible are sent to a particular district about 50 miles from Chicago because of the greater ease of supervision. The sheriff of the county in which this district lies is especially interested in keeping in touch with the boys and makes them feel that they can come to him if they get into any difficulty. Cooperation of public officials with probation officers is of peculiar importance when, of necessity, the officer is not readily accessible to his charges.

Boys under the guardianship of these officers are encouraged to go to school, but it is seldom that they attend beyond the age of 16. Those wishing to go to high school are not sent out on farms. The problem of securing education for even the younger boys presents difficulties, owing to the dislike of school authorities and parents for having city boys, many of them with undesirable records, attend the small country schools.

Commitment to child-placing societies.

A small proportion of dependent children, 4.6 per cent. as shown by Table XII, were committed to child-placing societies during the five-year period 1915–1919. The only societies of whose services the juvenile court now avails itself are the Illinois Children's Home and Aid Society, the Jewish Home Finding Society of Chicago,[8] and the

---

[8] Now a division of the Jewish Social Service Bureau.

Catholic Home Finding Association of Illinois. The effect of this order is not essentially different from the preceding, except that the care of the child passes to others than court officers. Children committed to these societies are placed in family homes or in institutions and are supervised by agents of the societies. No reports are required from these agencies, but the Illinois Home and Aid Society reports every three months to the chief probation officer regarding children received for placing but not for adoption. The court, however, takes no action upon these reports and a change in the status of the child is made only at the request of the society.

Commitment to hospitals and schools for defectives.

The juvenile court law gives the court authority to place a delinquent or dependent child found to be in need of medical care in a public or private hospital or institution for special treatment.[9] In a small number of cases, less than 1 per cent of each group in the period 1915 to 1919,[10] the child was committed to such institutions. Most of these children were placed in the county hospital and the county tuberculosis sanitarium, but a few were sent to the State school for the blind and to a home for destitute crippled children in Chicago. In these cases in which a child is to be placed in a public institution at county expense the procedure is commitment to the county agent.

Deportation.

A few children each year are deported.[10] This means usually that they are turned over to the county authorities to be returned to other counties or States in which the family has a legal residence.

Commitment to institutions.

An order for commitment to an institution is a last resort on the part of the court. Most delinquent children are tried on probation or are placed in family homes before it is finally thought to be necessary to place them in institutions. In cases of dependent children perhaps even greater effort is made to find a suitable and normal home environment before resorting to commitment to an institution. Nevertheless, from Tables XI and XII it appears that in 22.1 per cent of the cases of delinquent boys, 39.9 per cent of the cases of delinquent girls, and 40.7 per cent of the cases of dependent children, the child was committed to an institution, a higher proportion of the last two groups than that of cases in which the child was placed on probation. This is largely due to the fact that for dependent children every possible plan is tried before bringing the case into court, while the seriousness of the offense and the difficulty of supervising a girl in the old sur-

[9] Hurd's Revised Statutes 1919, ch. 23, sec. 177b.
[10] See Tables XI and XII, pp. 70 and 71.

roundings often makes commitment the only possible plan for the delinquent girl.

Dependent children.—The juvenile court law provides for the commitment of dependent children to "some suitable State institution," to a manual-training or industrial school, or to a private association.[11] As a matter of fact, only one institution for dependent children supported by public funds is in existence, the Soldiers' Orphans' Home at Normal, Ill. This institution is at present used by other counties of the State for dependent children as well as for soldiers' orphans, but is used by Cook County only for its original purpose. With the exception of a few orphanages, therefore, the institutions to which dependents can be sent are those organized under the acts establishing industrial schools for girls and manual-training schools for boys.[12] Under these acts any seven persons with the approval of the governor and the secretary of State may incorporate to maintain an institution for the education and care of dependent children.[13] When organized under these acts they have certain privileges not given to other private associations, by far the most important of which is the right to receive from the county $15 a month for each girl and $10 a month for each boy committed to their care by order of the court. Under these circumstances it is not surprising that in Cook County one after another of the institutions caring for dependents has reorganized under the industrial or manual training school act [14] until there are now 18 such schools in the county, 10 for boys and 8 for girls. Most of the schools are organized for children of foreign-born parents, along national and religious lines, and the court, as required by law, exercises scrupulous care in committing children to institutions where they will be given religious training in accordance with the faith of their parents.

The policy of the court with reference to the commitment of dependents to institutions has always been to avoid commitment whenever possible, in accordance with the principles set forth by the White House Conference of 1909 that "Children of worthy parents or deserving mothers should, as a rule, be kept with their parents at home" and that "Homeless and neglected children, if normal, should be cared for in families, when practicable." [15] The court has been hampered in carrying out this policy by the fact that there has been no public money available for the support of children in boarding homes and the resources of private agencies have been inadequate. Under these circumstances the court has been forced to commit to institutions

---

[11] Hurd's Illinois Revised Statutes, 1919, ch. 23, sec. 175.

[12] See p. 3.

[13] Hurd's Illinois Revised Statutes, 1919, ch. 122, secs. 320–347.

[14] Ibid., ch. 23, sec. 185.

[15] Proceedings of the Conference on the Care of Dependent Children, Held at Washington, D. C., Jan. 25, 26, 1909, p. 8. Washington, 1909,

children whom it was necessary to separate from their parents; unless the separation promised to be of such long duration that more or less permanent placing in a family home was possible.

When the parent or parents are financially able to contribute to the support of their children in an institution the court has authority to order the payment of a stated sum each month.[16] This money is not paid directly to the institution, but to the clerk of the court and is turned over by him to the county treasurer, who pays the institution. If parents fail to make the payments ordered, they may be brought before the court on contempt proceedings and punished by commitment to the county jail. The process, however, is cumbersome, and enforcement of orders by this means is very difficult. In recent years the major part of the time of one officer has been devoted to this work, with the result that collections on orders for support of children, either under guardianship or in institutions, have increased from $1,107.66 in 1912 to $48,513.84 in 1920.[17]

Delinquent boys.—Two public institutions are available for the care of delinquent boys, one the St. Charles School for Boys, maintained by the State, and the other the Chicago and Cook County School for Boys, jointly maintained by the city of Chicago and by Cook County. The policy of the court is against commitment of first offenders except for the most serious offenses, and against commitment until the boy has been given every chance to make good under some other treatment. Boys who have committed serious offenses and frequent repeaters are sent to the St. Charles School for Boys for an indefinite period that may legally extend through minority unless the boy is previously released. For first commitments or in cases of less serious nature the boy is usually sent to the Chicago and Cook County School for Boys, where the period of detention is shorter, varying from a few weeks to perhaps a year, depending upon behavior.

The Chicago and Cook County School for Boys was established in 1915 to take the place of the John Worthy School in the house of correction. It will be recalled that separate housing of the boys committed to the house of correction had first been brought about. Later a school in the confines of the institution was organized and the segregation of the boys was effected. In 1915 the use of that school was replaced by commitment to a farm school.

Table XIV shows the number of boys committed to these various institutions in each of the years 1915–1919.

---

[16] Hurd's Illinois Revised Statutes, 1919, ch. 23, sec. 190.
[17] Charity Service Reports, Cook County, Ill., 1920, p. 240.

TABLE XIV.—*Institution to which committed, by year; cases of delinquent boys committed to institutions, 1915–1919.*[1]

Institution.	Cases of delinquent boys committed to institutions.					
	Total.	1915	1916	1917	1918	1919
Total............................	2,603	425	379	453	493	853
Chicago and Cook County School......................	1,130	3	153	202	252	529
John Worthy School........................	166	166				
St. Charles School for Boys..........................	1,307	256	226	251	241	333

[1] Figures for fiscal years ending Nov. 30. Charity Service Reports, Cook County, Ill.; 1915–1919. For 1920 the figures are: Chicago and Cook County School, 444; St. Charles, 193. For 1921 they are: Chicago and Cook County School, 460; St. Charles, 178.

About 60 per cent of the commitments in 1919 were to the Chicago and Cook County School, the remainder to St. Charles.

Delinquent girls.—Delinquent girls may be committed to one of three institutions, the State Training School for Girls at Geneva, the House of the Good Shepherd—a Catholic home—and the Chicago Home for Girls, Protestant, though nondenominational. The last two receive per diem payments from the city of 40 cents a day for each girl, paid through the city house of correction. Only girls from the city would be sent to either of these institutions. The Chicago Home for Girls also receives a considerable sum from private contributions.

Table XV gives the number of girls committed to each of these institutions in the five years, 1915–1919.

TABLE XV.—*Institution to which committed, by year; cases of delinquent girls committed to institutions, 1915–1919.*[1]

Institution.	Cases of delinquent girls committed to institutions.					
	Total.	1915	1916	1917	1918	1919
Total............................	1,333	257	210	279	286	301
Chicago Home for Girls.......................	234	54	40	57	44	39
State Training School for Girls at Geneva............	439	81	61	85	97	115
House of the Good Shepherd......................	660	122	109	137	145	147

[1] Figures for fiscal years ending Nov. 30. Charity Service Reports, Cook County, Ill., 1915–1919. For 1920 the figures are: Chicago Home for Girls, 31; Geneva, 84; House of the Good Shepherd, 100. For 1921 they are: Chicago Home for Girls, 54; Geneva, 50; House of the Good Shepherd, 132.

With certain exceptions, delinquent girls are sent to the State school in only the more serious cases. About 60 per cent of them were committed in 1919 to the Chicago Home for Girls and the House of the Good Shepherd. The State school will not receive pregnant girls and these are committed to the Chicago Home for Girls.

Transfer to the criminal court.

The juvenile-court law provides that the court may in its discretion permit a delinquent child to be proceeded against in accordance with the laws of the State governing the commission of crimes or violations of city ordinances.[18] This authority has been exercised in serious cases involving a few boys each year. The delinquent petition is dismissed, and the boy is held to the grand jury for indictment on a criminal charge. In Table XVI the number of such cases is given for each year since 1915.

TABLE XVI.—*Cases held to the grand jury by the juvenile court, by year; delinquent boys, 1915–1919.*[1]

Year.	Cases of delinquent boys.		
	Total.	Held to the grand jury.	
		Number.	Per cent.
Total	11,799	70	0.6
1915	2,326	24	1.0
1916	2,192	25	1.1
1917	2,328	7	0.3
1918	2,306	2	0.1
1919	2,647	12	0.5

[1] Figures for fiscal years ending Nov. 30. Charity Service Reports, Cook County, Ill., 1915–1919. In 1920, 17 cases were held to the grand jury; in 1921, 6.

The proportion of cases disposed of in this manner as compared with all cases of delinquent boys appears from Table XVI to be very small, less than 1 per cent during the five-year period 1915–1919. All these boys were at least 16 years of age. Many had been tried on probation or had been at one time committed to institutions for delinquent boys. A few had never been in court before but were nearly 17. The offenses charged were for the most part deeds of violence, daring holdups, carrying guns, thefts of considerable amounts, and rape. The decision of the judge in these cases usually depends upon his belief that the boy is too experienced in wrongdoing to be manageable in the State institution for delinquent boys and that he should therefore be committed to the State reformatory established for boys between 16 and 26. A boy can not, however, be committed to this institution under the juvenile-court law but must be transferred to a court having criminal jurisdiction. The judge is also cognizant of the fact that in many of these cases the officers of the court have tried for some time and have failed to effect any change in the boys. No detailed study of these cases has been possible. The following paragraphs, however, indicate the type of case dealt with by transfer to the criminal court:

George J. had never been in court before. With three other boys carrying a gun he held up a man and stole an automobile. The same week he and another boy robbed a store, using force with the storekeeper. He was held to the grand jury under $10,000 bond. The other boys were committed to the St. Charles School for Boys.

[18] Hurd's Illinois Revised Statutes 1919, ch. 23, sec. 177a.

Tony M. had been previously committed to the Chicago Parental School, to the Chicago and Cook County School for Boys, and to the St. Charles School for Boys. He was involved in two robberies, one the theft of an automobile.

Alex B. had previously been committed to the Chicago and Cook County School for Boys. He was accused of rape.

Joseph G. had once shot another boy and had been in the Chicago and Cook County School for Boys. He was involved with several other boys in a holdup.

William M. had been known to the court for four years. He and another boy with a revolver held up a man and took an automobile and a watch. The same night they held up a man and woman and took another watch and some money.

Herman S. had never been in court before. He was involved in two holdups, one with a gun.

Other procedure in cases of delinquent children.

Besides the methods of disposing of cases of delinquent children especially provided by law and included in the official reports of the court, other methods of treatment are sometimes used, usually to supplement an order specified in the law.

The detention home is theoretically a place for safe-keeping pending hearing and not a place for detention as a punishment. In rare instances, however, during the service of a temporary judge, children have been sent to the detention home during short continuances as a disciplinary measure.

Restitution for damages is another form of procedure not contemplated by the law. Fines as such are never imposed, but in case of theft a boy is not infrequently required to make good the actual pecuniary loss; and this practice of the court is sometimes extended to other offenses besides stealing. In one instance noted a boy was required to pay the doctor's bill of the boy he had stabbed. In another, a boy who had accidentally shot a companion was ordered to pay $2.50 a week until he had paid $20, the money to be given to the family of the injured child. The boys required to make restitution are all of working age and the amount ordered is paid in weekly installments at the office of the chief probation officer. A check is then mailed to the person who is to receive the money. During 1920 the chief probation officer received and paid out $3.706.23 in this manner.[19]

---

[19] Charity Service Reports, Cook County, Ill., 1920, p. 241.

SUBSEQUENT RELATIONSHIP OF THE COURT, THE CHILD, AND THE CUSTODIAL AGENCY.

The problem of retaining jurisdiction after a final order has been entered placing a child under the care of persons other than officers of the court is one of very real significance; it is, however, a problem that has not as yet been satisfactorily dealt with in Illinois. If jurisdiction over the child is to continue, the court must be able to exercise its authority in three ways: (1) By inspection or visitation to make sure that the child is receiving the proper treatment and is returned to his own home at the earliest possible moment; (2) by requiring from the custodial agency regular reports showing the disposition of each child under its care; and (3) by the exclusive power of release. Under the Illinois law, as at present interpreted, the court does not possess complete authority to exercise any of these powers.

The following provisions of the juvenile-court law apply alike to dependent, neglected, and delinquent children whether committed to the care of a guardian, to an institution, or to an association:

The guardianship[1] under this act shall continue until the court shall by further order otherwise direct, but not after such child shall have reached the age of 21 years. Such child or any person interested in such child may from time to time upon a proper showing apply to the court for the appointment of a new guardian or the restoration of such child to the custody of its parents or for the discharge of the guardian so appointed.[2]

Whenever it shall appear to the court before or after the appointment of a guardian * * * that the home of the child is a suitable place * * * the court may enter an order to that effect returning such child to his home under probation, parole, or otherwise. * * * Provided, however, That no such order shall be entered without first giving 10 days' notice to the guardian, institution, or association to whose care such child has been committed, unless such guardian, institution, or association consents to such order.[3]

The court may, from time to time, cite into court the guardian, institution, or association to whose care any dependent, neglected, or delinquent child has been awarded, and require him or it to make a full, true, and perfect report as to his or its doings in behalf of such child; and it shall be the duty of such

---

[1] Whenever a child is committed to an institution, the head of that institution is appointed guardian. This should not be confused with the appointment of a reputable citizen as guardian, which is an order quite distinct from commitment. Guardianship in the provision quoted means *custody* in general, whether that of a guardian, institution, or association.

[2] Hurd's Illinois Revised Statutes 1919, ch. 23, sec. 177c.

[3] Ibid., ch. 23, sec. 177d.

guardian, institution, or association, within 10 days after such citation, to make such report either in writing verified by affidavit, or verbally under oath in open court, or otherwise as the court shall direct; and upon the hearing of such report, with or without further evidence, the court may, if it see fit, remove such guardian and appoint another in his stead, or take such child away from such institution or association and place it in another, or restore such child to the custody of its parents or former guardian or custodian.[4]

With regard to associations it is provided that—

The court may at any time require from any association, receiving or desiring to receive, children under the provision of this act, such reports, information, and statements as the judge shall deem proper or necessary for his action, and the court shall in no case be required to commit a child to any association whose standing, conduct, or care of children, or ability to care for the same, is not satisfactory to the court.[5]

These provisions of the juvenile court law seem to establish the following principles with regard to the court's jurisdiction: (1) Any disposition ordered by the court may be terminated only by a subsequent order of the court—that is, the court has sole authority to release; (2) any person may reopen the case by petition to the court; (3) the court may remove a child from custody with the consent of the guardian, institution, or association, or after 10 days' notice may remove the child *without* such consent; (4) the court may require a report from the custodian with regard to a particular child and may, with or without further evidence, remove the child from such custody; and (5) the court may at any time require such information as it desires from an association receiving children under the juvenile court law. These principles seem to give to the court a fair amount of control over the ultimate disposition of the child. The application of these principles formulated in the juvenile court law is, however, modified by the interpretation of the laws relating to State institutions for delinquent children and of the laws establishing industrial and manual-training schools for dependent children. Moreover, in some instances, even when the juvenile court's jurisdiction has appeared to be clear, the court has hesitated to press a claim against the opposition of an important and influential institution.

THE COURT AND THE GUARDIAN.

The question of the court's relation to the "reputable citizen" appointed as guardian is probably the least difficult both in theory and practice of the questions presented by these sections of the law. The policy of the court in this matter is in fact determined not so much by a principle of law as by a question of expediency. Judge Pinckney stated in 1911 before the county civil service commission[6] that

---

[4] Hurd's Illinois Revised Statutes, 1919, sec. 177e.
[5] Ibid., sec. 181.
[6] Testimony of Judge Pinckney in Breckinridge, S. P., and Abbott, E.: The Delinquent Child and the Home, Charities Publication Committee, New York, 1912, p. 213.

such citizens were chosen because of their reputable character and their recognized ability to care for the child and that interference by a probation officer or other representative of the court would seriously impair their service. The practice of appointing reputable citizens outside the court has, moreover, fallen into disuse almost, in recent years, and, as previously stated, the citizens usually appointed are the head of the child-placing division and the head of the delinquent boys' division, who are directly responsible to the chief probation officer.

THE COURT AND THE INSTITUTION.

The control exercised by the court over children placed in institutions is more limited than that over children placed under guardianship.

Institutions for delinquent children.

In the case of institutions for delinquent children none of the principles formulated above are held to apply. The Cook County board of visitors in 1912 reported on the question of release from these institutions as follows:

> The relation of the juvenile court to the two State institutions for delinquent children is governed definitely by statute. The custody during minority of every child committed to either of these institutions passes to the institution at the time of commitment. The responsibility for the child's care, training, and supervision rests with the institution. The length of stay of a boy in St. Charles School for Boys is determined by the superintendent and State board of administration, and so with the State Training School for Girls.[7]

The act establishing the St. Charles School for Boys[8] contains no reference to the manner of permanent release, although it is provided that the board of trustees may make such provisions as it sees fit as to placing boys in homes, obtaining employment for them, or returning them to their own homes. The act providing for the establishment of the State Training School for Girls at Geneva provides not only for parole but for permanent release by the governor of the State or by the board of trustees.[9]

As a matter of fact these two institutions and the Chicago and Cook County School for Boys[10] parole children without reporting to the court, and a violation of parole may mean return to the institution without another appearance in court. The State institutions are required by law to appoint agents to visit and supervise children released on parole. Permanent releases are made by these institutions without the knowledge of the court. They are also in some cases

---

[7] Report of the County Board of Visitors of Cook County, Ill., for the year ending Nov. 30, 1912, p. 22.

[8] Hurd's Illinois Revised Statutes 1919, ch. 23, secs. 191–215.

[9] Ibid., sec. 236.

[10] Established in 1915.

made by the court at the request of a parent or guardian after notice to the institution.

A somewhat different situation exists with regard to the court's relationship to private institutions receiving the custody of delinquent children. The authority of these institutions is defined only by the juvenile court law, not by separate acts such as those which govern the State schools for delinquent children. The power of a private institution to parole a child without consulting the court is not questioned, but the juvenile court law provides for the appointment by the institution of an agent to visit homes in which children are paroled " for the purpose of ascertaining and reporting to said court whether they are suitable homes." [11] The law evidently contemplated such control on the part of the court over homes in which children are placed by the institutions as may be exercised through visitation of those homes.

In the matter of permanent release by private institutions some conflict of opinion exists. The chief probation officer made an effort in 1918 to secure an agreement on the part of the private institutions to release children only through the court, but one institution, on legal advice, maintained its right under the law to effect permanent releases without court action; the assistant State's attorney assigned at the time to the juvenile court, concurred in this opinion of the institution's authority, and the effort was pushed no further. Another view of the law is at least possible, and it is to be hoped that a more liberal view of the court's power may find the opportunity of submitting the matter to judicial determination by the higher court, so that the juvenile court's claim of continuing jurisdiction over the child and exclusive authority permanently to release a child from a private institution may be affirmed, or, if finally denied by the court, obtained through amendment of the law.

The authority to require reports [12] has never been interpreted by the court as applying to public institutions, nor has the court had any power of visitation and inspection. Public institutions receiving delinquent children are subject to the inspection and control of the Illinois Department of Public Welfare, and private institutions must be certified by the same body.

Institutions for dependent children.

More serious difficulties have been met with, however, in retaining jurisdiction over dependent children. The institutions receiving these children are more numerous than those receiving delinquents, and all are under private management.

---

[11] Hurd's Illinois Revised Statutes 1919, ch. 23, sec. 180.
[12] See p. 96.

The apparent intent of the juvenile court law was to limit release to the court and to subject all institutions receiving dependent children to a certain amount of control by the court.[13] It was specifically provided,[14] however, that the juvenile court law should not in any way conflict with the earlier laws providing for the establishment of the industrial and manual-training schools.[15] These acts provided for discharge at any time by the court committing, with the restriction in the case of the industrial schools that the power could be exercised only if the girl was still in the school. But the acts also provided [16] that any girl committed to an industrial school or any boy committed to a training school might be " discharged therefrom at any time, in accordance with the rules thereof, where, in the judgment of the officers and trustees, the good of the girl (or boy) or the school would be promoted by such discharge," and discharge might also be ordered by the governor of the State. The industrial and manual-training schools have therefore claimed the right to dispose of children without reference to the court. As early as 1907 the chief probation officer pointed out [17] that this procedure had already in many cases rendered ineffectual the work of the court, since children were returned almost immediately to homes that the court had declared unfit for them. An effort was made at that time to prevent the continuance of this practice by informal agreement with the institution, but the effort was unsuccessful. In 1912 the Hotchkiss committee, after investigating the relationship of the court and the institutions, made the same criticism and proposed the following remedy:

The law should be so amended as to make each institution responsible to the court at least for continued custody of every child committed to its care. In case a child escapes from such custody notice should at once be filed with the court which should then have power to institute appropriate measures for the child's apprehension. The return of a child without court consent to an environment which the court has just found to be unfit is a humiliating travesty on judicial procedure, and is in no way necessary to uphold the autonomy of institutions.[18]

While there has been no amendment in accordance with these suggestions the practice of the industrial schools has in the last few years been somewhat modified. For a great many years the institutions had been represented at the court by police officers, commissioned as probation officers, whose primary duty it was to convey to their respective institutions the children committed. In 1917 these

---

[13] See pp. 91–92 for provisions applying to these institutions.

[14] Hurd's Illinois Revised Statutes 1919, ch. 23, sec. 188.

[15] Ibid., ch. 122, secs. 333a and 347.

[16] Ibid., ch. 122, secs. 332 and 345. The words of the two acts are practically identical in these sections.

[17] Charity Service Report, Cook County, Ill., 1907, p. 123.

[18] The Juvenile Court of Cook County, Ill. Report of a Committee Appointed under Resolution of the Board of Commissioners of Cook County, p. 17. Chicago, 1912.

officers were removed by the general superintendent of police at the time of a reorganization of the police department which abolished "special details." The police department felt that the work which these officers performed could not strictly be called police work. Several of the institution superintendents felt that the institutions should not bear the expense of an officer to convey children to the institution following commitment. In the emergency the court dealt directly with the managing officers of institutions until some plan for institutional representation at the court should be worked out. The court had already made a first step in dealing directly with the institutions through the inauguration of an effort during the previous year to keep in touch with dependent children committed to institutions. To the officer in charge of this work was assigned the new task of making arrangements with the institution authorities for the admission of children, conveying children to the institutions, and conducting correspondence in matters relating to the welfare of the children. This plan still continues in effect, and the result has been most satisfactory to both the court and the institutions. Misunderstandings which were almost inevitable when transactions were made through a third person have to a large extent disappeared.

Moreover, in January, 1917, Judge Arnold obtained from the superintendents of the industrial and manual-training schools, whom he had called together for conference, an agreement to give the court 10 days' notice of an intended discharge or parole. The court was in this way given an opportunity to make an investigation and to suggest any plans it deemed advisable in connection with the disposition of the child. This arrangement has resulted in closer cooperation between the court and the institutions, though the schools have not always rigidly adhered to the agreement.

The power to require reports from these institutions, as interpreted by the court,[19] is limited to specific instances in which complaint has been made with regard to particular institutions. Thus the court does not have the authority to require periodic reports from institutions concerning their general organization or their disposition of children committed by the court. A report required in a specific instance may be made under oath and is not subject to verification by representatives of the court. For assurance that the institutions are in general performing their functions in a satisfactory manner, the court relies upon the annual certification of the State department of public welfare.

Under authority of section 18 of the juvenile court law[20] a board of visitation to inspect institutions receiving children from the juve-

---

[19] The interpretation is that stated by Judge Pinckney in 1911 before the county civil service commission. Later judges have for the most part followed his interpretations of the law.

[20] Hurd's Illinois Revised Statutes 1919, ch. 23, sec. 186.

nile court may be appointed by the county judge. Under section 19 this power may be exercised in counties of over 500,000 by the judge of the juvenile court.[21] It was originally held, however, that this authority lay with the county judge alone. Thus during 20 years of the court's existence the only board of visitation created was that appointed by the county judge of Cook County in 1911 and lasting only a short time. This board employed an executive secretary paid from private funds and made an investigation of the 33 institutions then receiving children on commitment from the juvenile court. The board reported to the county judge on conditions prevailing during the year ended November 30, 1911.[22] The services of a paid secretary were not retained, however, and the board ceased to function after the presentation of their report. In 1920 the judge of the juvenile court for the first time decided that authority to appoint such a board of visitation lay within his powers, and a board of two members was appointed. One member was the former chief probation officer, who was at the time superintendent of the United Charities; the other was a physician. A few institutions were visited by these gentlemen acting as a board. They are both very much overworked men; they had no secretary nor provision for clerical help, and up to the present time, except so far as the institutions visited may have profited from suggestions made by them, no obvious results of the experiment can be pointed to.

RECOVERY OF CHILDREN WHO ESCAPE FROM INSTITUTIONS.

The possibility of escape from an institution raises the interesting question of responsibility for the recovery of a runaway child. Two cases of runaway children were among the records read for this study. A 16-year-old boy who had been committed to the Chicago and Cook County School for Boys ran away from the school. A letter was received by the court from a social agency in a town in a neighboring State saying that the boy was being held in the county jail there. The juvenile court replied that the parents refused to pay his return transportation; and since the school had no funds for this purpose, the social agency would have to dispose of him as best it could.

The other case is that of a 14-year-old delinquent girl. She had once run away from home with a woman of questionable character, taking $195 from her mother and going to Mississippi. Her mother had sent her money to return. When she ran away a second time, the mother appealed to the court, and the girl was found in Chicago. She was then committed to the State Training School for Girls at Geneva, and after eight months escaped from the institution. A month later

[21] Hurd's Illinois Revised Statutes, 1919, sec. 187.
[22] Report of the County Board of Visitors of Cook County, Ill., for the year ending Nov. 30, 1911. Chicago, 1912.

the mother received a letter from a probation officer in a Mississippi town asking for authority to place the girl in the house of correction. The mother notified the court, and the court in turn informed the authorities at the institution of the situation. These authorities requested the probation officer in Mississippi to take her into custody and sent the court a notice of this action, saying, "if we are able to return her to the school, we will notify you."

In neither of these cases, then, did the court exercise the right to deal independently with the child but rather treated the costs of securing the return as a burden to be borne by the institution.

The expense incurred by a public authority of another locality within the State in returning these children to their homes could presumably be collected as a charge against Cook County. In practice this collection is not made, but Cook County often bears the expense of returning to their homes runaway children from other counties.[23] The court itself, however, and the institutions from which they escape seem to be unable to authorize such expenditure or to expedite in any way the transfer of the children.

FOLLOWING UP THE DEPENDENT CHILD AND HIS FAMILY.

Since February, 1916, the court has made an effort to keep in touch with families of dependent children who have been committed to institutions. This work grew out of an inquiry conducted by the county bureau of public welfare, which was established by the board of commissioners of Cook County in April, 1914. This bureau investigated the cases of a number of children who had been in institutions for a considerable time and who were not frequently visited by relatives. In some cases the results were startling, and the reunion of relatives and children through the bureau was in some cases dramatic. When the value of such investigations became apparent, the court itself took over this part of the work of the bureau of public welfare, and in February, 1916, began the practice of assigning officers to visit the families of children in institutions.

This work is at present under the direction of the head of the family-supervision division and under the immediate supervision of the assistant to the head. Investigation and supervision of families of dependent children in institutions are assigned to the regular district officers. The volume of work was very great when this system

---

[23] The problem of the "runaway" to Cook County (Chicago) is an interesting one. Six hundred and eleven such children were dealt with by the probation staff during the year 1919. In approximately 85 per cent of these cases, the parents or near relatives supply transportation for the return of the child. In those cases in which the relatives are not financially able to do this, the county agent on recommendation of the court supplies the transportation. (Charity Service Reports, Cook County, Ill., 1920. pp. 241–42.)

was established; but, with the better technique of investigation of new cases developed within the past few years, constant improvement in the follow-up work is expected. A periodic investigation and report is required by the head of the family-supervision division for every child in an institution, the interval between reports varying with the circumstances of the particular case. Through this periodic review an effort is made to restore the child to community life, either in his own home or a foster home, at the earliest possible moment.

COOPERATION WITH OTHER AGENCIES.

SOCIAL AGENCIES.

As a case-work agency dealing with family problems, the juvenile court necessarily has relations with private organizations in Chicago that are working in the same field.

Attention has been called in a preceding section [1] to the court's use of the confidential exchange, or the registration bureau, as it is called in Chicago, to learn what agencies have known the family under investigation; consultation with these agencies, either by reading their records or by personal interviews, is a part of the work of investigation. It has also been pointed out that complaints revealing situations upon which no court action can be taken yet requiring treatment are referred by the court to an agency organized to handle the particular difficulty.

In other ways, too, the court cooperates with outside agencies. These can best be made clear by a discussion of the relation of the court with two agencies with which perhaps it comes in closest contact, namely, the Juvenile Protective Association and the Jewish Social Service Bureau.

The Juvenile Protective Association [2] is the successor of the Juvenile Court Committee organized in 1899 to pay the salaries of probation officers, there having been no provision for salaries in the juvenile court law. While this defect in the law was remedied in 1905,[3] the committee continued its support of four officers until 1909, when it was reorganized as the Juvenile Protective Association and turned its attention to community conditions affecting child life. The association, however, continues its case work for the protection of children found in dangerous or unwholesome surroundings. Its work is largely with the same classes of children as those dealt with by the court, and close relations with the court are necessary in order to avoid duplication and disagreement. At the present time the division of work between the two organizations is briefly as follows: The Juvenile Protective Association confines its attention to cases of a less serious nature, in which it is thought court action will prove to be unnecessary. Cases that seem to call for court action are referred directly to the court without preliminary investigation by the association. The association also does work that the court does not feel it can undertake, such as the investigation of anonymous

[1] See p. 37.
[2] It was known for a brief time as the Juvenile Protective League.
[3] See p. 6 of this report.

100

complaints and work of a detective nature. All such work that comes to the attention of the court is turned over to this association. In turning over cases that seem too trivial to require court action, the court uses its own discretion. If the situation is such that action, but not necessarily court action, appears to be required at once, the case is ordinarily referred to the association. If, on the other hand, this does not become evident until the officers of the court have made a partial or complete investigation, it is often thought better for the court, which is familiar with the facts and through its officer has established relations with the family, to continue the work. This is especially true if it seems at all probable that court action may be necessary later.

The Juvenile Protective Association on its side finds it difficult to know immediately what cases will require court action. A condition seeming to call only for friendly supervision may on further investigation prove to require more drastic treatment or one originally not serious may in the course of months or years become such that court action is necessary. To avoid the duplication of work that would occur in cases of this kind if the association turned them over to the court as soon as it saw the necessity for court action, the court and the association have agreed that if the association has done much work on the case before court action is seen to be necessary or before the case is referred to the court by an outsider, the association is to complete the investigation, which the court will accept. For this purpose workers of the association are commissioned as volunteer probation officers by the juvenile court. In making their investigations they are not subject to the supervision of the head of the investigation division, but they bring cases involving dependent children before the dependent-case-conference committee before they file petitions.

The court's method of cooperating with the agencies that care for Jewish families, until recently known as the Jewish Aid Society, the Jewish Home Finding Society of Chicago, and the Bureau of Personal Service (now organized as the Jewish Social Service Bureau) is somewhat different from its method of working with other agencies in the city. The Jewish agencies maintain in relation to the court the same policy that they hold with reference to most organizations, namely, that Jewish families can be dealt with more intelligently by Jewish workers and Jewish organizations and that these organizations alone should work with them. The court has acquiesced in this policy to a large extent, and at the present time the great majority of Jewish cases are handled by Jewish agencies with the power and authority of the court behind them. All complaints that are received regarding Jewish families are turned over to the Jewish Social Service Bureau for investigation. This agency investigates and keeps a record of its work in its own office: it does not, however, report to the court the details of the inquiry or what action it has taken.[3a] If it is thought that court action is necessary, a conference is held of representatives of the three Jewish agencies. Dependent cases are taken before the dependent case conference committee only if the action contemplated requires spending public money for the support of the child. The relation of the officers of the Jewish agencies to complaints of delinquent boys is like that of the court probation officers; that is, investigation of delinquent boys' cases is made by the Jewish agencies in those cases in which the complaint is made directly to the court; in other cases the police probation officers investigate the complaint of Jewish boys as they investigate cases of non-Jewish boys.

In cases of dependent children and of delinquent girls, if the court orders probation or appoints a guardian, a representative of the Jewish agencies is always named as the probation officer or guardian. If the order is " guardianship with the right to place in a home," the agency makes no further report to the court. If, on the other hand, the order is probation, the representative of the agency is nominally at least under the supervision of the head of the family-supervision division and submits written reports to the court in accordance with rules covering reports on probation cases.

The court comes in constant contact with the United Charities since many cases, both dependent and delinquent, have at some time been known to that agency. No formal plan of cooperation now exists. At one time the society maintained an officer at the court, and recently one visitor of the society was assigned to all cases involving action in any court. These plans, however, have at the present time been abandoned. The probation officers are invited by the United.Charities to attend district case conferences but rarely find themselves able to accept this invitation.

Successful cooperation often depends, of course, upon the willingness of other social agencies, both public and private, to carry through plans initiated by officers of the court. The work of the court can be rendered futile by the failure of the agency on which it must rely for special service. The following case illustrates the very great waste of effort caused by such lack of cooperation on the part of an agency through which alone the object sought by the court in behalf of the family could have been obtained.

Three children, a girl of 7, a boy of 5, and a girl of 1 year, all had glandular tuberculosis. Their mother had an active case of pulmonary tuberculosis. The father of the two older children had deserted, and the baby was an illegitimate child. In March, 1919, the case was placed on probation, and in June the proba-

---

[3a] Since July, 1921, complete reports of investigations in these cases have been made to the court.

tion officer placed the mother and her three children in a county tuberculosis sanitarium. In July she was given a pass by the sanitarium to go to the juvenile court with all the children, but she did not appear in court and did not return to the sanitarium. It was October before the family was again located and December before the probation officer had persuaded the mother to return to the sanitarium. When the ambulance arrived, however, she escaped with the baby through the back door, abandoning the two older children. The case of these two children was brought into court for rehearing on January 7, 1920. The following is a brief summary:

January 7, 1920: Case in court. Continued for three months in order to locate mother. Children to be placed meantime in tuberculosis sanitarium. Publication for mother ordered.

April 7, 1920: Case in court. Mother still missing. Sanitarium will keep children for another three months. Case continued.

May 12, 1920: Case in court. Mother still not located. Continued for publication for father.

August 10, 1920: Probation officer learns from sanitarium that on July 27, 1920, the children had been released to an uncle who had come for them, and the sanitarium had no record of their whereabouts. The "uncle" was unknown to the court.

August 11, 1920: Case in court. Family not located. Case dismissed.

RELATIONSHIP TO OTHER COURTS.

As explained in an earlier section, the juvenile court has no jurisdiction over adults except in the matter of enforcing an order for the support of a child removed from its own home. The lack of criminal jurisdiction has two important results. The first is that it becomes necessary for the probation officer handling the child's case, whenever court action against a parent or another adult is needed in behalf of a child, to institute proceedings in another court. The second is that a number of dependent or neglected children whose parents have been prosecuted in another court by persons outside the juvenile court never come to the attention of juvenile probation officers and never benefit from the services of the court.

Reports of the juvenile court contain repeated references to the first of these difficulties and point out the waste involved in the necessity of having to carry cases into other courts and in sometimes having two probation officers at work on the same family, one representing the adult probation department, the other the juvenile court. In 1916, for example, the report of the court contained the following statement:

In studying the records of dependent children one can not help reaching the decision that the present overlapping of courts in Cook County is nothing short of ridiculous. In the same case the parents might be taken before the municipal court of domestic relations or the children before the juvenile court of Cook County or both parents and children might be taken before the different courts. Some day the courts will be combined. If that is not done in the near future, the adult and juvenile probation forces should be united so that the probation officers will at least work under one head.[4]

---

[4] Charity Service Reports, Cook County, Ill., 1916, p. 299.

Neither of these hopes has been so far fulfilled, but the court has made some progress in its cooperation with other courts. The offenses for which adults have been prosecuted most frequently by juvenile court officers are those of contributing to delinquency or dependency, nonsupport, abandonment, adultery, abduction, rape, bastardy, crimes against children, incest, abortion, selling liquor to children, and disorderly conduct. Within the city of Chicago, most of these cases may be prosecuted in the domestic-relations branch of the municipal court, which has jurisdiction in all criminal cases except those punishable by death or imprisonment in the penitentiary and in all cases which may be transferred to it by the circuit, the superior, and the criminal courts of Cook County.[4a] The more serious cases are held to the grand jury and tried in the criminal court of the county. In 1915 the juvenile court reported that 72 cases had been taken into the criminal court on charges made by wards of the court.[5] The offenses charged in these cases were rape and assault to rape, 41; crimes against children, 21; contributing to delinquency, 1; incest, 4; crime against nature, 1; seduction, 1; inducing female to enter house of prostitution, 1; and harboring females, etc., 2.

The charges in 348 cases taken into the court of domestic relations during 1916 are shown in Table XVII. The most frequent charges by juvenile court officers in this court are contributing to delinquency or to dependency, nonsupport, and bastardy.

TABLE XVII.—*Charge; cases against adults prosecuted by juvenile court officers in the court of domestic relations, year ending Nov. 30, 1916.*[1]

Charge.	Cases against adults.
Total	348
Contributing to delinquency	114
Contributing to dependency	104
Nonsupport	80
Bastardy	31
Rape	4
Crimes against children	5
Disorderly conduct	4
Selling liquor to minors	5
Abortion	1

[1] Charity Service Reports, Cook County, Ill., 1916, p. 300. In 1920, 261 cases were prosecuted in the municipal and criminal courts; in 1921, 456 cases.

Since 1915 an assistant State's attorney has been assigned to the juvenile court to advise the probation officers concerning cases taken into other courts, and no prosecution may be begun without her assent and the assurance that the evidence is sufficient.

[4a] Hurd's Illinois Revised Statutes 1919, ch. 37, sec. 265. See p. 13.
[5] Charity Service Reports, Cook County, Ill., 1915, p. 229.

So long as cases of abandonment, contributing to dependency and delinquency, bastardy, etc., can be prosecuted without the children involved ever coming to the attention of the juvenile court, the development of a uniform policy of child care in Chicago is impossible. The report of the court of domestic relations for the year 1917 [6] shows that during that year 5,651 children were involved in 3,687 cases of non-support alone. Children were also concerned in 319 cases of contributing to delinquency, 137 cases of contributing to dependency, and 435 bastardy cases.

No investigation has been made as to the number of children under the jurisdiction of other Chicago courts who have never been brought to the attention of the juvenile court; but probably few of these children were known to the juvenile court. Many cases heard by the court of domestic relations, however, are taken into court by a social agency such as the United Charities and the provision for the children and the supervision of the family under such an agency may be as satisfactory as that possible through juvenile-court action. But many dealt with by the court of domestic relations are not under the care of any social agency.

Formerly a juvenile-probation officer was assigned to the court of domestic relations to present cases in that court and to receive cases that might be transferred from the court of domestic relations to the juvenile court. This custom has been discontinued, however, and the cooperation between the two courts is far from complete. Both courts have at various times expressed the opinion that their work should be combined under one court having jurisdiction in all cases involving family life. In a recent report of the court of domestic relations the presiding judge expressed the opinion of that court as follows:

As has been pointed out before, the domestic-relations branch would at once enter upon a greater program of usefulness to the public were the law-givers to enlarge its jurisdiction to take in all matters affecting the family that require judicial adjustment. If it be admitted that public policy of the present day and faultless administrative methods of justice call for special service, then, obviously, it follows that such special courts should be endowed with ample powers to handle their special problems. This argument means that all family troubles ought to be taken care of in one tribunal, doing away with a multiplicity of courts, with conflicting interests and consequent confusion, expense, delay, waste of time of litigants and lawyers, armies of witnesses, and scores of jury panels.[7]

It is obvious that both the juvenile court and the court of domestic relations are conscious of the need of change in the structure of the

---

[6] Tenth and Eleventh Annual Reports of the Municipal Court of Chicago for the years Dec. 6, 1915, to Dec. 2, 1917, inclusive, p. 98.
[7] Tenth and Eleventh Annual Reports of the Municipal Court of Chicago, for the years Dec. 6, 1915, to Dec. 2, 1917, inclusive, p. 97.

judicial system, so that the work they may be said to share may be
more efficiently and satisfactorily done. To determine what the
nature of that change should be will require careful examination of
the constitutional limitations as well as the accumulation of a large
body of data as to the exact nature and volume of the service to be
rendered. The two courts do not exercise jurisdiction over the same
geographic area, as the jurisdiction of the court of domestic relations
extends over the city only, while that of the juvenile court covers
the entire county. The court of domestic relations is a branch of the
municipal court,[8] which as the successor of the earlier justice of the
peace and city magistrates court, is a court of less dignity and of
lower judicial rank. The judges of the municipal court, who are
elected for terms of six years, in whose hands lies the appointment
of a certain number of the members of the adult probation department, have never adopted the policy initiated by Judge Pinckney of
making appointments from an eligible list prepared by a nonpolitical
expert committee on the basis of competitive examination. The
services of the adult probation department are by the terms of the
statute under which the department is organized[9] much more restricted than those of the juvenile probation staff, as they can be
utilized only when the accused has been convicted. These limitations were discussed at length in 1915 in a report to the city council
by a committee of which Prof. Charles E. Merriam was chairman,[10]
and conditions remain to-day substantially as they were at that time.

Under the clerk of the municipal court a social-service department
has been organized. But in that department no principle of selection
corresponding to the juvenile-court examinations has been applied;
the staff consisted during 1919 and 1920 of only seven persons,
though during the year 1919, 16,931 complaints were received, resulting in the issuing of 3,986 warrants, while in 1920, 38,441 complaints
were received and 3,342 warrants issued.[11] Obviously in the present
organization of the court of domestic relations no such basis exists
for the development of a general family court as might be found
in the juvenile court. The development of the juvenile court into a
tribunal competent to deal with the various problems both civil and
criminal that now characterize the treatment of the family groups
of which dependent and delinquent children are members will require constitutional interpretation and possibly constitutional amendments that will demand a study of the entire judicial system of
Cook County. Family problems in Cook County are, moreover,

[8] Hurd's Illinois Revised Statutes 1919, ch. 37, sec. 264 fol.
[9] Ibid., ch. 38, sec. 509b.
[10] Report of the City Council Crime Committee of the City of Chicago, Mar. 22, 1915,
p. 60 fol.
[11] Twelfth, Thirteenth, and Fourteenth Annual Reports of the Municipal Court of
Chicago, Dec. 2, 1917, to Dec. 5, 1920, p. 154.

dealt with not only by the circuit court and the court of domestic relations but also by the superior, probate, and county courts, all of them constitutional tribunals. The constitution confers, too, upon the criminal court of Cook County the criminal and quasi-criminal jurisdiction that is exercised by the circuit courts in other counties.[12] Such jurisdiction is not, however, specifically denied to the circuit court by the constitution; and it is possible that over certain classes of offenses concurrent jurisdiction with the criminal court might be granted to the circuit court and that agreements similar to that already arrived at in the handling of truant children might place the handling of the problems of the adult involved in a family situation in the juvenile branch of the circuit court.[13]

One difficulty now constantly confronting the juvenile court, however, is the large number of cases as well as the great variety of problems. It is therefore difficult to contemplate any considerable increase in the court's burden. If certain questions of jurisdiction now at issue between the juvenile court and other courts, such as that of jurisdiction over older boys, continued jurisdiction over children committed to institutions, or bastardy jurisdiction, could be so determined as to fix the court's responsibility for those groups of problems, other adjustments looking toward a corresponding reduction of the court's burden might be contemplated. Nor can the ultimate development of the court be profitably discussed without at the same time giving thorough consideration to the development of the public-relief agencies of the community, and to the provision of greater facilities for doing certain work with which the court is already charged, as, for example, giving to it adequate provision for " placing out " the children under its care *with* as well as *without* the payment of board. In this discussion, it is, however, impossible to go into these questions of enlarged community resources for child care.

---

[12] Constitution of 1870, Art. VI, sec. 26. Hurd's Illinois Revised Statutes 1919, p. LXVII.

[13] Since this was written the Illinois Constitutional Convention, now sitting, has formulated proposals for the consolidation of the courts of Cook County that would obviate the difficulties referred to. The convention's plan contains express sanction for the establishment of a juvenile or domestic relations court as a branch of the contemplated consolidated court. See Report of the Committee on Phraseology and Style of the Illinois Constitutional Convention of 1920. Report No. 18, p. 16.

LIST OF REFERENCES TO ILLINOIS STATUTORY SOURCES.

Constitution of 1870, Art. VI, sec. 26 (Hurd's Illinois Revised Statutes, p. LXVII).

Session Laws:
  1830–31, p. 103, sec. 43.
  1879, p. 309.
  1883, p. 168.
  1891, p. 52, sec. 9.
  1893, p. 23, secs. 16 and 17.
  1895, p. 295.
  1899, p. 131.
  1901, p. 141.
  1905, pp. 151, 152.
  1907, pp. 59, 70.
  1911, p. 126.
  1917, p. 536.
  1919, pp. 780–782.
  1921, p. 162.

Revised Laws of Illinois:
  1827, p. 124, secs. 4, 29, 46, 47, 48, 50.
  1833, p. 209, sec. 158.
  1867, p. 42, sec. 16.

Hurd's Illinois Revised Statutes:
  1874, ch. 75, sec. 11.
  1897, ch. 118.
  1919, p. LXVII;
    ch. 4, sec. 1;
    ch. 17, sec. 4
    ch. 23, secs. 169, 170, 171, 172, 173, 175, 177, 177a, 177b, 177d, 177e, 178, 179, 180, 181, 183, 185, 186, 187, 188, 190, 190d, 191–215, 271, 298 fol., 313, 324, 328, 341;
    ch. 37, secs. 264 fol., 265;
    ch. 38, secs. 283, 509b;
    ch. 122, secs. 144, 320–347.

INDEX.

Abbott, E., and Breckinridge, S. P.:
  Administration of the Aid to Mothers
    Law in Illinois, footnotes on
    pages 9, 18, 41.
  Truancy and Nonattendance in Chi-
    cago Schools, 18 (footnote).
  See also Breckinridge, S. P., and Ab-
    bott, E.
Adjustment of cases without court action:
  Agency cooperation in, 100–102.
  Extent and method of, 42–46.
  In delinquent boys' cases, 41.
  In delinquent girls' cases, 39.
  Informal complaint giving opportunity
    for, 35.
Adoption:
  Appointment of guardian with author-
    ity to consent to, 12–18, 79.
  Investigations, 42.
  Proceedings, 13.
Adults:
  Lack of jurisdiction over, 16.
  Relationship between juvenile and
    other courts in cases involving,
    103–104.
Age groups under court's jurisdiction, 11,
  12, 15, 19.
Age of criminal responsibility, 1.
Aid to mothers cases:
  Conference committee, 41–42, 62.
  Disposition, 64, 68, 70.
  Hearings, 62.
  Investigation, 36, 38, 41–42.
  Jurisdiction, 11, 12.
  Number, 17–18.
  Records, 34.
  Supervision of, 12, 31.
Aid to mothers division:
  Committee reviewing investigations
    made by, 38, 42.
  Function, 22, 31.
  Investigations of applications for moth-
    ers' pensions by, 36, 38, 41–42.
  Records, 34.
  Staff, 31.
  Supervision by, 12, 31.
Aid to mothers law:
  Disposition of cases under, 68.
  Funds for pensions granted under,
    9–10.
  History of, 9–10.

Annual reports:
  Citations, 14, 52–53, 80.
  Contents, 33.
  Statistics from, 17–21, 43–44.
Anonymous complaints, 36, 101.
Appointment of probation officers, 7–8,
  28–30.
Arnold, Judge Victor P., 26 (footnote).
Arrangement of court room, 58–59.
Arrest of children, 1, 35, 57.
Assistant to judge in girls' cases:
  Appointment, 27–28.
  Legal status, 28.
  Methods, 61–62.
  Powers, 28.
Attorney, representation by, 60.

Bastardy, 12, 13–14, 45, 104, 105.
Board of Commissioners of Cook County:
  Appropriation of funds for mothers'
    pensions by, 10.
  Committee to investigate court ap-
    pointed by, 7, 15.
  Determination of probation officers' sal-
    aries by, 30.
  Management of detention home by,
    30, 51.
  Power to select probation officers, 6, 7.
  Taking over of medical examinations
    by, 47.
Breckinridge, S. P., and Abbott, E., The
    Delinquent Child and the Home,
    footnotes on pages 6, 18, 20, 27,
    92.
  See also Abbott, E., and Breckinridge,
    S. P.
Bureau of Personal Service (Jewish Social
    Service Bureau), 6, 36, 101.
Bureau of social registration, 37, 40, 100.

Case records:
  Access to, 34.
  Filing, 34.
  Information included in, 33–34, 73, 74.
  Lack of study of, 21.
  Making out of, at detention home, 54.
  Use of, in probation work, 73.
Case stories, 57–58, 82–83, 89–90, 97–98,
  102–103.
  Continued for definite period, 66–68.
  Of children placed on probation, 75–78.
  Of neglect, 22, 23, 24–25, 45, 46.

111

Cases, classes of, under court's jurisdiction, 11–14.
Cases cited:
    County of McLean v. Humphreys, 104 Ill. 378, 3 (footnote).
    Dunn v. Chicago Industrial School, 280 Ill. 613, 3, (footnote).
    Gilbert et al. v. Sweitzer, 211 Ill. App. 438, 8 (footnote).
    Hosking v. So. Pac. Co., 243 Ill. 320, 13 (footnote).
    Lindsay v. Lindsay, 257 Ill. 328, 8 (footnote).
    P. v. Olson, 245 Ill. 288, 13 (footnote).
    People v. C., B. & Q. R. R. Co., 273 Ill. 110, 7 (footnote).
    People v. Chicago, Lake Shore and Eastern R. R. Co., 27 Ill. 447, 10 (footnote).
    Petition of Ferrier, 103 Ill. 367, 3 (footnote).
    Witter v. Cook County Commissioners, 256 Ill. 616, 7 (footnote).
Catholic Home Finding Association of Illinois, 85.
Chancery jurisdiction, 5.
Character of the court, 11.
Charity Service Reports, Cook County. See Cook County Charity Service Reports.
Chicago and Cook County School for Boys, 87, 88, 93.
Chicago Bar Association, 5.
Chicago Board of Education:
    Assignment by, of teacher to detention-home school, 9.
    Compulsory-education, department of, 12, 42, 70.
    Cooperation of, in securing passage of juvenile court act, 5.
Chicago Home for Girls, 88.
Chicago Parental School for Boys, 69.
Chicago Parental School for Girls, 69.
Chicago Woman's Club, 4.
Chief probation officer:
    Duties, 30–31.
    Examinations for position of, 7.
    Membership on committee passing on mothers' pension cases, 62.
    Report of, 14, 33, 49, 52–53.
    Reports to, of child-placing agency receiving children for placement, 85.
    Reports to, of officer in charge of police probation officers, 40.
    Representation on dependent-case-conference committee, 37.
    Responsibility of, for children placed under guardianship of court officers, 93.
    Restitution for damages received and paid out by, 90.
    Suspension of, by president of board of county commissioners, 7.

Child-placing division:
    Appointment of head of, as guardian, 80, 82, 93.
    Clubs established for wards of, 81–82.
    Conditions of placement in homes by, 80–81.
    Distinction between "child placing" under, and supervision of child in home other than his own by family-supervision division, 72.
    Function, 31, 80.
    Number of cases cared for by, 80.
    Records of, 81
    Reports of officers, 82.
    Requirements formulated by, for homes in which wards of the court are placed as mothers' helpers, 80–81.
    Savings handled by, 82.
    Staff, 31.
    Supervision by, 82–83.
Child-placing societies, commitment to, 71, 84–85.
Children's Hospital Society, 47.
Circuit court:
    Chicago juvenile court as branch of, 11.
    Hearing by juvenile court of adoption cases filed in, 12.
    Jurisdiction of, over dependency cases, 3.
    Jurisdiction of, over family cases, 106–107.
    Selection of judge of juvenile court by judges of, 26.
    Selection of probation officers delegated to judge of juvenile court by judges of, 7.
Civil-service appointees to probation staff, 29.
Civil-service commission, 6, 7.
Civil-service method of appointment, 28.
Colorado Revised Statutes, 63 (footnote).
Commissioners of Cook County. See Board of Commissioners of Cook County.
Complaints:
    Anonymous, 36, 101.
    Clearing of, at confidential exchange, 37.
    Handling of, by police probation officers, 32, 40–41.
    In delinquent boys' cases, 32, 39–41.
    In delinquent girls' cases, 39.
    In dependent children's cases, 36–37.
    Informal adjustment of, 42–46.
    Preliminary scrutiny of, 36–37.
    Substitution of, for petitions, 35.
    Supervised, 38, 44, 45–46.
    Treatment of, regarding Jewish families, 101–102.
Compulsory-education department, Chicago board of education, investigation of truancy cases by, 12, 42, 70.
Concurrent jurisdiction, 13, 107.

Confidential exchange (Registration bureau), clearing complaints at, 37, 40, 41, 100.
Constitutionality :
Of appointment of probation staff, 6–8.
Of juvenile court law, 8.
Contested cases, 26, 60, 62.
Continuance :
For definite period, 65, 68.
General, 63–64, 68, 69, 70, 71.
Continuing jurisdiction, 91, 94.
Cook County, jurisdiction in, 11.
Cook County Board of Visitors, 93, 97.
Cook County Charity Service Reports, 33, and footnotes on pages 1, 6, 14, 20, 28, 31, 41, 47, 49, 51, 52, 53, 55, 58, 65, 73, 80, 87, 90, 98, 103, 104.
Cook County Detention Hospital, 8.
Cooperation :
Of employers with juvenile court, 74.
Of other courts with juvenile court, 103–107.
Of public officials with probation officers, 84.
Of social agencies with juvenile court, 30, 36, 37, 100–103.
County agent :
Commitment to, of children placed in public institutions at county expense, 85.
Membership of, on committee passing on mothers' pension applications, 62.
Payment of funds to parents by, 9.
County board of commissioners. See Board of Commissioners of Cook County.
County bureau of public welfare, 98.
County of McLean v. Humphrys, 3 (footnote).
Court order :
Continued for definite period, 65–68.
Continued generally, 63–65.
Dismissed, 63–65.
Final order. See Final order.
Payment for support of dependent child in institution, 16, 38, 87.
Court procedure :
At hearings, 59–60.
Need for reforming, prior to passage of juvenile court law, 4.
Crimes against children, 104.
Criminal code, 1, 2.
Criminal court :
Jurisdiction, 107.
Procedure in cases of older boys on probation committing new offense, 15–16.
Transfer of juvenile-court cases to, 88–90, 104.
Trial of children committing serious offenses, 14–15.
Criminal procedure, 35.
Criminal responsibility, age of, 1.
Custodial agencies, relation of, to juvenile court, 91–99.

Defectives, schools for, commitments to, 70, 85.
Delinquency, contributing to, 104, 105.
Delinquent boys :
Age, 19, 21.
Division in charge of, 31, 36, 39–41, 72, 74.
Institutions for, 87–88.
Investigation of cases involving, 36, 39–41.
Offenses, 18–19, 20, 89.
Delinquent boys' division :
Care of boys under guardianship, 83–84, 93.
Conditions of placement in farm homes by, 83.
Function, 31.
Investigations by, 36, 39–40.
Monthly report of officers of, 84.
Probationary supervision by, 72, 74.
Reports of boys placed on farms to officers of, 84.
Staff, 31.
Delinquent children :
Age distribution, 18, 19, 21.
Commitment to institutions, 70, 85–86, 87–88.
Definition, 11–12, 14, 15.
Detention, 49, 51, 54, 55, 90.
Disposition of cases involving, 63–68, 70–71, 87–88.
Guardians appointed for, 78–84.
Hearings, 58, 59–60.
Investigation of cases involving, 35–36, 39–41.
Jewish, 101–102.
Number of cases involving, 17–18, 19, 20.
Offenses, 18–19, 20–21.
Probationary supervision of, 71–78.
Problems of, 18, 25.
Sex, 18, 19.
Delinquent Child, The, and the Home, by Breckinridge, S. P., and Abbott, Edith, 20.
Delinquent girls :
Age, 19, 21.
Divisions in charge of, 31, 36, 39, 72.
Hearings, 27–28, 61–62.
Institutions for, 88.
Investigation of cases involving, 39, 61.
Offenses, 18–19, 20–21.
Dependency, contributing to, 104, 105.
Dependent-case-conference committee, 30–31, 37–39, 102.
Dependent children :
Age distribution, 21.
Commitment to child-placing societies, 71, 84–85.
Commitment to institutions, 38, 60, 85, 86–87.
Definition, 12, 15, 22.
Detention, 51, 54.
Disposition of cases involving, 63–68.
Guardians appointed for, 70, 71, 78–81.

Dependent children—Continued.
    Hearings, 60–61.
    Investigation of cases involving, 36–39.
    Jewish, 101–102.
    Number of cases involving, 17–18, 21.
    Problems of, 21–25, 75–78.
    Sex, 21.
    Supervision of cases involving, 71–74.
Deportation, 70, 71, 85.
Deputy chief probation officer, 30–31, 37.
Detention:
    Before 1899, 1, 4.
    First detention facilities provided, 8–9.
    Juvenile court laws, provisions in, regarding, 5, 8, 35, 49.
    Policy, 49, 52–53.
    Use of police stations, 53.
Detention home:
    Average daily population, 51.
    Average length of stay in, 51.
    Building, 8–9, 53–54.
    Clothing of children, 56.
    Daily routine, 55–56.
    Dental work, 55.
    Dietary, 56.
    Equipment, 53–54.
    Investigation of, by Hotchkiss committee, 51.
    Management of, 51.
    Medical, psychological, and psychiatric examinations, 47–48.
    Number cared for, 50.
    Overcrowding, 51–53.
    Reception of children, 54–55.
    Recreation, 56.
    Report of matron of, 33.
    Return to, after hearing, 50, 69.
    School, 9, 53, 55–56.
    Sources from which children were received, 50.
    Use of, as disciplinary measure, 53, 90.
Development of the court, 5–10.
Discharge of probation officers, 28–29.
Dismissed cases, 63–64, 68, 69, 70, 71.
Dispensary in juvenile-court rooms, 47.
Disposing of children for money, 24–25.
Disposition of cases:
    Adjusted without court action, 43–44.
    Dismissal and continuance, 63–68.
    Final order—
        Delinquency cases, 70.
        Dependency cases, 71.
        Effect, 68.
        Feeble-minded cases, 69.
        Mothers' pension cases, 70.
        Truancy cases, 69.
    Supplementary methods of treatment of delinquent children, 90.
    See also Appointment of guardian, Commitment, Deportation, Probation, and Transfer to criminal court.
Domestic-relations branch of municipal court, 13, 104, 105–106.

Dunn v. Chicago Industrial School, 3 (footnote).
Employers, visits to, 36, 74, 80–81, 83, 84.
Equipment of juvenile detention home, 53–54.
Evidence:
    As to moral character of parents, 38.
    In adoption cases heard by juvenile-court judge, 13.
Examinations:
    Mental, 42, 46–48.
    Physical, 46–47.
Exclusive jurisdiction of juvenile court, 11, 15.
Family problems, jurisdiction over cases involving, 103–107.
Family-supervision division:
    Follow-up work of, 98–99
    Function, 31.
    Investigations by, 36, 39.
    Representation on dependent-case conference committee, 37.
    Return to court by, of cases not showing improvement, 74.
    Staff, 31.
    Supervision by, 72, 74.
Farm placements, 31, 83–84.
Feeble-minded cases:
    Detention, 50.
    Diagnosis, 47–48.
    Disposition, 64, 68, 69.
    Investigation, 42.
    Hearings, 62.
    Jurisdiction over, 13.
    Number, 18.
Fifteenth Biennial Report of the Board of State Commissioners of Public Charities of the State of Illinois (1898), 5 (footnote).
Filing system, 34.
Final order of court:
    Delinquency cases, 70.
    Dependency cases, 71.
    Effect, 68.
    Feeble-minded cases, 69.
    Mothers' pension cases, 70.
    Truancy cases, 69.
    See also Appointment of guardian, Commitment, Deportation, Probation, and Transfer to criminal court.
Fines, 1 (footnote), 90.
Follow-up work with dependent child and family, 31, 82, 98–99.
Foreign-language-speaking officers, 32.
Funds to parents act, 9.
    See also Aid to mothers act.
Gilbert et al. v. Sweitzer, 8.
Grand jury:
    In cases of children committing serious offenses, 14, 70, 89.
    Investigation of court by, 28.
Guardian:
    Consent to adoption, by, 12–13.
    Contact with child's own home, 82.

Guardian—Continued.
Frequency of appointment of, 70, 71, 79.
Order, 78–79.
Persons appointed, 80, 83, 102.
Placing of children by, 80–84.
Subsequent relation of court to, 91–93.

Health, parental responsibility for, 24.
Healy, Dr. William, 47–48.
Individual Delinquent, 18 (footnote).
Mental Conflicts and Misconduct, 18 (footnote).
Hearings:
Adoption cases, 13.
Aid to mothers cases, 62.
Compulsory attendance at, 57–58.
Contested cases, 26, 60, 62.
Delay in, 52, 57, 65.
Delinquent boys' cases, 59, 60.
Delinquent girls' cases, 61–62.
Dependent children's cases, 60–61.
Feeble-minded children's cases, 62.
Number, 35, 58, 64, 69, 70, 71.
Summons, 57–58.
Time and place, 58–59.
Truancy cases, 12, 59–60.
Home visits, 34, 40, 72, 74.
Hosking v. So. Pac. Co., 13 (footnote).
Hospitals, commitment to, 70, 85.
Hotchkiss committee, 15 (footnote), 51, 95.
House of correction, 3, 4, 87–88.
House of the Good Shepherd, 88.
Hurley, T. D.:
Development of the Juvenile Court Idea, 4 (footnote).
Juvenile Courts and What They Have Accomplished, 4 (footnote).

Illegitimacy, 12, 13–14, 45, 104, 105.
Illinois Children's Home and Aid Society, 6, 84, 85.
Illinois Department of Public Welfare, 48, 94.
Illinois Federation of Women's Clubs, 5.
Illinois Home for Juvenile Offenders, 2.
Illinois Industrial Association, 8.
Illinois State Board of Charities, 4, 5.
Illinois juvenile court act:
Date enacted, 2, 3, 5.
History of, 3–5.
Original provisions, 5.
See also Juvenile court law.
Illinois State Conference of Charities, 4.
Imprisonment of minors in penitentiary, 1 (footnote), 2.
Incompetent probation officers, dismissal of, 28–29.
Indictment, 14, 35, 70.
Industrial schools:
Acts providing for, 3, 86.
Follow-up work with families of children committed to, 31.
Procedure in commitment to, 60.
Number of, 86.
Relation of court to, 92, 95–96.

Informal adjustment of cases. See Adjustment of cases without court action.
Inspection of custodial agency, 91, 94.
Institute of Juvenile Research, 47–48, 53, 62, 69.
Institutions:
Certification of, 94.
Commitment to, of—
Delinquent boys, 70, 85, 87–88.
Delinquent girls, 70, 85–86, 88.
Dependent children, 38, 60, 85, 86–87.
Feeble-minded children, 69.
Truants, 69–70.
Follow-up work with families of children committed to, 30–31, 98–99.
Placement of children in private, by child-placing division, 80.
Recovery of children escaping from, 97–98.
Relation of court to, subsequent to commitment of—
Delinquent children, 30–31, 93–94.
Dependent children, 94–97.
Interpreters, 29, 32.
Investigation:
Adoption cases, 13, 42.
Aid-to-mothers cases, 41–42.
Bastardy cases, 13–14.
By private agencies, 36, 100–102.
Delinquent boys' cases, 39–40.
Delinquent girls' cases, 39.
Dependent children's cases, 36–39.
Divisions and agencies making, 35–36.
Elimination of complaints not requiring, 36–37.
Feeble-minded cases, 13, 42.
Police probation officers', 40–41.
Prior to filing petition, 35.
Truancy cases, 42.
Investigation division:
Adjustment of complaints, 43–44.
Function, 31.
Investigation of cases, 35–37, 39–40, 42.
Reception of complaints, 35.
Relation to dependent-case-conference committee, 37–38.
Reports on adoption cases, 42.
Staff, 31.
Investigation of juvenile court, 6–7.

Jail:
Commitment of children to, 2, 3.
Detention of children in, 1, 2, 49.
School for boys in, 4.
Jewish agencies, 6, 36, 38, 100, 101.
Jewish Aid Society, 101.
Jewish Social Service Bureau (Jewish Home Finding Society of Chicago), 36, 84, 100, 101.
John Worthy School, 87, 88.
Judge of juvenile court:
Duties, 12, 27.
Method of conducting hearings, 59–60.
Policy with reference to serious offenses, 14–15.

Judge of juvenile court—Continued.
  Qualifications, 27.
  Salary, 26.
  Selection, 26.
  Substitute, 26.
  Woman assistant hearing delinquent girls' cases, 27–28.
Jurisdiction :
  Age groups, 11, 12, 15, 19, 21.
  Area covered, 11, 106.
  As branch of circuit court, 12–14.
  Classes of cases, 11–14, 43–44.
  Cook County, jurisdiction in, 11.
  Duration, 15.
  Lack of criminal, 103.
  Original and exclusive, 11–12.
  Over adults, 16, 61, 103, 104.
  Over children accused of committing serious offenses, 14–15, 88–90.
  Over family cases, 105–107.
  Policy with reference to exercise of concurrent, 12–13, 14, 15, 105, 107.
  Retention of, after final order, 91–92.
  Retention of, by use of general continuance order, 64–65.
  See also Follow-up work with dependent child and family ; Guardian, subsequent relation of court to ; Institution, relation of court to, following commitment ; and Recovery of children escaped from institutions.
Jury, 1, 35.
  In dependency cases, 3, 60–61.
Justice of the peace, 14, 32, 106.
Juvenile court building, 9, 53, 58–59.
Juvenile court law :
  Act of 1899, 5, 8, 11.
  Amendments enacted, 5, 6, 9, 10 (footnote), 79, 100.
  Appointment of guardian, 78–79.
  Authority for mental and physical examinations under, 46.
  Board of visitation, 96–97.
  Commitment to institutions, 85, 86, 87.
  Constitutionality, 7, 8.
  Delinquent child as defined by, 11–12, 14, 15.
  Dependent or neglected child as defined by, 12, 15, 22.
  Efforts to secure enactment, 3–5.
  Initiation of case, 35.
  Legal status of minors prior to passage of, 1–3.
  Related acts—
    Aid to mothers, 9–10.
    Detention home, 9.
    Domestic-relations branch of municipal court, 104, 106.
    Industrial and manual training schools, 3, 60, 86, 95.
    Parental schools, 12.

Juvenile court law—Continued.
  Relation of court to private institutions, 94.
  Retention of jurisdiction over committed children, 91–92, 95.
  Transfer of cases to criminal court, 88–89.
  See also Jurisdiction.
Juvenile Court of Cook County, Ill., The, Report of a Committee Appointed under Resolution of the Board of Commissioners of Cook County, Aug. 8, 1912, 7 (footnote), 15 (footnote), 51 (footnote).
Juvenile Protective Association (Juvenile Court Committee), 6, 8, 36, 38, 100.
Juvenile Psychopathic Institute (Institute of Juvenile Research), 47–48, 53, 62, 69.

Lathrop, Julia C., Development of the Probation System in a Large City, 4 (footnote), 8 (footnote).
Legal papers, 33–34.
Legal relationship of detention home and juvenile court, 51.
Legal status of probation staff, 5, 6–8.
Legal status of woman assistant to judge, 28.
Lindsay v. Lindsay, 8 (footnote).

Mack, Judge Julian W., 26 (footnote), 27.
  Legal problems involved in the establishment of the juvenile court, 27 (footnote).
Manual training schools, 3, 31, 60, 86, 92, 95–96.
Mary A Home, 81, 82.
Mary B Home, 81, 82.
Massachusetts, probation system, 4, 5.
Massachusetts Acts and Resolves, 1878, 4 (footnote).
Medical care, 46, 47.
  In detention home, 53–55.
Medical examinations, 46–47.
Mental examinations, 42, 46–48.
Merriam, Prof. Charles E., 106.
Mothers' helpers, 80–81.
Mothers' pensions. See Aid to mothers cases.
Municipal court :
  Domestic-relations branch, 13, 104, 105–106.
  Tenth and eleventh annual reports of, 105 (footnote).
  Twelfth, thirteenth, and fourteenth annual reports of, 106 (footnote).

Nationality as basis of assignment of probation cases, 32.
Neglected child, 5, 9, 12, 63.
  See also Dependent children.

Negro probation officers. 32.
New York system of detention. 4–5.
Nonsupport, 104, 105.
Number of children brought into court, 17–18.
Number of families assigned to a probation officer, 73.
Number of probation officers, 29–30.

Offenses of delinquent children, 18–19, 20–21.
Offices. 53, 58–59.
Organization of the court:
Judge. 12, 26–27, 59–60.
Probation officers—
Appointment and discharge, 28–29.
Number. 29–30.
Organization, 30–32.
Police probation officers, 32–33.
Salaries, 30.
Records. 33–34, 40–41.
Reports, 33, 40.
Woman assistant to judge, 27–28, 61–62.
Origin of the court, 1–5.
Original, exclusive jurisdiction of juvenile court, 11, 15.
Outlying districts, probation work in, 32.
Overcrowding of juvenile detention home, 51–53.

P. v. Olson, 13 (footnote).
Parental schools, 12, 42, 69–70.
Parental school act, 12.
Parole. 93, 96.
Payment by parent for institutional care of child, 16, 38.
Penitentiary, imprisonment of minors in, 1, 2.
People v. C., B. and Q. R. R. Co., 7 (footnote).
People v. Chicago, Lake Shore & Eastern R. R. Co., 10 (footnote).
Petition:
By whom filed. 35.
Change of, 68.
Dismissal of, in transferred cases, 89.
For appointment of guardian, 12.
For commitment to industrial or training school, 3.
In cases of feeble-minded children, 13, 42, 69.
In cases reported by police, 39, 40.
Investigation prior to filing of, 35, 37–38, 39.
Presence at hearing of officer filing, 59, 61.
Public record, 34.
Petition of Ferrier, 3 (footnote).
Physical examinations, 46–47.
Pinckney, Judge Merritt W., 1, 26 (footnote), 27, 92–93, 106.
Place of hearing. 58–59.
Police magistrate, 14, 35.

Police probation officers:
Assignment, 6.
Investigations by. 36, 40–41, 42, 43.
Limitation of duties. 33, 65.
Number, 31.
Organization, 31, 32–33.
Presence at hearings. 59.
Records. 40–41.
Reports. 40.
Representatives of institutions, 95–96.
Supervision of work of, 32.
Value of. 32, 33.
Police stations:
Conferences with boys, parents, and complainant at, 41.
Detention of children in. 8, 49, 53.
Reception of complaints at, 32, 33.
Policy of juvenile court:
Application of probation system. 71.
Carrying out of, by chief probation officer. 30.
Commitment to institutions. 85, 86.
Detention, 49, 52–53.
Dismissal and continuance. 63–68.
Exercise of jurisdiction over older boys, 15.
Forming of, by judge, 27.
Guardianship, 92–93.
Separation of families because of poverty, 22.
See also Cooperation with other agencies.
Preliminary procedure:
Adjustment without court action, 42–46.
Complaint and petition, 35.
Investigation, 35–42.
Physical and mental examinations, 46–48.
Private nature of social records. 34.
Probation:
Child-placing as distinguished from, 72.
Continuance for definite period compared with, 65.
Delinquent children placed on. 70, 72.
Dependent children placed on, 71, 72.
Effect of order, 71.
Frequency of, as compared with other orders, 79.
Homes in which children are placed during. 72.
In truancy cases. 69–70.
Jurisdiction of court over older boys on, who commit new offenses, 15, 88–89.
Policy in application of. 71.
Standards of probation work, 73–75.
Supervision of delinquent boys on, 74–75.
Supervision of delinquent girls and dependent children on, 72–74.
Probation department:
Development, 5–8.
Organization. 30–32, 65.
Records, 34.
Reports. 34, 40,

Probation officers:
Appointment, 5–8, 28.
Assignment, 31, 105.
Average number of families assigned to, 73.
Discharge, 28–29.
Examinations, 7–8.
Number, 5–6, 29–30.
Salaries, 5–6, 8, 30.
Selection, 5–6, 7–8.
See also Chief probation officer, and Police probation officers.
Procedure. See Court procedure, Hearings, and Preliminary procedure.
Proceedings of the Conference on the Care of Dependent Children, held at Washington, D. C., Jan. 25, 26, 1909, 86 (footnote).
Psychological and psychopathic examinations, 46–48.
Publication of cases, 58.
Publicity, avoidance of, at hearings, 59.

Qualifications of probation officers, 28.

Reconstructing homes, 72–73.
Records:
Aid to mothers division, 34.
Case. See Case records.
Child-placing division, 81.
Clearing new cases with court, 41.
Other records and forms, 34.
Probation department, 34.
Social, private nature of, 34.
Recovery of children escaped from institutions, 97–98.
Registration bureau (Confidential exchange), clearing complaints at, 37, 40, 41, 100.
Rehearings, 41, 68, 70.
Relation of court, child, and custodial agency, 91–99.
Relation of juvenile court and other courts, 103–107.
Release, power of, 82, 91–92, 93–94, 95, 96.
Report of the County Board of Visitors of Cook County, Ill., 93 (footnote), 97 (footnote).
Report of the City Council Crime Committee for the City of Chicago, March 22, 1915, 106 (footnote).
Reports:
Annual, of court. See Annual reports.
Charity Service. See Cook County Charity Service Reports.
Chief probation officer's, 14, 33.
Monthly, for division heads, on probation work, 34, 40.
Monthly, of officers of delinquent boys' division, 84.
Of child-placing division officers, 82.
Of custodial agency to court, 91–92, 93.
Of dependent-case-conference committee, 38, 39.
Of Institute of Juvenile Research, 48, 62.

Reports—Continued.
Of investigation division, in adoption cases, 42.
Of matron of detention home, 33.
Of probationers to probation officers, 74, 84.
On feeble-minded cases, 62.
On follow-up work with families of dependent children in institutions, 99.
On results of private hearings of delinquent girls' cases by woman assistant to the judge, 27–28, 61–62.
School. See School reports.
Restitution for damages, 90.
Retention of jurisdiction:
After final order, 91–92.
By use of general continuance order, 64–65.
See also Follow-up work with dependent child and family; Guardian, subsequent relation of court to; Institutions, relation of court to following commitment; and Recovery of children escaped from institutions.
Return of child to his own home, 91, 95, 99.

Runaway children, 34, 97–98.

St. Charles School for Boys, 87, 88, 93.
Salaries of probation officers, 5–6, 8, 30.
Schedule of court hearings, 58.
School reports, 39, 73, 74.
Schooling, provisions for, for children in working homes, 81, 84.
Schools for defectives, commitments to, 85.
Sectarian institutions, 3.
Separate hearings, 4.
Serious offenses, children accused of committing, jurisdiction over, 14–15.
Settlements, reporting of probationers at, 74.
Social agencies, cooperation with juvenile court, 30, 36, 37, 100–103.
Social records:
Private nature of, 34.
Use of, in investigation, 40.
Social-service department of municipal court, 106.
Soldiers' Orphans' Home, Normal, Ill., 86.
Standards:
Realization of, in investigations of dependency cases, 36.
Standards of probation work, 73–75.
State criminologist, 48.
State penitentiary, 1.
State reformatory, 2, 3.
State school for the blind, 85.
State school for the feeble-minded, Lincoln, Ill., 56, 69.
State Training School for Girls, Geneva, Ill., 88, 93, 97.
State's attorney, 13, 14, 37, 94, 104.

Statistical information in annual report of juvenile court. 33.
Status of probation officers, 5, 6–8.
Stevens, Mrs. Alzena P., 5.
Summons, 3, 4, 35, 57–58.
Supervised complaint, 38, 44, 45–46.
Supervision :
    Boys under guardianship, 83–84.
    Children on parole, 93.
    Children on probation, 63, 71–78.
    Detention home, 51.
    Families of dependent children, 12, 63, 98–99.
    Guardians appointed by court, 92–93.
    In cases continued for a definite period, 65–68.
    Institutions receiving children, 93–97.
    Police probation officers, 32.
    Probation staff, 30–31.
    Wards of child-placing division, 82–83.
Support of dependent children :
    By parent, 16, 38, 87.
    Public funds for, 86.
Support order, dependent children committed to institution, 16, 38, 87.
Supreme court, 8, 14, 15, 26.
Suspension of probation officers, 29 (footnote).

Territorial assignment of probation work, 31.
Thurston, H. W., Ten Years of the Juvenile Court of Chicago, 9 (footnote), 58 (footnote).
Time of hearings, 58–59.
Transfer of cases to criminal court, 88–90, 104.
Trial of children prior to passage of juvenile court law, 1.

Truant cases :
    Disposition, 64, 68, 69–70.
    Hearings, 59–60.
    Investigation, 36.
    Jurisdiction, 12.
    Numerical importance, 18.
Truant officers, 12, 32, 36, 59–60, 69, 70.
Tuthill, Judge Richard S., 26 (footnote).
Types of cases heard by juvenile court :
    Definition of, 11, 12.
    Numerical importance of various, 17–18.

United Charities, 102, 105.

Visitation and Aid Society of Chicago, 3–4, 6.
Visitation of institutions receiving children, 91, 94, 96–97.
Visits to homes of probationers, 72, 73, 74.
Vocational bureau, 78.
Volunteer probation officers, 5–6, 32, 36, 101.

Wages, deductions from, for support of dependent child in institution, 16.
Warrant, 35, 57.
Whipping, 1 (footnote).
White House conference of 1909, 86.
Wines, Dr. Frederick W., 4–5.
Witnesses, 60.
Witter v. Cook County Commissioners, 7 (footnote).
Woman assistant to judge in girls' cases. See Assistant to judge in girls' cases.
Woman physician to examine delinquent girls, 47.
Working homes for girls, 80–83.

Y. W. C. A. 78.

UNITED STATES DEPARTMENT OF LABOR

FRANCES PERKINS, Secretary

CHILDREN'S BUREAU

KATHARINE F. LENROOT, Chief

THE CHILD, THE FAMILY AND THE COURT

A STUDY OF THE ADMINISTRATION OF JUSTICE IN THE FIELD OF DOMESTIC RELATIONS

GENERAL FINDINGS AND RECOMMENDATIONS

BY

BERNARD FLEXNER, REUBEN OPPENHEIMER
and KATHARINE F. LENROOT

Bureau of Publication No. 193

(Revised edition)

Reprinted in 1939

UNITED STATES

GOVERNMENT PRINTING OFFICE

WASHINGTON : 1939

CONTENTS

Page

Letter of transmittal_____ v
Introduction_____ 1
  Changing conceptions of the function of law and the administration
    of justice_____ 1
    Social jurisprudence_____ 1
    Cities and the law_____ 2
    Overlapping jurisdiction_____ 3
    A new judicial technique_____ 4
    New courts_____ 4
  Purpose and method of study_____ 5
The substantive law of domestic relations_____ 8
  Husband and wife_____ 8
  Parent and child_____ 9
  Guardian and ward_____ 10
Specialized courts dealing with family problems_____ 12
  The juvenile court_____ 12
  The family court or court of domestic relations_____ 13
    History_____ 13
    Extent of the family-court movement_____ 15
    Fundamental problems involved_____ 17
Procedural changes in specialized courts_____ 18
  Conservatism in legal procedure_____ 18
  Examples of the new procedure_____ 18
  The law in action_____ 19
Function of the law in family problems_____ 23
  The limits of effective legal action_____ 23
  Enforcement of the law of domestic relations_____ 24
Interrelation of juvenile and family-court cases_____ 25
  Early studies of overlapping_____ 25
  Study of families dealt with in juvenile and domestic-relations cases
    in Hamilton County, Ohio, and Philadelphia, Pa_____ 26
    Volume of cases_____ 27
    Interrelation of cases_____ 27
    Social agencies dealing with the families_____ 27
    Characteristics of the families_____ 28
Present judicial organization for dealing with juvenile and family cases 30
  Court systems having jurisdiction over cases included in the study 30
  Jurisdiction in delinquency and dependency cases_____ 31
  Jurisdiction in other juvenile and family cases_____ 32
  Possibilities of consolidating jurisdiction_____ 32
Family courts and courts of domestic relations in action_____ 34
  Consolidation of jurisdiction_____ 34
    Jurisdiction conferred by law or rule of court_____ 34
    Jurisdiction exercised in practice_____ 35
  Extension of accepted standards of juvenile-court organization and
    procedure_____ 38
    The judge_____ 38
    The probation staff_____ 39
    Precourt work and investigation of cases_____ 42
    Hearings and orders_____ 44
    Probationary supervision_____ 45
    Record system_____ 47
    Extent of courts' conformity to standards_____ 48
  Effect of family-court organization on juvenile-court work_____ 49

Page

Fundamental considerations in the extension of the new judicial technique_____ 51
    Safeguarding the juvenile court and consolidating the gains made__ 51
    Flexibility of program_____ 52
    Adequacy of personnel_____ 53
    Utilization and stimulation of community resources_____ 53
    Research and the development of scientific methods_____ 54
Application of the new technique to specified types of cases_____ 55
    Offenses against children_____ 55
    Nonsupport and desertion_____ 57
    Establishment of paternity and enforcement of support of children born out of wedlock_____ 58
    Divorce and annulment of marriage_____ 59
        General considerations_____ 59
        Alimony_____ 60
        Custody of children_____ 60
        Jurisdiction_____ 60
    Adoption and guardianship_____ 62
    Commitment of mentally defective and insane children_____ 62
    Public aid to dependent children in their own homes_____ 63
Conclusions_____ 64
Appendix A.—Family courts and courts of domestic relations in the United States_____ 67
Appendix B.—Study of families dealt with in juvenile and domestic-relations cases in Hamilton County, Ohio, and Philadelphia, Pa_____ 71

LETTER OF TRANSMITTAL

United States Department of Labor,
Children's Bureau,
Washington, D. C., March 19, 1937.

Madam: There is transmitted herewith a reprint of the revised and enlarged edition of The Child, the Family, and the Court; a Study of the Administration of Justice in the Field of Domestic Relations which was issued in 1933. This report, first published in 1929 as Part I, General Findings and Recommendations, is based upon legal research and field observations and was written by Bernard Flexner and Reuben Oppenheimer, lawyers who have devoted much study to the problems of juvenile and family courts, and Katharine F. Lenroot, of the Children's Bureau.

Descriptive material concerning 26 courts with special organization for dealing with family cases constitutes the supporting data for the section of this report entitled "Family Courts and Courts of Domestic Relations in Action" (p. 34). Publication of this material, together with a statistical study of families dealt with in juvenile and domestic-relations cases in Hamilton County, Ohio, and Philadelphia, Pa., now being included as Appendix B of this report, has been greatly delayed, first because of pressure of emergency work and second because of limitation of printing funds. A few copies of the report describing the individual courts are available in manuscript form for loan to students of family-court problems. The list of references included as Appendix B in the first edition has been revised and is available in mimeographed form.

Although great diversity is found in the organization and administration of juvenile courts, there is fairly general agreement among specialists regarding the broad principles which should govern their jurisdiction and procedure. No such condition prevails with reference to so-called family courts or courts of domestic relations, although the need for development of constructive service to families coming to the attention of the courts because of domestic difficulties is more widely recognized each year. Proposals for legislation often lack an adequate basis of information concerning the operation of existing court systems and the legal framework and social setting in which the new courts must find their place. The study was undertaken in the hope that it might help to meet this need.

Throughout the study the domestic relations court committee of the National Probation Association, the National Association of Legal Aid Organizations, and the National Desertion Bureau have been consulted. The report was read in manuscript by the following judges or former judges of juvenile or family courts: Hon. L. B. Day (Omaha), Hon. Charles W. Hoffman (Cincinnati), Hon. Paul W Guilford and Hon. Edward F. Waite (Minneapolis), Hon. Samuel O. Murphy (Birmingham), Hon. James Hoge Ricks (Richmond); and by the following probation officers: Mary E. McChristie, referee and supervisor, delinquent girls' department, court of domestic relations, Cincinnati; Fred R. Johnson, recorder's court, Detroit; and Patrick J. Shelly, magistrates' courts, New York City. Prof. Felix Frankfurter and the late Prof. Ernst Freund, of the law schools of Harvard University and the University of Chicago; Dr. Sheldon Glueck, department of social ethics, Harvard University; Charles L. Chute, general secretary, National Probation Association; John S. Bradway, secretary, the National Association of Legal Aid Organizations; Charles Zunser, secretary, National Desertion Bureau; Judge W. Bruce Cobb, secretary, courts committee, Brooklyn Bureau of Charities; and Frank E. Wade, attorney and former member of the New York State Probation Commission, Buffalo, also read the manuscript.

The bureau is deeply indebted to these authorities for their careful consideration of the report and their valuable criticisms. The suggestions made were considered by a small group called together by the National Probation Association, April 25, 1928, and certain of them have been incorporated in the report. The principal conclusions were presented at the annual conference of the National Probation Association held in Memphis, April 30 to May 2, 1928, and were indorsed in resolutions adopted by the association.

Since the publication of the first edition of the report the domestic-relations court of Multnomah County, Oreg., has been reorganized and given much broader jurisdiction; a state-wide domestic relations court act has been enacted in New Jersey; a court with juvenile and domestic-relations jurisdiction has been established for Mecklenburg County, N. C., and authorized for Forsyth County in the same State; and by a law just passed in New York State the New York City children's court and the domestic-relations work of the magistrates' courts have been combined into a family court of juvenile and limited adult jurisdiction. The tabulation in Appendix A of family courts and courts of domestic relations in the United States of which the Children's Bureau has information has been revised, and elsewhere in the text certain references have been made to recent developments. Although administrative changes—for the most part improvements— in personnel and methods have been made in some of the courts, they have not been so general nor so substantial as greatly to affect the general findings presented in 1929.

Respectfully submitted.

KATHARINE F. LENROOT, *Chief.*

Hon. FRANCES PERKINS,
Secretary of Labor.

THE CHILD, THE FAMILY, AND THE COURT

INTRODUCTION

CHANGING CONCEPTIONS OF THE FUNCTION OF LAW AND THE ADMINISTRATION OF JUSTICE

A deep and general interest has developed during recent years in the operation of law where it impinges upon the problems of family life. Court systems and processes have been studied and seriously criticized in relation to the treatment of such questions as the delinquency and dependency of children, offenses against children, desertion and nonsupport, divorce, annulment of marriage, the establishment of paternity, and adoption and custody. In the consideration of problems such as these all society is vitally interested. What is the function of law in their treatment? How is it endeavoring to perform its function? What steps shall be taken to remedy such deficiencies as exist?

A number of elements unite to make these questions of peculiar importance in the United States at the present time: (1) Legal theory is entering a new stage of development, the era of "sociological," or "social," jurisprudence, in which it will consider more than ever before the realization of human interests. (2) There is a growing pressure from the cities for organization of justice and improvement of legal procedure to meet the exigencies of urban development. (3) The jurisdictions of the courts overlap, and different judges pass upon different angles of what is really one problem of family life. (4) A new judicial technique is developing, in which the courts rely in large part upon such nonlegal sciences as medicine and psychology. (5) The last quarter century has witnessed the establishment of a number of special and in many respects novel tribunals, including particularly juvenile courts and courts of domestic relations.

SOCIAL JURISPRUDENCE

Before the beginning of the present century legal thinkers began to realize that too much of a gap existed between the methods of jurisprudence and those of other social sciences. There was a reaction from the schools of legal thought represented by Maine and Austin,[1] which regarded law from either the standpoint of history or that of logical analysis. Law, it was felt, must be oriented to life. The point of view of both bench and bar was too narrow, as was pointed out by Mr. Justice Holmes when he was a member of the Supreme Court of Massachusetts:

> I think that the judges themselves have failed adequately to recognize their duty of weighing considerations of social advantage. The duty is inevitable, and the result of the often proclaimed judicial aversion to deal with such

---

[1] See Ancient Law; Its Connection with Early History of Society and Its Relation to Modern Ideas, by Henry James Sumner Maine (1822-1888) (Henry Holt & Co., New York, 1907), and Lectures on Jurisprudence, by John Austin (1790-1859) (Soney & Sage, Newark, N. J.).

1

considerations is simply to leave the very ground and foundation of judgments inarticulate and often unconscious, as I have said.   When socialism first began to be talked about the comfortable classes of the community were a good deal frightened.   I suspect that this fear has influenced judicial action both here and in England, yet it is certain that it is not a conscious factor in the decisions to which I refer.   I think that something similar has led people who no longer hope to control the legislatures to look to the courts as expounders of the constitutions and that in some courts new principles have been discovered outside the bodies of those instruments, which may be generalized into acceptance of the economic doctrines which prevailed about 50 years ago and a wholesale prohibition of what a tribunal of lawyers does not think about right.   I can not but believe that if the training of lawyers led them habitually to consider more definitely and explicitly the social advantage on which the rule they lay down must be justified, they sometimes would hesitate where now they are confident and see that really they were taking sides upon debatable and often burning questions.[2]

The efficiency of the law is being more and more considered not according to the theoretical accuracy of its philosophy but in the light of its results.

Our philosophy will tell us the proper function of law in telling us the ends that law should endeavor to attain; but closely related to such a study is the inquiry whether law, as it has developed in this subject or in that, does in truth fulfill its function—is functioning well or ill.   The latter inquiry is perhaps a branch of social science calling for a survey of social facts rather than a branch of philosophy itself, yet the two subjects converge, and one will seldom be fruitful unless supplemented by the other.   "Consequences can not alter statutes but may help to fix their meaning."   We test the rule by its results.[3]

The purpose of "sociological jurisprudence" is succinctly stated by its foremost expounder, Dean Pound, of the Harvard Law School: "The main problem to which sociological jurists are addressing themselves to-day is to enable and to compel lawmaking, and also interpretation and application of legal rules, to take more account, and more intelligent account, of the social facts upon which law must proceed and to which it is to be applied."[4]

CITIES AND THE LAW

This new point of view has made it apparent that, while the substantive doctrines of the common law and the court systems of the United States are the product of the late eighteenth and early nineteenth centuries, the rise of cities and the decided urban trend present new and acute problems with which the judges of a century ago were not confronted.   It is indeed true that "our largest city now contains in 326 square miles a larger and infinitely more varied population than the whole 13 States when the Federal judicial organization, which has so generally served as a model, was adopted."[5]   A recent report states:

When the latest census figures were published we learned that for the first time in our history the population of the United States had become predominantly urban.   By 1920 more than half of our people had become dwellers in cities, and this development proceeds apace with no sign of abating.   From 1790 to 1800, while the structural framework of our present legal system was being securely laid, there were only six cities or towns that could boast of more

[2]Holmes, Oliver Wendell: The Path of the Law.   Harvard Law Review, vol. 10, No. 8 (Mar. 25, 1897), pp. 467–468.
[3]Cardozo, Benjamin Nathan: The Growth of the Law, p. 112.   Yale University Press, New Haven, 1924.
[4]Pound, Roscoe: Scope and Purpose of Sociological Jurisprudence.   Harvard Law Review, vol. 25, No. 6 (April, 1912), pp. 512–513.
[5]Pound, Roscoe: The Administration of Justice in the Modern City.   Harvard Law Review, vol. 26, No. 4 (February, 1913), p. 303.

than 8,000 inhabitants, and their aggregate population was only 4 per cent of the total population of the country. The most recent census statistics reveal that American civilization, taken as a whole, has definitely passed from the simpler conditions of agricultural and frontier life to the complex, intricate, and more ruthless conditions of an industrialized society.[6]

It has been pointed out in this same report that in 1918 there were about 37,500,000 people in the United States with incomes from any source whatever, of whom more than 20,250,000 had incomes of less than $1,200 a year; and the authors question whether many of these 20,250,000 are able to avail themselves of those equal rights before the law which are the proudest boast of American liberty. Three factors are specified that "impede the even course of justice when its protection is sought by a wage earner or by any person of small means"—delay, the expense involved in the payment of court costs and fees, and the necessity of employing lawyers.[7] William Howard Taft, Chief Justice of the United States Supreme Court, has said:

I think that we shall have to come, and ought to come, to the creation in every criminal court of the office of public defender, and that he should be paid out of the treasury of the county or the State. I think, too, that there should be a department in every large city, and probably in the State, which shall be sufficiently equipped to offer legal advice and legal service in suits and defenses in all civil cases, but especially in small-claims courts, in courts of domestic relations, and in other forums of the plain people.[8]

The general realization of the significance of this urban development in relation to the problems of the law is shown by still another highly important recent study: In January, 1921, the Cleveland Foundation committee authorized a survey of criminal justice in that city. The report of the survey, which was in charge of Dean Roscoe Pound and Mr. Felix Frankfurter, professor of administrative law, both of the Harvard Law School, shows the deficiencies of the administration of criminal law in a typical large American city.[9] In his summary Dean Pound points out the following problems for solution: Reshaping of the substantive criminal law, organization of the administration of justice, unification of courts, organization of the prosecuting system, organization of administrative agencies, adequate provision for petty prosecutions, preventive methods, justice in family relations, and the unshackling of administration.

OVERLAPPING JURISDICTION

It has been charged repeatedly in recent years that the courts, particularly in the larger cities, are doing piecemeal justice in the domain of domestic relations. The arraignment has been phrased by Dean Pound as follows:

Two signal cases of waste of judicial power, the multiplicity of independent tribunals, and the vicious practice of rapid rotation which prevails in the great majority of jurisdictions, whereby no one judge acquires a thorough experience of any one class of business, may only be noticed. As an example of the possibilities of the first it has been observed that in Chicago to-day, at one and the same time, the juvenile court, passing on the delinquent children; a court of equity, entertaining a suit for divorce, alimony, and the custody of children;

[6] Growth of Legal Aid Work in the United States, by Reginald Heber Smith, of the Boston bar, and John S. Bradway, of the Philadelphia bar, with preface by William Howard Taft, Chief Justice, United States Supreme Court, p. 1. U. S. Bureau of Labor Statistics Bulletin No. 398. Washington, 1926.
[7] Ibid., pp. 7, 16-17.
[8] Ibid., p. iv.
[9] Criminal Justice in Cleveland; Reports of the Cleveland Foundation Survey of the Administration of Criminal Justice in Cleveland, Ohio. Directed and edited by Roscoe Pound and Felix Frankfurter. Cleveland Foundation, Cleveland, Ohio, 1922.

a court of law, entertaining an action for necessaries furnished an abondoned wife by a grocer; and the criminal court or domestic-relatiɔns court, in a prosecution for desertion of wife and child—may all be dealing piecemeal at the same time with different phases of the same difficulties of the same family.[10]

A NEW JUDICIAL TECHNIQUE

The technique worked out by the common law for the attainment of justice in court is based upon the presentation of the evidence and argument by opposing attorneys before a judge who decides each case according to established principles on the legally admissible evidence of the witnesses   To-day in a juvenile court or a court of domestic relations much of the evidence is taken outside the court by court officials, and it is based in great part on medicine, psychiatry, and the impressions of trained observers.   There may be no lawyers— the judge represents both parties and the law.   In a juvenile-court proceeding the prosecuting officer as a general rule has no place, and in the domestic-relations court he often acts as a friend of the accused. Social environment is given consideration.   The probation officer occupies a position of great importance, furnishing "an impartial investigating service."[11]   These are not the methods of the old common law; they are the instruments forged by a jurisprudence which realizes that law, like medicine, is social engineering.

NEW COURTS

With the development of a new legal technique has come the establishment of new tribunals.   Courts of small claims and municipal courts have swept away certain of the formalities of common-law pleading.   Workmen's compensation commissions not only are based upon a legislative departure from common-law principles of master and servant but are working out a procedure as flexible as their conception is sound.   Public-service commissions have accustomed the public to decisions affecting the fundamentals of modern existence based upon broad economic policies rather than legal precedents. Juvenile courts represent a growth in legal theory rather than a departure from it; but their methods in dealing with children are for the most part unknown to common-law procedure or to chancery procedure.[12]   Courts of domestic relations already exist in a number of cities and deal in various degrees with problems of family life that come to the attention of judicial agencies.

The existence of these courts, particularly of the juvenile and domestic-relations courts, has heightened public interest in the problems with which they deal.   Dicey has pointed out that—

Laws foster or create law-making opinion.   This assertion may sound, to one who has learned that laws are the outcome of public opinion, like a paradox; when properly understood it is nothing but an undeniable though sometimes neglected truth * * *.   Every law or rule of conduct must, whether its author perceives the fact or not, lay down or rest upon some general principle, and must, therefore, if it succeeds in attaining its end, commend this principle to public attention or imitation, and thus affect legislative opinion.[13]

---

[10] Pound, Roscoe: The Administration of Justice in the Modern City.   Harvard Law Review, vol. 26, No. 4 (February, 1913), p. 313.
[11] Eliot, Thomas D.: The Juvenile Court and the Educational System.   Journal of Criminal Law and Criminology, vol 14, No. 1 (May, 1923), pp. 25–45.
[12] See The Legal Aspect of the Juvenile Court, by Bernard Flexner and Reuben Oppenheimer, p. 21 (U. S. Children's Bureau Publication No. 99, Washington, 1922).
[13] Dicey, Albert Venn: Lectures on the Relation between Law and Public Opinion in England during the Nineteenth Century (second edition), p. 41.   Macmillan Co., New York, 1914.

A study of the operation of the law upon the problems of human relationship must, it is obvious, be pragmatic, entered into without preconceived theories and based upon factual observation. The problems of family life run through the substantive law, as they run through all society. If a study of their treatment by the law meets the same difficulty that is encountered in the writing of history, which Maitland compared to tearing a seamless web,[14] it is also true that tearing the web of law is likely to produce a cross section of the interrelations between the workings of justice and the life of the community. Finally, in a study of the efficiency of judicial agencies it is necessary to keep in mind the demarcations of the field in which the law can hope to operate efficiently.

PURPOSE AND METHOD OF STUDY

As the field of the Children's Bureau is naturally limited to questions affecting the welfare of children, and as the primary concern of the public in family relationships is the care and protection of children, this study has been planned to cover those cases— and only those cases—in which the status or welfare of children is necessarily and primarily affected,[15] including the following:

1. Children's cases covered by juvenile-court laws, including cases of delinquent, dependent, and neglected children.
2. Offenses against children, including contributing to delinquency and dependency and specified crimes against children.
3. Cases of desertion and nonsupport of children.
4. Cases of divorce and separate maintenance when children are involved.
5. Proceedings for the establishment of paternity and the enforcement of support of children born out of wedlock.
6. Children's cases usually within the jurisdiction of the probate courts, including adoption, guardianship of the person, and commitment of mentally defective and insane children.

This classification corresponds closely to that proposed by a committee of the National Probation Association in 1917 as the jurisdiction that should be vested in family courts, except that the committee report recommended the inclusion of cases of divorce and of desertion and nonsupport where wives only were involved. (See p. 15.) In most of the States jurisdiction over these classes of cases is greatly divided at the present time, and in many of them the same class of case may be handled by a number of different courts.

The aim of this study is to show: (1) The place of specialized family courts in the juridical structure; (2) the development of specialized courts dealing with juvenile and family problems; (3) the

---

[14] " Such is the unity of all history that anyone who endeavors to tell a piece of it must feel that his first sentence tears a seamless web." Pollock, Frederick, and Frederick William Maitland: The History of English Law Before the Time of Edward I (second edition), vol. 1, p. 1. Little, Brown & Co., Boston, 1899.
[15] Excluding child-labor cases, in which the action is usually against the employer.

present judicial organization for dealing with these problems; (4) the proportion of cases of delinquency and dependency which also involve cases of other types (for example, problems of nonsupport or desertion); (5) the organization and methods of work of courts especially established to deal with the cases included in the study and the extent to which they are equipped to give constructive social service; and in the light of these facts to determine the general outlines of a program for more effective judicial organization in this field.

In order to obtain information concerning statutory provisions relating to jurisdiction and procedure, a compilation was made of pertinent sections of the laws of each State and Territory under the headings suggested by the list of types of cases, with additional general material concerning jurisdictional provisions, probation and parole, and compensation to prisoners. For subjects covered by existing compilations or summaries only brief summaries of the most essential points were prepared. The laws were then summarized State by State, according to the same outline as that used in the compilation. This material furnished basic information for the studies of court systems in selected communities and was also used in the preparation of a chart, which has been published separately,[16] showing for each State the courts having jurisdiction over cases covered by the study.

Statistical studies of families dealt with in juvenile and domestic-relations cases were made by the Children's Bureau in Hamilton County, Ohio, and in Philadelphia, that in the latter city being made in cooperation with the statistical department of the Philadelphia municipal court. These communities were selected because the organization and record systems of the courts dealing with the majority of family and children's cases made such information relatively easy to obtain and because in Philadelphia valuable assistance was offered by the statistical department of the court.

The descriptive material regarding courts with special organization for dealing with family cases was obtained by visits to nearly all these courts.[17] The first visits were made in the fall of 1923 and the last in June, 1927. Data concerning the courts first studied have been supplemented through later visits or through correspondence and study of their annual reports. Because of the limitations of the inquiry it was possible to make only comparatively brief visits to the courts. Thorough study of the case work done was not attempted, but information was obtained for each court concerning jurisdiction, personnel (including method of appointment, salaries, qualifications, assignment of work, volume of work of individual officers), methods

---

[16] Analysis and Tabular Summary of State Laws Relating to Jurisdiction in Children's Cases and Cases of Domestic Relations in the United States, by Freda Ring Lyman. U. S. Children's Bureau Chart No. 17. Washington, 1930. (Exhausted. Available only in libraries.)

[17] Information was obtained concerning 26 courts in the following cities and counties: (1) Four family courts with juvenile and broad adult jurisdiction: Hamilton County (Cincinnati), Mahoning County (Youngstown), Montgomery County (Dayton), Summit County (Akron), Ohio. (2) Five family courts with juvenile and limited adult jurisdiction: Jefferson County (Birmingham), Ala.; Multnomah County (Portland), Oreg.; Norfolk, Va.; Richmond, Va.; St. Louis, Mo. (3) Five domestic-relations courts without juvenile jurisdiction: Boston, Mass.; Buffalo, N. Y.; Chicago, Ill.; New York City; Newark, N. J. (4) Eight juvenile courts with broad jurisdiction: District of Columbia; Denver, Colo.; Dutchess County, N. Y.; Essex County (Newark), N. J.; Hudson County (Jersey City), N. J.; Marion County (Indianapolis), Ind.; New York City; Rockland County, N. Y. (5) Four municipal and district courts that have juvenile and domestic-relations jurisdiction and special organization for domestic-relations work: Douglas County, (Omaha), Nebr.; Polk County (Des Moines), Iowa; Philadelphia, Pa.; Springfield, Mass. (By 1929 legislation the court of Multnomah County, Oreg., now belongs in the first group and the New Jersey courts belong in the second group.)

of receiving complaints and of adjusting cases without court hearing, methods of investigation, hearings, court orders, probation, and other follow-up work.

The present report gives a general view of the legal aspects of the subject, of the efforts made to provide methods of organization and treatment adapted to modern conditions, and of the degree of success attained, together with suggestions as to the general principles that should govern the establishment of new courts or the reorganization of existing courts.

THE SUBSTANTIVE LAW OF DOMESTIC RELATIONS

Blackstone, writing in the middle of the eighteenth century, declared that there are three great relations in private life: Master and servant, husband and wife, and parent and child. To these he added the legally created relation of guardian and ward. The industrial revolution has changed in large part the relation of master and servant to one of employer and employee and thus removed this contact from the field of domestic relations; otherwise Blackstone's classification is still generally followed.

It is impossible even to outline in a few pages all the doctrines that constitute the law of domestic relations.[1] Courts are only the medium through which law is put in force. Changes in procedure, however radical and far-reaching, are changes only in the way legal principles are administered. It is advisable before considering courts and procedure dealing with the law of domestic relations to consider briefly some of the doctrines of the law itself.

HUSBAND AND WIFE

The creation of the marital relation requires, first, a valid contract between the parties; this implies that they are able to understand and that they do understand what they are doing. Second, they must be persons whom the law permits to enter the marital status; they must be physically competent and of proper age, and there must be no bar of consanguinity or race. Third, they must enter the status in the manner provided by law; in almost all the States there must be a religious ceremony or a civil ceremony and the giving of public notice or the issuance of a license, as may be required by the particular jurisdiction.

In the United States the various requirements and disqualifications are generally fixed by statute and vary in the different States, so that cases for the annulment of marriage often involve questions of conflict of State laws. As to questions of contractual capacity the law of the State where the ceremony was performed is generally held to govern; but if the laws of the State in which one or both of the parties were domiciled at the time of the marriage prohibit it on some ground of public policy, the marriage is generally held invalid even though it was valid in the State in which the ceremony took place.

The rights conferred by the marital relation at common law have been considerably altered by statutes. It is no longer true, as it was in Blackstone's day, that "the very being or legal existence of

---

[1] For good textbook discussions see A Treatise on the Law of Marriage, Divorce, Separation, and Domestic Relations, by James Schouler, Sixth Edition by Arthur W. Blakemore (Matthew Bender & Co., Albany, N. Y., 1921), Handbook on the Law of Persons and Domestic Relations, by Walter C. Tiffany, Third Edition by Roger W. Cooley (West Publishing Co., St. Paul, Minn., 1921); Cases on the Law of Persons and Domestic Relations, by William Edward McCurdy, vol. 1 (Callaghan & Co., Chicago, 1926); and Cases on Domestic Relations, by Joseph Warren Madden (West Publishing Co., St. Paul, Minn., 1928).

8

the woman is suspended during the marriage." At common law and under many of the statutes the husband is under the legal duty to support and maintain his wife according to his station in life and to his means. He is not relieved from this liability because the wife has separate means. In most States the statutes give a wife who has been deserted by her husband or who is living apart from him because of his fault the right to bring a civil action for maintenance. In many States, likewise, for a husband to leave his wife without means of support is made a criminal offense.

With certain exceptions, sometimes recognized when the wife leaves the husband because of his fault, the domicile of the wife merges with that of the husband and changes with his.

The rights of husband and wife in each other's property during life and the rights of one at the other's death, the validity and effect of prenuptial and postnuptial settlements, the rights of husband and wife to contract, as affected by marriage, though fixed by the common law, have all been greatly modified by statute. In general, disabilities of married women have been removed; they can contract freely in their own interest, and can own, acquire, use, and enjoy property of their own. A number of States have the institution of "community property" derived from Spanish law, in which, especially with respect to property acquired after marriage, husband and wife are treated as a property-owning entity.

Divorce is of two kinds: Divorce a mensa et thoro, which suspends the effect of marriage so far as cohabitation is concerned, and divorce a vinculo, which dissolves the marriage. Whether or not divorce is to be allowed, and if it is, upon what grounds, are determined by the laws of each State.

PARENT AND CHILD

A child is legitimate at common law when he was born or begotten during the lawful marriage of his parents. Statutes in this country generally make a child legitimate also when his parents marry subsequently to his birth. As a general rule the legitimacy or illegitimacy of a child is determined by the law of his parents' domicile at the time of birth.

Adoption was unknown to the common law but is generally recognized in the United States by statute. In general the consent of the parents of the child or of the surviving parent must be had to an adoption, unless they have abandoned the child or have forfeited the right to custody. Judicial proceedings are generally necessary for adoption. With few exceptions adoption places the parties in the legal relation of parent and child.

The rights of children to inherit from their parents vary according to the statutes of each State. There is usually a distinction between the rights of legitimate and of illegitimate children.

Whereas at common law it was occasionally held that a parent is under no legal obligation to support his children, the obligation to support minor children is now generally imposed upon the parent, either by the common law or by statute. In most States failure of the parent to support his minor children is made a criminal offense. By the weight of authority the obligation of the parents to support their children is not affected by divorce.

A father was under no legal obligation to support his illegitimate children at common law, but to-day he is generally chargeable with their maintenance by statute. In most States the mother has a statute remedy to enforce support from the father; this remedy is generally known as "bastardy proceedings," though the tendency is to substitute the term "illegitimacy proceedings" or "proceedings for the establishment of paternity."

A parent is under the legal duty to protect his children and generally has the right to their services and earnings. But the common law recognizes no legal obligation of the father to educate them.

The custody of children belonged under common law to the father, and upon his death it belonged to the mother. To-day statutes usually give the juvenile courts jurisdiction to remove children from their parents' custody when the unfitness of the children's surroundings is clearly apparent. Such statutes represent growth in common-law doctrines rather than a departure from them,[2] and their constitutionality has been almost uniformly upheld. Juvenile-court statutes also give the courts power to remove delinquent children from the custody of their parents.

In case of divorce the custody of the children is determined according to the circumstances of each case and may be changed from time to time by decree.

The domicile of a legitimate child is that of his father, at least before he is emancipated; the domicile of an illegitimate child is usually that of his mother.[3] Upon divorce the parent to whom the child is awarded has the power to fix the child's domicile. Under the doctrine that the sovereign through his proper court is the protector of every person within his jurisdiction who needs protection, it has been held that a court may take away a foreign child from his parent or proper domiciliary guardian.

Offenses against children are strictly part of the criminal law, not of the law of domestic relations. Such offenses include not only actual attacks and mistreatment but, under statutes, causation of or contributing to a child's delinquency or dependency. Statutory actions of this kind generally lie not only against parents, guardians, or persons having custody but against strangers as well. Infants have certain contractual rights and disabilities, which are sometimes treated as part of the law of domestic relations but which are outside the scope of this study.

To prevent future dependency and to recognize the State's interest in children many statutes provide for pecuniary aid to mothers who can not support their children and whose husbands are dead, have abandoned them, or are not in a position to aid in their children's support. Such aid, frequently called "mothers' pensions," is in some States under the jurisdiction of a court; in others under that of an administrative board.

GUARDIAN AND WARD

The law often intrusts the person or the estate of an infant to a person other than the parent. Children have always been regarded

---

[2] See, for example, the case of Shelley v. Westbrooke (Jac. 266), in which Shelley was deprived of the custody of his children because he declared himself an atheist.

[3] In Minnesota, however, complaint in proceedings to establish paternity may be filed in the county of the mother's residence, that of the alleged father's residence, or that in which the child is found if he is likely to become a public charge upon the county. (Gen. Stat. 1923, sec. 3261.)

as the wards of chancery, and there are early instances in which equity acted to protect unfortunate minors even when no property right was involved, although the early chancery jurisdiction was generally exercised when some property interest was at stake. A guardian is often named for children by will or deed. A court within whose jurisdiction the minor lives or has property may appoint a guardian for such minor. Unlike a parent, a guardian is not entitled to his ward's services and earnings. He is a trustee, and usually he must account from time to time for his ward's estate to the court which appoints him.

Juvenile-court statutes generally provide for the commitment of dependent or neglected children to persons, institutions, or societies that will give them proper care. When a child is committed to the guardianship of an individual or an institution the proceeding is not equivalent to an adoption but is only a police measure of the State, affecting the incidents but not the existence of the legal status between parent and child. Such a guardian has no rights over the property of the child but has certain rights over his person.[4]

---

[4] Courts are given statutory authority to appoint guardians for persons of unsound mind and for inebriates as well as for children.

SPECIALIZED COURTS DEALING WITH FAMILY
PROBLEMS

THE JUVENILE COURT

As early as 1890 children's courts were introduced in South Australia by ministerial order, and they were subsequently legalized under a State act in 1895. Legislation looking to the same end was passed in the Province of Ontario, but practically nothing was done under it. Before this date Massachusetts, New York, and several other American States had statutes providing for the separate hearing of children's cases. Adult probation had been in use in Massachusetts for many years, but in 1899 laws were passed in Illinois and in Colorado under which the first real juvenile courts in the United States were established in Chicago and Denver.[1]

Since that time all the States except two—Maine and Wyoming—have adopted legislation providing special court organization for dealing with juvenile cases. Every city in the country with a population of 100,000 or more has a court especially organized for children's work.[2]

What are the basic conceptions that distinguish juvenile courts from other courts?

Children are to be dealt with separately from adults. Their cases are to be heard at a different time and preferably in a different place. The children are to be detained in separate buildings. If institutional guidance is necessary they are to be committed to institutions for children. Through its probation officers the court can keep in constant touch with the children who have appeared before it. Taking children from their parents is, when possible, to be avoided; on the other hand, parental obligations are to be enforced. The procedure of the court must be as informal as possible. Its purpose is not to punish but to save. It is to deal with children not as criminals but as persons in whose guidance and welfare the State is peculiarly interested. Save in the cases of adults, its jurisdiction is equitable, not criminal, in nature.[3]

It is probably the most remarkable fact in the history of American jurisprudence that these conceptions were adopted almost universally in less than 25 years. The initial battle was hard, but the victory, so far as nominal acceptance of the fundamental ideas of the juvenile court is concerned, has been almost complete. Legal writers, legislatures, lawyers, and laymen have come to recognize that the law must differentiate in its treatment of adults and of children.

How far these conceptions have been put into successful practice is another matter. For the present it is enough to state that they have been proved workable. It is interesting to note, however, that

---

[1] Flexner, Bernard, and Roger N. Baldwin: Juvenile Courts and Probation. Century Co., New York, 1914.
[2] Lenroot, Katharine F., and Emma O. Lundberg: Juvenile Courts at Work; A Study of the Organization and Methods of Ten Courts. U. S. Children's Bureau Publication No. 141. Washington, 1925. (Exhausted. Available only in libraries.) In 1931 Maine passed a law extending the jurisdiction of municipal courts over offenses committed by children under 15 years of age and providing certain special procedure in these cases. (Act of Apr. 3, 1931, ch. 241, Laws of 1931, p. 273.)
[3] See The Legal Aspect of the Juvenile Court, pp. 8–9.

12

their growth has been in the way of a circle. In the beginning few doubted that the law should treat adults and infants in most respects the same. Then it was seen that the law must provide special treatment for children. To-day the vanguard of thought is recognizing that many of the principles of socialized treatment—such as study of the characteristics of the individual and the environment in which he lives and constructive supervision during probation—are applicable and should be extended gradually to the whole field of criminal justice and in part to certain questions of domestic relations now dealt with under civil procedure. Thus, in these respects at least, adults and infants are again treated alike.

THE FAMILY COURT OR COURT OF DOMESTIC RELATIONS

HISTORY

Partly as a result of the extension of the ideas underlying juvenile courts and partly as a result of the development of probation in criminal cases a number of new tribunals have been created. They are referred to generally as "courts of domestic relations" or "family courts." This movement has progressed along two different lines which have tended to converge in the family courts of the broadest jurisdiction.

The earliest development was the extension of the jurisdiction of juvenile courts. The first juvenile courts were given jurisdiction over children's cases only. Very early the necessity that the court have power to deal with certain types of closely related adult cases became apparent. Colorado enacted in 1903 special legislation making contributing to delinquency or dependency an offense within the jurisdiction of the juvenile court. Nearly all juvenile courts now have jurisdiction over certain types of adult cases, though the nature of this jurisdiction varies greatly from State to State. The juvenile-court standards drafted by a committee appointed by the United States Children's Bureau and adopted by a conference held under the auspices of the Children's Bureau and of the National Probation Association in 1923 recommended that cases of contributing to delinquency or dependency, nonsupport or desertion of minor children, and determination of paternity and the support of children born out of wedlock, as well as adoption cases and cases of children in need of protection or custodial care by reason of mental defect or disorder, should be brought within the jurisdiction of the juvenile court.[4]

In 1910 a domestic-relations division was established in the city court at Buffalo, under the provision in the law creating the city court [5] which authorized the chief judge of this court to determine the parts into which the court should be divided. This domestic-relations division had jurisdiction over all criminal business relating to domestic or family affairs, including bastardy cases.[6] Cases of wayward minors between the ages of 16 and 20 years, inclusive, also were

---

[4] Juvenile Court Standards; report of the committee appointed by the Children's Bureau, August, 1921, to formulate juvenile-court standards, adopted by a conference held under the auspices of the Children's Bureau and the National Probation Association, Washington, D. C., May 18, 1923.   U S. Children's Bureau Publication No. 121. Washington, 1923.

[5] N. Y., act of May 29, 1909, ch. 570, Laws of 1909, pp. 1654–1659.

[6] Jurisdiction in bastardy cases was transferred to the Erie County court by act of Apr. 15, 1926, ch. 386, Laws of 1926, p. 703, which amended ch. 14 of the Consolidated Laws as added by act of Apr. 1, 1925, ch 255, sec. 1, Laws of 1925, p. 508.

assigned to this division. A law of 1924 specifically authorized the establishment of a domestic-relations court as part of the city court, and equity jurisdiction as well as criminal jurisdiction was conferred upon this court as authorized by the constitution of New York State.[7] In several cities the example of Buffalo in setting apart by law or rule of court a division of a municipal court to deal with domestic-relations cases, chiefly nonsupport and desertion, has been followed. In discussing this type of court Mr. Frank E. Wade, of Buffalo, for many years a member of the New York State Probation Commission, has said:

> During the past 10 or 15 years three distinct court systems or procedures, all related under various names and dealing exclusively with the family, have been enacted into law in many parts of the United States. The earliest was the so-called domestic-relations court. This in the main has been an inferior criminal court, having exclusive jurisdiction of nonsupport and assault cases between husbands and wives. Taking family trouble out of the slime of the old police court was at the time considered a great step forward. Many of these courts are functioning in all parts of the United States and doing a splendid work, especially through the probation departments, in enforcing support orders.[8]

The Chicago court of domestic relations, a branch of the municipal court, is of the same general type as the Buffalo court. In 1921 Judge Harry A. Fisher, then a judge of the municipal court, outlined the advantages of these courts as follows:

> The advantages of having such a court are in the main the possibility of establishing a social-service department in connection with it, which is required to make investigation of cases and when possible to avoid bringing these matters before the court either by effecting reconciliations or by obtaining voluntary contributions for the support of the families, and to look after a proper collection of the money ordered for the support of wife or child. A separate court for these matters also develops expertness on the part of the judge who is assigned to preside over it. It separates these cases from the other cases that are usually brought before the criminal branches of the court, and, above all, makes it possible to treat these cases from a social point of view. The proceedings are less formal, and the court is not limited to the trial of bare issues of fact. It is in a position to call to its aid the numerous private social agencies which exist in the city and which are able to help solve many domestic problems. In fact, our court has become much more a great social agency than a court. The judicial power is resorted to only where coercion is necessary.[9]

In 1914 the first family court in the United States to exercise jurisdiction over both domestic-relations and juvenile cases was created in Hamilton County (Cincinnati), Ohio, as a division of the court of common pleas. For the first time divorce cases were brought under the jurisdiction of a court especially organized to deal with cases affecting child welfare and family life. Similar courts have been established in six other Ohio counties and in certain other communities, and the Cincinnati court has been regarded generally as the pioneer in the movement for family courts as distinguished from domestic-relation courts with adult jurisdiction only.

The aim of the family court, in the language of Judge Charles W. Hoffman, of the domestic-relations court of Cincinnati, Ohio, a leader in the movement for their establishment, is provision "for the consideration of all matters relating to the family in one court of exclusive

---

[7] N. Y., act of Apr. 25, 1924, ch. 424, Laws of 1924, p. 777, adding Art. III A (sec. 80) to Laws of 1909, ch. 570, in accordance with Art. VI, sec. 18, of the constitution as amended by concurrent resolution of the senate (Apr. 8, 1921) and assembly (Apr. 16, 1921), Laws of 1921, pp. 2534–2535. Art. VI of the constitution was itself amended in 1925 (Laws of 1926, pp. 1583–1595).

[8] Discussion in Proceedings of the National Probation Association, 1924, p. 191.

[9] Quoted in Courts of Domestic relations, by Edward F. Waite (Minnesota Law Review, vol. 5, No.3 (February, 1921), pp. 164–165).

jurisdiction, in which the same methods of procedure shall prevail as in the juvenile court and in which it will be possible to consider social evidence as distinguished from legal evidence. In fact, providing for a family court is no more than increasing the jurisdiction of the juvenile court and designating it by the more comprehensive term of family court." [10]

In 1917 a committee of the National Probation Association recommended the establishment of family courts with jurisdiction in the following classes of cases:

(a) Cases of desertion and nonsupport; (b) paternity cases, known also as bastardy cases; (c) all matters arising under acts pertaining to the juvenile court known in some States as the children's court, and all courts, however designated in the several States, having within their jurisdiction the care and treatment of delinquent and dependent children and the prosecution of adults responsible for such delinquency and dependency; (d) all matters pertaining to adoption and guardianship of the person of children; (e) all divorce and alimony matters.[11]

Commenting on this report, Judge Edward F. Waite has said:

In this grouping there appear to be three underlying ideas: The interest of the State in the conservation of childhood, the intimate interrelation of all justiciable questions involving family life, and the need for administrative aid in the wise solution of such questions.[12]

EXTENT OF THE FAMILY-COURT MOVEMENT [13]

The terms "family court" and "court of domestic relations" (often used interchangeably) indicate different types of organization, including at least the following:

1. *A family court of juvenile and broad adult jurisdiction, including children's cases, cases of divorce, desertion or nonsupport, and contributing to delinquency or dependency.*

The divisions of domestic relations in the courts of common pleas of Franklin, Hamilton, Lucas, Mahoning, Montgomery, Stark, and Summit Counties, Ohio, the domestic-relations courts of Multnomah County, Oreg. (by law of 1929), and of Cabell County, W. Va., and the division of domestic relations of the first circuit court of Hawaii are examples of this type.[14]

2. *A family court of juvenile and limited adult jurisdiction, including some of but not all the types of cases listed in paragraph 1.*

The juvenile and domestic-relations courts in New Jersey (by law of 1929) and Virginia (under state-wide systems) and in Jefferson and Montgomery Counties, Ala., also the domestic-relations court of Mecklenburg County, N. C. (by 1929 law), have jurisdiction over cases of desertion and nonsupport, but these courts do not have jurisdiction over divorce.[15]   The domestic-relations court of St. Louis, Mo., on the other hand, has jurisdiction over divorce but not over desertion and nonsupport.

---

[10] Hoffman, Charles W.: Social Aspects of the Family Court. Journal of Criminal Law and Criminology, vol. 10, No. 3 (November, 1919), pp. 409–422.
[11] Proceedings of the National Probation Association, 1917, p. 85.
[12] Waite, Edward F.: Courts of Domestic Relations. Minnesota Law Review, vol. 5, No. 3 (February, 1921), p. 167.
[13] See Appendix A, p. 67.
[14] A Tennessee law of 1929 (Private Acts of 1929, ch. 675), authorized a court of this type in Hamilton County, which, however, was held unconstitutional by the State supreme court Dec. 15, 1930 (Newton **v.** Hamilton Co., 161 Tenn. 634; 33 Sw. (2d) 419).
[15] The domestic-relations court of Monongalia County, W. Va., which was established in 1923 and went out of existence in 1929, belonged to this group (Laws of 1923, ch. 134; Laws of 1927, ch. 92). A North Carolina law of 1931 (ch. 221) authorized such a court in Forsyth County, but it was not established by 1933.

3. *A juvenile court of broad jurisdiction, not including jurisdiction over divorce.*

The outstanding example of courts of this type is that in Denver, Colo. Its jurisdiction includes children's cases, mothers' aid, adoption, contributing to delinquency or dependency, offenses against children, desertion or nonsupport, illegitimacy (action technically under the charge of contributing to dependency), and children whose custody is in controversy in divorce cases under a general provision relating to cases in which custody of a child is involved. The juvenile courts of Marion County, Ind., and of the District of Columbia also have broad adult jurisdiction. The New York State children's court act attempted to vest such jurisdiction in children's courts, but judicial decisions appear to have limited their jurisdiction in adult cases.[16] These are only a few of the juvenile courts that have broad jurisdiction. In 17 States and the District of Columbia the juvenile court has jurisdiction over cases of desertion and nonsupport; in 6 States and the District of Columbia it has jurisdiction over proceedings for the establishment of paternity; in 24 States and the District of Columbia it has jurisdiction over contributing to delinquency and dependency. In some of these States only certain juvenile courts have this jurisdiction.

4. *A domestic-relations court without juvenile jurisdiction and with adult jurisdiction over cases of desertion or nonsupport and sometimes illegitimacy and certain offenses against children (divorce not being included).*

The domestic-relations courts of Buffalo, Chicago, and Boston and the family courts of New York City and Newark are of this type. The Newark family court also has jurisdiction in morals cases; and cases of wayward minors are assigned to the Buffalo court, which has both equity and criminal jurisdiction.[17]

5. *A municipal or district court with juvenile and domestic-relations jurisdiction and special organization, by law or rule of court, for domestic-relations work.*

Among the courts of this type are the Philadelphia municipal court and the district court of Springfield, Mass., with separate juvenile and domestic-relations divisions, and the district courts of Douglas County, Nebr., and Polk County, Iowa,[18] with juvenile and domestic-relations divisions. The two latter courts, but not those of Philadelphia or Springfield, have divorce jurisdiction. Courts of this type may be established by rule of court without special legislation.

In this report the term "family court" will be used in general to indicate a court with combined juvenile and domestic-relations jurisdiction and the term "domestic-relations court" to indicate a court or division with jurisdiction over adult cases only. Individual courts will generally be referred to by the term used locally.

Unified probation departments, usually serving a county, have been established in a number of communities in which no unified family court has been created.[19] Through these departments that serve several courts a considerable degree of coordination in the social

---

[16] As In re Cole (212 App. Div. 427; 208 N. Y. S. 753), People *v.* De Pue (217 App. Div. 321; 217 N. Y. S. 205). As to family court see City of New York *v.* Kaiser (125 Misc. 637; 210 N. Y. S. 598).
[17] For provisions of a new law (1933) for New York City see Appendix A, p. 67.
[18] See Appendix A, p. 67.
[19] See recommendation in Report to the Crime Commission of New York State of the Subcommission on Adjustment of Sentences, by W. Bruce Cobb, p. 30 (Albany, Feb. 28, 1927).

treatment of family problems can be accomplished. Ohio has a state-wide law authorizing the establishment of such departments at the option of the county.[20] New Jersey is organized on this basis. The probation department of Ramsey County, Minn., serving the St. Paul courts, is also an example of this type of coordinated service.[21] Programs of county organization for social work, designed primarily for rural communities and small cities, may make social service by a unified county department available to all the courts. For example, in North Carolina the county superintendent of public welfare is responsible for the probationary supervision of both children and adults.[22]

In spite of the diversity of organization indicated by these various types of courts described, the family-court movement, as has been shown, has gained wide recognition in the past 20 years. To summarize: In addition to the many States in which the juvenile court has more or less broad jurisdiction over domestic-relations cases, the family court combining juvenile jurisdiction with jurisdiction over certain types of adult cases has been established in the entire State in New Jersey and Virginia, in seven counties in Ohio, and in one or more communities in Alabama, Missouri, North Carolina, Oregon, West Virginia, and the Territory of Hawaii.[23]

The domestic-relations court with adult jurisdiction only has been established in parts of four States: Illinois, Massachusetts, New Jersey, and New York. In other States, including Iowa, Nebraska, and Pennsylvania, and also in Massachusetts, organization for juvenile and domestic-relations work has been developed by municipal, district, or superior courts.

FUNDAMENTAL PROBLEMS INVOLVED

It is apparent that the family court, or court of domestic relations, embodies two desires—first, to extend the new method of legal treatment of certain classes of cases, best exemplified in juvenile courts; second, to prevent duplication of jurisdiction by various tribunals. In other words, these new courts involve a problem of legal procedure and a problem of judicial organization.

---

[20] Ohio, act of Mar. 24, 1925, Laws of 1925, p. 423, Code 1930, secs. 1554–1 to 1554–5.
[21] Doyle, John J., Chief Probation Officer, Ramsey County Courts, St. Paul, Minn.: The Family in Court—A Unified Probation Staff. Proceedings of the National Probation Association, 1926, pp. 59–63.
[22] See Public Child-Caring Work in Certain Counties of Minnesota, North Carolina, and New York, by H. Ida Curry (U. S. Children's Bureau Publication No. 173, Washington, 1927) and The County as an Administrative Unit for Social Work, by Mary Ruth Colby (U. S. Children's Bureau Publication No. 224, Washington, 1933).
[23] An Oklahoma law of 1925 (act of Apr. 11, 1925, ch. 128, Laws of 1925, p. 182) established family courts in counties of 90,000 population. The district judges of Tulsa County declined to assume jurisdiction, stating that, in their opinion, the law was unconstitutional, and no court has been established in Oklahoma County, the only other county of this size. An Alabama law of 1931 (No. 401) to create a court of domestic relations in counties of 105,000–300,000 inhabitants (Mobile County) with jurisdiction over juvenile cases, contributing to delinquency or dependency, nonsupport, and (for investigation only) divorce cases involving minor children was held unconstitutional on the ground that the procedure for its adoption violated the provision of the State constitution (sec. 106 of 1901) requiring publication of notice of intention to apply for passage of local laws (Kearley v. State ex. rel. Hamilton etc., 137 So. 424).

PROCEDURAL CHANGES IN SPECIALIZED COURTS

CONSERVATISM IN LEGAL PROCEDURE

It is a maxim of legal history that it is easier to effect a change in the substantive law than it is to effect a change in procedure. The natural conservatism of the bar is most in evidence when a change in the way cases are handled is proposed. Nor is this conservatism unjustified. Abstract justice becomes unimportant if the method of obtaining justice is not suited to the needs of the community. The common law was several centuries in working out its system of procedural rights. Almost from the first these procedural rights have been jealously guarded, as witness the construction of the phrases "law of the land" in Magna Charta, and "due process of law" in the fourteenth amendment to the United States Constitution. In view of this conservatism[1] the speedy adoption of the procedure involved in the establishment of juvenile courts is all the more remarkable.

EXAMPLES OF THE NEW PROCEDURE

Typical hypothetical cases before and after the establishment of the juvenile court will illustrate best the far-reaching nature of the change due to the new procedure:

In the middle of the nineteenth century a boy 13 or 14 years old set fire to a stable. He was indicted by the grand jury, and because he could not give bail he was sent to jail until he was tried before a petit jury in a crowded court room. The State's attorney presented his evidence, consisting of proof that the boy committed the act with which he was charged and that he was old enough to know what he was doing. The boy's attorney offered evidence to the contrary. The judge ruled on questions of evidence. Hearsay evidence was not admissible. No one thought of offering testimony as to the boy's surroundings. He was convicted and sent to the penitentiary, in which he served his sentence in the company of the usual hardened convicts in a penal institution.

That boy's grandson to-day sets fire to a garage in a jurisdiction that has a modern juvenile court. Complaint is made. The boy is brought in and is sent to a juvenile detention home in which are no adults except the persons in charge. There he is examined physically and mentally. In the meantime a court probation officer investigates the boy and his environment. He finds that the boy's grandfather was sent to prison, that his family is poor, that they have moved from State to State, that he has had little schooling, and that he has been associating with vicious companions. A plan is made for the boy's care and training. His case is heard in a room informally arranged in which there are no spectators except those immediately concerned in the case and no lawyer except the judge. The judge hears the complaint and reads the reports of the physician, the psychiatrist, and the probation officer. The boy admits the act complained of. (If he had not admitted it the judge would have heard testimony and decided the question of fact.) The judge talks to the boy and to his parents and places him on probation. The cooperation of social agencies is enlisted and a better job is found for the boy's father. The probation officer con-

---

[1] See The English Struggle for Procedural Reform, by Edson R. Sunderland (Harvard Law Review, vol. 39, No. 6 (April, 1926), pp. 725–748).

sults the school authorities and arranges for the boy to have school work that will hold his interest. He puts the boy in touch with recreational activities that will occupy his spare time in a wholesome way. The boy comes to the probation office regularly to report progress and to talk over his problems. The probation officer visits the boy and his family at frequent intervals and endeavors to bring the mother and father to a better understanding of their son and his needs. Finally, the boy is discharged from probation, or, if he continues in his old ways, he may be committed to a training school for boys.

If this boy in the hypothetical case of to-day had been referred to court because he did not have a suitable home or proper parental care similar procedure would have been followed. The fact of dependency would have been determined, his physical and mental condition would have been studied, and his environmental conditions would have been ascertained, and the case would have remained under the jurisdiction of the court, with officers of the court actively engaged in supervision, until discharge or commitment for foster-home or institutional care was deemed advisable.

What is the law doing in these cases? First, generally, as in cases of contract and property, it is determining an event. It determines whether or not the boy set fire to the garage, as it might determine whether a deed was actually signed or whether a seller failed to deliver an order. Second, it is determining a condition—the boy's health, mentality, and environment—again the factual question. Third, it is treating the event in the light of the condition, just as it may weigh considerations of public policy against considerations of individual interest in deciding whether a noise from a factory constitutes a public nuisance and should be enjoined. Fourth, it gives the case continued treatment, as it continues to supervise the administration of a trust in equity.

In such cases concerning minors the law formerly included only the first step. Taking the next three steps involved a method of approach new in this type of case but already known to the law in other cases. The great departure consists in the way the additional steps are taken—in the consideration of such factors as environment, of which the common law took no cognizance; in the action of court officials in investigating and reporting on questions of fact; and in the active participation of the court in endeavoring to improve environmental conditions.

THE LAW IN ACTION

It is apparent that the court in its new procedure is combining three distinct acts. It not only determines the facts, it seeks them out, and it may itself apply the treatment indicated. It unites the judicial process of the judge with the processes of the grand jury, of the posse, and of the district attorney, and it continues administrative supervision.

That the facts which the agencies of the court unearth include elements of psychology and psychiatry unknown a few decades ago to laymen as well as to lawyers is here immaterial. The content of judicial decisions always varies. Some centuries ago the courts were concerned mainly with questions of land tenure; to-day problems of corporation law bulk large. Nor is it unprecedented for a court to take into account considerations of economics and social polity.

The judicial process is generally influenced, consciously or subconsciously, by the thought of the era in which it is functioning,[2] as witness the legal history of labor problems. The most important change is that these courts combine three distinct functions: Investigation, decision, and treatment. This combination of functions is often said to result in an "administrative tribunal," but such phraseology is both loose and dangerous. People are too prone to give a complex situation a name; then because they can recognize its tag they believe that they understand its nature. Courts have always had their agencies by which the decisions of the judges were made effective, from the clerks who recorded them to the sheriffs who acted upon them. The law has always had, too, its agencies of investigation, from the time when the judges traveled from county to county to pass upon the breaches of the king's peace which the assizes had revealed. On the other hand, decision of course is not a purely judicial rôle; from early times there have been executives and legislators. The remarkable fact is that these new tribunals study the whole situation, formulate their policies, issue the orders for carrying them out, and decide when and how they are being violated and what shall be done about their violation. "Administrative" is too colorless a word.

The New York State Judiciary Constitutional Convention of 1921 was of the opinion that "extensive legislative, executive, and judicial powers are being vested and combined in administrative bodies in distinct and reckless disregard of the sound principle of the separation of governmental powers, which was deemed so essential to the true protection of individual rights by the wise founders of our republican form of State governments.[3] As a matter of constitutional law there is no Federal requirement that the executive, legislative, and judicial functions of the States be kept separate.[4] The various State constitutions generally provide for a separation of functions; but there is no clear legal demarcation, and the question of the jurisdiction to be given to the courts is generally one of policy rather than one of law.[5]

It is true that the jurisdiction of these new courts is defined by the legislature, but their jurisdiction is sometimes as broad as the limits of family problems. It is true also that parties are given the right of appeal and the right to be represented by counsel, but the parties are represented by lawyers in relatively few cases, partly because of poverty, partly because the court itself not only acts as judge but also takes an active part as an investigator and as a friend of the parties. The relatively small proportion of appeals is attributable partly to lack of funds and partly to the absence of lawyers.

Under the new procedure precedent means little except as it represents experience. The question whether or not to take a child away from his parents and commit him to an institution is not governed by what seemed advisable in a previous reported decision. In fact, the decisions of these courts are not generally reported; the judge is

---

[2] See The Nature of the Judicial Process, by Benjamin N. Cardozo (Yale University Press, 1921, reprinted in 1925).
[3] Report to New York Legislature of Judiciary Constitutional Convention of 1921, p. 11. Legislative Document (1922) No. 37.
[4] Prentis v. Atlantic Coast Line, 211 U. S. 210, 213. See also Constitutional Aspects of American Administrative Law, by Cuthbert W. Pound (American Bar Asssociation Journal, vol. 9, No. 7 (July, 1923), pp. 409-416).
[5] See Power of Congress over Procedure in Criminal Contempts in Inferior Federal Courts; A Study in Separation of Powers, by Felix Frankfurter and James M. Landis (Harvard Law Review, vol. 37, No. 8 (June, 1924), pp. 1010-1113).

not restrained by the knowledge that his judgments will be read and criticized by fellow members of his profession, a knowledge generally regarded as one of the most salutary checks of the common law.

Likelihood of appeal and the existence of printed reports are vividly present to other "administrative" tribunals, such as public-service commissions and even industrial-accident commissions, where financial interests, large or small, are at stake. The judge of a family court, without these checks, has opportunities well-nigh oriental in scope. Nor is this tremendous power over the lives and happiness of thousands confined to the judge. It is shared by the officials of the courts, particularly the probation officers, who are intrusted with the preliminary investigations and the follow-up work. Indeed, in some family courts only a relatively small proportion of the cases come before the judge's bench.

The danger of this system is the danger of all magisterial justice. The common law as it emerged from feudal times is essentially a system of checks and balances and is fundamentally a practical institution. Its procedure in particular reflects a long history of struggle against abuses of freedom. Because it is a practical institution it is changing its procedure. The celerity and businesslike organization of the English High Court of Justice are far removed from the leisurely processes of Coke and Blackstone. The rush of modern civilization, the problems brought on by the industrial revolution, and the growth of huge cities have necessitated a new judicial technique. But that technique as it is being worked out in family courts is not unlike the manorial courts of feudalism itself.

The distinction between the new procedure and the old common-law ways can not be overemphasized. The old courts relied upon the learning of lawyers; the new courts depend more upon psychiatrists and social workers. The evidence before the old courts was brought by the parties; most of the evidence before the new courts is obtained by the courts themselves. The old courts relied upon precedents; the new courts have few to follow. The decisions of the old courts were reported, studied, and criticized by lawyers, and their rooms were filled with lawyers; the decisions of the new courts are seldom reported, and their hearings are attended by probation officers trained in social service. The judgments of the old courts were final, save for appeal; in the new courts appeals are infrequent, and the judgment of the court is often only the beginning of the treatment of the case. In the old courts the jury was a vital factor; in the new courts, in practice, the jury is discarded. The system of the old courts was based upon checks and balances; the actual power of the new courts is practically unlimited. Justice in the old courts was based on legal science; in the new courts it is based on social engineering.

In other words, whatever analogies may be drawn with old common-law cases and customs, the vivid fact emerges of departure from an attempt to obtain justice by precedent and abstract reason and of return to an attempt to reach justice in the individual case.

From one aspect the new freedom may be the old tyranny. "The powers of the court of Star Chamber were a bagatelle compared with those of American juvenile courts and courts of domestic relations. If those courts chose to act arbitrarily and oppressively they could cause a revolution quite as easily as did the former."[6]

The new socialized procedure is gaining ground steadily and has affected not only the treatment of juvenile and domestic-relations cases but also general criminal procedure. Fundamentally and applied within its proper sphere the theory of the new procedure is sound because it is adapted to modern conditions. It can be successful in practice, however, only if it lives up to its theory. It must be supplied with the exceptionally able, trained man and woman power that its success demands. It must be regarded not as an end but as a means toward legal and social development. It must be treated frankly as an experiment requiring constant watching and study. Emotionalism must be shed, errors must be acknowledged when they are found, and facts must be dealt with. Finally undue haste to abolish the safeguards and the science of the common law must be avoided. It must be remembered that law is only a part of life, only one science among many to be used for social betterment; but it must be borne in mind, too, that law can not make over life.

---

[6] Pound, Roscoe: The Administration of Justice in the Modern City. Harvard Law Review, vol. 26, No. 4 (February, 1913), pp. 302–328.

FUNCTION OF THE LAW IN FAMILY PROBLEMS

THE LIMITS OF EFFECTIVE LEGAL ACTION

What is the proper field for the new procedure as applied to domestic relations? Obviously it can not be made to cover the whole substantive law. It is not adapted, for example, to deal with pre-nuptial property agreements. It can not compel the enforcement of connubial rights beyond ordering the payment of money or prohibiting certain acts. In short, the law has inherent limitations as applicable here as elsewhere.

Dean Pound, in discussing before the Pennsylvania Bar Association the question how far the law can hope to go, pointed out five limitations, the first one growing out of the difficulties involved in ascertainment of the facts to which legal rules are to be applied. As a matter of fact, nothing is more difficult than to get the truth in a family tangle. The suppression of vital elements by the parties, or ignorance of their existence, combined with the innate delicacy and many-sidedness of the problems, makes it practically impossible in many cases for the court to uncover the real situation. He continues as follows:

Another set of limitations grows out of the intangibleness of duties which morally are of great moment but legally defy enforcement. I have spoken already of futile attempts of equity at Rome and in England to make moral duties of gratitude or disinterestedness into duties enforceable by courts. In modern law not only duties of care for the health, morals, and education of children but even truancy and incorrigibility are coming under the supervision of juvenile courts or courts of domestic relations. * * *

A third set of limitations grows out of the subtlety of modes of seriously infringing important interests which the law would be glad to secure effectively if it might. Thus grave infringements of individual interests in the domestic relations by talebearing or intrigue are often too intangible to be reached by legal machinery. * * *

A fourth set of limitations grows out of the inapplicability of the legal machinery of rule and remedy to many phases of human conduct, to many important human relations, and to some serious wrongs. One example may be seen in the duty of husband and wife to live together and the claim of each to the society and affection of the other. * * *

Finally, a fifth set of limitations grows out of the necessity of appealing to individuals to set the law in motion. All legal systems labor under this necessity. But it puts a special burden upon legal administration of justice in an Anglo-American democracy. For our whole traditional polity depends on individual initiative to secure legal redress and enforce legal rules. It is true the ultraindividualism of the common law in this connection has broken down. We no longer rely wholly upon individual prosecutors to bring criminals to justice. We no longer rely upon private actions for damages to hold public-service companies to their duties or to save us from adulterated food. Yet the possibilities of administrative enforcement of law are limited also, even if there were not grave objections to a general régime of administrative enforcement. For laws will not enforce themselves. Human beings must execute them, and there must be some motive setting the individual in motion to do this above and beyond the abstract content of the rule and its conformity to an ideal justice or an ideal of social interest.[1]

---

[1] Pound, Roscoe: The Limits of Effective Legal Action. Report of the Twenty-second Annual Meeting of the Pennsylvania Bar Association, 1916, pp. 233–238.

The law, after all, beyond giving money compensation, is much more adapted to deal with negatives than with positives. It can keep a baseball player from working for a team other than the one with which he signed, but it can not compel him to play for that team. It can order a man not to live with a woman other than his wife, but it can not give the wife her husband's society. The most it can do generally by way of affirmative action is to order a thing done and punish the defendant for contempt if he refuses.

ENFORCEMENT OF THE LAW OF DOMESTIC RELATIONS

In view of its inherent limitations how far should the law endeavor to go in the solution of domestic difficulties? The answer is simple: The law should enforce to the best of its ability the fulfillment of the legal rights and obligations of the family. These rights and obligations are formulated by common law and statute, as has been outlined in a preceding section. If the substantive law itself goes too far, beyond the practical boundaries of effective legal action, the law itself—not its functioning—needs overhauling. The law, it must always be kept in mind, is only one of the social agencies. There are others, such as the church and social-welfare organizations, which may be much better equipped to deal with certain aspects of family problems. But the substantive law in general does not go too far. Here and there, of course, it needs revision. In some States it may include matters with which the law should not concern itself; in others the arsenal of legal remedies is incomplete. Uniform desertion and nonsupport laws are needed, and the varying doctrines of divorce are not all in accord with modern thought. But it can be said as a general proposition that for the most part the doctrines of the substantive law of domestic relations as it exists to-day are just and that it stays within the limitations of the law pointed out by legal thinkers and tested by the practical experience of centuries.

The problem to-day is not so much what the law of domestic relations should be as how the law should be enforced. In other words, the first concern of students of the subject should be not the limitations of legal doctrine but the limitations of its enforcement.

Enforcement of the law of domestic relations involves the two elements of judicial technique and court organization. The new technique has been discussed. The problem of court organization, like the problem of procedure, is not confined to domestic relations but runs throughout the judicial structure. The two problems, which are in some measure interrelated, must be kept distinct so far as possible in aid of clear thinking on these questions of the law and the family.

The effective limits of the enforcement of the law are after all pragmatic. If the law can be enforced more adequately, if its final aim of justice can be obtained more completely through the new socialized procedure and socialized courts, those means must be found—provided always that in seeking to do justice no injustice is committed. The criticism of unwarranted meddling with the most intimate personal relations of humanity is not new and is not always unfounded. A meddlesome and ill-equipped family court may do far more harm than the old common-law tribunal, whose mischief at least was limited.

INTERRELATION OF JUVENILE AND FAMILY-COURT CASES

Reference has already been made to "the intimate interrelation of all justiciable questions involving family life." (See p. 15.) A number of instances of conflict of jurisdiction between juvenile courts and courts awarding custody of children in divorce cases have come before courts of last resort,[1] and conflict also occurs between divorce courts granting alimony and courts having jurisdiction over criminal non-support actions. Machinery established in some jurisdictions for the collection of support orders in the criminal courts is not always available for the collection of money ordered as alimony for the support of children of divorced parents. Careful methods of investigation that have been developed in the best juvenile courts for the protection of dependent children whose custody is to be transferred have not been available for the protection of children who are to be given permanently in adoption.

To eliminate piecemeal justice in the field of domestic relations has been one of the aims of the family-court movement. Evidently there is a real problem in the overlapping of jurisdiction in cases involving the law of domestic relations, in that a number of courts may be passing upon different phases of the same family problem. Relatively little information is available, however, concerning the actual extent to which the same families are dealt with by more than one court or in more than one type of juvenile or domestic-relations case.

EARLY STUDIES OF OVERLAPPING

A study of the extent of duplication between the children's court and the family court of New York City, which has jurisdiction over cases of nonsupport, desertion, and abandonment, showed relatively little overlapping in the two courts in a period of three years and four months (January 1, 1919, to May 1, 1922). Only 2.4 per cent of 7,563 cases coming before the children's court during this period had ever been in the family court, and only 1.1 per cent had been in both courts within a period of six months at any time in their history. It must be borne in mind, however, that both the children's court and the family court had limited jurisdiction at the time of this study.[2]

A Minneapolis study covering a small number of cases known to social agencies indicates considerable overlapping. It was found that 33 of 89 families dealt with in 1921 and 1922 in divorce cases (over which the district court has jurisdiction) were known also to the juvenile branch of that court; that 54 of the men had been before the municipal court on charges of nonsupport, assault and battery, or drunkenness; and that 36 of them had been dealt with previously by the district court on desertion charges. Nineteen of the 89 families had appeared in all three courts (district, juvenile, and municipal), 37 others in two courts; and many of them had appeared repeatedly. The proportion of families with records in more than one court probably was higher than if an unselected group of families, including both

[1] For example: In re Hosford (107 Kans 115; 190 Pac. 765); Spade v. State (44 Ind. App. 529; 89 NE. 604); Brana v. Brana (139 La. 306; 71 So. 519); State v. Trimble (306 Mo. 657; 269 SW. 617).
[2] See the report of a study made by the committee on criminal courts of the Charity Organization Society of the City of New York (Annual Report, Forty-first Year, Oct. 1, 1922, to Sept. 30, 1923, pp. 32-33, Bulletin No. 470, Apr. 30, 1924).

those known to social agencies and those not known, had been studied.[3]

Much overlapping appeared in the statistics presented by the Philadelphia municipal court for 1922, as 16 per cent of 3,771 new cases received in the juvenile division of this court were known to have records in other divisions of the court, 12.1 per cent in the domestic-relation division.[4]

STUDY OF FAMILIES DEALT WITH IN JUVENILE AND DOMESTIC-RELATIONS CASES IN HAMILTON COUNTY, OHIO, AND PHILADELPHIA, PA.

In order to obtain information concerning the volume of cases involving juvenile and domestic-relations problems, the extent to which the same family was dealt with in cases of different types and by two or more organizations, and something of the characteristics of the families and the extent to which they had been dealt with by social agencies, studies were made by the Children's Bureau in Hamilton County, Ohio, and Philadelphia, Pa.

Hamilton County, in which Cincinnati is situated, was the pioneer community in the development of a family court with broad juvenile and domestic-relations jurisdiction (the domestic-relations division of the court of common pleas). In this city juvenile and divorce cases and certain other types of domestic-relations cases are dealt with by this family court, which has a central record system. Domestic-relations cases (chiefly desertion or nonsupport) not dealt with by the family court are given through the Ohio Humane Society the type of service usually rendered by a probation department. Statistical data for the year 1923 were obtained from the records of the family court, the humane society, and the probate court—which has jurisdiction over adoption, guardianship, and commitment of mentally defective persons. In Philadelphia practically all the juvenile and domestic-relations work except that relating to divorce cases is centered in the municipal court, which has juvenile, domestic-relations, misdemeanants, and criminal divisions, and a central record system and statistical department. The Philadelphia study was a joint undertaking of the Children's Bureau and the court's statistical department, which gave valuable assistance. In addition to municipal-court records, the records of the court of common pleas were consulted and information was obtained concerning 284 divorce cases involving children under 18 years of age. Although the Hamilton County study covered the entire year 1923, the Philadelphia study, because of the large number of cases passing through the court, covered only the month of October, 1923.[5]

---

[3] The 89 families were chosen from a much larger group known to social agencies, and detailed information was obtained as to their social histories and court records. The families known to the social agencies represented 30 per cent of an unselected group of individuals applying for divorces cleared through the social-service exchange on the basis of the surnames and first names of the men and women as given in the newspapers. See Where Courts Interlock, by Mildred D. Mudgett (Family, vol. 4, No. 3 (May, 1923), pp. 51–55). The social-service exchange is a clearing bureau maintained for the use of social case work agencies to prevent duplication in case work and to assist in investigations. When a case is registered with the exchange the names of agencies previously registered are given to the registering agency.

[4] Ninth Annual Report of the Municipal Court of Philadelphia, 1922, p. 449.

[5] For detailed presentation of the findings of this study see Appendix B, p. 71, and for the jurisdiction of the courts see Appendix A, p. 67.

VOLUME OF CASES

The studies indicate a considerable volume of domestic-relations work in Cincinnati (Hamilton County) and Philadelphia. More than 5,000 families (5,286), or approximately 4 per cent of all the families in Hamilton County, were dealt with in the year 1923 by the family court, the humane society (with or without court action), and the probate court in juvenile and domestic-relations cases (including divorce cases in which children were involved). In a single month (October, 1923) the Philadelphia municipal court dealt with 6,728 families, or approximately 2 per cent of the total families in Philadelphia, in juvenile and domestic-relations cases exclusive of divorce, adoption, and certain other types of cases included in the Hamilton County study.

The family court in Hamilton County, which has jurisdiction over all the cases included in the study except cases of adoption, guardianship, and feeble-mindedness, actually dealt with only 68 per cent of all the families in that community included in the study. Many dependency and neglect cases and the great majority of the desertion or nonsupport and illegitimacy cases were dealt with by agencies other than the family court.

INTERRELATION OF CASES

Many families presented two or more different types of family problems, some of the kind usually coming within the jurisdiction of a juvenile court and others involving such issues as divorce, desertion or nonsupport, illegitimacy, or adoption. Such overlapping is significant in relation to efforts to consolidate court work in juvenile and domestic-relations cases. One-eighth of the Hamilton County families (13 per cent) were dealt with in more than one type of case during the year. Six per cent of the Philadelphia municipal-court cases were dealt with in more than one type of case in a single month (October). Fourteen per cent of the juvenile cases in Philadelphia, the same percentage of desertion or nonsupport cases, and 20 per cent of the illegitimacy cases had been dealt with in cases of other types during the year ended October 31, 1923.

Forty-one per cent of the Hamilton County families dealt with in dependency or neglect cases in 1923 were dealt with also in that year in cases of other types, usually domestic relations. Twenty-six per cent of the families dealt with in divorce cases were known in cases of other types, chiefly desertion or nonsupport. The greatest amount of overlapping was found to exist between dependency or neglect and desertion or nonsupport, divorce and desertion or nonsupport, and offenses against children and delinquency. Thirteen per cent of 284 divorce cases dealt with by the Philadelphia court of common pleas were known to the municipal court during the year in which divorce petitions were filed, and 47 per cent had been known to the municipal court before or during the year, practically all of them to the domestic-relations division of the court.

SOCIAL AGENCIES DEALING WITH THE FAMILIES

Many of the families dealt with by the courts in juvenile and domestic-relations cases (and, in Hamilton County, by the humane society) had required various types of community social service. In

Hamilton County 53 per cent of the families dealt with were reported by the social-service exchange as known to Hamilton County agencies other than the courts or the humane society, or as known to the family court or the humane society in cases of other types than those included in the study. Thirty-three per cent were known to more than one agency. Among families dealt with in desertion or non-support cases, 53 per cent—and among those dealt with in divorce cases, 36 per cent—had social-agency records. More than one-third of all the families included in the study had been known to family-welfare agencies.

The Philadelphia percentages approximated very closely those for Hamilton County, 58 per cent of the families dealt with by the municipal court in juvenile and domestic-relations cases having been known to social agencies, 36 per cent to more than one agency, and 24 per cent (a considerably smaller percentage than in Hamilton County) to family-welfare agencies. Among families dealt with by the Philadelphia court in more than one type of case, 89 per cent had social-agency records.

It is clear that use of the social-service exchange and of the information available in the case records of the agencies is exceedingly important in the work of family courts.

CHARACTERISTICS OF THE FAMILIES

Information concerning race of mother and age of parents was obtained for Hamilton County but not for Philadelphia. The percentage of colored mothers in Hamilton County was almost three times as high as the percentage of colored in the whole population. Many of the parents were young or in early middle life. In 36 per cent of the families the mother was between 21 and 30 and the father between 21 and 40 years of age. Both parents were 21 and under 30 years of age in 17 per cent of the families dealt with in dependency and neglect cases, 21 per cent of those dealt with in divorce cases, and 29 per cent of those dealt with in desertion or nonsupport cases. Less than one-fourth of the mothers (23 per cent) had reached the age of 40.

The number of living children in the Hamilton County families dealt with in the course of a year in juvenile and domestic-relations cases was 10,681, an average of 2.4 per family in the 4,477 families with living children (excluding unborn children). In Philadelphia 17,143 children, an average of 2.8 per family, were reported in the 6,017 families with living children dealt with in the course of one month by the municipal court in juvenile and domestic-relations cases.

The Hamilton County families studied which had been dealt with in divorce cases included only those that had minor children; of these, 54 per cent had children under 7 years of age and 21 per cent had children under 3 years of age. Seventy-three per cent of the families dealt with in desertion or nonsupport cases had children under 7, and 47 per cent had children under 3 years of age. These cases are thus seen to involve, very frequently, provision for the care and protection of young children, a task which can be performed only when the court has facilities for social investigation, planning, and supervision. Of the whole group of Hamilton County families for which age of children was reported, 53 per cent had children under the age of 7 years and

28 per cent had children under the age of 3 years.   The Philadelphia percentages were very similar—52 per cent with children under 7 and 27 per cent with children under 3.   The types of cases included in the two communities were somewhat different.

As was to be expected, many broken homes and complicated family situations were included in the groups for which information was obtained.   In only 23 per cent of the Hamilton County families were all the children the children of both husband and wife and all living with both parents.   Corresponding information was not available for Philadelphia.   In 12 per cent of the Hamilton County families and 13 per cent of the Philadelphia families none of the children was with either parent.

PRESENT JUDICIAL ORGANIZATION FOR DEALING WITH JUVENILE AND FAMILY CASES

COURT SYSTEMS HAVING JURISDICTION OVER CASES INCLUDED IN THE STUDY

At the present time in most States jurisdiction in juvenile and domestic-relations cases is divided among (1) specialized juvenile, family, or domestic-relations courts; (2) criminal courts; and (3) courts of probate and chancery jurisdiction. Attempts to consolidate jurisdiction therefore must take into consideration these three classes of courts, constitutional limitations relating to the establishment of courts, and the vested jurisdiction of existing courts.

The number of courts having jurisdiction over family cases of course depends in the first instance upon the general judicial organization of the State. This country seems to take a peculiar zest in the formation of new courts. Many States have courts which do not coordinate with the other judicial units but whose jurisdiction overlaps theirs in almost every particular; and the cure for this situation is often taken to be creation of another court. This condition is by no means nation-wide. In some jurisdictions there is real evidence that the business aptitude for organization for which Americans are supposed to be famous has permeated into the judicial system. In others there is a marked lack of coordination.

Original jurisdiction in criminal cases is usually divided between courts that deal with cases on indictment or information (as the court of general criminal jurisdiction) and courts of summary jurisdiction (justices of the peace, municipal courts, police courts) that have power to dispose of minor cases immediately and hold only the more serious cases for the grand jury or the court of general criminal jurisdiction. Sometimes the same domestic situation may be dealt with as a misdemeanor and disposed of in a municipal or police court or may be dealt with as a felony by the grand jury and higher criminal court. This is particularly true of nonsupport and desertion cases (as in Arkansas, California, and Indiana). In fact, in some jurisdictions (for example, Indianapolis and St. Louis) three or four types of courts may deal with nonsupport: City courts, courts of inferior criminal jurisdiction, courts of general criminal jurisdiction, and (as in Indianapolis) the juvenile court under a law relating to contributing to dependency.

In considering chancery and probate jurisdiction it is found that in many States cases of adoption and guardianship are dealt with in the probate or county court, and cases of divorce and annulment of marriage are dealt with in the superior, district, or circuit court or in some other court of general civil and criminal jurisdiction. In some States, however, divorce and annulment cases come under the jurisdiction of a chancery court without criminal jurisdiction, as in Arkansas and Mississippi. On the other hand, adoption and guardianship jurisdiction is sometimes vested in a court of general criminal and civil jurisdiction, as in California, where the superior court has

30

exclusive probate and juvenile jurisdiction, and in Iowa, where the district court has exclusive probate jurisdiction. In the latter State the probate division of the district court handles guardianship matters, and all courts of record (including both the district court and the division of this court designated the juvenile court) have jurisdiction over adoption.

A summary of the number of different court systems in each State that have jurisdiction over the various cases included in this study is of interest in this connection.[1] Specific offenses against children, which are classed as misdemeanors or felonies and are handled usually by any criminal court having jurisdiction over the grade of offense indicated, are excluded; and juvenile and domestic-relations courts that are divisions of larger courts have not been counted as separate courts. Possibly some local courts that may have jurisdiction under special laws or under ordinances not published in the codes have not been counted.[2] In only 3 States is jurisdiction over the cases specified vested in only two courts. In the District of Columbia and 8 States it is divided among three courts; in 17 States four or five courts may have jurisdiction; in 15 States, six or seven courts; and in 5 States, eight or more courts.[3]

JURISDICTION IN DELINQUENCY AND DEPENDENCY CASES

One of the first points to be considered with reference to the jurisdiction that should be vested in the juvenile or family court is whether juvenile jurisdiction includes all young people who should be brought under the protection of the special procedure that has been developed. This involves two questions: (1) The age jurisdiction of the juvenile court, and (2) exceptions or modifications in juvenile-court jurisdiction with reference to serious offenses committed by children.

The tendency clearly is to raise age jurisdiction to 18 years at least. About half the States extend the delinquency jurisdiction of the juvenile court to both boys and girls, or to girls only, under 18 years of age; and in a few States jurisdiction extends to a higher age. Considerable work, however, remains to be accomplished if the standard adopted in 1925 by the National Probation Association in its standard juvenile court law be regarded as a desirable goal.[4] To reach this it would be necessary to raise age limits to 18 years throughout the State in some or all classes of cases (boys' or girls', dependency and neglect, or delinquency) in 29 States [5] and the District of Columbia, and to

---

[1] See p. 15 of this report and also Analysis and Tabular Summary of State Laws Relating to Jurisdiction in Children's Cases and Cases of Domestic Relations, p. 1.

[2] It has been impossible to ascertain in every instance whether city and municipal courts should be considered one or two types of court, and the same is true of justice of the peace and police courts. In the absence of information to the contrary they have been counted as two courts. Of course not all the courts authorized by law are operating in all jurisdictions, and sometimes several courts are presided over by the same judge and served by the same staff. For example, in New Jersey the judge of the court of common pleas is also judge of the courts of quarter sessions and special sessions and of the juvenile court (except in counties of the first class), and he may be judge of the orphans' court, all these courts having jurisdiction over cases included in the study.

[3] Two courts have jurisdiction in Arizona, Kentucky, Louisiana; 3 in California, Nebraska, Nevada, North Dakota, Oregon, Utah, Washington, Wyoming; 4 in Colorado, Idaho, Minnesota, Mississippi, Montana, New Hampshire, Rhode Island, South Dakota, Texas, Vermont; 5 in Alabama, Georgia, Kansas, Massachusetts, New Mexico, Oklahoma, Wisconsin; 6 in Connecticut, Florida, Illinois, Indiana, Iowa, North Carolina, Pennsylvania, West Virginia; 7 in Arkansas, Delaware, Maine, Maryland, Michigan, Ohio, Virginia; 8 in Missouri, South Carolina, Tennessee; 9 in New York; and 13 in New Jersey.

[4] A Standard Juvenile-Court Law, prepared by the committee on standard juvenile-court laws (revised edition) National Probation Association (Inc.), New York, 1933.

[5] Alabama, Connecticut, Delaware, Florida, Georgia, Illinois, Indiana, Kansas, Kentucky, Louisiana, Maine, Maryland, Massachusetts, Michigan, Missouri, Montana, New Hampshire, New Jersey, New York, North Carolina, Oklahoma, Pennsylvania, Rhode Island, South Carolina, Tennessee, Texas, Vermont, West Virginia, and Wisconsin.

eliminate exceptions to juvenile-court jurisdiction or modifications of it in cases of serious offenses in 27 States [6] and the District of Columbia. These changes would prevent overlapping of jurisdiction in cases of children under the age of 18 years.

JURISDICTION IN OTHER JUVENILE AND FAMILY CASES

In 33 States, in parts of 5 others, and in the District of Columbia the juvenile court or the court of which it is a part has at least concurrent jurisdiction over cases of contributing to delinquency or dependency; and in 29 States, parts of 10 others, and the District of Columbia such courts have jurisdiction over some or all types of offenses against children. In 28 States, the District of Columbia, and parts of 15 States such courts have jurisdiction in cases of desertion or nonsupport. In 3 States, parts of 3 others, and the District of Columbia the juvenile court or family court has jurisdiction over cases of establishment of paternity, and in more than a third of the States such jurisdiction is vested in courts having juvenile divisions. Jurisdiction over divorce is vested in juvenile or family courts in 1 State and parts of 4 others; and courts having juvenile divisions are given such jurisdiction in 8 States and parts of 13 others.

In few States is jurisdiction over adoption or guardianship cases, or the commitment of mentally defective or insane children, vested in the juvenile court; but in a number of States the court of which the juvenile court is a part has such jurisdiction. In more than half the States possibilities exist for coordination of work in these cases through court assignment and utilization of the social-service machinery of the juvenile division.

POSSIBILITIES OF CONSOLIDATING JURISDICTION

As is indicated by the preceding analysis, certain types of judicial organization greatly simplify the problem of centralizing jurisdiction. For example, in certain of the western States, such as Nebraska, the district courts have very broad general jurisdiction, including cases under the juvenile-court law, nonsupport and desertion cases, and divorce cases. There it was possible without special legislation to reassign cases and to create a special docket, establishing divisions of domestic relations of broad scope. In Hamilton County and other Ohio counties a similar situation existed, the court of common pleas having jurisdiction over juvenile cases, divorce cases, cases of failure to provide for minor children, and illegitimacy cases. Accordingly the Ohio laws creating family courts are very brief and involve no difficult legal problems. Over the two last-named classes of cases, however, municipal courts in Ohio also have jurisdiction, which is frequently exercised in at least two of the Ohio cities having family courts.

In contrast to the relatively simple situation in Nebraska, which makes consolidation easy, is the very complicated system in New York City, where jurisdiction is divided among the children's court;

---

[6] Arkansas, Colorado, Delaware, Florida, Georgia, Idaho, Illinois, Indiana, Iowa, Louisiana, Maine, Massachusetts, Mississippi, Missouri, Montana, New Hampshire, New Mexico, New York, North Carolina, Oregon, Pennsylvania, Rhode Island, South Carolina, Tennessee, Utah, Vermont, and Wyoming. The standard law would permit the juvenile court to waive jurisdiction in the case of a child 16 years of age or over charged with an offense that would amount to a felony in the case of an adult.

the magistrates' courts, which deal with deserting and nonsupporting husbands as "disorderly"; the court of special sessions, with jurisdiction in illegitimacy cases; the surrogate's court, with jurisdiction in adoption cases; and the supreme court, with divorce jurisdiction. The children's court has been given certain enlarged powers with reference to families of children before the court as delinquent, neglected, or dependent, and in three boroughs "family divisions" of the magistrates' courts have been developed to deal with desertion and nonsupport cases.[7] In a number of States possibilities exist for further consolidation in the juvenile or family division of jurisdiction over the classes of cases included in this study or for utilization of the social-service machinery of that division without legislative action.

---

[7] By a law of 1933 the family courts have been merged with the children's court, and the domestic-relations jurisdiction has been considerably broadened (N. Y., act of Apr. 26, 1933, ch. 482).

FAMILY COURTS AND COURTS OF DOMESTIC RELATIONS IN ACTION

The efficacy of a court can not be judged by the number of cases that come before it nor by the amount of money it handles. Most courts can be judged according to their published opinions, but family courts rarely make law. They must be tested by results, and it is results that are hardest to evaluate. However, the court's jurisdiction, the number and quality of personnel, the equipment, actual observation of hearings, and information concerning methods or organization and administration are all indicative of the extent to which the court succeeds in correcting the individual family and community maladjustments with which it deals.

CONSOLIDATION OF JURISDICTION

It has been pointed out that one of the aims of the family-court movement has been elimination of the overlapping jurisdiction of various tribunals. How far this aim is realized depends in the first place upon the content of the legislation under which the courts operate and in the second place upon the extent to which the new courts actually exercise jurisdiction. The first factor is affected by the constitutional limitations regarding the establishment of new courts and the conferring of exclusive jurisdiction upon these courts and the legal status of the courts upon which jurisdiction is conferred (as whether their jurisdiction is limited and whether provision is made for jury trials). The second factor is largely dependent upon the extent to which public opinion, as expressed through prosecuting authorities, bench and bar, and cooperating social agencies, supports the new court.

JURISDICTION CONFERRED BY LAW OR RULE OF COURT

The four family courts of juvenile and broad adult jurisdiction that were studied in Hamilton, Mahoning, Montgomery, and Summit Counties, Ohio, have jurisdiction over all types of cases included in the study except cases of adoption and guardianship. The family court of Multnomah County, Oreg., also has very broad jurisdiction.

The family courts of juvenile and limited adult jurisdiction that were studied furnish an interesting contrast. Desertion and non-support cases, but not divorce cases, are included in the jurisdiction of the New Jersey and Virginia courts and in that of Jefferson County, Ala., whereas in the court of St. Louis, Mo., the reverse is true. Offenses against children are dealt with by the Virginia courts and that of Jefferson County but not by those of New Jersey and St. Louis. The jurisdiction of the New Jersey, Jefferson County, and St. Louis courts covers one or more of the types of cases that usually are dealt with by a probate court. The Virginia courts have power to commit mentally defective children who are within their jurisdiction for other reasons.

34

The jurisdiction of the juvenile courts included in the study is in some instances so broad as to make the line between this group and the preceding group little more than an arbitrary division.[1] All of them have jurisdiction over contributing to delinquency or over other offenses against children, though in the District of Columbia and New York City such jurisdiction is quite limited. All have jurisdiction over desertion or nonsupport, though in Indianapolis, Ind., the procedure is in reality a contributing-to-neglect procedure; but in New York City such jurisdiction is limited to cases in which the child is already before the court on a charge related to juvenile jurisdiction. The New York and District of Columbia courts have jurisdiction over proceedings for the establishment of paternity. None has divorce jurisdiction. Adoption jurisdiction is vested in the New York and Denver courts, though in New York City it is limited to cases in which the child is already before the court. Power to commit mentally defective children and at least certain powers with reference to guardianship are also vested, with certain exceptions, in the courts of this group.

The jurisdiction of the five domestic-relations courts without juvenile jurisdiction that were studied (see p. 16) is limited for the most part to cases of desertion and nonsupport, though two courts have jurisdiction over cases of establishment of paternity and three over at least certain types of cases of offenses against children. None of these courts has divorce jurisdiction nor jurisdiction over adoption, guardianship, or the commitment of mentally defective children.

The municipal and district courts with organization for juvenile and domestic-relations work are a group concerning which information is difficult to obtain, because they may be established by rule of court without special legislation. Jurisdiction has been given by law over divorce to one of the four courts studied, over adoption to one, over commitment of mentally defective children to two. In addition, nearly all types of cases included in the study may be assigned to these courts. Cases of offenses against children, however, and cases of establishment of paternity were not usually assigned to the juvenile and domestic-relations divisions.

JURISDICTION EXERCISED IN PRACTICE

Much of the adult jurisdiction of the family court or court of domestic relations is concurrent with that of other courts. In each of the four Ohio counties whose family courts of juvenile and broad adult jurisdiction were studied the chief city has a municipal court with limited criminal and civil jurisdiction, including concurrent jurisdiction over nonsupport, illegitimacy, and offenses against children; and each county has a probate court with jurisdiction over adoption, guardianship, and commitment of mentally defective children. In each community also is a humane society, a very old organization that has been granted special privileges by State law. This society had been accustomed to prosecute cases of neglect, abuse, or nonsupport and desertion in the municipal court; and in Hamilton and Mahoning Counties it continued to prosecute them

---

[1] For the location of the juvenile courts studied see footnote 17, p. 6, and for the extent to which they are representative of a larger group see p. 16. Legal authority was given in 1923 for designating the Denver court "for convenience" the family court.

in the municipal court after divisions of domestic relations had been established in the courts of common pleas. In 1923 in Hamilton County only 14 per cent of the families dealt with in cases of desertion or nonsupport and not in cases of other types and 10 per cent of those dealt with in illegitimacy cases only were handled by the family court. The remainder were dealt with by the humane society, informally or through the municipal court. (See Appendix B, p. 73.) The Mahoning County division of domestic relations did not exercise jurisdiction over desertion or nonsupport except in cases of failure to pay alimony and cases in which the children were cared for apart from both parents, and illegitimacy jurisdiction was not exercised. All or most of the nonsupport cases in Montgomery and Summit Counties were reported to be heard in the family courts, but only the Montgomery County court heard paternity cases. Thus in these four Ohio communities consolidation of jurisdiction had not approached in practice the extent to which it is authorized by law. The court of Multnomah County, Oreg., was not exercising to any extent its jurisdiction over nonsupport or contributing to delinquency.

In the family courts of juvenile and limited adult jurisdiction that were studied the situation was found to be as follows: The jurisdiction of the Virginia courts was exclusive in the cases designated by law as coming under their control. The volume of business had not been so great in any community as to make it necessary to separate the court into two divisions. The jurisdiction of the court of Jefferson County, Ala., was similar to that of the Virginia courts and was exclusive over juvenile cases and desertion and nonsupport cases, and also over cases of contributing to delinquency or dependency. This court had had two separate divisions, presided over by different judges, holding sessions in different places, staffed by different officers, and having relatively little provision for coordination of work. Little social-service work was done in adult cases. In 1927 the situation was improved by legislation establishing in place of the existing court a juvenile and domestic-relations court with a single judge.[2] The court of St. Louis, Mo., likewise was divided into distinct juvenile and divorce divisions with little coordination of activities except that the judge presiding over one of the divorce divisions was assigned also to the juvenile division. In the two New Jersey counties many domestic-relations cases within the jurisdiction of the county family courts were dealt with by other courts. Practically all the probation work in these two communities was done through county probation bureaus serving all the courts in the county. Each of these bureaus had a domestic-relations division, so that the social-service work in these cases was coordinated even though jurisdiction was divided.

Among the juvenile courts of broad jurisdiction that were studied several had succeeded in consolidating jurisdiction to a considerable degree, if not to the full extent authorized by law. The District of Columbia juvenile court was exercising jurisdiction in the majority of cases of desertion or nonsupport, and it had exclusive jurisdiction in illegitimacy cases. It was not exercising the very limited jurisdiction that it possessed over cases of offenses against children, and its jurisdiction in cases of serious offenses committed by children was limited to preliminary examinations.

---

[2] Ala., act of Aug. 2, 1927, No. 225, Acts of 1927, pp. 238–250.

The judge of the Denver juvenile court interpreted the legislation under which it operated to mean that it had exclusive jurisdiction in the first instance as to the custody and disposition of all children under the age of 21 years in both delinquency and criminal cases; but it might direct that children under 21 not included in the definition of delinquency who were brought to court on criminal charges should be tried either in the criminal court or under criminal procedure in the juvenile court.[3]   The juvenile court had concurrent jurisdiction in criminal cases against adults if the offense charged was against the person or concerning the morals or protection of a person under the age of 21 years.   The Colorado laws relating to contributing to delinquency and dependency were very broad, and concurrent jurisdiction in desertion and nonsupport cases was vested in the juvenile court.   In 1923 an arrangement was made with the district attorney whereby the juvenile court was given authority to investigate all nonsupport cases in which fathers failed to pay for the support of their children.   If court action was justified, charges of contributing to dependency instead of nonsupport charges were filed in the juvenile court.   It was stated in 1924 that illegitimacy cases were dealt with by the juvenile court under charges of contributing to dependency, that divorce cases in which children were involved were often referred to the juvenile court for investigation, and that cases of rape and of other offenses against children, jurisdiction over which was concurrent, were dealt with by the juvenile court.   Much unofficial court work was done in cases involving questions of divorce, insufficient support, nonsupport, and family trouble.

In New York City, prior to the 1933 law effective October 1, jurisdiction in nonsupport cases was divided between the juvenile and domestic-relations courts.   In Indianapolis, Ind., such jurisdiction was divided between the juvenile and municipal courts.   In Indianapolis nonsupport cases were dealt with in the juvenile court under a contributing-to-neglect law and in the municipal court under a nonsupport law.   In New York City the jurisdiction of the children's court in adult cases was limited to cases in which the child was before the court as delinquent or neglected.   In exercising even this jurisdiction the court had been proceeding very slowly, partly because questions had been raised as to the validity of certain parts of the act.   It exercised its nonsupport jurisdiction first by undertaking the collection of orders for the support of children placed in institutions or under the care of agencies; after this work had been well developed it began to collect support for neglected and delinquent children in their own homes.

The state-wide children's court act of New York State attempted to give to the children's court jurisdiction in all juvenile and family cases involving the welfare of children under the age of 16 years, except cases of divorce and alimony and adult cases involving offenses of the grade of felony, the jurisdiction to be exclusive except over truancy, adoption, guardianship, custody, contributing to delinquency, and other offenses against children.   But decisions of the New York State supreme court, appellate division, weakened this jurisdiction, as has been stated (see p. 16), and limited the jurisdiction of the children's courts throughout the State substantially to that conferred upon the New York City court.   Information

---

[3] The judge elected in 1927 interpreted the delinquency jurisdiction of the court somewhat less broadly

obtained in the course of this study indicated that the courts were proceeding slowly in exercising adult jurisdiction.

The five domestic-relations courts without juvenile jurisdiction that were studied had little opportunity to consolidate jurisdiction in various types of cases. The jurisdiction actually exercised by these courts has already been described. (See p. 35.)

The four municipal and district courts with juvenile and domestic-relations divisions that were studied had succeeded in centralizing the treatment of a variety of juvenile and family cases. In Philadelphia and in Springfield the juvenile and domestic-relations divisions were separate, though in Springfield the probation office was not divided into distinct departments but served all parts of the court. In Polk County, Iowa, and in Douglas County, Nebr., a single division had dealt with juvenile and domestic-relations cases. Later the work of these courts was reported to be departmentalized to some extent.

EXTENSION OF ACCEPTED STANDARDS OF JUVENILE-COURT ORGANIZATION AND PROCEDURE

Inasmuch as one of the two main objects of family-court organization was to extend to family cases the point of view and methods developed in the juvenile court it is pertinent to inquire into the extent to which the organization and methods of the new courts conform to generally accepted standards of juvenile-court procedure. It must be borne in mind that with perhaps .a few notable exceptions these juvenile-court standards have not yet been put fully into practice in juvenile courts themselves; also that almost no attempt has been made to modify the rules of criminal procedure as applied to cases involving nonsupport and desertion (aside from those dealt with by juvenile courts under laws on contributing to dependency) or offenses against children.[4]

The principal juvenile-court standards applicable to family courts or courts of domestic relations [5] and the extent to which courts of various types included in the study approached the respective standards may be summarized as follows:

THE JUDGE

1. *The judge should be chosen because of his special qualifications for the work. The term of office should be sufficiently long to make specialization possible, preferably not less than six years. The judge should be able to devote such time to the work of the court as is necessary to hear each case carefully and thoroughly and to give general direction to the work of the court.*

With few exceptions the judges, probation officers, and staffs of juvenile courts and family courts or courts of domestic relations are not adequately paid. The wonder is, not that the judges and their assistants are not better but that so many capable officials are at work.

The position of judge of a family court requires qualities of the highest order: Broadmindedness, executive ability, tact, knowledge of the law, knowledge of the principles governing social work, and

---

[4] Chancery procedure in contributing to delinquency and dependency cases has been developed in Denver, Colo., and equity jurisdiction, along with criminal jurisdiction, is being developed in nonsupport cases in New York State.

[5] Adapted from Juvenile-Court Standards, pp. 2-10.

knowledge of people. To these must often be added ability to convince appropriating authorities and the general public that sufficient funds must be made available. These specifications are rarely filled.

The terms of consecutive service of the judges of courts other than juvenile courts included in the study ranged from the 6-year terms in Ohio, in Norfolk and Richmond, Va., and in Jefferson County, Ala., to assignments of three weeks in Boston. With the exception of the Philadelphia municipal court, which had short assignments in the domestic-relations division, and of the St. Louis court, which had 2-year assignments, the terms of service in all the courts having both juvenile and domestic-relations jurisdiction were four to six years. The juvenile courts with broad jurisdiction included in the study also had long terms—4, 6, or 10 years. Only one of the five domestic-relations courts without juvenile jurisdiction—that in Newark, N. J.—had a long term of service (four years) for the judge; in the others the judge as a rule served for periods of a few weeks or a few months. In New York City, however, some of the judges have served in the family court for much longer periods.

In a number of the courts the judges did not have sufficient time to "hear each case carefully and thoroughly and to give general direction to the work of the court." The volume of divorce business was very heavy in the Ohio courts, and in three of the four courts studied this occupied the major portion of the judge's time. These Ohio courts, however, gave much more time to the consideration of individual divorce cases than some of the other courts having divorce jurisdiction included in the study; for example, one that heard 60 to 70 divorce cases in a single day. The judges of some of the courts gave a great deal of time, both in formal hearings and otherwise, to considering the problems of individual cases.

THE PROBATION STAFF

2. *Not more than 50 cases should be under the supervision of one probation officer at any one time. Probation officers should be chosen from an eligible list secured by competitive examination. The minimum qualifications of probation officers should include a good education, preferably graduation from college or its equivalent or from a school of social work; at least one year in case work under supervision; good personality and character; tact, resourcefulness, and sympathy. The compensation of probation officers should be such that the best types of trained service can be secured. The salaries should be comparable with those paid to workers in other fields of social service. Increases should be based on records of service and efficiency.*

It is very difficult to measure the volume of preliminary work, such as interviewing and investigating, that each probation officer does, but the number of probationers under the supervision of each officer can be ascertained and a comparison made. In only five or six of the courts studied did the case loads even approximate the standard of 50 cases per officer, and two of these courts were serving rural counties. For instance, in one court having jurisdiction over juvenile and nonsupport cases the two juvenile officers had 74 and 130 cases, respectively, and the adult officers had 160 to 198 cases; in addition they made investigations and served as bailiffs and court attendants. In another court with similar jurisdiction no case super-vision of adult probationers and very little of juveniles was at-tempted; some of the juvenile officers did not even know for how many probationers they were responsible. In one juvenile court with broad jurisdiction the juvenile-delinquent case load was in con-formity with the standards (boys 51, girls 33); but the officer super-vising neglected and dependent children was responsible for 159 families, and the adult probation officers were responsible for 96 to 132. Other courts had as many as 200, 250, and 500 adult proba-tioners under a single officer; and some frankly stated that they attempted little or no supervision in adult cases. In general the juvenile-case loads were lighter than the adult-case loads.[6]

As appointment based upon a system of competitive examination is comparatively infrequent in probation work, it is encouraging to find that in the majority of the courts included in the study appoint-ments were made from eligible lists established after examinations held by civil-service commissions or other agencies. In the New Jersey courts, for example, initial appointments were made from State civil-service registers, and provision was made for regular in-creases in salary after promotional examinations. Several courts failed to obtain full value from the merit system of appointment because some of the staff members assigned to social-service work were appointed as constables or other court officials not covered by the competitive-examination system. As a rule, the probation departments in which appointments were made from lists established through competitive examination did not prescribe definite standards of education and experience. The New Jersey examinations, how-ever, did prescribe such standards, though they were usually very low with reference to education, and examinations for the New York City domestic-relations court required one year's social-service experience, though experience in a volunteer capacity was sometimes accepted.[7]

Not many members of the probation departments had the training and experience outlined in the standards as desirable—graduation from college or its equivalent or from a school of social work and at least one year in case work under supervision. This may be explained in part by the salaries paid, which as a rule were markedly inadequate, and in part by the fact that probation work in most communities has not yet been placed upon so firm a professional basis as social work done by private family-welfare organizations or by child-caring agencies with high standards. Opportunities for training and for professional advancement and recognition are believed to be less, and young workers with good general education and professional prepa-ration are not so eager to enter this field. Yet the case loads carried by probation officers are much heavier in most courts than the case loads of workers in private organizations of the kind mentioned, and the work is more difficult and more responsible than that of many private agencies.

Several of the chief probation officers and some of the other officers were law-school graduates. A few women probation officers were graduate nurses. In one court none of the probation officers had

[6] Later information indicated some improvement in case loads in a number of the courts studied.
[7] The probation laws of New York State were strengthened greatly by legislation enacted in 1928 pro-viding that probation officers shall be selected because of definite qualifications as to character, ability, and training. (Acts of Mar. 9 and 21, 1928, chs. 313 and 460, Laws of 1928, pp. 795, 1013.)

had training or previous experience in social work; one officer had been a public-health nurse. In another court the staff dealing with adult domestic-relations cases was composed exclusively of persons who had had experience only as constables or sheriffs or in courthouse clerical work. In a court with a separate domestic-relations division only one of eight investigators had any training or previous experience related to the work, and her training had been limited to a period of six months.

A few of the courts had staffs better prepared by education and in some cases by experience. Thus in the District of Columbia juvenile court nearly all the probation officers were college or law-school graduates, and several had had previous experience in social work. One of the six members of the staff of the domestic-relations division of the Boston municipal court's probation department was a member of the bar and had had four years' unusually successful experience in the juvenile court of Boston; and the one woman officer—also a member of the bar—had had experience in settlement work and in a family-welfare society. Three had had no previous social-service experience; one had been an attorney, one the chief clerk of the probation department, and one was a law student. One had family-welfare experience.

Several of the executives of probation departments serving domestic-relations courts and other courts and one devoting full time to domestic-relations and juvenile-court work received in 1931 salaries ranging from $5,600 to $9,000, and a number received $3,000 to $4,100; but some received $2,500 to $2,850 or even as little as $1,920. Most of the chief probation officers received salaries too low for positions of such responsibility. In probation departments with supervisors of divisions as well as chief probation officers 5 had salaries ranging from $2,000 to $3,000, 5 had a higher range (to $5,000 in one court), and 2 had a lower range. Salaries of investigators and probation officers ranged from $1,080 to $3,400; only a few probation officers received less than $1,800 or more than $3,000.[8]

On the whole the most adequate salary scale was found in the probation departments of Essex and Hudson Counties, N. J., which served all the courts in their respective counties. In Essex County the chief probation officer received $9,000, the assistant chief probation officer received $5,000, the probation officers in charge received $3,600, and the probation officers received $2,160 to $3,360. In Hudson County the chief probation officer received $7,500, officers in supervisory positions received $3,500 to $3,800 (except one receiving a nominal salary), and the salaries of probation officers were $2,400 to $3,400.

Information on salaries summarized for 20 probation departments serving large cities included in the study[9] showed that in 13 of these the chief probation officer received in 1931 less than $3,500 or some of the probation officers received less than $1,800, or both these conditions existed. Information subsequent to 1931 has not been obtained.

---

[8] In some courts persons assigned to the investigation of cases are termed "investigators," the term "probation officer" being reserved for those supervising persons on probation. Information on salaries presented in the first edition of this report related to the year 1927. From 1927 to 1931 there had been improvement in salaries in some courts, but on the whole there was little change.

[9] Two of these were in New York City, the children's court and the magistrates' court of which the family court was a part.

PRECOURT WORK AND INVESTIGATION OF CASES

3. *The judge or a probation officer designated by him should examine all complaints and after adequate investigation should determine whether formal court action is to be taken. It should be the duty of the court to bring about adjustment of cases without formal court action whenever possible.*

Social investigation should be made in every case and should be set in motion at the moment of the court's earliest knowledge of the case. Psychiatric and psychological study should be made at least in all cases in which the social investigation raises a question of special need for study and should be made before decision concerning treatment, but only by a clinic or an examiner properly qualified for such work.

These standards would apply to cases of nonsupport and desertion and to other family difficulties as well as to juvenile cases; and it is sometimes urged that so far as they relate to conciliation service and social investigation they are applicable to divorce cases, at least where children are involved. (See p. 59.) For the purpose of this summary only juvenile cases, nonsupport and desertion cases, and divorce cases will be considered, as these usually represent the most important classes numerically.

Most of the courts with juvenile jurisdiction included in the study were following the tendency noted in most juvenile courts throughout the country in placing considerable emphasis on the unofficial adjustment of children's cases, especially cases of delinquency.[10] The practice varied from that in courts adjusting only a small minority of children's cases unofficially to that in courts like the family court of Hamilton County, Ohio, which adjusted nearly all children's cases unofficially.

Nineteen courts (not including two courts serving rural counties) were dealing with considerable numbers of nonsupport and desertion cases. In 12 of these emphasis was placed on unofficial adjustment, and in most of the others some work was done along this line, either by the court or by a cooperating private agency. Some courts had developed a comprehensive technique for this kind of service, including individual interviews with the complainant and defendant, home visits, and joint interviews, with agreements to pay through the court in many cases. Such agreements were approved by the judge in the New York and Philadelphia courts, and under the law these had all the force of official court orders. Needless to say, the services of attorneys in these cases were not required, though defendants were often represented by attorneys. All that was necessary to initiate action was for the mother to tell her story to an officer of the court.

Eight courts included in the study had divorce jurisdiction. In three of these considerable emphasis was placed on conciliation service in divorce cases, either before or after the filing of the petition or libel. In a fourth court two probation officers gave full time to

---

[10] Juvenile courts receive many complaints which are regarded by some judges as not requiring formal judicial treatment or official determination of the status of the child. For instance, complaints of trivial offenses can often be settled with a warning to the child, and it would involve needless expense for the court and trouble for all concerned to insist on service of notice and formal hearing. As the juvenile court becomes well established in the community parents and others bring to the attention of its officers problems of conduct or of environment which call merely for advice or for direction to the social agency best equipped to handle the difficulty. In addition to giving advice which does not involve assuming responsibility for the child, many courts make a practice of supervising children whose parents desire them to have the benefit of such oversight and guidance without the formality of hearing and of determination of delinquency. (Juvenile Courts at Work, p. 109.)

adjusting domestic controversies of various kinds, but this work was not closely related to the divorce business of the court.

All or practically all the juvenile cases were investigated in most of the courts having juvenile jurisdiction. Sometimes investigations were not made in unofficial delinquency cases. In one court the investigations in many juvenile cases were made by police officers. In some courts investigations were not made in all juvenile cases; one usually postponed home investigations until after the child had been placed on probation. The investigation varied from a few items entered on a small card to complete investigations reviewed by the chief probation officer or other supervisory officer. In several courts juvenile cases were not cleared with the social-service exchange as a matter of routine.

All but 3 of the 19 courts (not including 2 courts serving rural counties) dealing with considerable numbers of desertion and nonsupport cases made some attempt to obtain social histories in these cases, but 4 courts usually limited the investigation to office interviews, sometimes supplemented by verification of earnings and by histories obtained from social agencies knowing the families. One of these courts consulted the social-service exchange in all cases; another consulted the exchange in cases in which warrants were issued. Ten courts made outside investigations in all cases, in all official cases, or in many cases, and another court made them in cases requiring extradition and in probation cases after the defendant had been placed on probation. A twelfth court made investigations in cases in which differing statements as to earnings were made by husband and wife and in some other cases, and consulted the social-service exchange in all official cases after court hearing. The investigations varied from those in which little history was recorded to those in which comprehensive studies of the family history, economic conditions, present difficulty, and care of the children were made.

Investigations in divorce cases include those made to prevent collusive divorce and social investigations made primarily to determine what the provision should be, through custody and alimony orders, for the welfare of the children. The latter type of investigation involves determination of the parents' fitness to have custody of the children, their financial ability, and arrangements that can be made for avoiding the conflicts with reference to the children's care, education, and guidance often incident to divorce or separation and frequently disastrous in their effects on the children.

In four of the eight courts having divorce jurisdiction investigations in divorce cases were not usually made, though in one court the judge ordered investigation if he was in doubt concerning the custody of the children; one court obtained fairly comprehensive information through office interviews; and three made investigations that included home visits. One of the courts not making investigations had formerly made them in all cases, covering chiefly the character and reputation of the parents and the alleged grounds for divorce; another had made them in cases involving children under the age of 14 years, covering the condition of the children and the arrangements that should be made for their care but not covering the grounds for divorce. In the former court a later judge had discontinued the practice; in the latter the policy of making investigations had been abandoned, except in case of special need, because the probation officer who had made the investigations had resigned and his successor's work in that field had been unsatisfactory. One of the three courts making investigations that included home visits made them in all divorce cases; another made them in uncontested divorce cases and in cases involving children; and the third made them in cases involving minor children. In two courts the investigation covered the causes of divorce, though in one of these the emphasis was being placed increasingly on the care of the children,[11] and in the third court it was concerned primarily with the condition of the children and the provision that should be made for their care.

Few courts had made adequate provision for physical and mental examination of either children or adults. Special child-guidance clinic or psychiatric service was available to 6 of the 20 courts with juvenile jurisdiction for which information on this point was obtained (not including courts serving rural counties). In some of the other courts such service was available for a limited number of cases, and some provided facilities for psychological testing without psychiatric study. A full-time psychologist was on the staff of one of these courts.

In a few courts facilities for physical and mental examinations were available for nonsupport and desertion cases when need was indicated. Three courts were parts of a municipal-court organization with a medical and psychiatric department in which physical and mental examinations were made. In one of these courts it was said that in nonsupport and desertion cases the wives and children of the defendants as well as the defendants themselves were sometimes referred to the psychiatric department.

HEARINGS AND ORDERS

4. *Hearings should be held promptly, and unnecessary publicity and formality should be avoided.*

Sufficient resources should be available for home supervision or for institutional care, so that in disposing of each case the court may fit the treatment to the individual needs disclosed.

Juvenile hearings were conducted informally in all the courts having juvenile jurisdiction.[12] The general public was excluded from all juvenile hearings, but in some courts a considerable number of persons—staff members, representatives of social agencies, and visitors—were present.

Most of the courts with jurisdiction over nonsupport and desertion cases, illegitimacy cases, and cases of contributing to the delinquency or dependency of children conducted the hearings in a simple and informal manner unless the cases were contested or unless jury trials were demanded. As a rule, persons not concerned in the cases were not present. Some courts, however, conducted hearings in a formally arranged court room, and all persons interested in cases to

---

[11] Investigations in this court were condemned severely by a committee appointed by the bar association to inquire into the legal status and activities of the investigators of the courts of domestic relations. The reports of the investigators were criticized as including hearsay evidence, coming between attorneys and clients, and assuming undue authority. It was stated that although the condition of the children was inquired into, the investigations concerned mainly the grounds for divorce. (See Report of Committee Appointed to Inquire into the Legal Status and Activities of the Investigators of the Courts of Domestic Relations, St. Louis Bar Association, Oct. 8, 1923.) Thereafter, although the practice of making investigations continued, the investigators curtailed their work in certain directions; but by 1929 the services connected with the adjustment of domestic difficulties before filing of petitions had been resumed.

[12] In the New York City court each case had two hearings, the first being conducted more formally than the second.

be heard during the session were present, as were spectators in some instances. In these courts the cases involving especially difficult testimony, such as illegitimacy cases, were sometimes heard in the judge's private office, and some of the court rooms were so arranged that the spectators were at a distance from the bench and could not hear proceedings conducted in low tones.

In one of the courts having jurisdiction over divorce cases the divorce hearings were conducted in a small, informally arranged room with few persons in attendance, and in another they were conducted in a small uncrowded court room. In six courts they were conducted in ordinary court rooms, the sessions of one part of one of these courts being held in a large crowded room, under conditions no better than those prevailing in divorce courts where no attempt at special organization for domestic-relations work had been made. The court that held public hearings under undesirable conditions had a rule providing for chamber hearings in the discretion of the court, with the consent of the parties; and reports of the proceedings in such chamber hearings were not given to the public. The rule in this court further provided for cooperative arrangements with the press looking toward the elimination of newspaper publicity in divorce cases, except for bare recital of filing of suits, grounds alleged, and decrees granted.

The inadequacy of the resources for constructive supervision of probationers at the disposal of most of the courts has been indicated in the discussion of the probation staff. Facilities for caring for children who had to be provided for outside their own homes usually were inadequate in some respects, a situation prevailing in most juvenile courts throughout the country.

The courts having jurisdiction over nonsupport used probation or its equivalent [13] in these cases, the defendants often being required to give security for compliance with the order of the court. In a number of communities 50 cents or more a day was paid for the support of families of defendants sentenced to the workhouse or to hard labor. The highest payment per diem provided was in Norfolk and Richmond, Va., where families of prisoners sentenced to labor on the roads received from 50 cents to $1 a day for the wife and 25 cents additional for each child, the maximum amount being $1.75.

In some courts—that in Chicago, for example—probation was not used in illegitimacy cases, and no constructive supervision was given except through cooperating private agencies. In Boston, on the other hand, the procedure was criminal and probation could be ordered, and constructive case work was done over long periods with defendants and with mothers and children.

PROBATIONARY SUPERVISION

5. *A definite plan for constructive work, even though it be tentative, should be made and recorded in each case and should be checked up at least monthly in conference with the chief probation officer or other supervisor.*

Reporting, when rightly safeguarded, is a valuable part of supervision, but it should never be made a substitute for more constructive methods of case work. Frequent home visits are essential to effective supervision,

---

[13] Sometimes the defendant was placed on parole under suspended sentence, sometimes simply under court order to support.

knowledge of the assets and liabilities of the family, and correction of unfavorable conditions.

Reconstructive work with the family should be undertaken whenever necessary, either by the probation officer himself or in cooperation with other social agencies. Whenever other agencies can meet particular needs their services should be enlisted.

Provision should be made by the court for collection of orders in non-support and illegitimacy cases, and for assistance, when necessary, in the collection of alimony orders.

For the 21 courts with juvenile jurisdiction included in the study information was obtained concerning methods of probationary supervision in children's cases: In 4 of these courts little attempt was made to give intensive supervision in these cases, though 1 selected a few of the most urgent cases for probationary supervision, and in 2 of them it was not even possible to ascertain the number of active cases on probation.[14] In only a few of the courts was fairly intensive work done in children's cases, including the formulation of a plan which was reviewed at intervals by the judge or a probation officer, frequent home visits, and enlistment of the cooperation of outside agencies to meet the needs of the children and their families. Some of the courts were doing the most thorough case work possible in view of the large numbers of cases under the supervision of each probation officer. The reporting system was usually relied upon, at least in boys' cases. Nearly all the courts stated that the aim was to make home visits monthly, and some of them attempted to visit more often, but pressure of work prevented frequent visits in many instances. Cooperation with social agencies was also generally stated to be the practice.

Fourteen of the group of 19 courts exercising jurisdiction in non-support and desertion cases attempted to give probationary supervision, though in many of them constructive case work was impossible in the majority of cases because of the heavy case loads carried by the probation officers. Five of these 14 formulated definite plans in the beginning of the probation period, and usually required reports from the probationers (one requiring them under exceptional circumstances only), made an effort to visit the families monthly, semi-monthly, or more often, and enlisted the cooperation of social agencies in meeting special needs.[15] Nine of the 14 courts gave some probationary supervision but were unable to give much intensive service. They made some home visits, referred the families to social or health agencies if special problems existed, and kept in touch with probationers through reports, usually in connection with payment of orders to support. In one court all such cases were supervised by a private organization. The remaining courts in this group attempted practically no case work with the families of probationers, limiting their service mostly to collection of the amounts ordered.

The eight courts having divorce jurisdiction gave little or no follow-up supervision in divorce cases involving children. Such supervision, given in some cases by one court, had been discontinued for a time as a result of adverse criticism by the bar association, and was later resumed to some extent.[16]

---

[14] Later information for two of these courts indicated some improvement.
[15] Two of these courts, in Essex County, N. J., were served by the same probation departmen t.
[16] See footnote 11, p. 44.

Information on methods of collecting money ordered by the court for the support of probationers' families was obtained for the courts studied that exercised jurisdiction in cases of nonsupport and desertion. Payments were made through the cashier's office, the clerk's office, a special auditing department, or the probation department; and for one court through the overseers of the poor. Some courts required the mothers to call in person for their money, and some mailed the checks. In several courts a careful system of checking the regularity of payments and sending notices to men delinquent in payments had been developed; in others the initiative in following up delinquent accounts rested with the mothers, assistance being given by the courts when complaints were received. A collection fee of about 10 cents a week was charged in one court.

Alimony ordered in divorce cases was paid through tne court or probation office in five of the eight courts having divorce jurisdiction. In a sixth the alimony usually was paid through the court, and a seventh gave assistance in collecting delinquent accounts when complaints were made. The eighth court gave no assistance whatever in this matter; if payments were in arrears, the wife had to employ a lawyer to represent her in civil proceedings or to start a criminal action for nonsupport in another court. In one court the payments were made to a probation officer, who then sent out checks to the women. This officer kept record of the accounts and followed up delinquent accounts by letter.

Most of the eight courts dealing with illegitimacy cases [17] had the payments ordered in such cases made through the court in the same way in which payments were made in nonsupport cases. Case work with mothers and children was attempted in three courts, though in one the case load was extremely heavy; and a fourth had a comprehensive program for the care of children born out of wedlock through aid to expectant and nursing mothers and other measures. In one court the cases came through the overseers of the poor, and no social-service work was attempted by the court. Except for reference to social agencies and hospitals no case work in illegitimacy cases was done in the remaining three courts.

RECORD SYSTEM

6. *Every court should have a record system which provides for the necessary legal records and for social records covering the investigation of the case and the work accomplished. The records of investigation should include all the facts necessary to a constructive plan of treatment. The records of supervision should show the constructive case work planned, attempted, and accomplished, and should give a chronological history of the supervisory work.*

In the majority of the courts included in the study the social records did not meet the standards specified in either juvenile or adult cases. The records of supervision were as a rule less complete than the records of investigation.

---

[17] Excluding those dealing only with an occasional case, in one of which illegitimacy cases were included in the general nonsupport jurisdiction of the court.

EXTENT OF COURTS' CONFORMITY TO STANDARDS

The extent to which the organization and procedure of the courts included in the study conformed to the standards outlined may be stated as follows:

1. In a majority of the communities whose courts were studied the establishment of family courts brought cases involving family problems to the consideration of judges who regarded this work as a specialty and who were sincerely interested in developing better standards. This situation did not exist, however, in some of the courts, especially the domestic-relations courts without juvenile jurisdiction, in which the periods of the judges' service were usually very short.

2. In a majority of the courts probation officers were appointed from eligible lists established through competitive examinations. Salaries were markedly inadequate in 13 of the 20 probation departments serving large cities included in the study for which information on this point was obtained. Not many probation officers had adequate preparatory training and experience, and the probation departments of all but five or six courts were so understaffed that the officers were carrying excessively heavy case loads and could not give enough attention to the cases intrusted to them. Officers supervising adults were usually responsible for a much larger number of probationers than were officers supervising juveniles.

3. In most of the courts considerable emphasis was placed on unofficial adjustment in nonsupport and other domestic-relations cases, as well as in juvenile cases; and a comprehensive techinque had been worked out in some courts. Conciliation service in divorce cases had been relatively less developed. The majority of courts made field investigations in some of or all the nonsupport and desertion cases, and a few made thorough studies; husbands and wives involved in nonsupport cases were not given physical or mental examinations except in occasional instances or if the need for examination was obvious. Field investigations were made in divorce cases in three of the eight courts having divorce jurisdiction.

4. Court proceedings in nonsupport and desertion cases and other domestic-relations cases (excluding divorce) were for the most part simple and informal, and persons not concerned in the cases were not usually present. In some courts, however, these conditions did not prevail. Little improvement had been made in divorce hearings except in two or three courts.

5. In only a few of the courts having juvenile jurisdiction for which information was obtained concerning probationary supervision in children's cases was even fairly intensive work done in these cases. Methods of collecting money through the court in nonsupport and desertion cases had been rather well developed, though in some courts no follow-up of delinquent accounts was made as a matter of routine. Probationary supervision was attempted by 14 of the 19 courts exercising jurisdiction in nonsupport and desertion cases, but inadequate staff in most of them made intensive work difficult or impossible. Little or no follow-up supervision was given in divorce cases involving children, though assistance in collecting alimony was usually available.

6. Social records in most courts did not give an adequate picture of the problems involved and the work accomplished.

EFFECT OF FAMILY-COURT ORGANIZATION ON JUVENILE-COURT WORK

One of the questions frequently raised in discussions of the advisability of consolidating in one court the jurisdiction over juvenile cases and certain types of adult cases is the effect that such consolidation may have upon the juvenile work of the court. It is argued that the original purpose of the juvenile court was separation of children's cases from adult cases in order to avoid contacts between children and adult offenders, to remove the stigma connected with bringing children to a court which also deals with criminal cases, and—of special importance—to permit the court to center all its attention on the juvenile problem. On the other hand, those advocating the consolidation in one court of children's cases, cases of adults offending against children, cases of nonsupport and desertion, and cases of divorce are impressed with the desirability of enabling the court dealing with children to dispose of related problems that closely affect their welfare and to extend the safeguards of the juvenile court to children who must appear as witnesses in cases against adults.

In the study of the Ohio courts special attention was given to these considerations. So far as could be observed the only serious difficulty involved in the exercise of the extensive jurisdiction that these courts possessed was the overloading of the judge with divorce cases. The proportion of the judge's time devoted to divorce business was naturally much greater than the proportion that the divorce cases bore to the total number of cases dealt with, inasmuch as all divorce cases were heard by the judge, whereas many of the other cases (especially in Hamilton County, Ohio) were handled unofficially by the probation department. Contested divorce cases also occupied a very much longer time than cases of any other type. Three of the four Ohio courts studied were devoting three and a half or four of the five and a half working days of the week to the divorce business of the court, and the fourth (that in Mahoning County) was giving two and a half days to it.

The organizing of the St. Louis domestic-relations court had practically no effect on the work of the juvenile court, as the juvenile division was entirely separate from the domestic-relations division. The juvenile court of Jefferson County (Birmingham), Ala., had been weakened by the organizing of the domestic-relations court, as the law provided for dual control by the two judges, but this situation was corrected by making provision for a single judge. (See p. 36.) The chief probation officer, acting as referee, heard some of the children's cases, but both the judge and the chief probation officer were overburdened. Juvenile-court work in New York State and in Virginia was greatly strengthened by the legislation that had been enacted. As has been pointed out (p. 37), the New York children's courts were proceeding cautiously in the exercise of adult jurisdiction. In most of the juvenile courts with broad jurisdiction the adult jurisdiction had developed gradually, and as a result there had been no disorganization of the juvenile work. The adult jurisdiction of the Philadelphia municipal court had little effect on the juvenile work, as the juvenile work and the domestic-relations work were done by separate divisions. The juvenile division had the services of the medical department, the central record bureau, the statistical division, and other service divisions maintained by the court.

In courts in which the combined juvenile and adult business is not too heavy for one judge and the juvenile work alone would not occupy his full time, the combination of juvenile and adult jurisdiction has enabled the judge to devote all his time to problems connected with child and family welfare. With a few exceptions probation officers already engaged in juvenile work have not been burdened with adult cases as a result of the organization of family courts, the juvenile case loads generally being lighter than the adult case loads, as has been pointed out. But in many communities the juvenile court was greatly in need of a larger, better-organized staff, and it may be questioned whether the time, effort, and money devoted to domestic-relations cases should not have been directed first of all toward improving the service rendered in children's cases. In some communities juvenile-court work undoubtedly has been damaged through the effect the family-court movement has had upon public opinion. It is a mistake to regard the juvenile court as a task accomplished, as a foundation upon which to rear the structure of a family court, before the juvenile court has been given sufficient attention and intelligent criticism to enable it to fulfill its aims

FUNDAMENTAL CONSIDERATIONS IN THE EXTENSION OF THE NEW JUDICIAL TECHNIQUE

SAFEGUARDING THE JUVENILE COURT AND CONSOLIDATING THE GAINS MADE

The family-court movement has been in large part an outgrowth of the juvenile court. It has been the result of practical experience which has demonstrated to judges, lawyers, and social workers that problems of child welfare and of family welfare are inextricably intertwined and that the new technique is needed in dealing with certain types of family problems. Obviously the welfare of the child is at stake not only in a delinquency or neglect proceeding but also in a nonsupport proceeding against the father, in an action for the legal separation or divorce of his parents, or in a proceeding to establish the child's paternity. The child, in fact, is the primary reason for the concern of the public with the adults involved in such situations.

In developing the new judicial technique it is important to consolidate the gains made in dealing with certain aspects of the problem which have been attacked first before attempting to cover other sectors. The ideas underlying the juvenile court have been adopted almost universally, but the fact that a legislative body has enacted a principle does not mean that the principle has yet been put into wholly effective operation. Many rural communities and small towns throughout the country have no facilities for dealing with children in need of the protection that a juvenile court can give. Even in many of the larger cities the juvenile court still has an inadequate staff, lacks the means for intensive study of the child, and obtains results chiefly through the method of trial and error instead of through scientific study followed by treatment adapted to the needs discovered.

The primary importance of children's cases has been recognized by the law itself, which has always been peculiarly interested in them. The necessity of treating juvenile cases adequately is universally recognized by legal thinkers, educators, and social economists. The new judicial technique is well adapted to the handling of juvenile cases, and it has been shown that the juvenile court which is based upon that technique can live up to the expectations of its founders. Entirely apart from the relative importance of adult cases and of juvenile cases, if the new machinery and the new technique are not properly fulfilling their existing functions in children's cases, it can hardly be expected that new functions will be performed better.

If the personnel qualified to administer these delicate questions of family relations is insufficient, either in caliber or in number, to handle adults as well as children, questions of domestic relations involving adults should not be allowed to interfere with the work of the juvenile court. It is far better that justice be administered properly and thoroughly in one field, particularly when that field is very important, than that new courts try to do too much and as a consequence do nothing well.

Hopes and aspirations should not be allowed to obscure facts. The condition of the juvenile court is a fact, ascertainable in each jurisdiction in which it functions. The greatest service that can be performed to-day by those interested in the administration of justice in domestic relations is to see that the juvenile court in their community is properly organized and is properly carrying on its functions. For the most part, except in rural communities, the initial effort of founding juvenile courts is past, but there remains to be done the equally important work of making the juvenile court as stabilized and as competent in its field as are most courts of common law. That work should be given right of way.

This is not to say that the juvenile court necessarily must be continued as a separate court, nor that the extension of the new technique to cases of adults is necessarily inadvisable; but every question of change of court organization or of court technique with respect to domestic relations involving the juvenile court should be considered first of all in the light of its probable effect upon the handling of children's cases.

FLEXIBILITY OF PROGRAM

The point of view indicated in the preceding section would lead to different results in almost every jurisdiction. In some cases it would lead to temporary abandonment of proposals to consolidate in one court all cases of domestic relations and to revitalizing of interest in the work of the juvenile court. In other cases, where the material for the application of the new technique is better and more plentiful, it might lead to the establishment of an omnibus court that, depending largely upon the volume of business, would operate either as a unit or in two parts, one of which would deal with cases involving adults and the other with cases involving children. In still other cases it might lead to two separate courts—a domestic-relations court and a juvenile court.

In none of the communities whose courts were studied has there been developed a family court that exercises complete, exclusive, riginal jurisdiction over cases of all types included in the study. Attempts at consolidation have succeeded, here with reference to one aspect of the problem and there with reference to another; but in a number of communities the establishment of a family court has not eliminated overlapping jurisdictions. For instance, two different courts still hear nonsupport cases in some communities in which family courts have been established. In such communities it is possible without additional legislation to effect further consolidation through court rule, agreement among prosecuting authorities, and increasing public knowledge of the function of the family court.

One of the outstanding results of this study is the sharp realization that there can be no nation-wide formula for the legal adjustment of family problems. Local conditions vary, and the population of one State differs in both number and character from the population of another. Domestic relations themselves differ with geography. In a seaport city with a large foreign population, for example, the conflicts between parents raised in foreign lands and their children brought up in new surroundings may crowd the court; in an agricultural community conflicts may arise from dissatisfaction with rural life on the part of the younger generation. In one community there may be an excellent judge and a large and efficient probation staff supported by a group of lawyers and social workers who see that proper standards are maintained in domestic-relations courts; in another these vital elements may be absent. Fifty years ago the people of one State may have guessed better than the people of another as to the kind of court structure that the constitution should impose upon future generations; the court structure even of municipalities is often embodied in the State constitution or entrenched behind the ramparts of politics. All these variations and many more came to light in this study. In evaluating the work of family courts it must always be remembered, first, that generalizations are unsafe; second, that the problem of the law, the family, and the court can never be solved adequately unless local conditions are kept constantly in mind.

ADEQUACY OF PERSONNEL

Most of the statements favoring the establishment of family courts dwell on the advantages that should be derived from their foundation or extension; comparatively little reference is made to the handicaps under which such courts must labor without sufficient and adequately trained personnel. Yet without such personnel a family court may be worse than useless; instead of being an administrator of justice in the light of modern conditions and scientific study it may degenerate into an unwarranted and harmful meddler in domestic affairs.

It is useless to talk about making the administration of justice a process of social engineering if the first principle of both engineering and the administration of justice is not observed—supplying the tools with which the work must be done. It is futile to attempt to adapt law to an industrialized society unless the instruments of law are organized with the efficiency that industry itself has attained. One probation worker can no more handle 150 cases of juvenile delinquency adequately than a judge can adjudicate 150 points of law simultaneously. The new judicial technique, whatever advantages it may have, does not possess the ability to cure by waving a magic wand.

A scientific attitude toward the administration of the law of domestic relations implies recognition of the fact that most family courts are poorly equipped to fulfill the purposes for which they were founded. As quickly as possible the standards previously set forth for judges and probation officers (see p. 38) should be reached in existing courts, and enlarged powers should not be conferred nor new courts created until careful plans for administration have been formulated.

UTILIZATION AND STIMULATION OF COMMUNITY RESOURCES

If it is to be successful a family court must utilize to the fullest extent other social agencies in the community. Not only does a large part of the work carried on by family courts belong functionally as much to these other agencies as it does to the courts, but in many cases the outside groups are able to supply service that the court is not equipped to give.

Of course the outside agencies may have the same shortcomings as the family courts. They may not be properly oriented among themselves, and as a consequence their work may overlap as much as the old courts are accused of overlapping. Or, as this study discloses, the family court and the outside organizations may themselves overlap in their endeavors. Once more the difficulty of formulating a general rule without reference to local conditions becomes apparent.

If the resources of the community do not meet the needs discovered it is the duty of the court to inform the public from time to time and to cooperate to the fullest extent with other agencies in obtaining more satisfactory provision. For example, sufficient resources for foster-home care and institutional care of children may be lacking. Facilities for family-welfare service, including help in budget planning and in adjusting various family difficulties, may be inadequate. Provision for diagnosis and treatment of mothers and fathers incapacitated by physical or mental disability may be insufficient. For obtaining these and many other items of an adequate community program the court shares responsibility with other organizations.

RESEARCH AND THE DEVELOPMENT OF SCIENTIFIC METHODS

Few courts of any type are equipped to do research work. Child-guidance clinics working with juvenile courts in a number of communities have been accumulating information concerning the causes and methods of treatment of delinquency which is invaluable as a basis for developing programs of treatment and prevention.[1] In the field of marital maladjustments and other domestic difficulties research is equally necessary, but as yet little has been attempted. Exceptions are the studies of men and women involved in a selected number of domestic-relations cases in the Detroit recorder's court, made by the psychopathic clinic of that court, and the intensive study and treatment of a limited number of neglect cases by the psychopathic clinic maintained in connection with the juvenile court of Detroit, also the studies of causes of marital difficulties in a group of divorce cases dealt with by the Cincinnati court.[2] Some municipal courts (as in Chicago and Philadelphia) have a psychopathic laboratory or neuropsychiatric division. However, few family courts or courts of domestic relations can be expected under present conditions to be equipped with facilities for scientific research.

As the child-guidance movement has been initiated and for the most part carried on by private effort, so might nongovernmental endeavor be directed toward the establishment of domestic-relations clinics, possibly in connection with legal-aid bureaus. These clinics should be equipped to render diagnostic service and unofficial assistance in the medical, psychiatric, and social fields to those asking help in solving difficulties connected with marital or other family relations or referred by courts for such service. Such organizations, besides being of immediate assistance to the families with which they came in contact, would make available for the first time a factual basis for programs of prevention and treatment and for measurement of the efficiency of legal and nonlegal institutions as agencies dealing with family maladjustments.[3]

---

[1] For example, the early work of Dr. William Healy and Dr. Augusta F. Bronner in connection with the Chicago juvenile court and their present work in the Judge Baker Foundation in Boston, and the work of other child-guidance clinics.

[2] See One Hundred Domestic-Relations Problems, by Helen Flinn and Arnold L. Jacoby (Mentals Hygiene, vol. 10, No. 4 (October, 1926), pp. 732–742), and Sex Antagonism in Divorce, by Hornell Hart and M. E. McChristie (Proceedings of the National Probation Association, 1922, pp. 135–141).

[3] The tendency in the field of the physical sciences is also applicable to sciences dealing with human behavior and social organization, though its development is naturally much more difficult in the latter field. "Experts recognize that the day of arbitrary opinion is passing, that experimental research and service experience can best guide every item of the standard. With great gaps in our precise knowledge of the properties of matter and energy, empiricism still rules; but its domain narrows as research gives us measured data based on scientific methods." Standards Year Book, 1927, p. 6. U. S. Bureau of Standards Miscellaneous Publication No. 77. Washington, 1927.

APPLICATION OF THE NEW TECHNIQUE TO SPECIFIED TYPES OF CASES

In the review of various considerations applicable to the treatment of cases of domestic relations when they come into contact with law these cases in the main have been treated generically. At this point, however, the law of domestic relations, apart from the treatment of juvenile delinquency and dependency, which has already been considered, can be separated into its component parts. It is important to ascertain how each group of cases relevant to this study is affected by the possibilities and limitations of the new judicial technique and court reorganization, to endeavor to fix some limits as to what courts can and should hope to accomplish in these cases, and to orient their treatment with the principle of safeguarding the juvenile court.

It is necessary in considering each type of case to bear in mind, as has been emphasized in this report, that the program for a given community must be based upon careful analysis of local conditions and adaptation of general principles to local needs. The family-court movement is still in an experimental stage, and no final statement of principles with reference to the scope of the new courts can yet be made. In fact, in this stage of development it matters little what aspects of the family problem are brought within the jurisdiction of the new courts in various localities so long as effective standards of dealing with the problems selected are developed.

In the opinion of the writers any attempt to judge the efficacy of existing courts by a standardized outline of a so-called model court would be actually detrimental. Experiments in the treatment of the different types of cases coming within the general scope of this report are greatly to be desired, and local situations must determine the parts of the problem to be attacked first. It is extremely helpful to the whole movement, for example, when a court in one locality undertakes a demonstration of what socialized treatment of nonsupport cases really involves, while a court in another community may be developing such methods of cooperation with courts having divorce jurisdiction as will insure adequate treatment of matters affecting the custody and welfare of the children involved.

In considering any particular type of case with reference to any given local situation the first question to answer is "How can adequate administrative standards be developed best in this field?" When careful study of existing conditions indicates that further advance is possible in the direction of socialized treatment of family problems certain general considerations applicable to the various subjects coming within the jurisdiction of family courts in different communities may be helpful. These will be suggested in the following paragraphs.

OFFENSES AGAINST CHILDREN

Acts or omissions of adults in regard to children come under legal cognizance in three classes of cases: Those in which an adult is

accused of a crime against a minor, those in which the adult has failed
to fulfill a duty toward a minor, and those in which the adult is
accused of causing juvenile delinquency or dependency or of tending
to cause it.

Included in the first group of cases are certain types of offenses
against minors that clearly do not require thorough investigation of
environment or need for continuous treatment, as cases in which an
adult has stolen from a minor.   In some jurisdictions all such cases
come under the family court, but it is obviously unnecessary for them
to be handled by a court whose main object is socialized treatment
of children.   Certain other offenses are more closely analogous to
the third group of cases—those in which the adult is accused of
causing or attempting to cause juvenile delinquency.   These cases
affect or have a bearing upon the child's care and development and
should be considered from the social point of view.   They include
not only cases of sex offenses against children but also certain other
types of cases covered by criminal law, such as the purchase of junk
from minors.   Some of these types of cases are usually dealt with as
contributing to delinquency and can be treated very satisfactorily in
this manner.   Whether serious sex crimes should be dealt with in the
juvenile court is a more difficult question.   The children involved
need the protection given by the absence of the atmosphere of the
criminal court and of publicity, and they usually require careful study
and treatment in order that they may be helped to recover from the
effects of the exploitation they have suffered.   Nevertheless the
accused is charged with a most serious crime and is entitled to all
the safeguards provided by the criminal law.   In any event a method
of cooperation between the juvenile court and the prosecuting authorities such as has been developed in certain jurisdictions could be
adopted immediately,[1] and the criminal court could make it an inva-
riable practice to refer the minors involved to the juvenile court for
investigation and treatment.

The second group of cases, in which an adult has failed to fulfill a
duty toward a minor, is illustrated mainly by nonsupport and desertion cases, which will be discussed in the following section.   Failure
to comply with school-attendance laws or to furnish medical care,
and other types of failure to fulfill parental obligations are dealt with
sometimes under specific charges, sometimes under the general charge
of neglect, sometimes under the charge of contributing to delinquency
or dependency.   These cases are closely related to the dependency-
and-neglect jurisdiction of the juvenile court, and they should be
dealt with by the same tribunal and receive the same socialized
treatment.

The third group of cases can be taken as excluding crimes against
children and cases of desertion and nonsupport but including all
other cases in which the adult is accused of causing or tending to
cause juvenile delinquency or dependency.   As a rule they are closely
related to some juvenile problem already before the court, and jurisdiction over them belongs properly to the juvenile or family court.
Their number is not usually so great as to place that court under
undue strain.

---

[1] See Juvenile Courts at Work, pp. 221-224.

NONSUPPORT AND DESERTION

Such offenses as nonsupport and desertion of course bear a direct relation to juvenile delinquency and dependency. They are rarely the result of a deliberate desire to violate either the law or the traditional obligations of the family. Rather they are caused by economic conditions, poverty, and physical and mental limitations. In most cases the old criminal treatment is inadequate. Nor are intermittent police-court hearings and orders to pay money much more efficacious. Nonsupport is usually an evidence of home conditions seriously detrimental to the welfare of the children. As a general rule, much more than the enforcement of the payment of support orders is necessary. Physical examination and psychiatric study of one or more members of the family, medical care, and vocational and social adjustments may be needed. In these cases of adults the new judicial technique can be most helpful if properly administered. These also are the cases in which jurisdiction is often most confused. In some localities the police court, the criminal court, the juvenile court, the family court, and a number of social agencies all attack the same family problem.

The practical difficulties, however, of treating these cases in the new way are great. The volume of such cases in the larger cities is enormous. To unload them upon the juvenile court subjects it to undue strain unless a reallocation of jurisdiction of this kind can be accompanied by a proper supplementing of the juvenile-court staff. The same comment applies to the family court having juvenile and adult jurisdiction. Establishing a separate court of domestic relations concerned mainly with nonsupport and desertion cases may be the best solution in some communities, but in view of the close interrelation between these cases and juvenile cases the absolute separation of the two classes involves certain losses.

This class of cases exemplifies the necessity of trying to do one thing well; or, if it is being done well, to assure its future before attacking new problems with inadequate tools. It is true that children's cases often can not be treated adequately without proper treatment of the adults involved, but it may be better to proceed with this handicap than to undermine the quality of all the work being done.

This of course is the negative side of the picture. Great need exists for coordinating and improving the treatment of these cases, which have so important a bearing on the preservation of the home and the welfare of the children. As rapidly as the new technique can be extended to embrace them without hampering the development of the juvenile court such action should be taken. Whether they should be placed in the juvenile court, a separate court of domestic relations, or a family court of broad jurisdiction will depend upon circumstances; but whenever the combined volume of work will not be too great for a single court that organization appears to be preferable. Within the organization specialization of service is desirable; for example, certain probation officers should devote all their time to the conduct problems of children, and others should specialize on family problems, including cases of neglect, contributing to dependency, and nonsupport.

Some experiments have been made in the extension of equity procedure to nonsupport cases. The domestic-relations division of the city court of Buffalo has been given equity powers (see p. 14), and the New York State children's court act provides for civil proceedings in nonsupport cases and specifies that a judgment of "disorderly person" shall not be necessary in making an order.[2] It has been noted that in certain jurisdictions action to compel support is brought under a contributing-to-dependency statute. Contributing to dependency may be dealt with in Colorado either as a misdemeanor or under equity procedure, and the Denver juvenile court used equity procedure in all except the most seriously contested or extradition cases of nonsupport. Some provision for informal procedure in nonsupport cases is greatly to be desired. This can be accomplished not only by vesting the court with full equity powers but also by a provision such as that existing in the Philadelphia municipal court, in which voluntary agreements are confirmed by the judge without hearing and have the force of official orders. In any event criminal procedure should always be available for cases in which full justice can not be done through voluntary agreements and for cases in which the defendant is outside the court's jurisdiction.

After the question of the court through which the new technique is to be developed has been settled the relation between the court and the other family-welfare agencies of the community remains to be considered. Here again whether intensive family rehabilitation is to be undertaken by the staff of the court or by other family-welfare agencies must be determined in accordance with local resources and local needs. Whatever division of service may be adopted it is essential that the court include on its staff experienced family-welfare workers who are able to make adequate investigations, to carry on conciliation service, to formulate plans, and to utilize the resources of the community in making them effective. Medical and psychiatric clinics also must be available to the court if effective work is to be done in this field.

ESTABLISHMENT OF PATERNITY AND ENFORCEMENT OF SUPPORT OF CHILDREN BORN OUT OF WEDLOCK

Proceedings to establish paternity and to enforce support of children born out of wedlock have many problems in common with cases of nonsupport and desertion, involving as they do the determination of the amount of support that should be ordered and the collection of support orders. They are complicated by the difficulty of establishing paternity, the necessity for testimony of a most intimate and embarassing nature, and the urgent need for social service that will help the mother to reestablish herself in the community. They are closely allied with juvenile-court problems, inasmuch as very young mothers or fathers may be already under the jurisdiction of the juvenile court as delinquent or may need the guidance that the juvenile court can give.[3] All the safeguards that can be thrown around the proceeding—such as exclusion of the general public and protection of the mother from revolting cross-examination—

[2] The 1933 law establishing the domestic-relations court for New York City provides for both equity and criminal procedure and eliminates the "disorderly" charge.
[3] In various studies it has been found that one-ninth to nearly one-fourth of the unmarried mothers were under 18 years of age, and one-eighth to more than one-fourth of the fathers were under 21. See Case Work with Unmarried Parents and Their Children, by Katharine F. Lenroot (Hospital Social Service, vol. 12, No. 2 (August, 1925), p. 70).

are greatly to be desired. Except in the largest cities, the number of cases is not so considerable as greatly to overload the juvenile or family court. As rapidly as possible jurisdiction over these cases should be placed in a socialized court having jurisdiction of juvenile cases, or cases of nonsupport and desertion, or both. An added reason for combining nonsup; ort and illegitimacy jurisdiction is the fact that in more than one-third of the States the father of a child born out of wedlock is liable under the general nonsupport and desertion law.

DIVORCE AND ANNULMENT OF MARRIAGE

GENERAL CONSIDERATIONS

As far as judicial treatment is concerned divorce cases may be divided into two parts: The determination whether or not a divorce should be granted and the proceedings after this question has been settled, including alimony and custody of children.

Some confusion of thought exists between what the substantive law of divorce should be and how the law should be administered; and one school of thought believes that, whatever the law may be, the court should go beyond its strictly judicial functions and try to reconcile the difference between the parties.

Hearings in uncontested divorce cases are perfunctory in many jurisdictions. The real cause of disagreement often is not given in such cases, and sometimes it is not even realized by the parties. Frequently evidence is taken before a master in equity. Doubtless collusion between the parties is common. In contested cases the evidence adduced is more reliable, and a greater array of facts is presented than in uncontested cases; but even in these cases the real difficulty may not be ascertained. A correct diagnosis of marital difficulties is often more a matter for doctors and psychiatrists than for lawyers. The element of sexual maladjustment is coming to be more and more recognized. This element the parties either do not comprehend or will not testify to. In most States it does not of itself constitute a ground for divorce.

Whether divorces should be made easier or harder to obtain is outside the scope of this study. It is for the legislature of each State to determine that question. No court, whether a court of equity or a family court, can or should depart from the requirements which the legislature has laid down. In other words, much of the agitation on this subject should be directed toward the substantive law and not toward the method of its administration.

It is a real question how far the new judicial technique is applicable to cases of divorce. In theory the granting or refusing of a divorce involves only one judicial act, not continuous jurisdiction; but this could be said too, in theory, of juvenile delinquency and dependency. The new method of treatment of cases by the courts is frankly, in some respects, interstitial judicial legislation. Moreover, in two respects—alimony and custody of children—divorce cases do come before the court recurrently.

Determining whether or not a divorce should be granted does not involve the exercise of magisterial discretion that juvenile cases require.

Public opinion—as reflected to some degree in the statutes—has conceded that there should be no hard and fast rules in children's cases; but with respect to the granting of divorces the statutes and the common law speak too plainly to permit doubt. Divorces are to be granted only in certain well-defined cases and under certain conditions. The court, of course, should safeguard itself as much as possible from fraud and collusion, and in many jurisdictions reform is greatly needed. The social investigator in some jurisdictions has been called upon to make field investigations to determine whether fraud exists; but in general, until the existing rules of substantive law are changed, it would seem that the new technique can not and should not be applied to the question of severing marital relations unless the welfare of children is involved.

What has been said with respect to divorce applies also to cases where annulment of marriage is sought. Here, too, the question is chiefly one of substantive law.

ALIMONY

The awarding of alimony after a divorce has been granted involves different considerations. Here there is much more scope for judicial discretion. Several alimony hearings in the same case are usual, sometimes spread over a number of years, and the system of rotation of judges in effect in many courts of equity is not conducive to the most satisfactory handling of such cases. The allowance of alimony, after determination that one of the parties is entitled to it, is really a separate matter from the granting of the divorce, and the method of treatment is different. In short, alimony hearings are much more closely allied to hearings for nonsupport and desertion than to divorce proceedings, and the new technique is intrinsically applicable to both.[4]

CUSTODY OF CHILDREN

When children are involved in a divorce case their custody and welfare become the most important aspect of the whole proceeding from the standpoint of the State; and 38 per cent of the divorces reported in the United States in 1931 involved children.[5] Here certainly the new technique not only is in order but is required for proper determination of the interests involved. Divorce proceedings conducted according to the old rules of evidence are not calculated to bring out the various considerations that should be regarded in determining custody. The problems here are closely allied to the work of the court handling juvenile cases. Indeed if they are not brought to the juvenile court in their inception they may end there in cases of juvenile dependency or delinquency. Divorce cases also are allied closely to cases of nonsupport and desertion because courts dealing with nonsupport cases deal with many families involved later in divorce proceedings. (See p. 27.)

JURISDICTION

Jurisdiction over cases of divorce generally is given to-day to the equity courts. Although a number of students of the problem

---

[4] See the Michigan law providing for a "friend of the court" to oversee the collection and expenditure of alimony orders, making nonpayment of alimony and leaving the State a felony, and providing for payment of compensation to families of men sentenced to the house of correction for default in alimony payments. (Supp. 1922 (Cahill's), secs. 11499, 11450 (1)–(6).)

[5] Marriage and Divorce, 1931, pp. 47, 48. U. S. Bureau of the Census. Washington, 1932.

believe that the same judge, or at least the same court, should pass upon all aspects of divorce questions and that this judge or court should be the one having jurisdiction in children's cases and other family cases, all the objections to this omnibus treatment that were mentioned in discussion of desertion and nonsupport can be made in this connection also.   The volume of divorce cases is very large, and some of the work of the court would be likely to suffer under present conditions.   Observations of some courts where the experiment is being tried confirms this statement.   (See p. 49.)

Can jurisdiction in divorce cases be split?   As a general rule, it is hard to see why it should not be when practical circumstances make it inadvisable to give full jurisdiction to a family court.[6]   The juvenile court, for example, could determine custody after an equity court had granted the divorce, or the equity court could send the question of custody to the juvenile court for determination, just as it sometimes sends a question to a court of law to be determined by a jury.   At the present time some divorce cases are referred informally to the juvenile court for investigation as to the interests of the children.[7] In the absence of special legislation the practice of such informal reference by the divorce court to the juvenile court should be extended. Wherever jurisdiction is placed the court should be required to have evidence as to the number, ages, and whereabouts of the children entered upon the records before a decree is granted.   In 5 per cent of the 182,203 divorces in 1931 no information was available as to whether children were involved.[8]

Alimony cases involving the support of children might be heard by the juvenile court or by a socialized court dealing with cases of nonsupport and desertion, provided it was able to handle the increased volume of business.   Where a court of general civil and criminal jurisdiction, including divorce, has a juvenile or family division, as in some Ohio counties and in Iowa and Nebraska, it might be desirable to assign to the juvenile or family division entire responsibility for divorce cases involving children, leaving other divorce cases in the general equity or chancery division.   Such an arrangement in Hamilton County, Ohio, for example, would relieve the family-court judge of a large volume of work not involving children at all.   Of course local statutory and constitutional provisions in each jurisdiction would have to be taken into account.   If possible, the court determining custody and alimony for the support of the children should have

---

[6]In this connection it is of interest to note a comment made by the executive secretary of the Pennsylvania Children's Commission: " Differing from many States, Pennsylvania has a system of separating entirely the process for hearing and granting divorces from the process of awarding custody of the children. In all divorce cases the master appointed to hear the evidence ascertains the number, ages, and whereabouts of the children of the couple, and this information undoubtedly influences his recommendation to the court with regard to the granting or refusing of the petition. Questions of custody are settled, however, by a different process. Parents are expected to make a private arrangement and decide questions with regard to the care of their children. If either parent wishes to secure the custody of a child or to make a new arrangement to which the other parent does not acquiesce, the case comes into the common-pleas court on a writ of habeas corpus, and the judge awards the custody in accordance with what the evidence indicates will be in the best interests of the child. The consideration of custody apart from divorce decrees is thought to have advantages over the system of awarding custody in connection with the decree.   It tends to keep the issues in the divorce case more clearly defined and prevents the bitterness and recrimination characteristic of divorce cases in which both parents are eager to secure the custody of the child or children."   Child Welfare Conditions and Resources in Seven Pennsylvania Counties, by Neva R. Deardorff, p. 258. U. S. Children's Bureau Publication No. 176. Washington, 1927. (Available only by purchase from the Government Printing Office.)

[7] As in Denver, Colo., where divorce cases in which children were involved were generally referred to the juvenile court for investigation.

[8] Marriage and Divorce, 1931, pp. 47, 48.

continuing jurisdiction that would permit modifications of orders from time to time as changed conditions might make such modifications necessary or desirable.

It can be argued that such a subdivision of functions would only increase the confusion of jurisdictional alignment that already exists. But if such a subdivision would result in a better handling of the cases, particularly with respect to the important question of custody of the children, that should be sufficient reason for it. An apparent conflict in theory should not obstruct an actual accomplishment.

ADOPTION AND GUARDIANSHIP

Adoption legislation is departing from the purely legal point of view—according to which adoption may be consummated by notarial act or the court is expected merely to sanction a relationship as a justice of the peace solemnizes a wedding—toward the conception of adoption as essentially a process in social case work. Thus the newer laws provide for social investigation and for a trial period in the foster home before a decree is granted, the aim being to insure the welfare of the child and to avoid unnecessary severance of natural family ties.[9]

For the administration of these modern statutes facilities for social investigation are essential, and the judge should have a sound knowledge of the general principles of child-welfare work. The number of such cases to be disposed of during a year is usually small, and in most jurisdictions it would seem desirable to assign them to the juvenile court.[10]

Guardianship may be either of the person or of property. Guardianship of the person of infants, when not created by will or deed, is akin to adoption. Proceedings for the appointment of children's personal guardians and for their removal on the ground of unfitness can best be determined by the juvenile court with its facilities for investigation, although jurisdiction in these cases is generally given to the equity courts.

Guardianship of property involves no considerations that could make the new technique applicable. Property rights of children have always been protected by the common law, supplemented by equity, and there is no reason to disturb the situation. The new courts have enough to do, and generally more than enough, in trying to adjust the more intangible problems of personality.

COMMITMENT OF MENTALLY DEFECTIVE AND INSANE CHILDREN

It is no longer believed that all feeble-minded persons (to the extent to which society is able to provide for their care) should be segregated

---

[9] See Adoption Laws in the United States, especially pp. 17–18, 20, 25–26 (U. S. Children's Bureau Publication No. 148, Washington, 1925; exhausted; available only in libraries); also Jurisdictional and Social Aspects of Adoption, by Joseph W. Newbold (Minnesota Law Review, vol. 11, No. 7 (June, 1927), pp. 605–623). The last States to discontinue adoption by notarial act and to require court action were Texas and Louisiana. (Tex., act of May 21, 1931, ch. 177, Laws of 1931, p. 300; La., act of July 7, 1932, No. 46, Laws of 1932, p. 239.)

[10] Reporting on the adoption of children in Philadelphia County, Pa., the Pennsylvania Commission Appointed to Study and Revise the Statutes of Pennsylvania Relating to Children made the following recommendations: "The annual number of adoptions is so small that if properly placed in the judicial system the administration of this service would present none of the difficulties growing out of a great volume of work in which standards of performance must be temporarily, at least, sacrificed in the interests of serving great numbers of people. It should be possible for a community of the size of Philadelphia to give adequate attention to the three or four adoptions which occur in a week. Smaller communities which have a proportionately smaller number likewise can give the matter the requisite time to do a thorough piece of work." The commission did not recommend that adoptions be placed under the juvenile court, but the need for social investigation was emphasized. Report to the General Assembly Meeting in 1925, pt. 1, pp. 133–134, Harrisburg, 1925.

in institutions.   The question of commitment of a mentally defective child to an institution involves consideration of his home conditions, his own behavior, the special educational facilities available to him, and the possibility of supervision in the community that will safe-guard his own interests and those of the public.   Obviously the mere determination of the grade of mental defect is not sufficient; the process involves social investigation as well as psychological and psychiatric study.   Moreover, feeble-minded children often come before the juvenile court as delinquents or dependents, and the court should have power to select the type of care best adapted to each child's needs.   Hence it is desirable to give the juvenile court juris-diction over these cases, which are comparatively few in number, and over the very few cases of insane children.   Already juvenile courts in 9 States and in parts of 6 others have been given exclusive or concurrent jurisdiction over at least certain classes of mentally handicapped children.   In 4 States and in part of 1 other the juvenile court has jurisdiction over such children if they are already before the court on another charge.   A tendency may be noted also to extend the jurisdiction of the juvenile court to minors who are in need of special care because of physical handicap.[11]

PUBLIC AID TO DEPENDENT CHILDREN IN THEIR OWN HOMES

Chiefly because the movement for granting public aid to dependent children in their own homes (the so-called mothers' pension movement) was in the beginning an outgrowth of the juvenile-court movement, a number of States have placed administration of this aid in the court having juvenile jurisdiction.   This function is primarily administra-tive and not judicial, and logically it should be vested in a properly equipped public department rather than in a court.   Here again local conditions may modify this generalization.

---

[11] For example, New York and Ohio legislation of 1925 (N. Y., act of Apr. 1, 1925, ch. 227, Laws of 1925, pp. 461–470; Ohio. act of Apr. 6, 1925, Laws of 1925, pp. 106–107, Code, 1930, secs. 7803, 7803–1).

CONCLUSIONS

In this examination of the child, the family, and the court certain facts have been set forth and certain opinions of the writers based upon these facts expressed. The problem is extremely complicated, and often the same set of facts may be interpreted in different ways. The general conclusions growing out of the study, as viewed by those who have had it in charge, may be stated as follows:

1. In considering the attitude of the law toward domestic relations, two factors must be kept constantly in mind: First, that law is a process of social engineering, that the organization of the society with which it deals is changing, and that it must discover and perfect new tools to fulfill its functions; second, that it is necessary to ascertain and deal with the facts, that sentimentalism is as dangerous as ignorance, and that changes in legal processes should be conditioned upon practicability.

2. Great need exists for extending the new judicial technique as rapidly as possible to matters bearing upon family relations that come within the scope of this report. This technique includes informal adjustment of cases not requiring official court action, thorough social investigation, physical and psychiatric examinations when necessary, informal hearings conducted with a minimum of publicity, and constructive supervision of probationers. Without doubt the ideals of justice can be achieved more nearly by these methods properly administered than by wholly legalistic methods of dealing with these cases.

3. Because of variation in local conditions a nation-wide formula for the adjustment of family problems coming before the courts is impossible. Wide differences exist not only in constitutional provisions and court systems but also in the degree of public interest in a social approach to legal problems involving child welfare and family life. Nevertheless, efforts of all interested groups should be directed toward the establishment and maintenance of tribunals that will have broad powers to deal with family problems.

4. The proper treatment of children's cases must be assured. If the resources of a community are inadequate to meet the needs discovered in day-by-day contact with juvenile problems it is the duty of the judge and executive officers of the staff to call public attention to the deficiencies disclosed and to cooperate with other agencies in obtaining the facilities required. The juvenile court requires continuing study, constructive criticism, and constant support by the public, whether it continues to exist as a separate court or becomes part of a court of broader jurisdiction. In general, where juvenile courts have been established they should be brought to a high standard of efficiency before an attempt is made to extend their jurisdiction further. It may be, however, that in a given situation it would be easier to obtain

adequate administrative machinery for the juvenile court if it were absorbed into a new court with broad jurisdiction, but the plan for administration should always be worked out carefully in advance.

5. The new judicial technique seems particularly applicable to nonsupport and desertion, the support of children born out of wedlock,[1] and certain offenses against children, especially contributing to dependency and delinquency. Some of the new methods, especially investigation, should be extended also to cases of adoption, guardianship of the person of children, and commitment of mentally defective children.

Divorce cases present special problems. Only a minority of divorce cases (somewhat more than one-third) involve children. Where children are concerned three questions must be decided: Severance of marital relationships, custody of children, and alimony.

The problem of ascertaining the real causes of marital difficulties and of adjusting them without resort to divorce procedure is of the most delicate nature, and at least under present conditions it is not one which courts are equipped or can reasonably be expected to become equipped to solve. The question whether or not a divorce should be granted is governed by well-defined rules of substantive law, and the new methods of procedure developed in juvenile courts do not apply. Moreover, the addition of divorce jurisdiction to the family court tends to overload it with cases not involving children.

Alimony and custody are subject to the continuing jurisdiction of the court, and the new technique of investigation and supervision is required in order to safeguard the interests involved. The possibility of vesting in the juvenile or family court jurisdiction as to divorce cases involving children, or as to custody of children and alimony for the support of children, merits careful study and experimentation.

6. Depending upon local conditions, social treatment of the cases mentioned may be developed in one unified court having also juvenile jurisdiction, in one court with separate branches for juvenile and domestic-relations work, or in separate juvenile and domestic-relations courts. Unified jurisdiction is desirable when it can be obtained without the sacrifice of more important ends.

7. Wherever jurisdiction over domestic-relations cases can be centered in one court by some working agreement on the part of the several judges such action appears to be more desirable than appeal to a legislative body, provided an adequate social-service staff can be maintained. This plan lacks the dramatic quality of the establishment of a new court, but it has the advantage of ease of accomplishment and flexibility.

---

[1] Adjustment without official court hearing should not be permitted in illegitimacy cases unless paternity is acknowledged and the settlement approved by the court as making adequate provision for the child.

8. Attempts to obtain the passage of legislation providing for the establishment of family courts or courts of domestic relations invariably should be preceded by careful study of the constitutional and statutory provisions of the State regarding courts and court systems, study of existing methods of dealing with juvenile cases and adult cases involving family problems in the locality which the proposed court would serve, and education of the public as to the need for socialized treatment of juvenile and family problems, its cost and its value.

9. Whatever jurisdiction is vested in a juvenile court, a family court, or a court of domestic relations, the following conditions are essential if it is to develop into an efficient instrument of social justice:

(a) Freedom from political influence and selection of judges and probation staff based on qualifications for the work to be performed.

(b) Ample financial support, permitting the employment at adequate salaries of a staff sufficiently large to render all the service required in each case.

(c) Recognition of the fact that the socialized treatment which the court is intended to give can be performed only by men and women fitted by nature, education, and experience to carry on the delicate tasks intrusted to them. The services of the social case worker, the physician, the psychologist, and the psychiatrist, all are necessary to the proper development of this new legal institution.

10. To supplement the work of the new courts and also to render services in courts organized along the old lines, pending the extension of the new technique, the work of legal-aid bureaus and other social agencies should be strengthened and extended.[2] The staffs of these organizations should have a proper understanding of the functions and methods of the new courts and should maintain close cooperation with them.

A valuable contribution could be made toward the understanding and solution of marital difficulties and other domestic-relations problems if funds were made available for the development in selected communities of domestic-relations clinics, staffed by psychiatrists, psychologists, and social investigators. These clinics should be available to any person desiring help in adjusting troubles growing out of the marital relation.

11. Finally, there emerge from this study the significant facts of overlapping jurisdictions, inadequacy of treatment, and other failures of law to meet the family problems coming within its scope. Public responsibility for the correction of these conditions must be fulfilled, though the types of organization selected for dealing with them may vary.

---

[2] See Report of Joint Committee for the Study of Legal Aid, by the Association of the Bar of the City of New York and Welfare Council of New York City (Brooklyn, 1928), and Growth of Legal Aid Work in the United States.

Appendix A.—FAMILY COURTS AND COURTS OF DOMESTIC RELATIONS IN THE UNITED STATES

EXCLUSIVE OF JUVENILE COURTS OF BROAD JURISDICTION

State and Territory, and name of court	Legislation authorizing court	Date of establishment of court	Type of court	Territory covered by court	Jurisdiction conferred by law or rule of court
Alabama:[1]					
Juvenile and domestic-relations court of Jefferson County	Acts of 1927, No. 225, amended by Acts of 1931, No. 451.	[2] 1923	Independent	Jefferson County (includes city of Birmingham).	Delinquent, dependent, neglected, and mentally defective children; contributing to delinquency or dependency; desertion or nonsupport; child-labor and school-attendance case assault and battery on husband, wife, or children.
Juvenile and domestic-relations court of Montgomery County.	Acts of 1927, No. 201, amended by Acts of 1931, No. 70.	[2] 1927	____do____	Montgomery County (includes city of Montgomery).	Delinquent, dependent, neglected, and mentally defective children; contributing to delinquency or dependency; desertion or nonsupport.
Hawaii:					
Division of domestic relations, first circuit court of Hawaii.	Laws of 1921, ch. 183 (Rev. Laws 1925, secs. 2236, 2237).	1921	Branch of circuit court.	Honolulu County (includes city of Honolulu).	Delinquent and dependent children; contributing to delinquency or dependency; desertion or nonsupport; bastardy; divorce, separation, separate maintenance, annulment of marriage; guardianship.
Illinois:					
Domestic-relations branch of the municipal court of Chicago.	_____	1911	Branch of municipal court.	City of Chicago____	Contributing to delinquency or dependency; desertion or nonsupport; establishment of paternity; misdemeanor offenses against minors; certain sex offenses.
Iowa:					
Juvenile court and court of domestic relations of Polk County.	Code 1931, ch. 179____	[2] 1924	Branch of district court.[3]	Polk County (includes city of Des Moines).	Delinquent, dependent, neglected, and mentally defective children; contributing to delinquency or dependency; divorce; guardianship; adoption; mothers' aid.
Massachusetts:					
Municipal court of Boston, domestic-relations sessions.	_____	1912	Branch of municipal court.	Central district of Boston (10 wards).	Stubborn children 17 to 21 years of age; desertion or nonsupport; assault and battery on husband, wife, or children; establishment of paternity; school-attendance cases.
District court of Springfield, juvenile and domestic-relations sessions.	_____	1914	____do____	City of Springfield, also West Springfield and 5 other towns.	Delinquent, neglected, and wayward children; stubborn children under 21 years of age; contributing to delinquency; desertion or nonsupport; assault and battery and drunkenness involving husband and wife or children; establishment of paternity; school-attendance cases.

[1] An Alabama law of 1931 (No. 401) creating a court of domestic relations for Mobile County was held unconstitutional. See footnote 23, p. 17.

[2] Formerly a juvenile court.

[3] The juvenile court, although technically an independent court, is in fact a branch of the district court, presided over by district-court judges.

FAMILY COURTS AND COURTS OF DOMESTIC RELATIONS IN THE UNITED STATES—Continued

State and Territory, and name of court	Legislation authorizing court	Date of establishment of court	Type of court	Territory covered by court	Jurisdiction conferred by law or rule of court
Missouri: Court of domestic relations of St. Louis.	Laws of 1921, p. 225 (Supp. 1927, sec. 2634a).	1921	Branch of circuit court.	City of St. Louis	Delinquent, neglected, and mentally defective children; certain offenses of minors over 17; adoption; divorce; separate maintenance, annulment of marriage; civil actions relating to care, custody, or control of children not connected or associated with divorce or separate maintenance; child-labor and school-attendance cases.
Nebraska: Juvenile court and court of domestic relations of Douglas County.		1921	Branch of district court.	Douglas County (includes city of Omaha).	Delinquent, neglected, dependent, and mentally defective children; desertion or nonsupport; divorce, separate maintenance custody of children involved in divorce; mothers' aid.
New Jersey: Family court of Newark.	Laws of 1921, ch. 327, amended by Laws of 1924, ch. 252 (Cum. Supp. 1911–1924, secs. 160–213).	1921	Independent	City of Newark	Contributing to delinquency or dependency; desertion or nonsupport; misdemeanor offenses against children; preliminary hearing of assault and battery involving husband and wife; fornication and adultery in cases in which indictment and jury trial are waived; establishment of paternity
Juvenile and domestic-relations courts throughout the State.	Laws of 1929, ch. 157	1929	Independent	Each county in State (2 or more counties may combine after special election).	Delinquent, dependent, neglected, mentally defective, and truant children; contributing to delinquency or dependency; desertion or nonsupport; establishment of paternity; school-attendance cases; mothers' aid.
New York: Domestic-relations court of the city of New York.	Laws of 1933, ch. 482	⁴1933	...do...	The 5 boroughs of Greater New York.	Delinquent, neglected, and mentally defective children, also contributing to the delinquency or dependency of such children and children held as material witnesses and their adoption and guardianship; physically handicapped minors; truants; wayward minors; desertion or nonsupport; misdemeanor offenses against children; orders of protection (in effect limited separation) where children are involved.
Domestic-relations court of Buffalo.	Laws of 1924, ch. 424	⁵1910	Branch of city court.	City of Buffalo	Wayward minors 16 to 21 years of age; desertion or nonsupport; disorderly persons; all criminal business related to domestic relations or family affairs.

North Carolina:[6]					
Domestic-relations court of Mecklenburg County.	Laws of 1929, ch. 343	1929	Independent	Mecklenburg County (includes city of Charlotte).	Delinquent, dependent, and neglected children; mentally defective children who are delinquent, dependent, or neglected; contributing to delinquency or dependency; misdemeanor offenses against children; desertion or nonsupport; establishment of paternity; school-attendance cases; also preliminary investigation and recommendation in adoption cases and in divorce cases involving children.
Ohio:					
Franklin County court of common pleas, division of domestic relations.	Laws of 1927, p. 58 (Code 1930, sec. 1352–7).	1929	Branch of court of common pleas.	Franklin County (includes city of Columbus).	
Hamilton County court of common pleas, division of domestic relations, juvenile court, and marital relations.	Laws of 1914, first special session, p. 176 (Code 1930, sec. 1639), amended by Laws of 1931, p. 50.	1914	----do----	Hamilton County (includes city of Cincinnati).	Delinquent, neglected, dependent, and crippled children; mentally defective children who are delinquent, dependent, or neglected; contributing to delinquency or dependency; desertion or nonsupport; misdemeanor offenses against children; establishment of paternity; divorce; child-labor and school-attendance cases; mothers' aid.
Lucas County court of common pleas, division of domestic relations.	Laws of 1923, p. 157 (Code 1930, sec. 1532–6).	1924	----do----	Lucas County (includes city of Toledo).	(The jurisdiction in these 7 Ohio courts is the same except that divorce is not specifically granted to the Summit County division of domestic relations but is assigned to this division by the court of common pleas; the Lucas County division of domestic relations has exclusive jurisdiction over bastardy proceedings; and the Montgomery County division of domestic relations has concurrent jurisdiction over all criminal matters.)
Mahoning County court of common pleas, division of domestic relations.	Laws of 1917, p. 721 (Code 1930, sec. 1532–4).	1918	----do----	Mahoning County (includes city of Youngstown).	
Montgomery County court of common pleas, division of domestic relations.	Laws of 1915, p. 424 (Code 1930, sec. 1532–1).	1917	----do----	Montgomery County (includes city of Dayton).	
Stark County court of common pleas, division of domestic relations.	Laws of 1927, p. 95 (Code 1930, sec. 1532–8).	1929	----do----	Stark County (includes city of Canton).	
Summit County court of common pleas, division of domestic relations.	Laws of 1917, p. 703 (Code 1930, sec. 1532–5).	1919	----do----	Summit County (includes city of Akron).	
Oklahoma [7]					
Oregon:					
Department of domestic relations in the circuit court for Multnomah County.	Code 1930, secs. 28–845 through 28–855, 33–601 through 33–616.	[8]1929	Branch of circuit court.	Multnomah County (includes city of Portland).	Delinquent, neglected, dependent, and mentally defective children; contributing to delinquency or dependency; nonsupport; adoption; divorce; provision of medical and surgical treatment for sick or deformed indigent children.

4 Formerly the independent children's court of New York City and the New York City family courts (branches of the magistrates' courts). See footnote 7, p. 33.

5 Established by rule of court in 1910.

6 A law of 1931 authorized a domestic-relations court in Forsyth County, N. C., which includes the city of Winston-Salem, but no such court had been established by 1933. See footnote 15, p. 15.

7 A law of 1925 (ch. 128) applicable to Oklahoma and Tulsa Counties, Okla., authorized the creation of family courts, but no such courts had been established by 1933. See footnote 23, p. 17.

8 Formerly an independent court of domestic relations. See p. 15.

FAMILY COURTS AND COURTS OF DOMESTIC RELATIONS IN THE UNITED STATES—Continued

State and Territory, and name of court	Legislation authorizing court	Date of establishment of court	Type of court	Territory covered by court	Jurisdiction conferred by law or rule of court
Pennsylvania: Domestic-relations division of the municipal court of Philadelphia.		1914	Branch of municipal court.	City of Philadelphia.	Desertion or nonsupport.
Tennessee [9]					
Virginia: Juvenile and domestic-relations courts throughout the State.	Laws of 1922, chs. 481, 482, 483, (Code 1924, secs. 1945, 1953–a).	[10] 1922	Independent	Each county and each city (may combine by special agreement).	Delinquent, dependent, neglected, and mentally defective children; contributing to delinquency or dependency; desertion or nonsupport; misdemeanor offenses against children; misdemeanor offenses of one member of family against another; persons who knowingly contribute to marital disruption of home; child-labor and school-attendance cases.
West Virginia: [11] Domestic-relations court of Cabell County.	Acts of 1921, ch. 168	1921	do	Cabell County (includes city of Huntington).	Delinquent, dependent, neglected, and mentally defective children; contributing to delinquency or dependency; desertion or nonsupport; misdemeanor offenses against children; divorce, separate maintenance, annulment of marriage; adoption; school-attendance cases.

[9] A juvenile and domestic-relations court was authorized in Hamilton County, Tenn. (which includes the city of Chattanooga), by a law of 1929, which was declared unconstitutional in 1930. See footnote 14, p. 15.

[10] Such courts were established in Norfolk and Richmond in 1915 under a Virginia law of 1914 (ch. 57).

[11] A domestic-relations court was established in Monongalia County, W. Va., in 1923 and went out of existence Jan. 1, 1929, in accordance with a law of 1927. See footnote 15, p. 15.

Appendix B.—STUDY OF FAMILIES DEALT WITH IN JUVE-NILE AND DOMESTIC-RELATIONS CASES IN HAMILTON COUNTY, OHIO, AND PHILADELPHIA, PA.

A statistical study was made by the United States Children's Bureau in Hamilton County, Ohio (in which the city of Cincinnati is situated), in regard to the families dealt with in one year in juvenile and domestic-relations cases by the courts and the Ohio Humane Society, which gives the courts considerable assistance in dealing with family problems. The year chosen for the study was 1923. A similar study was made of the families dealt with by the municipal court of Philadelphia, Pa., in a single month—October, 1923—and of a group of divorce cases dealt with by the court of common pleas. The number of juvenile and domestic-relations cases dealt with in one month in the Philadelphia municipal court is larger than the yearly total in Hamilton County. (For the method of the study and a summary of the findings see p. 26 and for the jurisdiction of the courts see Appendix A, p. 67.)

FAMILIES DEALT WITH IN JUVENILE AND DOMESTIC-RELATIONS CASES IN HAMILTON COUNTY, OHIO

NUMBER OF FAMILIES DEALT WITH AND TYPES OF CASES

In 1923 the family court, the probate court, and the humane society (with or without court action) dealt with 5,286 families in cases of the types included in the study. These families represented 4 per cent of the 129,020 families in Hamilton County as enumerated in the 1920 census. An additional group of 359 families, with which the only contact during 1923 consisted in the payment of a support order through the cashier of the family court, were not included in the statistical study because of the lack of complete information concerning them. If the families with which payment of support orders was the only contact were included with the 5,286 families, the total dealt with (5,645), is somewhat more than 4 per cent of the number of families enumerated in the census.[1]

The general types of cases in which the 5,286 families were dealt with by the family court, the probate court, and the humane society (with or without court action in the municipal or other court) were as follows:

1. Juvenile cases (2,699), including delinquency, mothers' aid, dependency or neglect, adoption, guardianship, feeble-mindedness or epilepsy, crippled children.

---

[1] Fourteenth Census of the United States, 1920, vol. 3, Population, pp. 11, 778. Washington, 1922. The census, however, in 1920 defined a family as "a group of persons, whether related by blood or not, who live together as one household, usually sharing the same table." One person living alone was thus counted as a family, and the occupants of a hotel or institution, however numerous, were counted as a single family. The 1930 census affords information on number of private families, excluding institutions, hotels, boarding houses, and other quasi-family groups. Assuming that there had been no actual change in size of family in the 10-year period, it is estimated that the number of private families in Hamilton County in 1920 was 132,282. On this basis the percentage of the total number of families represented by the families included in the study would still have been 4. In the present study "family" was defined as follows: A unit consisting of father, mother, and minor child or children, or one parent and child or children, or prospective mother (if living away from her parental home) and her unborn child. Accordingly, groups consisting of more than one such unit, each maintaining a separate home and dealt with as a separate family, were entered on two schedules as two families. If the two units were dealt with as one—for example, if a married daughter and her child lived with her parents—they were counted as one unit. Adopted and foster children but not grandchildren were included in the term "children." The term "families dealt with" therefore includes any family thus defined with which there was any contact (other than mere payment of a support order) during the specified period in a case coming under one or more of the following heads: Delinquency; dependency or neglect; mothers' aid; desertion or nonsupport; divorce; support of illegitimate child; other domestic-relations cases (as quarreling, abuse, unfaithfulness); offenses against children; school-excuse and employment-certificate cases; adoption; guardianship of the person of minors; commitment of feeble-minded or epileptic children. Families of which any member was under supervision in cases of these types were included whether or not the family had been dealt with on new charges or complaints during the period covered. Desertion and nonsupport cases not involving children were not included unless the wife was known to be pregnant. Divorce cases not involving minor children were not included, and 93 families were excluded because of uncertainty as to whether any of the children was under the age of 21 years. Of the 359 families with which the only contact was payment of a support order, 258 were receiving payments in cases of divorce and alimony, 92 in cases of nonsupport or desertion, 7 in both divorce and nonsupport cases, and 2 in illegitimacy cases.

2. Domestic-relations cases (2,210), including desertion or non-support, contributing to dependency, divorce cases involving children, support of illegitimate children, any other case involving domestic relations.

3. Juvenile cases and domestic-relations cases (256), including combinations of the types listed in paragraphs 1 and 2.

4. Offenses against children (102), including cases of offenses against children alone (64), and cases in which families dealt with in other cases were involved (38). Cases of contributing to delinquency are included here.

5. School-excuse and employment-certificate cases (19), including families dealt with in cases of other types also (10).

DISTRIBUTION OF CASES AMONG AGENCIES DEALING WITH THE FAMILIES

The family court dealt with 3,574 families (68 per cent of all the families in this county included in the study). Of these families, 350 were known also to other courts or to the Ohio Humane Society.

The humane society dealt with 1,638 families, of which 1,116 were handled by that organization without reference to courts, 247 were dealt with by the humane society and the municipal court (57 also by the family court), 245 by the humane society and the family court (8 by other courts also), and 30 by the humane society and other courts.

The probate court dealt with 432 families, of which 56 were known to the family court or to the humane society or to both.

Of the 5,286 families 4,906 (93 per cent) were dealt with by one court or by the humane society alone or with the municipal court and 380 were dealt with by more than one court or by the humane society and a court other than the municipal court.

Table 1 shows the agencies dealing with the family and the general types of cases.

TABLE 1.—*General type of case; families dealt with in juvenile and domestic-relations cases by one or more of specified agencies in 1923, Hamilton County*

General type of case	Families dealt with											
	By 1 court or by humane society alone or with municipal court					By more than 1 court or by humane society with 1 or more courts other than municipal court						
				Humane society				Family court and—				
								Humane society				
	Total	Total	Family court	Alone	With municipal court	Probate court	Total	Alone	With municipal court	With probate or other court	Probate court	Other court	Humane society and probate or other court [1]
Total	5,286	4,906	3,224	1,116	190	376	380	237	57	8	42	6	30
Juvenile cases	2,699	2,617	2,065	176	-----	376	82	34	-----	-----	40	4	4
Domestic-relations cases	2,210	2,043	986	883	174	----	167	115	31	2	-----	-----	19
Juvenile cases and domestic-relations cases	256	136	67	56	13	----	120	84	22	5	2	-----	7
Offenses against children [2]	102	93	89	1	3	----	9	3	3	1	-----	2	-----
School-excuse and employment-certificate cases [3]	19	17	17	-----	----	----	2	1	1	-----	-----	-----	-----

[1] Includes cases in municipal court also.

[2] Includes 34 also dealt with in juvenile cases, 3 dealt with in domestic-relations cases, and 1 dealt with in a juvenile case and a domestic-relations case.

[3] Includes 7 also dealt with in juvenile cases, 1 dealt with in a domestic-relations case, and 2 dealt with in a juvenile case and a domestic-relations case.

Both the family court and the humane society were dealing with dependency and neglect cases, the family court alone dealing with only half the families known in such cases and not in cases of other types.

It appeared to be the policy of the court and the social agencies to keep at a minimum the number of dependency cases referred for court action. The Cincinnati Associated Charities rarely referred a dependency case to the family court, and other agencies dealing with dependent families seldom referred such cases.

Of the families known only in desertion or nonsupport cases, 86 per cent were dealt with by the humane society alone or by courts other than the family court, and 90 per cent of the families known only in illegitimacy cases were so dealt with. The family court dealt with all the families known only in divorce cases and with 60 per cent of the families dealt with in family-relationship cases such as quarreling or abuse. All but 2 of the 64 families known only in cases of offenses against children were dealt with by the family court alone.

Table 2 shows the type of case and the contact of the family court and the humane society with the families dealt with in Hamilton County.

TABLE 2.—*Type of case; families dealt with in juvenile and domestic-relations cases by the family court, by the humane society, and by both agencies in 1923, Hamilton County*

Type of case	Total	Families dealt with					
		By family court [1]		By humane society [2]		By family court and humane society [1]	
		Number	Per cent	Number	Per cent	Number	Per cent
Total	[3] 4,910	3,272	67	1,336	27	302	6
Juvenile cases	2,323	2,109	91	180	8	34	1
Delinquency	1,221	1,218	99	3	[4]		
Dependency or neglect	395	199	51	173	44	23	6
Mothers' aid	613	613	100				
Crippled child	4	4	[5]				
More than 1 type	90	75	83	4	5	11	12
Domestic-relations cases	2,210	986	45	1,076	49	148	7
Desertion or nonsupport	954	116	12	817	86	21	2
Divorce	688	688	100				
Support of illegitimate child	155	13	8	140	90	2	1
Quarreling, abuse, or other domestic trouble	174	104	60	66	38	4	2
Desertion or nonsupport and divorce	144	39	27			105	73
Desertion or nonsupport and other cases	65	6	9	53	82	6	9
Divorce and other cases	30	20	[5]			10	[5]
Juvenile cases and domestic-relations cases	256	69	27	76	30	111	43
Offenses against children	102	91	89	4	4	7	7
Alone	64	62	97	1	2	1	2
With other cases	38	29	[5]	3	[5]	6	[5]
School-excuse and employment-certificate cases	19	17	[5]			2	[5]

[1] With or without other courts.
[2] With or without courts other than the family court.
[3] Excludes 376 families dealt with by the probate court only.
[4] Less than 1 per cent.
[5] Not shown because number of families was less than 50.

On December 31, 1923, the family court or the humane society had 1,358 of the 5,286 families included in the study under supervision. Of these families 801 (59 per cent) were supervised by the probation department of the family court, 550 by the humane society, and 7 by both organizations.

It is evident that the comprehensive jurisdiction conferred by law on the family court of Hamilton County (see Appendix A, p. 69) was being only partly exercised in 1923, and that in dependency cases and domestic-relations cases other than divorce much still remained to be accomplished if the degree of consolidation which family courts are designed to secure was to become a reality.

FAMILIES WITH PREVIOUS COURT AND HUMANE-SOCIETY RECORDS

Table 3 shows the agency dealing with the family in 1923 and the court or humane-society record of the family before that year.

Information concerning court or humane-society record prior to 1923 was obtained for all families (except the 376 dealt with only by the probate court) through the case histories of the organizations dealing with the families in 1923. As the families known to the humane society in 1923 were not cleared through the family-court records for cases prior to 1923, nor the reverse process followed, it is probable that the information on previous court record is not entirely complete. If the case dealt with in 1923 had been carried over from the previous year, it was not counted as a previous record. For example, dependency cases in which the children had been temporarily committed to institutions before 1923 and recommitted in 1923 were considered pending cases. Courts outside the county were included if noted in the case history.

TABLE 3.—*Previous court or humane-society record; families dealt with in juvenile and domestic-relations cases by one or more of specified agencies in 1923, Hamilton County*

Court or humane-society record of family prior to 1923 [1]	Total	Families dealt with										
		By family court or by humane society alone or with municipal court				By more than 1 court or by humane society with 1 or more courts other than municipal court						
		Total	Family court	Humane society		Total	Family court and—					Humane society and probate or other court [2]
				Alone	With municipal court		Humane society			Probate court	Other court	
							Alone	With municipal court	With probate or other court			
Total	[3] 4,910	4,530	3,224	1,116	190	380	237	57	8	42	6	30
Previous court record	1,541	1,326	879	367	80	215	135	27	8	23	2	20
1 court or humane society	1,349	1,207	839	304	64	142	86	21	2	21	------	12
Family court	907	854	819	32	3	53	26	4	1	21	------	1
Humane society	405	318	3	255	60	87	59	16	1	------	------	11
Alone	246	193	2	163	28	53	35	8	1			9
With municipal court	159	125	1	92	32	34	24	8				2
Other court or court outside county	37	35	17	17	1	2	1	1				
More than 1 court, or humane society with specified courts	178	107	35	58	14	71	49	6	6	2	2	6
Family court with other courts	20	15	15	------	------	5	------	1	1	2	1	------
Humane society with—												
Family court	54	28	1	23	4	26	23	2	------	------	1	------
Family court and municipal court	58	31	4	21	6	27	20	2	4	------	------	1
Family court and other courts	2	------	------	------	------	2	1	------	------	------	------	1
Other courts	44	33	15	14	4	11	5	1	1	------	------	4
Court not reported	14	12	5	5	2	2	------	------	------	------	------	2
No previous court record reported	3,369	3,204	2,345	749	110	165	102	30	------	19	4	10

[1] Not including cases carried over into 1923 from previous year.
[2] Includes cases in municipal court also.
[3] Excludes 376 families dealt with by the probate court only.

Thirty-one per cent of the 4,910 families dealt with in 1923 by the family court or humane society or both were found to have been known previously to courts or to the humane society in cases of the types included in the study.

Of the families known in 1923 to the family court alone, 27 per cent had previous court or humane-society records. The proportion with previous records was somewhat higher for those dealt with in 1923 by the humane society, 34 per cent having such records. In each group the percentage with a previous record in the same organization was far higher than the percentage with a previous record in another organization. Of the families known in 1923 to the family court only, 25 per cent had previous records with the same organization alone and only 2 per cent with another organization. The corresponding percentages for families known only to the humane society or to that agency and the municipal court in 1923 were 24 known to the same organization only and 10 known to other courts. More than half the families (57 per cent) dealt with in 1923 by more than one court or by the humane society and a court other than the municipal court had records prior to 1923.

Table 4 shows the number of families dealt with in cases of specified types in 1923 and the number and percentage that had previous court records.

TABLE 4.—*Type of case and previous court or humane-society record; families dealt with in juvenile and domestic-relations cases.in 1923, Hamilton County*

Type of case	Families dealt with			
	Total	Having previous court or humane-society record		No previous court or humane-society record reported
		Number	Per cent	
Total	1 4,910	1,541	31	3,369
Juvenile cases	2,323	625	27	1,698
Delinquency alone and with other cases	1,290	377	29	913
Mothers' aid alone and with other cases (except delinquency)	623	91	15	532
Dependency or neglect	395	148	37	247
Other cases and other combinations	15	9	(2)	6
Domestic-relations cases	2,210	728	33	1,482
Desertion or nonsupport with divorce	144	78	54	66
Desertion or nonsupport alone and with other cases (except divorce)	1,019	361	35	658
Divorce alone and with other cases (except desertion or nonsupport)	718	230	32	488
Support of illegitimate child	155	25	16	130
Other cases	174	34	20	140
Juvenile cases and domestic-relations cases	256	143	56	113
Offenses against children	102	34	33	68
School-excuse and employment-certificate cases	19	11	(2)	8

1 Excludes 376 families dealt with by the probate court only.
2 Not shown because number of families was less than 50.

Most of the families dealt with in juvenile cases in 1923 who had previous records had been known to the courts or the humane society in juvenile cases; likewise the families dealt with in domestic-relations cases had been known previously chiefly in domestic-relations cases. Of the families known only in juvenile cases in 1923, however, 7 per cent had been known previously in domestic-relations cases alone or in cases of other types also. The same proportion (7 per cent) of families dealt with only in domestic-relations cases in 1923 had been previously dealt with in juvenile cases. More than half the families dealt with in both juvenile cases and domestic-relations cases in 1923 had been dealt with previously in one or both of these types of cases. (Table 5.)

TABLE 5.—*General type of case and type of previous court or humane-society record; families dealt with in juvenile and domestic-relations cases in 1923, Hamilton County*

General type of case	Total	Families dealt with					
		Having previous court or humane-society record prior to 1923					No previous court or humane-society record reported
		Total	Juvenile cases	Domestic-relations cases	Juvenile cases and domestic-relations cases	Offenses against children	
Total	1 4,910	1,541	576	699	225	41	3,369
Juvenile cases	2,323	625	446	73	86	20	1,698
Domestic-relations cases	2,210	728	67	566	80	15	1,482
Juvenile cases and domestic-relations cases	256	143	31	55	53	4	113
Offenses against children	102	34	23	4	5	2	68
School-excuse and employment-certificate cases	19	11	9	1	1		8

1 Excludes 376 cases dealt with by the probate court only.

The number of families dealt with in divorce cases during 1923 (not including those known in juvenile cases as well) was 862, many of them also being dealt with in domestic-relations cases of other types. Six per cent of these families had been known previously in juvenile cases (offenses against children in combination with juvenile cases included), 25 per cent in domestic-relations cases (11 per cent in cases of desertion or nonsupport), and 5 per cent in both juvenile and domestic-relations cases. Fourteen per cent of the families had been involved in a divorce proceeding prior to that pending in 1923.

Of the 1,163 families dealt with in 1923 in desertion or nonsupport cases, alone or in combination with domestic-relations cases of other types, 2 per cent had been dealt with previously in juvenile cases, 32 per cent in domestic-relations cases (8 per cent in divorce cases), and 4 per cent in both juvenile cases and domestic-relations cases.

INTERRELATION OF CASES IN THE YEAR COVERED BY THE STUDY

One-eighth of the 5,286 families (13 per cent) were dealt with in more than one type of case during 1923.

Table 6 shows the number of families appearing before the courts or the humane society in specified types of juvenile and domestic-relations cases and also dealt with in other cases of these types within the year.

Among the juvenile cases dependency or neglect was most likely to occur in combination with other types of cases, 41 per cent of the families known in dependency or neglect cases being also known in cases of other types, usually domestic-relations cases. Almost one-third (31 per cent) of the families dealt with in cases of feeble-mindedness or epilepsy were also dealt with in cases of other types, usually juvenile cases. Among the families dealt with in cases of desertion or nonsupport 28 per cent were also dealt with in cases of other types, for the most part either juvenile cases or divorce cases; and almost as high a percentage (26) of the families dealt with in divorce cases were known in cases of other types, chiefly cases of desertion or nonsupport. A very high percentage (45) of the families known in such domestic-relations cases as abuse, quarreling, and other domestic difficulty were dealt with also in cases of other types, chiefly desertion or nonsupport and juvenile cases. Only 13 per cent of the families dealt with in illegitimacy cases were known in cases of other types, in most instances juvenile cases. The percentage of families dealt with in cases of offenses against children known in other types of cases, chiefly delinquency cases, was 36. Ten of the 19 families dealt with in school-excuse and employment-certificate cases were dealt with in cases of other types.

TABLE 6.—*Type of case and interrelation of cases; families dealt with in juvenile and domestic-relations cases in 1923, Hamilton County*

Type of case [1]	Families dealt with												
		In 1 type of case		In more than 1 type of case									
				Total		Juvenile cases		Divorce cases		Desertion or nonsupport cases	Other domestic-relations cases	Offenses against children	School-excuse and employment-certificate cases
	Total	Number	Per cent	Number	Per cent	Alone	With domestic-relations cases	Alone or with domestic-relations cases except desertion or nonsupport	With desertion or nonsupport cases				
Juvenile cases:													
Delinquency	1,394	1,203	86	191	14	87	[2]21	10	4	28	6	[3]27	[4]8
Dependency or neglect	672	395	59	277	41	66	[2]23	27	16	91	40	[5]12	[6]2
Mothers' aid	651	601	92	50	8	44	-----	-----	-----	2	1	[7]1	[7]2
Crippled child	7	4	----	3	----	3	-----	-----	-----	-----	-----	-----	-----
Adoption	113	105	93	8	7	6	[8]1	-----	-----	1	-----	-----	-----
Guardianship	211	195	92	16	8	13	[8]1	1	1	-----	-----	-----	-----
Feeble-mindedness and epilepsy	109	75	69	34	31	27	[9]2	2	-----	1	2	-----	-----
Domestic-relations cases:													
Desertion or nonsupport	1,329	954	72	375	28	128	[10]31	144	-----	-----	65	[11]4	[12]3
Divorce	929	688	74	241	26	37	[13]27	-----	-----	144	30	[14]3	-----
Support of illegitimate child	178	155	87	23	13	14	[15]2	1	-----	6	-----	-----	-----
Other cases	318	174	55	144	45	42	[16]13	29	-----	59	-----	1	-----
Offenses against children	102	64	63	38	36	33	[17]2	-----	2	-----	1	-----	-----
School-excuse and employment-certificate cases	10	9	----	10	----	7	[8]2	-----	-----	1	-----	-----	-----

[1] Many families were dealt with in more than 1 type of case.
[2] Includes 1 divorce, 11 desertion or nonsupport, 2 nonsupport and divorce, with or without other domestic-relations cases.
[3] Includes 5 other juvenile cases, 1 nonsupport case.
[4] Includes 2 other juvenile cases and nonsupport, 1 other juvenile case.
[5] Includes 4 other juvenile cases, 1 divorce and nonsupport.
[6] Both nonsupport.
[7] Includes 1 other juvenile case.
[8] Nonsupport.
[9] Includes 1 nonsupport case.
[10] Includes 23 divorce cases.
[11] Includes 2 divorce also, 1 divorce and juvenile case, and 1 juvenile case.
[12] Includes 2 juvenile cases.
[13] Includes 23 desertion or nonsupport cases.
[14] Includes 2 nonsupport cases, 1 nonsupport and juvenile case.
[15] 1 nonsupport, 1 divorce.
[16] Includes 7 nonsupport cases, 3 divorce, 3 nonsupport and divorce.
[17] 1 nonsupport case, 1 divorce and nonsupport.

The figures for delinquency, dependency or neglect, desertion or nonsupport, and divorce are of especial interest. Of the 1,394 families dealt with in delinquency cases, 115 (8 per cent) were dealt with in other types of juvenile cases. Seventeen families (1 per cent) were dealt with in divorce cases, 48 families (3 per cent) in cases of desertion or nonsupport, and 27 (2 per cent) in cases of offenses against children.

Among 672 families dealt with in dependency or neglect cases, 93 (14 per cent) were also dealt with in juvenile cases of other types. Forty-seven families (7 per cent) were dealt with in divorce cases, and 123 families (18 per cent) were dealt with in cases of desertion or nonsupport.

Of the 1,329 families dealt with in cases of desertion or nonsupport 163 (12 per cent) were dealt with in juvenile cases, and 170 (13 per cent) were dealt with in divorce cases.

Of the 929 families dealt with in divorce cases, 64 (7 per cent) were dealt with in juvenile cases, and 170 (18 per cent) were dealt with in cases of desertion or nonsupport.

The most overlapping appeared to exist between dependency or neglect and desertion or nonsupport, and between divorce and desertion or nonsupport.

The analysis of interrelation of cases dealt with in 1923 and of previous court records has shown that problems of divorce and desertion or nonsupport occur in the same family in many instances and that two or more problems of other types included in this study are also present in considerable numbers of families. The following case histories (in which fictitious names have been used) illustrate this overlapping of problems:

The Newton family was known to both the family court and the humane society in 1923 and had been known the previous year to the humane society. Mr. and Mrs. Newton, aged 22 and 23 years, respectively, were separated, and the three children 1, 2, and 3 years of age were with Mrs. Newton. She had come to the humane society in 1922 for assistance in obtaining support from the father, and he had complained that Mrs. Newton was neglecting the children and failing to provide a proper home for them. An agreement to support was obtained, and the humane society was supervising on January 1, 1923. On the 5th of that month complaint against the mother was again made by Mr. Newton, and the society referred the case to the family court, which placed the children under care of a private agency. A little later a divorce complaint was filed, and the divorce case was still pending at the end of the year. In August the children were living with Mrs. Newton, and the father renewed his complaint that the home was improper. The family court ordered the children placed in a foster home by the private agency to which they were committed. The Newton family was known to a family-welfare agency.

Mr. Thompson, aged 22, and Mrs. Thompson, aged 23, were separated. A young daughter was living with Mr. Thompson, and a baby 1 year of age was in a boarding home. In May, 1923, Mrs. Thompson brought a charge of nonsupport. The case was handled by the humane society and the municipal court, and Mr. Thompson was ordered to support. The following month Mrs. Thompson filed a petition for divorce in the family court, and Mr. Thompson filed a cross petition alleging neglect. A divorce was granted to the wife. In the meantime the family court had dealt unofficially with the children as dependent and had arranged for their placement in a boarding home. The Thompson family had been known to a hospital and to a child-caring agency.

Mr. and Mrs. Andrews, who were separated, had two grown daughters and three sons, James, Jonas, and Paul, aged 18, 17, and 15 years. The boys were living with their mother. In January, 1923, a divorce was pending in the family court, but no action on this case was taken during the year. In July Jonas was charged with theft and was placed on probation, to live in his own home. A few days later Mrs. Andrews brought a nonsupport charge against the father in the family court. The case was dealt with unofficially, and Mr. Andrews agreed to support. The following month the same court dealt with James on an illegitimacy complaint and James married the girl involved. Jonas had been dealt with eight times before 1923 on delinquency charges ranging from truancy to immorality and robbery, and he had been for some time in the State institution for delinquent boys. James had been dealt with five times as a delinquent prior to 1923, and he also had been committed to the State institution. Paul had been before the court three times as a delinquent and had been on probation. The family had been dealt with by the family court three times prior to 1923 on nonsupport charges. In 1920 a divorce complaint had been filed by Mrs. Andrews, charging adultery and neglect, but the case was dismissed. The Andrews family had been known to the humane society and to a free dental clinic.

In the Donnelly family the father, aged 47, had seven children by a previous marriage, the younger children aged 18, 13, and 11 years. Mrs. Donnelly had three children by a former marriage, the youngest 20 years of age. Mr. and Mrs. Donnelly were separated. Mr. Donnelly's two youngest children were living with him, and Mrs. Donnelly's oldest son was with her. Mrs. Donnelly's 23-year-old daughter had been married and divorced. In October, 1923, Mr. Donnelly filed a divorce complaint, charging neglect. The complaint was dismissed. His 20-year-old and 18-year-old daughters had been on probation to the family court since 1920, on charges of theft and immorality. They had previously been dealt with as delinquents and for a time had been in a city institution for delinquent girls. Their older brother had been on probation as a delinquent. In 1916 Mr. Donnelly had been charged with contributing to the delinquency of one of his older daughters, then 17 years of age, but the case against him had been dismissed, though the daughter had been adjudged delinquent and committed to a State institution. In 1916 Mrs. Donnelly's daughter had also been adjudged delinquent and had been placed in a city institution. Mrs. Donnelly's three children had been before the juvenile court as dependents in 1909. The family had been known to family-welfare, medical, and health agencies.

Mr. and Mrs. Otto, aged 40 and 37 years, were separated. Their one child, Kate, who was 12 years old, was living with Mrs. Otto. In October, 1923, Mrs. Otto filed a divorce petition, charging cruelty and neglect. The case was dismissed. A little later Kate ran away from home and was brought before the court as a runaway. The case was pending at the close of the year. The Otto family had been known to family-welfare and child-welfare agencies and to the humane society.

Mr. and Mrs. Raymond, both 29 years of age, were separated. Two children, Randolph, aged 10, and Elizabeth, aged 7, were living with their mother. Randolph had been born out of wedlock before his mother's marriage to Mr. Raymond. In 1921 and 1922 the humane society, the municipal court, and the court of common pleas had dealt with the family on nonsupport charges, and Mr. Raymond had been ordered to support his wife and the children. In 1923 he agreed to support, but in June he was brought again before the court of common pleas, served a jail sentence, and was released under an order to support his family. In the meantime Randolph had been arrested for vagrancy; his case was investigated by the family court, but no action was deemed necessary. Three months later Mrs. Raymond complained to the court that Randolph was stealing from persons in the home. This case also was handled unofficially. The Raymond family had been known to family-welfare, medical, and health agencies.

SOCIAL AGENCIES DEALING WITH THE FAMILIES

More than half (53 per cent) of the 5,286 families dealt with by the family court, the humane society, or the probate court in 1923 were reported by the Cincinnati social-service exchange as known to Hamilton County agencies other than these organizations, or as known to the family court or the humane society in cases of other types than those included in the study. One-third (33 per cent) were known to more than one agency. If the humane society had dealt with a family in 1923 or earlier in cases included in the study, it was not listed among the registered agencies; otherwise it was included. As the probate court did not register cases with the social-service exchange, and the family court in 1923 did not register minor behavior cases, all cases not already registered (except mothers' aid cases) were cleared through the social-service exchange as a preliminary to calculating the numbers of cases dealt with by these courts and other social agencies. The juvenile division of the family court was registered in some humane-society cases in which no detailed information was available concerning the date of the court record or the nature of the case. The court was counted as a registering agency if it was not dealing with the family in 1923 and had not dealt with the family before 1923 in a case for which information concerning its nature was available but was entered on the records of the social-service exchange.

Table 7 shows the number and per cent distribution of families according to the number of social agencies reported as having known the families during and before 1923.   Table 8 shows the types of cases in which they came to the attention of the courts and the humane society, according to the number of social agencies reported.—

TABLE 7.—*Number of social agencies to which family was known; families dealt with in juvenile and domestic-relations cases in 1923, Hamilton County*

Reported number of social agencies to which family was known prior to and in 1923	Families dealt with	
	Number	Per cent distribution
Total _____	5,286	100
None _____	2,478	47
1 agency _____	1,083	20
2 agencies _____	654	12
3 agencies _____	401	8
4 agencies _____	260	5
5 agencies _____	163	3
6 or more agencies ___	247	5

TABLE 8.—*Type of case and number of social agencies to which family was known; families dealt with in juvenile and domestic-relations cases in 1923, Hamilton County*

Type of case	Total	Families dealt with					Not reported as known to social agencies
		Reported as known to social agencies prior to and in 1923					
		Total	Number of social agencies to which family was known				
			1	2 or 3	4 or 5	6 or more	
Total _____	5,286	2,808	1,083	1,055	423	247	2,478
Juvenile cases _____	2,699	1,481	533	550	241	157	1,218
Delinquency _____	1,203	595	239	195	107	54	608
Delinquency and other cases _____	87	75	14	25	17	19	12
Mothers' aid _____	601	416	148	169	66	33	185
Mothers' aid and other cases (except delinquency) _____	22	20	5	14	1	_____	2
Dependency or neglect ___	395	252	86	101	33	32	143
Adoption, guardianship, feeble-mindedness, epilepsy _____	[1] 376	109	37	40	15	17	267
Other cases and other combinations _____	15	14	4	6	2	2	1
Domestic-relations cases ___	2,210	1,051	467	402	131	51	1,159
Desertion or nonsupport ___	1,163	620	257	247	80	36	543
Alone _____	954	501	220	183	66	32	453
With divorce _____	144	80	28	41	8	3	64
With other cases _____	65	39	9	23	6	1	26
Divorce _____	718	256	125	91	33	7	462
Alone _____	688	238	118	83	30	7	450
With other cases (except nonsupport) ___	30	18	7	8	3	_____	12
Support of illegitimate child ___	155	90	41	40	8	1	65
Quarreling or other domestic trouble ___	82	31	17	6	5	3	51
Abuse _____	64	39	20	11	4	4	25
Unfaithfulness and immorality ___	14	8	3	4	1	_____	6
Other cases _____	14	7	4	3	_____	_____	7

[1] Includes 105 dealt with in adoption cases only, of which 14 were known to social agencies; 195 in guardianship cases only, of which 44 were known to social agencies; and 75 dealt with in cases of feeble-mindedness and epilepsy only, of which 51 were known to social agencies.

TABLE 8.—*Type of case and number of social agencies to which family was known; families dealt with in juvenile and domestic-relations cases in 1923, Hamilton County*—Continued

Type of case	Families dealt with						
	Total	Reported as known to social agencies prior to and in 1923					Not reported as known to social agencies
		Total	Number of social agencies to which family was known				
			1	2 or 3	4 or 5	6 or more	
Juvenile cases and domestic-relations cases_____	256	191	53	75	40	23	65
Dependency or neglect_____	174	131	44	52	25	10	43
With desertion or nonsupport_____	87	67	17	28	15	7	20
With divorce_____	26	17	7	8	1	1	9
With other cases or other combinations___	61	47	20	16	9	2	14
Delinquency and domestic-relations cases_____	48	34	5	14	11	4	14
Other combinations_____	34	26	4	9	4	9	8
Offenses against children_____	102	67	26	20	9	12	35
Alone_____	64	36	14	13	4	5	28
With other cases_____	38	31	12	7	5	7	7
School-excuse and employment-certificate cases [2]__	19	18	4	8	2	4	1

[2] With or without other cases.

More than half (55 per cent) of the families dealt with in juvenile cases, nearly half (48 per cent) of those dealt with in domestic-relations cases, three-fourths (75 per cent) of those dealt with in both juvenile cases and domestic-relations cases, and two-thirds (67 per cent) of those dealt with in cases of offenses against children were reported as known to social agencies. More than half (51 per cent) of the families dealt with in delinquency cases and nearly two-thirds (64 per cent) of those dealt with in dependency or neglect cases only were known to social agencies, not including families that were dealt with also in domestic-relations cases, cases of offenses against children, or school-excuse and employment-certificate cases. Families dealt with in adoption and guardianship cases only were known to social agencies less frequently (13 per cent and 23 per cent, respectively), but two-thirds (68 per cent) of the families dealt with in cases of feeble-mindedness and epilepsy and not in cases of other types had social-agency records. Of the families dealt with by the probate court alone nearly three-tenths (29 per cent) were known to social agencies and nearly one-fifth (19 per cent) to more than one such agency. More than half of the families dealt with in desertion or nonsupport cases (53 per cent), more than one-third of those dealt with in divorce cases (36 per cent), and almost three-fifths of those dealt with in cases for the support of children born out of wedlock (58 per cent) had social-agency records. Those dealt with in desertion or nonsupport cases do not include those also dealt with in juvenile cases, cases of offenses against children, or school-excuse and employment-certificate cases; and those dealt with in divorce cases do not include those also dealt with in cases of the types specified or in desertion or nonsupport cases.

Table 9 shows the number and percentage of families known to family-welfare agencies, medical and health agencies, and agencies dealing with delinquency, the prevention of delinquency, and the protection of children. The last group includes the Central Mental Hygiene Clinic, Big Brother and Big Sister organizations, and the Juvenile Protective League, also the humane society and the family court so far as they dealt with cases other than those included in the study.

TABLE 9.—*General type of case and number and per cent of cases known to social agencies of specified type; families dealt with in juvenile and domestic-relations cases in 1923, Hamilton County*

General type of case	Families dealt with in all cases	Families [1] dealt with who were reported as known to specified social agencies prior to and in 1923					
		Family-welfare agencies		Medical and health agencies		Agencies dealing with delinquency, prevention of delinquency, and protection of children	
		Number	Per cent	Number	Per cent	Number	Per cent
Total	5, 286	1, 782	34	1, 609	30	829	16
Juvenile cases	2, 699	1, 015	38	832	31	460	17
Domestic-relations cases	2, 210	579	26	615	28	275	12
Juvenile cases and domestic-relations cases	256	132	52	120	47	57	22
Offenses against children	102	44	43	33	32	29	28
School-excuse and employment-certificate cases	19	12	(2)	9	(2)	8	(2)

[1] Many families were known to more than 1 type of agency.
[2] Not shown because number of families was less than 50.

Family-welfare agencies had dealt with the most families (34 per cent); medical and health agencies were second (dealing with 30 per cent), and agencies dealing with delinquency, the prevention of delinquency, and the protection of children were third (dealing with 16 per cent). Two per cent of the families not dealt with by agencies of the types specified and a number of families known to such agencies were known to children's institutions, child-placing agencies, the department of education, and other agencies.

The individual agency registering the largest number of families in the group studied was the Associated Charities, which registered 1,207 families. The Bureau of Catholic Charities (which combines family-welfare service, a health center, institutions for children, and Big Brother and Big Sister work) was next, 561 families being reported as known to this agency. The vocational bureau and other divisions of the school department, including the attendance department and placement office, registered 453 families, and the humane society registered 401 families (in addition to families dealt with by this society in 1923 or earlier in cases of the types included in the study and entered under court record or previous court record.) Hospitals, dispensaries, and clinics, the Bureau for Prevention of Tuberculosis, and the Babies Milk Fund Association registered 1,609 families. The Children's Home, a private institution for dependent children which also places children, registered 161 families. Seventeen of these families and 91 others were registered with the Boarding Home Bureau, which was then an independent agency.[2] The Juvenile Protective Association registered 153 families, the Central Mental Hygiene Clinic (not established until January, 1923) registered 104, and the Federation of Churches (which does Big Brother and Big Sister work) registered 93.

Among the 5,286 families the number which were registered in the social-service exchange in 1923 for the first time was 1,223 (23 per cent), as compared with 2,808 (53 per cent) registered at any time. Of these 1,223 families 803 (66 per cent) had been registered with only 1 agency in 1923; 260 (21 per cent) had been registered with 2 agencies; 117 (10 per cent) had been registered with 3 agencies; and 43 (4 per cent) had been registered with 4 agencies or more.

Medical and health agencies registered 620 families in 1923; family-welfare agencies registered 403 families; and agencies dealing with delinquency, the prevention of delinquency, and the protection of children registered 270 families.

The family court depended upon social agencies for assistance in probation work to a considerable extent; both the court and the humane society frequently referred families for services of various kinds.

[2] Boarding-out work was divided later among the Children's Home, the Bureau of Catholic Charities, and the United Jewish Charities.

CHARACTERISTICS OF THE FAMILIES

Race and age of mother and age of parents.

Information concerning the race of the mother was obtained for 4,525 of the 5,286 families dealt with. The mother was white in 3,645 (81 per cent) of these families and colored in 880 families (19 per cent). The percentage of colored mothers was almost three times as high as the percentage of colored in the whole population (7 per cent in 1920).[3] The percentage of colored mothers was very low (6 and 9, respectively) in mothers' aid and divorce cases and very high in illegitimacy cases, in more than half (56 per cent) of which the mother was colored. For other cases the percentage of colored mothers ranged from 15 to 25. (Table 10.)

TABLE 10.—*Type of case and race of mother; families dealt with in juvenile and domestic-relations cases in 1923, Hamilton County*

Type of case	Families dealt with						
	Total	Race of mother reported					Race of mother not reported
		Total	White		Colored		
			Number	Per cent	Number	Per cent	
Total	5,286	4,525	3,645	81	880	19	761
Juvenile cases	2,699	2,302	1,863	81	439	19	397
Delinquency alone and with other cases	1,290	1,231	926	75	305	25	59
Mothers' aid alone and with other cases (except delinquency)	623	617	582	94	35	6	6
Dependency or neglect	395	365	288	79	77	21	30
Adoption	105						105
Guardianship	195						195
Feeble-mindedness or epilepsy	75	73	56	77	17	23	2
Other cases or other combinations	16	16	11	(1)	5	(1)	
Domestic-relations cases	2,210	1,866	1,489	80	377	20	344
Desertion or nonsupport alone and with other cases	1,163	1,050	828	79	222	21	113
Divorce alone and with other cases (except desertion or nonsupport)	718	579	524	91	55	9	139
Support of illegitimate child	155	151	67	44	84	56	4
Other domestic-relations cases	174	86	70	81	16	19	88
Juvenile cases and domestic-relations cases	256	243	200	82	43	18	13
Dependency or neglect and domestic-relations cases	174	167	142	85	25	15	7
Delinquency and domestic-relations cases	48	45	31	(1)	14	(1)	3
Other combinations	34	31	27	(1)	4	(1)	3
Offenses against children alone and with other cases	102	96	77	80	19	20	6
School-excuse and employment-certificate cases alone and with other cases	19	18	16	(1)	2	(1)	1

[1] Not shown because number of families was less than 50.

In 3,169 of the 5,286 families dealt with the mother was living and her age was ascertained. Eleven per cent of the mothers were under 21 years of age and 32 per cent were between 21 and 29 years of age. Less than one-fourth of the mothers (23 per cent) had reached the age of 40.

Table 11 shows the age of the mother in all reported cases and for four groups of cases: Dependency or neglect, mothers' aid, divorce, and desertion or nonsupport. As the mother's age was reported for less than 25 per cent of the families dealt with in delinquency cases, this group and the groups in which the numbers of cases are small are not shown separately.

[3] Fourteenth Census of the United States, 1920, vol. 3, Population, p. 778. Washington, 1922.

TABLE 11.—*Age of mother; families dealt with in all types and in selected types of juvenile and domestic-relations cases in 1923, Hamilton County*

Age of mother	Families dealt with in all cases		Families [1] dealt with in selected types of cases							
			Dependency or neglect		Mothers' aid		Divorce		Desertion or nonsupport	
	Number	Per cent distribution	Number	Per cent distribution	Number	Per cent distribution	Number	Per cent distribution	Number	Per cent distribution
Total	5,286	------	672	------	651	------	929	------	1,329	------
Age of mother reported	3,169	100	388	100	637	100	757	100	1,109	100
Under 18 years	67	2	6	2	------	------	5	(2)	28	3
18 years, under 21	270	9	29	7	------	------	46	6	148	13
21 years, under 30	1,013	32	165	43	48	8	310	41	516	47
30 years, under 40	1,095	35	135	35	277	43	279	37	303	27
40 years, under 50	565	18	44	11	248	39	81	11	93	8
50 years or over	159	5	9	2	64	10	36	5	21	2
Age of mother not reported or mother dead	2,117	------	284	------	14	------	172	------	220	------

[1] Many families were dealt with in more than 1 type of case.   [2] Less than 1 per cent.

TABLE 12.—*Age of mother and father; families dealt with in all types and in selected types of juvenile and domestic-relations cases in 1923, Hamilton County*

Age of mother and father	Families dealt with in all cases	Families [1] dealt with in selected types of cases		
		Dependency or neglect	Divorce	Desertion or nonsupport
Total	5,286	672	929	1,329
Age of mother reported	3,169	388	757	1,109
Mother under 21 years	337	35	51	176
Father under 21 years	56	3	6	29
Father 21 years, under 30	205	18	37	127
Father 30 years and over	22	4	5	10
Father's age not reported or father dead	54	10	3	10
Mother 21 years, under 30	1,013	165	310	516
Father under 21 years	8	--------	1	4
Father 21 years, under 30	496	52	156	306
Father 30 years, under 40	351	70	130	171
Father 40 years and over	44	9	21	19
Father's age not reported or father dead	114	34	2	16
Mother 30 years, under 40	1,095	135	279	303
Father under 30 years	42	6	17	19
Father 30 years, under 40	435	63	174	167
Father 40 years and over	295	40	86	102
Father's age not reported or father dead	323	26	2	15
Mother 40 years or over	724	53	117	114
Father under 40 years	35	7	11	10
Father 40 years and over	350	31	106	95
Father's age not reported or father dead	339	15	--------	9
Age of mother not reported or mother dead	2,117	284	172	220

[1] Many families were dealt with in more than 1 type of case.

One of the striking facts brought out by the figures in Table 11 is the youth of the mothers involved in desertion or nonsupport cases. Almost one-sixth (16 per cent) were under the age of 21 years and more than three-fifths (62 per cent) were under 30. These were not childless wives but were women bringing action against their husbands for the support of themselves and their children. Almost half the mothers involved in divorce cases (48 per cent) were under the age of 30, and 7 per cent were under the age of 21. On the other hand, 91 per cent of the mothers applying for mothers' aid were 30 years of age or older.

Table 12 shows the ages of the parents in the families dealt with. In 2 per cent of the families in which the parents were living and their ages known both the mother and the father were under 21 years of age. In 21 per cent both were 21 and under 30 years of age; in another 15 per cent the mother was 21 and under 30 and the father was 30 and under 40; thus in 36 per cent of the families the mother was between 21 and 30 and the father between 21 and 40. Families in which the mother was 30 but under 40 years of age and the father 30 or over comprised 31 per cent of the total for which age of mother and father was reported. Both parents were 21 and under 30 years of age in 17 per cent of the families dealt with in dependency or neglect cases, 21 per cent of those dealt with in divorce cases, and 29 per cent of those dealt with in desertion or nonsupport cases. The mother was of this age and the father 30 but under 40 years of age in 23 per cent of the families dealt with in dependency or neglect cases, 17 per cent of those dealt with in divorce cases, and 16 per cent of those dealt with in desertion or nonsupport cases.

Number and ages of the children.

For 4,589 families the number of minor children was reported. (Table 13.) In more than two-fifths of the families (41 per cent, including families in which there was only an unborn child) there was but one minor child. Two children were reported for 1,056 families (23 per cent), and three or more children for 1,638 families (36 per cent). Excluding unborn children, the total number of minor children in the 4,477 families who had living children was 10,681, an average of 2.4 per family.

Of the 4,508 families in which the numbers and ages of the children were reported, 112 (2 per cent) had an unborn child only, 3,197 (71 per cent) were families in which all the children were under the age of 16 years, 893 (20 per cent) were families in which some of the children were under 16 and some were between 16 and 21 years, and 306 (7 per cent) were families in which all the children were between the ages of 16 and 21 years.

TABLE 13.—*Number of minor children in family by age groups; families dealt with in juvenile and domestic-relations cases in 1923, Hamilton County*

Number of minor children in family	Families dealt with					
		Ages of minor children				
	Total	All under 16	Some under 16, some 16 but under 21	All 16 but under 21	Not reported	Child unborn
Total	5,286	3,197	893	306	778	112
Number of minor children in family reported	4,589	3,197	893	306	81	112
1 [1]	1,783	1,534		234	15	
2	1,056	811	169	59	17	
3	724	447	248	12	17	
4	412	224	174	1	13	
5	248	113	126		9	
6	133	37	91		5	
7	68	21	44		3	
8	33	6	25		2	
9	14	3	11			
10	4	1	3			
11	2		2			
Child unborn	112					112
Number of minor children in family not reported	697				697	

[1] The number with 1 child only is probably somewhat overstated. Of the 324 families dealt with by the probate court only in which the ages of the children were reported, 234 (72 per cent) appeared to have only 1 child. The information concerning children in the families dealt with by the family court or the humane society was incomplete in a number of cases.

Table 14 shows the number of children of specified ages in the families dealt with by the courts or the humane society in cases of various types.

Of the 896 families (with minor children) dealt with in divorce cases, for which numbers and ages of children were reported, 54 per cent had children under 7 years of age and 21 per cent had children under 3 years of age. The corresponding percentages for the 1,273 families with numbers and ages of children reported which were dealt with in cases of desertion or nonsupport were 73 having children under 7 years of age and 47 having children under 3 years. Of the group of families dealt with in desertion or nonsupport cases, 18 per cent had children under 1 year of age. Of all the families included in the study for which numbers and ages of children were reported, 53 per cent had children under the age of 7 years and 28 per cent had children under the age of 3 years.

TABLE 14.—*Number of minor children in family, by age groups: families dealt with in all types and in selected types of juvenile and domestic-relations cases in 1923, Hamilton County*

Number of children of specified ages in family	Families dealt with in all cases	Families [1] dealt with in selected types of cases				
		Delin-quency	Depend-ency or neglect	Mothers' aid	Divorce	Desertion or non-support
Total	5,286	1,387	672	651	929	1,329
Number of children under 21 years:						
1	1,783	243	179	37	497	551
2	1,056	180	160	159	220	324
3	724	154	108	199	107	159
4	412	105	70	101	49	112
5	248	88	35	73	20	47
6	133	54	24	35	8	18
7 or more	121	64	22	24	1	19
Unborn child only	112	4	3	----	9	62
Not reported	697	495	71	23	18	37
Number of children under 16 years:						
None [2]	418	133	18	1	114	71
1	1,794	256	192	89	448	573
2	1,061	170	154	202	211	323
3	606	120	96	177	79	148
4	332	82	59	87	32	98
5	177	67	30	46	9	38
6	66	25	15	15	3	10
7 or more	54	26	8	10	----	12
Not reported	778	508	100	24	33	56
Number of children under 7 years:						
None [2]	2,136	646	230	341	412	348
1	1,511	119	162	147	385	566
2	614	73	118	104	81	256
3	201	32	50	29	17	83
4	41	9	11	6	1	17
5	5	----	1	----	----	3
Not reported	778	508	100	24	33	56
Number of children under 3 years:						
None [2]	3,234	777	381	539	708	670
1	1,081	88	147	73	177	494
2	185	13	41	15	11	105
3	8	1	3	----	----	4
Not reported	778	508	100	24	33	56
Number of children under 1 year:						
None [2]	4,026	847	511	606	848	1,045
1	473	32	56	20	48	225
2	9	----	5	1	----	3
Not reported	778	508	100	24	33	56

[1] Many families were dealt with in more than 1 type of case.
[2] Includes families with no children under the age specified but with unborn children.

Composition of family and whereabouts of the children and the parents.

The number of families dealt with by the courts or the humane society in 1923, excluding those dealt with only by the probate court—concerning which information was incomplete—and those in which there was only an unborn child, was 4,718. These included unmarried mothers and their children, as well as legally constituted family groups; and adopted children were considered as own children. In 625 families (13 per cent) there were stepchildren. One-third of these families (208) included children of husband and wife and stepchildren also. (Table 15.)

In only 1,039 (28 per cent) of the 3,694 families for which whereabouts of all the living children was reported were all the children with both parents (including step-parents). In 1,933 cases (52 per cent) they were all with one parent. In 290 families (8 per cent) the children were separated, some of them being with one or both parents; and in 432 families (12 per cent) none of the children was with either parent. In only 859 families (23 per cent) were there no stepchildren and were all children living with both parents.

TABLE 15.—*Composition of family and whereabouts of children; families dealt with in juvenile and domestic-relations cases in 1923, Hamilton County*

Composition of family [1]	Families dealt with						
		Whereabouts of children reported					Whereabouts of children not reported or child unborn
	Total	Total	All with both parents	All with 1 parent	None with either parent	Separated, some with parent or parents	
Total_____	[2] 4,910	3,694	1,039	1,933	432	290	1,216
Composition reported—families with children_____	4,718	3,681	1,033	1,930	430	288	1,037
No stepchildren in family [3]_____	4,093	3,226	859	1,805	360	202	867
Stepchildren in family_____	625	455	174	125	70	86	170
Stepchildren and children of husband and wife_____	208	150	55	35	13	47	58
Children of husband only_____	96	58	19	11	23	5	38
Children of wife only_____	285	218	94	74	33	17	67
Children of each_____	36	29	6	5	1	17	7
Composition not reported_____	80	13	6	3	2	2	67
Child unborn_____	112	------	------	------	------	------	112

[1] Adopted children are considered as own children.
[2] Excludes 376 families dealt with by the probate court only.
[3] Includes unmarried mothers and their children.

Table 16 shows the composition of the families dealt with in 1923 by the family court or the humane society in relation to cases of various types. Stepchildren were reported in 21 per cent of the families dealt with in divorce cases and in 10 per cent of those dealt with in desertion or nonsupport cases. The percentage with stepchildren was higher in families dealt with in dependency and neglect cases (20) than in those dealt with in delinquency cases (15).

TABLE 16.—*Composition of family; families dealt with in all types [1] and in selected types of juvenile and domestic-relations cases in 1923, Hamilton County*

Composition of family	Families dealt with in all cases		Families [2] dealt with in selected types of cases									
			Delinquency		Dependency or neglect		Mothers' aid		Divorce		Desertion or nonsupport	
	Number	Per cent distribution	Number	Per cent distribution	Number	Per cent distribution	Number	Per cent distribution	Number	Per cent distribution	Number	Per cent distribution
Total_____	[1] 4,910	-----	1,387	------	672	------	651	------	929	-----	1,329	-----
Composition reported—families with children_____	4,718	100	1,325	100	657	100	650	100	914	100	1,263	100
No stepchildren in family_____	4,093	87	1,127	85	523	80	639	98	724	79	1,136	90
Stepchildren in family__	625	13	198	15	134	20	11	2	190	21	127	10
Composition of family not reported, or child unborn_	192	-----	62	------	15	------	1	------	15	------	66	-----

[1] Excludes 376 families dealt with by the probate court only.
[2] Many families were dealt with in more than 1 type of case.

It has been noted that in 12 per cent of the families for which the whereabouts of the children was reported, none of the children was living with either parent. The percentages for the various types of cases ranged from 10 per cent in families dealt with in delinquency cases to 27 per cent in families dealt with in dependency or neglect cases. Among families dealt with in divorce cases with children whose whereabouts was reported, 16 per cent—about one family in every six—had already been so disintegrated at the time the divorce petition was filed that none of the children was living with either parent. All the children were with the mother only in 50 per cent of all the families, but in only 3 per cent were they all with the father only. The percentage in which the children were with the mother only was lowest in families dealt with in delinquency (18 per cent) and highest in those dealt with in mothers' aid cases (90 per cent).

Table 17 shows the whereabouts of children in families dealt with in 1923 by the family court or the humane society in cases of various types.

TABLE 17.—*Whereabouts of children; families dealt with in all types [1] and in selected types of juvenile and domestic-relations cases in 1923, Hamilton County*

Whereabouts of children	Families dealt with in all cases		Families [2] dealt with in selected types of cases									
			Delinquency		Dependency or neglect		Mothers' aid		Divorce		Desertion or nonsupport	
	Number	Per cent distribution	Number	Per cent distribution	Number	Per cent distribution	Number	Per cent distribution	Number	Per cent distribution	Number	Per cent distribution
Total	[1]4,910		1,387		672		651		929		1,329	
Families with children whose whereabouts was reported	3,694	100	770	100	559	100	603	100	680	100	1,180	100
All with both parents or step-parents	1,039	28	456	59	152	27	12	2	27	4	311	26
All with mother	1,833	50	142	18	148	26	540	90	441	65	652	55
All with father	100	3	33	4	30	5			26	4	13	1
Separated, some with parent or parents	290	8	59	8	79	14	45	7	75	11	71	6
None with either parent	432	12	80	10	150	27	6	1	111	16	133	11
Whereabouts of children not reported, or child unborn	1,216		617		113		48		249		149	

[1] Excludes 376 families dealt with by the probate court only.
[2] Many families were dealt with in more than 1 type of case.

FAMILIES DEALT WITH BY THE PROBATE COURT

Cases of adoption.

The probate court dealt with 113 families in adoption cases in 1923. The adoption of more than one child was sought in 6 of these families. In 74 families the child or children whose adoption was sought were of legitimate birth; in 39 families the child was of illegitimate birth. Information concerning the status of the child's parents had been recorded for only 38 of the 74 families in which the children were of legitimate birth and for 23 of the 39 children born out of wedlock. In only 3 of the former families was the child known to be a full orphan; in 21 it was known that 1 parent was dead; in 9 both parents were known to be living, and in 5 families 1 parent was living and the status of the other was unknown. The mothers of 23 of the 39 children born out of wedlock were known to be living, and the status of 16 was not reported.

In 21 of the 113 families the child was a juvenile-court ward, and in 7 families the child was a ward of the court as a result of a divorce proceeding. In 65 families consent to adoption was given by a social agency, in 5 by both parents, in 38 by 1 parent, in 4 by an individual not the parent; in 1 instance the person giving consent was not reported.[4]

In 20 families the child was under 1 year of age, in 38 the child or children were 1 year old but less than 3 years old, and in 55 families the child was 3 years of age or older.

The law specifies that no decree of adoption shall be made until the child has resided in the home of the petitioner at least six months, "unless the court for some special reason which shall be entered in the record deems it best to waive this requirement."[5] However, in 55 of the 99 families in which adoption was granted, the child had been in the adoptive home less than one year. In 42 families the child had lived in the home one year or longer, and in 2 the time in the home was not reported.

It was known that investigations had been made in respect to 57 of the 99 families in which adoption was granted. No investigation appeared to have been made in 39 instances, and in 3 it was not known whether or not there had been an investigation. Among the persons and agencies making investigations were the State department of public welfare, the Bureau of Catholic Charities, various child-placing agencies and children's institutions, probation officers, and attorneys.[6]

Petitions for adoption were granted in 99 families. In 12 families adoption cases were pending at the end of the year. In two families the disposition of the adoption cases was not reported. No petition was reported as denied.

Cases of guardianship.

The probate court dealt with 211 families in which guardianship of children was petitioned, including 208 in which guardianship of both person and estate was sought, and with 3 in which only guardianship of the person was desired. Guardianship was granted in 186 cases, 24 cases were pending at the close of the year, and the disposition of 1 case was not reported. No instance of denial of the petition for guardianship was reported. The number of children in these families whose guardianship was petitioned for was as follows:

	Number of families
Total families	211
1 child	124
2 children	47
3 children	22
4 children	9
5 children	5
6 children	3
7 children	1

Cases of mentally defective children.

Provision for mentally defective children was difficult because the State institution was overcrowded, and children had to remain on the waiting lists for extended periods. The number of families dealt with in this type of case in 1923 was 109 (98 with feeble-minded children, 10 with epileptic children, and 1 with both feeble-minded and epileptic children). The application for admission was

---

[4] The law requires consent to adoption as follows: (1) By the child if over 13 years of age; (2) by each of the living parents or by the mother of a child of illegitimate birth except (a) by one of the parents if the other has failed or refused to support the child for two consecutive years, (b) by the juvenile court if both the parents have failed or refused to support the child for two consecutive years, (c) by the parent or person to whom a juvenile court has awarded legal custody and guardianship because of dependency or because of the mental, moral, or other unfitness of one or both parents, subject to the approval of the juvenile court, (d) by the parent or other person awarded custody by a decree of divorce, subject to the approval of the divorce court, (e) by the legal guardian if the parents are dead or their residence has been unknown at least a year or if the juvenile court has deprived them of legal custody and guardianship because of their unfitness, (f) by an institution or agency having legally acquired custody and control of the child if the State department of public welfare has certified such institution or agency as approved. (Ohio, Code 1930, sec. 10512–11, added by Laws of 1931, p. 472.)

[5] Ohio, Code 1930, sec. 10512–20 (added by Laws of 1931, p. 475).

[6] Through its study group on adoptions the Cleveland Conference on Illegitimacy made a study of the 311 adoptions that were consummated in Cuyahoga County (in which Cleveland is situated) between July 1, 1922, and June 30, 1923. The following statement was made in an article by the chairman of the committee reporting this study: "In Ohio the intent of the law is clearly that the court shall have specific information concerning both the family and child through investigation. It was intended, although the law says 'may,' that the State board of charities [now the department of public welfare], county home, or some accredited children's agency should make the investigation and verify the allegations in the petition. However, in practice, frequently blanks are filled in by the attorney of the foster parents, some court attaché, or even not prepared at all. Only 29 reports in the 66 cases studied were found filed. In 37 cases no reports were attached to the record. Of the 29 reports 27 were by agencies, 1 by the next friend, and 1 not given." See A Study of Adoptions in Cuyahoga County, by Lawrence C. Cole (The Family, vol. 6, No. 9, p.259).

made for 1 child by 99 families, for 2 children by 9 families, and for 3 children by 1 family. More than two-thirds of the children were between the ages of 7 and 16 years. The petition was signed by the parents in the case of 86 of the 109 families, by courts in the case of 15 families, by social agencies in the case of 3 families, and by other persons or agencies in the case of 5 families.

Children from only 50 of the 109 families were admitted to institutions in 1923. In 16 families admission was applied for and in 43 the children were committed to the care of an individual or agency pending admission.

FAMILIES DEALT WITH IN JUVENILE AND DOMESTIC-RELATIONS CASES IN PHILADELPHIA, PA.

The Philadelphia study included juvenile and domestic-relations cases brought before the municipal court of Philadelphia in October, 1923, and a group of divorce cases in which there were children under 18 years of age. (These latter cases, which were dealt with by the court of common pleas, were cleared through the central registration bureau of the municipal court; see p. 93.)

NUMBER OF FAMILIES DEALT WITH AND TYPES OF CASES

In October, 1923, the municipal court dealt with 6,728 families in cases of the types included in the study. The general types of cases in which these families were dealt with were as follows:

1. Juvenile cases (2,902), including delinquency, incorrigible and runaway children 16 to 21 years of age, dependency, neglect, and cases of mentally defective children.
2. Domestic-relations cases (3,535), including desertion or non-support, illegitimacy, and friendly-service cases dealt with by the domestic-relations division.
3. Juvenile and domestic-relations cases (291), including combinations of the types listed in paragraphs 1 and 2.

The 6,728 families dealt with during the month of October, 1923, represent 2 per cent of the 402,946 families enumerated for Philadelphia in the 1920 census.[7]

It will be noted that cases of adoption, guardianship, and contributing to the delinquency of children and neglect of children (adult cases), which were included in the study of interrelation of cases made in Hamilton County, Ohio, were not included in the study made in Philadelphia. In 1923 the juvenile division of the municipal court of Philadelphia disposed of 145 new official adult cases, holding them to the grand jury or otherwise disposing of them.

Six per cent of the 6,728 families included in the inquiry were dealt with in more than one type of case during October, 1923. Table 18 shows the number and per cent of families dealt with in each type of case that were also dealt with in cases of other types. The percentages ranged from 9 in desertion or nonsupport and delinquency to 29 in dependency or neglect cases. In the inquiry in Hamilton County, Ohio, the percentage of families dealt with in more than one type of case was 13, as has been stated, that for desertion or nonsupport cases was 28, and that for cases of dependency or neglect was 41. (See p. 76.) It must be remembered, however, that the figures for Hamilton County cover an entire year and include divorce and certain other types of cases not included in the Philadelphia study. Among the juvenile cases in Philadelphia, as in Hamilton County, dependency or neglect was found to occur most frequently in combination with cases of other types.

The numbers of families dealt with in juvenile cases, desertion or nonsupport, or illegitimacy cases in October, 1923, which had been dealt with in other types of cases included in the study at any time during the year ended October 31, 1923, were also ascertained. (Table 19.)

---

[7] Fourteenth Census of the United States, 1920, vol. 3, Population, p. 864. For definition of the family in the census and as used in this study see footnote 1, p. 71. The number of families in Philadelphia in 1920 calculated on the basis of the 1930 definition of private family was 428,721, but the percentage would have remained the same. The figures given in this section refer to children under 21 years of age and (if not over 16 years) not married nor living outside the city, whereas the figures for Hamilton County, Ohio, were based on the total number of minor children whether those between 16 and 21 were married and living outside the city or not.

TABLE 18.—*Type of cases and interrelation of cases; families dealt with in juvenile and domestic-relations cases by the municipal court in October, 1923, Philadelphia*

Type of case [1]	Total	In 1 type of case		In more than 1 type of case											
				Juvenile cases						Desertion or nonsupport cases		Illegitimacy cases			
				Alone		With desertion or nonsupport cases		With illegitimacy cases							
	Total	Number	Per cent	Number	Per cent	Number	Per cent	Number	Per cent	Number	Per cent	Number	Per cent	Number	Per cent
Juvenile cases:															
Delinquency or incorrigibility [2]	2,501	2,272	91	229	9	71	3	9	(3)	3	(3)	[4] 107	4	39	2
Dependency or neglect	727	516	71	211	29	70	10	9	9	4	1	[5] 115	16	13	2
Mentally defective children	51	41	80	10	20	5	10	----	----	1	2	4	8	----	----
Desertion or nonsupport cases	3,080	2,818	91	262	9	230	7	----	----	5	(3)	----	----	27	1
Illegitimacy cases	778	690	89	88	11	56	7	5	1	----	----	27	3	----	----

[1] Many families were dealt with in more than 1 type of case.
[2] Includes cases of incorrigible, disorderly, and runaway children 16 to 21 years of age.
[3] Less than 1 per cent.
[4] Includes 3 families also dealt with in illegitimacy cases.
[5] Includes 2 families also dealt with in illegitimacy cases.

TABLE 19.—*General type of case; families dealt with by the municipal court during October, 1923, and number and per cent dealt with in cases of other types during the year ended October 31, 1923, Philadelphia*

General type of case	Families dealt with				
	Total	In specified type of case only, during year ended Oct. 31, 1923		In cases of other types during year ended Oct. 31, 1923	
		Number	Per cent	Number	Per cent
Juvenile cases [2]	3,193	2,750	86	443	14
Desertion or nonsupport cases	3,080	2,662	86	418	14
Illegitimacy cases	778	624	80	154	20

[1] Many families were dealt with in more than 1 type of case.
[2] Includes cases of delinquency, dependency, or neglect, and mentally defective children and of incorrigible, disorderly, and runaway children 16 to 21 years of age.

DISTRIBUTION OF CASES AMONG THE DIVISIONS OF THE COURT'S PROBATION DEPARTMENT

Families dealt with by more than one division.

Cases of the types with which this study is concerned were dealt with by five divisions of the probation department (not including the medical department, which supervised persons on probation from all the divisions). These were the juvenile, domestic-relations, women's criminal, men's misdemeanants, and women's misdemeanants divisions. For the purpose of the study the two misdemeanants divisions, which handled incorrigible boys and girls, have been treated as one division. Juvenile cases (including cases of children under 16 and of incorrigible children 16 to 21 years of age) were dealt with by the juvenile and misdemeanants divisions, desertion or nonsupport cases by the domestic-relations division, and illegitimacy cases by the women's criminal division.

Of the 6,728 families, 377 (6 per cent) were dealt with by two or three divisions in October, 1923, in cases of the types included in the study. The divisions dealing with the family in that month were as follows:

Number of families

Total families	6, 728
Families dealt with by only 1 division of the court's probation department	6, 351
Juvenile division	2, 216
Misdemeanants division	627
Domestic-relations division	2, 818
Women's criminal division	690
Families dealt with by 2 divisions	362
Juvenile and misdemeanants divisions	59
Juvenile and domestic-relations divisions	200
Juvenile and women's criminal divisions	36
Misdemeanants and domestic-relations divisions	22
Misdemeanants and women's criminal divisions	18
Domestic-relations and women's criminal divisions	27
Families dealt with by three divisions	15
Juvenile, misdemeanants, and domestic-relations divisions	8
Juvenile, misdemeanants, and women's criminal divisions	2
Juvenile, domestic-relations, and women's criminal divisions	5

Table 20 shows the total number of families dealt with by each division of the court's probation department in October, 1923, and the numbers and percentages of families dealt with during that month by other divisions in cases of the types included in the study.

TABLE 20.—*Distribution of cases by divisions of probation department; number and percentage of families dealt with by one and by more than one division of the probation department of the municipal court in October, 1923, Philadelphia*

Division of probation department	Total	Families dealt with			
		By 1 division of probation department		By more than 1 division of probation department	
		Number	Per cent	Number	Per cent
Juvenile division	2, 526	2, 216	88	310	12
Misdemeanants division	736	627	85	109	15
Domestic-relations division	3, 080	2, 818	91	262	9
Women's criminal division	778	690	89	88	11

Of especial interest in considering the amount of overlapping in the work of the several divisions is the extent to which different divisions were giving probationary supervision to the same family at the same time. Of the 6,728 families included in the study, 4,363 (65 per cent) were under probationary supervision on October 31, 1923, including a few under supervision in cases of types with which the study was not concerned. Excluding 59 families that were under supervision of the medical department only, the total was 4,304, and 164 (4 per cent) of these families were under the supervision of more than one division (not including those under supervision of the medical department and one other division). Thirteen families were under the supervision of three divisions. The most frequent combinations were the juvenile and domestic-relations divisions (60 families), the juvenile and men's misdemeanants (17 families), the juvenile and women's criminal (17 families), the juvenile and women's misdemeanants (14 families), the women's misdemeanants and women's criminal (13 families), and the women's misdemeanants and domestic relations (11 families).

FAMILIES WITH PREVIOUS COURT RECORDS

Of the 6,728 families dealt with by the municipal court in October, 1923, in cases included in the study, 1,255 (19 per cent) had previously been known in such cases to one or more divisions other than those dealing with the family in that month.

Table 21 shows the number of families dealt with in October that had been dealt with previously by one division and by two or more divisions, and the divisions dealing with these families.

TABLE 21.—*Previous court record in divisions of the probation department other than that dealing with family in October, 1923; families dealt with by one or more specified divisions of the probation department of the municipal court in October, 1923, Philadelphia*

Court record in other divisions of probation department prior to October, 1923[1]	Families dealt with										
		By 1 division of probation department				By more than 1 division of probation department					
								Juvenile or misdemeanants and—			
	Total	Total	Juvenile or misdemeanants	Domestic relations	Women's criminal	Total	Juvenile and misdemeanants	Domestic-relations	Women's criminal	Other combinations	Domestic-relations and women's criminal
Total	6,728	6,351	2,843	2,818	690	377	59	222	54	15	27
Not known previously to other divisions	5,473	5,182	2,245	2,398	539	291	43	185	36	[2] 13	14
Known previously to 1 other division	1,079	1,001	515	376	110	78	15	31	18	[3] 2	12
Known previously to 2 or more other divisions	176	168	83	44	41	8	1	6			1

[1] Previous court record in the same division as that dealing with the family in October, 1923, not included nor court record in type of case not covered by the study.
[2] Includes 8 dealt with by the juvenile, misdemeanants, and domestic-relations divisions; 2 dealt with by the juvenile, misdemeanants, and women's criminal divisions; and 3 dealt with by the juvenile, domestic-relations, and women's criminal divisions.
[3] Dealt with by juvenile, domestic-relations, and women's criminal divisions.

Of the 3,193 families dealt with by the juvenile and misdemeanants division, 21 per cent had been previously dealt with in juvenile or family cases by some other division than that dealing with the family in the period covered by the study. Of the 3,080 families dealt with by the domestic-relations division, 15 per cent had been previously dealt with by other divisions. Of the 778 families dealt with by the women's criminal division, 24 per cent had been dealt with previously.

A relation between desertion or nonsupport and delinquency is suggested by the fact that of the 3,080 families dealt with in desertion or nonsupport cases 1,323 (43 per cent) had children between the ages of 10 and 21 years, and in 230 of these families (17 per cent) one or more of the children had been known to the juvenile, misdemeanants, or criminal divisions because of delinquency or crime. More than one child (including a few children under 10 years of age) had been delinquent in 74 families.

INTERRELATION OF DIVORCE WITH THE MUNICIPAL-COURT CASES COVERED BY THE STUDY

The Philadelphia municipal court does not have jurisdiction over divorce. Records were obtained for 284 families with children under 18 years of age to which divorce decrees had been granted by the court of common pleas before

June 30, 1924, the petitions having been filed between January 1 and August, 1923.[8]

The 284 families included in the study represented 18 per cent of the total number of Philadelphia families to which divorces were granted in 1923.[9] Information regarding the number of children under the age of 18 years was obtained for 276 of the 284 families. Eight families were known to have children under this age, but the number of children was not reported. The 276 families had 385 children, an average of 1.4 per family, as compared with an average of 1.8 for the State as a whole for families with children of all ages.[10]

Of the 276 families reporting ages of children, 35 (13 per cent) were reported as having children under the age of 3 years and 141 (50 per cent) as having children under the age of 7 years. Two-thirds of the families (67 per cent) had only one child under the age of 18.

Thirty-six of the 284 families (13 per cent) were known to the municipal court in the year ended October 31, 1923, the year in which the divorce petitions were filed. Ninety-seven additional families had been known to the municipal court previously, making almost half the families (47 per cent) known to the municipal court at some time prior to the end of the fiscal year.

The major cause for divorce among the 284 families was desertion, this being the only cause stated for 135 families and one of the causes for 33 others. These 168 families represented three-fifths of the group. Eighty of the families in which desertion was the sole alleged cause or one of the alleged causes of divorce had been known to the municipal court during or before the year specified— almost exactly the same proportion as for the whole group (48 per cent as compared with 47 per cent). Approximately the same percentage (47) among the families in which cruelty and indignities, but not desertion, were alleged were known to the municipal court.

Table 22 shows the cause alleged for divorce in the Philadelphia divorce cases involving children, and the municipal-court record.

TABLE 22.—*Alleged cause of divorce and municipal-court record; families with children under 18 dealt with by the common-pleas court in divorce cases from January to August, 1923,[a] Philadelphia*

Alleged cause for divorce	Families dealt with in divorce cases					
	Total	Known to municipal court				Not known to municipal court
		Total	In fiscal year in which petition was filed	Before fiscal year in which petition was field	After fiscal year in which petition was filed	
Total	284	140	36	97	7	144
Desertion	168	81	14	66	1	87
Alone	135	63	10	53	--------	72
With cruelty or indignities [b]	[c] 26	16	3	12	1	10
With other cases	[d] 7	2	1	1	--------	5
Cruelty or indignities [b]	98	50	18	28	4	48
Alone	96	49	17	28	4	47
With adultery	2	1	1	--------	--------	1
Adultery	17	9	4	3	2	8
Commission of crime	1	--------	--------	--------	--------	1

[a] Includes only cases in which the decree was granted before July 1, 1924.
[b] Includes 1 or both causes.
[c] Includes 1 case of adultery also.
[d] Includes 5 cases of adultery and 2 of commission of crime.

[8] Only so many of the August cases were included as were necessary to bring to 300 the number of divorce cases included. Later exclusions reduced the total number of divorce cases to 284. (The Hamilton County study included cases in which petitions for divorce had been filed as well as those in which they had been granted.
[9] According to the census 1,578 divorces were granted. See Marriage and Divorce, 1923, p. 54 (U. S. Bureau of the Census, Washington, 1925). But the census figures relate to the calendar year 1923, whereas the figures here given represent families in which divorce petitions were filed during approximately the first seven months of 1923 and decrees were granted prior to June, 1924.
[10] Marriage and Divorce, 1923, p. 40.

Fifty of the one hundred and forty families in divorce cases that had been known to the municipal court had been dealt with by that court in unofficial cases only. All but 5 of the 140 had been known to the domestic-relations division and 121 had been known to that division only. Twelve had been known to the juvenile and domestic-relations divisions, 2 to the domestic-relations division and other divisions, 3 to the juvenile division only, and 2 to the misdemeanants or criminal divisions. The number of families known to the domestic-relations division comprised 48 per cent of the total number (284) for which information was obtained. Thus almost half of this group of divorce cases involving children under the age of 18 years had been known to the domestic-relations division of the municipal court of Philadelphia.

Many of these families had come to the attention of the municipal court more than once, as follows:

Number of families

Total families_____ 140

Dealt with once_____ 68
Dealt with twice_____ 30
Dealt with 3 times_____ 17
Dealt with 4 times_____ 8
Dealt with 5 times_____ 17

The types of complaints made to the municipal court with regard to these 140 families were as follows:

Number of families

Total families_____ 140

Domestic-relations cases_____ 135

Desertion or nonsupport_____ 67
Desertion or nonsupport with abuse, quarreling, improper home, or other charge [11]_____ 33
Desertion or nonsupport with juvenile cases or cases of offenses against children_____ 6
Abuse, quarreling, improper home, custody of child, and other charge [11]_____ 29
Other cases_____ 5

SOCIAL AGENCIES DEALING WITH THE FAMILIES

As the municipal court of Philadelphia registered with the social-service exchange nearly all the types of cases with which this study is concerned, it was possible to ascertain approximately the extent to which families dealt with by the court were known to social agencies of various types.[12]

More than half the families included in the study (58 per cent) were reported as known to social agencies at some time, and more than one-third (36 per cent) were known to more than one agency. The corresponding percentages found in Hamilton County, Ohio, were 53 and 33, but the Hamilton County cases included divorce, adoption, and guardianship, which were not included in Philadelphia (for other differences in method see p. 79) and covered the entire year of 1923. Eighteen Philadelphia families had been known to 15 or more agencies, one to 20 agencies, and two to 24 agencies.

Table 23 shows the per cent distribution of the total number of families according to the number of agencies to which the families were known. Table 24 shows the numbers and percentages of families known to social agencies, by type of case and by type of social agency.

[11] Including a few families also dealt with in children's cases. These cases included some "friendly service" cases dealt with unofficially by the domestic-relations division.
[12] Of the 6,728 families included in the municipal-court study, 627 were dealt with by the misdemeanants division only. The two branches of this division were not registering cases with the social-service exchange when the study was made. A number of families in this group, however, were reported as known to social agencies, though the percentage was smaller than in any other group. (See Table 24, p. 96.)

TABLE 23.—*Number of social agencies to which families were known; families dealt with in juvenile and domestic-relations cases by the municipal court in October, 1923, Philadelphia*

Reported number of social agencies to which family was known prior to and in October, 1923	Families dealt with	
	Number	Per cent distribution
Total	6,728	100
None	2,840	42
1 agency	1,463	22
2 agencies	766	11
3 agencies	519	8
4 agencies	335	5
5 agencies	246	4
6 agencies	182	3
7 or more agencies	377	6

TABLE 24.—*Type of case and number and percentage of cases known to social agencies of all types and of specified types; families dealt with in juvenile and domestic-relation cases by the municipal court in October, 1923, Philadelphia*

Type of case	Families dealt with in all cases	Families dealt with who were reported as known to social agencies prior to and in October, 1923															
		All agencies		Family-welfare agencies		Medical and health agencies		Child-caring agencies and institutions		Agencies dealing with delinquency, prevention of delinquency, and protection of children		Settlements and recreational agencies		Other agencies	
		Number	Per cent	Number	Per cent	Number	Per cent	Number	Per cent	Number	Per cent	Number	Per cent	Number	Per cent
Total	6,723	3,888	58	1,606	24	2,949	44	1,112	17	1,027	15	267	4	714	11
Delinquency	1,599	865	54	343	21	667	42	250	16	254	16	78	5	181	11
Dependency or neglect	515	440	85	265	51	339	66	253	49	194	38	63	12	68	13
Mentally defective child	41	35	(2)	19	(2)	32	(2)	7	(2)	3	(2)	1	(2)	4	(2)
Incorrigible, runaway, or disorderly child	627	170	27	42	7	90	14	45	7	45	7	7	1	24	4
Desertion or nonsupport	2,818	1,463	52	618	22	1,045	37	253	9	288	10	73	3	237	8
Illegitimacy	690	526	76	77	11	471	68	126	18	67	10	4	1	90	13
More than 1 type of case	438	389	89	242	55	305	70	178	41	176	40	41	9	110	25

[1] Many families were known to more than 1 type of agency.
[2] Not shown because number of families was less than 50.

Nearly nine-tenths (89 per cent) of the families dealt with in more than one type of case by the court had been known to social agencies. The percentages known to agencies of all types correspond rather closely to the similar figures for Hamilton County, Ohio, except that the Philadelphia figures for families dealt with in cases of dependency or neglect and of illegitimacy and known to social agencies were considerably higher (85 per cent as compared with 64 per cent for dependency and neglect and 76 per cent as compared with 58 per cent for illegitimacy cases; see p. 81.)

Forty-four per cent of the families had been known to medical and health agencies, including hospitals, dispensaries and clinics, the visiting nurse society, child-health centers, and other health agencies. The corresponding percentage for Hamilton County was 30. Family-welfare agencies ranked next, 24 per cent of the families being reported as known to them, whereas in Hamilton County the family-welfare agencies dealt with the largest proportion of families (34 per cent). A surprisingly large group of families (17 per cent) had been known to child-caring agencies and institutions. In Hamilton County the proportion of families known to such agencies was much smaller.[13] Fifteen per cent of the Philadelphia families and 16 per cent of the Hamilton County families were known to agencies dealing with delinquency, the prevention of delinquency, and child protection. (Table 9.) In view of the importance of wholesome recreation in the prevention of juvenile delinquency, it is interesting to note that only 4 per cent of all the Philadelphia families and only 5 per cent of those dealt with in delinquency cases had been known to settlements and recreational agencies. Doubtless, however, registration with the social-service exchange by agencies of this type was much less complete than registration by most of the other types of social agencies.

The individual agency registering the largest number of families was the Society to Protect Children from Cruelty, 970 families having been known to this agency. The Society for Organizing Charity (now the Family Society) was next, registering 947 families. Almost a third of the families known to the former agency (308) were dealt with in nonsupport or desertion cases and in no other type of case, the next largest number (222) having been dealt with in delinquency cases. Of the 947 families known to the Society for Organizing Charity, 354 were involved in desertion or nonsupport cases and 219 in delinquency cases. Each of these agencies was reported for more than twice as many families as any other single agency. The Philadelphia Children's Bureau was reported as knowing 428 families; the Catholic Children's Bureau, 365; the department of public health and charities, 301; the Jewish Welfare Society, 168; the Jewish Children's Aid Society, 162; and the White-Williams Foundation (an organization doing vocational counseling and visiting-teacher work in the public schools), 146. Six other agencies were reported as having known as many as 100 families. (For the agencies most frequently registering the families in Hamilton County, Ohio, see p. 82.)

CHARACTERISTICS OF THE FAMILIES

Number and ages of the children.

Information on the number of minor children in the family was obtained for 6,017 families (not including 690 families dealt with only in illegitimacy cases and 21 other families for which information on composition of family was not reported). In nearly one-third of these families (32 percent) there was but one minor child (including families in which there was only an unborn child or in which the child had died and the father was paying arrears on a support order or on funeral and confinement expenses). The corresponding percentage for Hamilton County, Ohio, was 41; but the Hamilton County figures included certain groups not represented in the Philadelphia figures (families dealt with only in illegitimacy cases and cases of divorce, adoption, and guardianship).[14] In 21 per cent of the families there were two children, and 47 per cent had three or more. Excluding unborn children, the total number of minor children in the 6,017 families was 17,143, an average of 2.8 per family, as compared with an average of 2.4 per family in Hamilton County.

Table 25 shows the number of minor children in families by age groups. In 63 per cent of the families all the children were under 16 years of age. This percentage was somewhat smaller than that in Hamilton County (71). Families in which all the children were between 16 and 21 years represented 7 per cent of the total in Philadelphia.

---

[13] The differences in the proportions known to family-welfare and to children's agencies are partly accounted for by the fact that family-welfare agencies in Hamilton County included the child-caring work and the Big Brother and Big Sister work of the Bureau of Catholic Charities and the United Jewish Social Agencies.
[14] The probate court in Hamilton County, which deals with adoption, guardianship, and commitment of mentally defective children, had only very incomplete social data. Doubtless a number of families with only one child recorded had in reality more than one child.

TABLE 25.—*Number of minor children in family by age groups; families dealt with in juvenile and in desertion or nonsupport cases by the municipal court in October, 1923, Philadelphia*

Number of minor children in family	Families dealt with in juvenile and in desertion or nonsupport cases					
	Total	Ages of minor children				
		All under 16	Some under 16, some 16 but under 21	All 16 but under 21	Not reported	Child unborn or dead
Total	6,038	3,782	1,757	418	21	60
Number of minor children in family reported	6,017	3,782	1,757	418	----------	60
1	1,907	1,631	----------	276	----------	----------
2	1,270	911	245	114	----------	----------
3	937	541	374	22	----------	----------
4	651	315	330	6	----------	----------
5	501	189	312	----------	----------	----------
6	321	110	211	----------	----------	----------
7	206	49	157	----------	----------	----------
8	101	14	87	----------	----------	----------
9	41	19	22	----------	----------	----------
10	15	2	13	----------	----------	----------
11	3	----------	3	----------	----------	----------
12	4	1	3	----------	----------	----------
Child unborn or dead	60	----------	----------	----------	----------	[1] 60
Number of minor children in family not reported	21	----------	----------	----------	21	----------

[1] Includes some families in which the father was paying arrears on a support order or funeral or confinement expenses.

Table 26 shows the numbers of children of specified ages in families dealt with in cases of desertion or nonsupport and in juvenile cases (including delinquent, dependent, neglected, and mentally defective children, and incorrigible, disorderly, and runaway children between the ages of 16 and 21 years).

TABLE 26.—*Number of minor children in family by age groups; families dealt with in juvenile and in desertion or nonsupport cases by the municipal court in October, 1923, Philadelphia*

Number of children of specified ages in family	Families [1] dealt with in juvenile and in desertion or nonsupport cases		
	Total	Juvenile cases [2]	Desertion or nonsupport cases
Total	6,038	3,193	3,080
Number of children under 21 years:			
1	1,907	808	1,138
2	1,270	487	822
3	937	527	460
4	651	414	269
5	501	368	164
6	321	248	96
7 or more	370	305	83
Unborn or dead	60	20	43
Not reported	21	16	5

[1] Some families were dealt with in both juvenile and desertion or nonsupport cases.
[2] Includes cases of delinquent, dependent, neglected, and mentally defective children and incorrigible, disorderly, and runaway children 16 to 21 years of age.

TABLE 26.—*Number of minor children in family by age groups; families dealt with in juvenile and in desertion or nonsupport cases by the municipal court in October, 1923, Philadelphia*—Continued

Number of children of specified ages in family	Families dealt with in juvenile and in desertion or nonsupport cases		
	Total	Juvenile cases	Desertion or nonsup-port cases
Number of children under 16 years:			
None [3]	446	329	128
1	2,072	888	1,233
2	1,305	531	816
3	872	471	451
4	580	387	233
5	356	257	119
6	225	177	62
7 or more	149	125	33
Not reported	33	28	5
Number of children under 7 years:			
None [3]	2,900	1,881	1,098
1	1,687	604	1,155
2	956	422	583
3	339	179	187
4	85	49	42
5	13	9	6
6	2	2	----------
Not reported	56	47	9
Number of children under 3 years:			
None [3]	4,356	2,526	1,979
1	1,309	501	873
2	288	100	205
3	20	11	13
4	5	4	1
Not reported	60	51	9
Number of children under 1 year:			
None [3]	5,431	2,938	2,697
1	535	196	368
2	10	5	7
Not reported	62	54	8

[3] Includes families with no children under the age specified but with unborn or dead children.

In 9 per cent of all the families dealt with in juvenile cases and cases of desertion or nonsupport there were known to be living children under 1 year of age (not including unborn children); 27 per cent had children under the age of 3 years; 52 per cent had children under 7 years; 93 per cent had children under 16. Among families dealt with in desertion or nonsupport cases 36 per cent had children under 3 years of age and 64 per cent had children under 7 years of age. The corresponding percentages in desertion or nonsupport cases in Hamilton County were 47 and 73.

Whereabouts of the children and the parents.

Some or all of the children were living with one or both parents or with step-parents in 87 per cent of the 5,927 families dealt with in juvenile cases and cases of desertion or nonsupport for which whereabouts of children was reported. In 13 per cent the children were not with the parents. The percentages of families dealt with in various types of cases in which none of the children was with either parent were as follows: In cases of delinquency and incorrigibility, 15; of dependency or neglect, 34; of desertion or nonsupport, 7. (The corresponding percentages for Hamilton County were delinquency, 10; dependency or neglect, 27; desertion or nonsupport, 11.)

In 24 per cent of the families dealt with in juvenile cases and in cases of desertion or nonsupport some or all of the children were not living with either parent. The whereabouts of the children not living with their parents was as follows:

Number of families

Total families _____ 1, 427

Children living with relatives_____ 457
Children married_____ [15] 17
Children living or working away from home_____ [16] 93
Children in foster or adoptive home_____ 202
Children in institution_____ 392
Children separated, some in foster homes or institutions____ 170
Children elsewhere_____ 45
Whereabouts not reported_____ 51

Table 27 shows the whereabouts of the children in families dealt with in juvenile cases and in cases of desertion or nonsupport.

TABLE 27.—*Whereabouts of children and type of case; families dealt with in juvenile and in desertion or nonsupport cases by the municipal court in October, 1923, Philadelphia*

Whereabouts of children	Families dealt with in juvenile and in desertion or or nonsupport cases	Families [1] dealt with in selected types of cases		
		Delinquency or incorrigibility	Dependency or neglect	Desertion or nonsupport
Total_____	6, 038	2, 501	727	3, 080
Families with children whose whereabouts was reported_____	5, 927	2, 446	724	3, 022
Some or all children with one or both parents_____	5, 139	2, 073	467	2, 808
With both parents (or parent and step-parent)_	2, 414	1, 448	161	869
With mother only_____	2, 286	455	223	1, 729
With father only_____	405	162	81	186
Parent not reported_____	[2] 34	8	2	24
Children not with either parent_____	788	373	257	214
Whereabouts of children not reported, or child unborn_	111	55	3	58

[1] Many families were dealt with in more than 1 type of case.
[2] Includes 29 families in which the parents were divorced or separated and 5 in which the parental status was not reported.

Both own parents or step-parents were in the home in 41 per cent of the families in which whereabouts of children was reported. In a very few cases a stepfather and stepmother were in the home, both own parents being absent. Only the mother was in the home in 38 per cent of the families and only the father in 7 per cent. The percentage of families in which both parents were in the home was considerably higher in Philadelphia (41) than in Hamilton County, Ohio (28). This difference is due in part at least to the inclusion of mothers' aid cases and divorce cases in the Hamilton County figures.

[15] In 7 other families some of the children were married and living away from home.
[16] Including children in boarding schools and in the Army or the Navy.

IN RE GAULT
AND
THE FUTURE OF JUVENILE LAW

Norman Dorsen
and
Daniel A. Rezneck

In Re Gault and the Future of Juvenile Law

NORMAN DORSEN* AND DANIEL A. REZNECK**

"The prophecies of what the courts will do in fact," said Justice Holmes, "are what I mean by the law."[1] Predicting the future development of the law in the wake of *In re Gault*[2] is a risky business. The case represented the Supreme Court's first foray into the no-man's land of federal constitutional rights of juveniles, but it will obviously not be the last.[3]

So far-reaching a decision will initiate a lengthy process of constitutional adjudication, accompanied by legislative change and alteration of administrative and judicial practices. This process will unfold primarily in the state courts, legislatures and other governmental agencies, which bear initial and major responsibility for implementing *Gault* and piecing out its full implications.

The Supreme Court can be expected to participate only sporadically in this process of change, through the review of cases carefully

---

*Professor of Law and Director of the Arthur Garfield Hays Civil Liberties Program, New York University School of Law.

**Member of the firm of Arnold & Porter, Washington, D.C., and Adjunct Professor of Law, Georgetown Law Center.

The authors were counsel for appellants in the United States Supreme Court in the *Gault* case. They gratefully acknowledge the assistance of Stephen Gillers, a third year law student at New York University, in preparing the manuscript for press.

After the preparation of this article, the Supreme Court granted certiorari in another juvenile case. In the Matter of Whittington, No. 701, O.T. 1967. One of the authors of this article, Daniel A. Rezneck, is co-counsel for petitioner Whittington in the Supreme Court.

1. Holmes, *The Path of the Law*, 10 HARV. L. REV. 457, 461 (1897).

2. 387 U.S. 1 (1967).

3. The Whittington case raises issues relating to standard of proof and other fact-finding procedures in juvenile delinquency hearings, as well as questions of interrogation and detention of juveniles, all left unresolved by the Court in Gault, see pp. 3-5, *infra*.

Gault's precursor, Kent v. U.S., 383 U.S. 541 (1966), ostensibly was decided on statutory grounds as an interpretation of the District of Columbia Juvenile Court Act, although the constitutional mandates which emerged in *Gault* were obviously close to the surface.

1

selected to focus on critical problems of the juvenile system. The Court will no doubt tread carefully, aware that, even if *Gault* had never arisen, this would have been a time of change in the juvenile courts. The ferment is evidenced by major statutory changes in recent years[4] and comprehensive studies of juvenile justice such as that recently concluded by the National Crime Commission.[5] The Supreme Court's role therefore may consist primarily of formulating basic minimal procedural standards for the conduct of juvenile justice, without undertaking to frame a detailed code of juvenile procedures. What form these standards are likely to take is the subject of this paper.

In determining the implications of *Gault*, it is necessary to take account of what the Court held and what it did not hold, the rationale that emerges from its decision and those theories that were rejected. We will first state the precise holdings and the specific reservations of the Court in *Gault*, then set out the underlying principles of the decision, and finally consider its impact on certain important issues of juvenile justice.

I. What Gault Held

The Supreme Court first held that the Due Process Clause of the Fourteenth Amendment applies to proceedings in state juvenile courts to adjudicate a juvenile a delinquent.[6] It then proceeded to "ascertain the precise impact of the due process requirement" upon proceedings which determine whether a juvenile is delinquent by reason of having violated a criminal statute, when the consequence of this determination may be commitment to an institution.[7]

---

4. *E.g.*, N.Y. Family Court Act, (1962); Illinois Juvenile Court Act, Ill. Stat. Ann. Ch. 37, §§ 701-707 (Supp. 1966).

5. The President's Commission on Law Enforcement and Administration of Justice, Task Force Report: Juvenile Delinquency and Youth Crime (1967) [hereinafter "Task Force"].

6. 387 U.S. at 12-13. This was in accord with the decision of the Arizona Supreme Court on this point.

7. *Id.* at 14. Gerald Gault was adjudicated a delinquent under a section of the Arizona Code defining delinquency to include a violation of state law. He was found to have violated an Arizona statute making it a misdemeanor to use obscene language in the presence or hearing of a woman, a crime carrying a penalty of imprisonment of not more than two months and $5 to $50 fine. He was committed to the state industrial school under a provision authorizing detention up to the age of 21, *i.e.*, 6 years in his case.

The Court's specific holdings are as follows:

(a) A juvenile charged with delinquency, and his parents or guardian, must be given written notice of "the specific charge or factual allegations" against him at the "earliest practicable time" in advance of any hearing to adjudicate the merits of the charge, and in any event "sufficiently in advance" of such hearing to permit preparation.[8]

(b) Before such a hearing may be held, the juvenile and his parents must be notified of the juvenile's right to be represented by counsel retained by them, or, if they are unable to afford counsel, that counsel will be appointed to represent the juvenile.[9]

(c) The privilege against self-incrimination is applicable in such a hearing and the juvenile must be advised that he does not have to testify or make a statement.[10]

(d) Absent a "valid confession adequate to support" a determination of delinquency, an adjudication at such a hearing must be based on the sworn testimony of witnesses who are available for confrontation and cross-examination.[11]

II. What Gault Did Not Hold

Gault did not hold that all the procedural guarantees applicable in the case of an adult charged with crime apply in juvenile delinquency proceedings. The Court reiterated its view, as expressed in *Kent*,[12] that "We do not mean . . . to indicate that the hearing to be held must conform with all of the requirements of a criminal trial. . . ."[13]

Thus, even with respect to an adjudicative hearing to determine delinquency based on a law violation, the Court reserved the following questions:

(a) Whether, and to what extent, the juvenile court may admit hearsay or other testimony normally inadmissible under the rules of evidence.[14]

---

8. *Id*. at 33.
9. *Id*. at 41.
10. *Id*. at 55.
11. *Id*. at 56.
12. 383 U.S. at 555.
13. 387 U.S. at 30.
14. *Id*. at 11.

(b) What the correct burden of proof is in such a proceeding.[15]

(c) Whether there is a right to have a transcript or other record kept of the proceeding.[16]

(d) Whether there is a right to appeal from an adjudication of delinquency in such a proceeding.[17]

(e) Whether a juvenile court judge must state the grounds for his finding when he is the trier of fact.[18]

Gault is silent on other major procedural questions relating to the conduct of adjudicative hearings, including:

(a) The right to trial by jury.

(b) The right to a public proceeding.

(c) The right of compulsory process to secure witnesses for the defense.

All other questions relating to juvenile proceedings were reserved by the Court. It divided juvenile proceedings into three phases—pre-judicial, adjudicative, and dispositional—and emphasized that its holdings were directed only to the adjudicative stage. The Court said: "We are not here concerned with the procedures or constitutional rights applicable to the pre-judicial stages of the juvenile process, nor do we direct our attention to the post-adjudicative or dispositional process."[19]

Thus the Court declined to decide certain critical questions relating to the pre-judicial stage, to wit:

(a) Whether juveniles are entitled to invoke the constitutional guarantee against unreasonable searches and seizures.

(b) Whether juveniles who have been taken into custody have rights to bail, a hearing to test the legality of pre-hearing detention, and other safeguards against unlawful confinement.

(c) Whether the admissibility of pre-hearing statements made by

---

15. *Id.*

16. *Id.* at 58.

17. *Id.* Both (c) and (d) were tendered to the Court for decision by appellants in Gault.

18. *Id.*

19. *Id.* at 13.

juveniles to police or probation officers is governed by the requirements of *Miranda* v. *Arizona*.[20]

(d) Whether juveniles have a right to counsel prior to the adjudicative hearing stage and, if so, at what point.[21]

Likewise, the court reserved all questions as to the dispositional phase. It even declined to state "whether ordinary due process requirements must be observed with respect to hearings to determine the disposition of the delinquent child."[22] It also did not pass on the power of courts to determine the adequacy of treatment being received by a committed juvenile, but it emphasized the serious inadequacies in dispositional resources.[23]

The reasons for the Court's wariness to rule on problems of the pre-judicial and dispositional stages of juvenile proceedings are not far to seek. They transcend the traditional judicial reluctance to decide questions not necessary for decision or inadequately developed in the record below.

The Court clearly regards both the pre-judicial and dispositional phases as flexible and adaptable to the special needs of juveniles. These stages offer the states unique possibilities for furthering the rehabilitative goals that have historically characterized the philosophy of the juvenile court movement. The Court is unwilling to strait-jacket, with procedural requirements derived from the criminal law, phases of the juvenile process which are undergoing change and where creative thinking about new techniques is now taking place.[24]

Thus the Court, in an important footnote, called attention to the recommendation of the National Crime Commission that "Juvenile Courts should make fullest feasible use of preliminary conferences to

---

20. 384 U.S. 436 (1966).

21. 387 U.S. at 12, 13.

22. *Id*. at 27.

23. *Id*. at 22-23 n. 30. Earlier, in Kent, the Court had said that some questions of treatment are "not within judicial competence." 383 U.S. at 543.

24. Adjudication of delinquency, on the other hand, is the determination whether the juvenile has committed an act which may make it necessary for society, acting through the juvenile court, to exert a sanction against him. In itself the adjudicative process has relatively little to contribute to the rehabilitative goal, and the justification for departing from historic methods for the determination of guilt is far weaker.

dispose of cases short of adjudication."[25] In the same note the Court highlighted the "consent decree" procedure urged by the Commission, under which a juvenile may submit to court supervision with his consent and that of his legal representative, without an adjudication that he is delinquent and without the possibility of commitment to an institution.[26]

With regard to the dispositional phase—whose *raison d'etre* is to carry out the philosophy which animated the juvenile court movement —the Court seems implicitly to recognize that the procedures should be adapted to the goal of individualized treatment. Here the analogy to the criminal process is least compelling, and the relevance of practice and procedures drawn from the criminal law least demonstrable.

A possible limitation of great importance on the sweep of *Gault* should be observed. The case involved an adjudication of delinquency based on a violation of law that would have been a crime if committed by an adult. It did not involve delinquency based solely on "truancy" or "incorrigibility" or one of the other categories that states have created to justify a determination of delinquency arising from a juvenile's status. It has been estimated that so-called "truants" or "incorrigibles" account for over 25% of the total number of alleged delinquents appearing in juvenile courts.[27]

It might be argued that a juvenile charged with being a delinquent solely on the basis of "truancy" or "incorrigibility" would not

---

25. 387 U.S. at 31 n. 48. New York and Illinois have provided statutory authority for these conferences, with a view toward formalizing them to some extent while preserving "the virtues of informal negotiation." *See Task Force,* p. 21; N.Y. Family Court Act § 734 (1962); Ill. Juvenile Court Act, Ill. Stat. Ann. Ch. 37, §§ 703-08 (Supp. 1966).

Moreover, even where such conferences have not been statutorily sanctioned, the intake process of the juvenile court provides the opportunity for informal adjustment and disposition of juvenile cases in which the goal of individualized treatment can be pursued. In many juvenile courts about half the cases are informally adjusted at intake, without the necessity for adjudication. *Task Force,* p. 5. The National Crime Commission reported that:

"Intake is set apart from the screening process used in adult criminal courts by the pervasive attempt to individualize each case and the nature of the personnel administering the discretionary process." *Id.* at 14.

26. The consent decree procedure may enable the juvenile court judge to "short-circuit the more rigorous procedural requirements [of the adjudicative stage] and continue to make use of the flexibility and other advantages of informality where he thought it desirable." *Task Force,* p. 40.

27. *Task Force,* p. 4.

be entitled to the rights recognized in *Gault,* even if he faces the stigma of a delinquency adjudication and the possibility of commitment. The theory would presumably be that if the conduct charged is not a crime when committed by an adult, rights drawn from the criminal law would have no application.

Gault leaves the matter unclear. The Court stated that it was dealing with proceedings "by which a determination is made as to whether a juvenile is a 'delinquent' as a result of *alleged misconduct on his part,* with the consequence that he may be committed to a state institution."[28] This language appears broad enough to embrace delinquency adjudications carrying the threat of commitment, even if the specific misconduct relied on is not a crime when committed by an adult. At least the rights declared fundamental by *Gault*—notice, counsel, confrontation and cross-examination, and the privilege against self-incrimination—should apply to any proceeding carrying the possible consequences of an adjudication of delinquency and institutionalization.[29]

This aspect of juvenile court law is in flux, however. There is discernible a legislative trend to treat "truants" or "incorrigibiles" differently from those juveniles who commit law violations: to adjudicate the former as "persons in need of supervision" (known as "PINS") and to reserve the label "delinquency" for the latter.[30] An effort is made thereby to eliminate the stigma of a delinquency adjudication from these juveniles.[31]

---

28. 387 U.S. at 13. (Emphasis supplied.)

29. The United States Court of Appeals for the District of Columbia Circuit has already indicated its view that the notice requirement of *Gault* applies to a proceeding in which a juvenile was charged with being "beyond control." In the Matter of Elmore, No. 20, 497, (D.C. Cir. May 23, 1967).

30. *See* New York Family Court Act § 712 (1962); Illinois Juvenile Court Act, Ill. Stat. Ann. Ch. 37, §§ 702-03 (Supp. 1966). Compare 387 U.S. at 24 n. 31.

31. It has been urged that such persons should not be subject to institutionalization. *See* Burns & Stern, *The Prevention of Juvenile Delinquency, Task Force,* Appendix S, p. 398.

The National Crime Commission has said:

". . . especially in instances of conduct that is delinquent but would not be criminal for an adult, it is of the greatest importance that all alternative measures be employed before recourse is had to court." *Task Force,* p. 26.

When such cases require court action, they "should be dealt with separately from criminal cases in treatment and perhaps in court proceedings as well." The Commission suggests that ultimately the jurisdiction of juvenile courts should perhaps be narrowed to divest power over such cases altogether. *Id.,* p. 27.

Removal of both the stigma of delinquency and the threat of commitment might well justify a difference in procedural treatment between "PINS" and juveniles accused of law violations.[32] It cannot be assumed that the application of particular procedural rights in juvenile courts by the Supreme Court in cases involving alleged law violations which are adult crimes will necessarily carry over in all respects to all categories of juveniles over whom the juvenile court exercises jurisdiction.[33] As we shall discuss below, *Gault* need not be interpreted as imposing procedural inflexibility on differing categories of juvenile court adjudication, any more than it does on the pre-judicial and dispositional phases of the process.[34]

III. The Underlying Rationale of Gault

The theoretical basis of *Gault* is far from self-evident. Indeed, Justice Harlan complained that the Court had failed "to provide any discernible standard for the measurement of due process in relation to juvenile proceedings . . . ."[35]

The Court's basic rationale can be discerned, however, from the theories it rejected either explicitly or implicitly, those which had previously been enunciated to justify the use of noncriminal procedures in juvenile courts and those which were applied by the concurring opinions of Justices Black and Harlan.

---

32. Compare the treatment by the Model Penal Code of the American Law Institute (Proposed Official Draft 1962).of so-called "welfare offenses" for violations of housing code and pure food and drug laws. Section 1.04 provides that "no other sentence than a fine, or fine and forfeiture or other civil penalty is authorized upon conviction" and that "a violation does not constitute a crime and conviction of a violation shall not give rise to any disability or legal disadvantage based on conviction of a criminal offense." The effect of reducng a crime to a violation in the Code is to permit absolute liability, that is, to omit the ordinary requirement of culpability for criminal conduct. See Section 2.05.

33. *A fortiori,* this is true of such categories as "neglected" or "dependent" children; such persons even now are not classified as delinquents and the juvenile court's jurisdiction over them is not based on adjudication of misconduct of any kind by them.

34. Mr. Justice Harlan was concerned about this problem and urged that "it would therefore be imprudent, at the least, to build upon these classifications rigid systems of procedural requirements which would be applicable, or not, in accordance with the descriptive label given to the particular proceeding." 387 U.S. at 77.

35. *Id.* at 67.

The Court made clear that the so-called *parens patriae* theory—that the juvenile court stands *in loco parentis* to a juvenile who never had the right to personal liberty anyway, but only to parental custody and care—is inadequate to determine the appropriate procedures in an adjudicative hearing. While not altogether rejecting the *parens patriae* philosophy, the Court indicated that the doctrine's appropriate sphere of operation is in the dispositional phase and in shielding the juvenile against such prejudicial byproducts of the juvenile process as broadside disclosure of his contacts with juvenile authorities.[36]

The Court also made short shrift of the notion that the "civil" label frequently attached by courts to juvenile proceedings justifies denying rights accorded in criminal proceedings, in view of the possible incarceration of the juvenile against his will.[37]

The Court also rejected the *"quid pro quo"* theory sometimes advanced to justify denial of procedural rights to juveniles: that in return for denying the juvenile rights, the state gives him "treatment" and rehabilitation instead of punishment and retribution. As it had in *Kent*,[38] the Court reiterated its doubts that juveniles in fact receive the individualized care and treatment which is the professed objective of the juvenile court system.[39]

In determining what procedural guarantees to recognize in *Gault,* the Court did not adopt the rationales formulated by concurring Justices. Justice Black advanced two theories:

(1) That because Gault was charged with a crime under state law and ordered confined for up to six years, and the Bill of Rights enumerates the guarantees of persons charged with crimes, and all these guarantees are made applicable to the states by the Fourteenth Amendment, Gault was therefore entitled to all rights he was asserting which are enumerated in the Bill of Rights.[40]

(2) That if Gault had been an adult, he would have been entitled to all the guarantees of the Bill of Rights, and that to deny him

---

36. *Id*. at 24-25, 27.

37. The Court acknowledged that the "civil" label has its appropriate place —in protecting the juvenile from being branded a criminal as a consequence of a delinquency adjudication. *Id*. at 23-24.

38. 383 U.S. at 555.

39. 387 U.S. at 22-23 n. 30.

40. *Id*. at 61.

any of these rights solely because he was a juvenile was to deny him the equal protection of the laws in contravention of the Fourteenth Amendment.[41]

Although the Court emphasized that Gault was charged with a crime under Arizona law and faced the threat of confinement, it was careful to indicate that these factors do not automatically invoke all procedural guarantees of adults accused of crime. Thus, in dealing with the privilege against self-incrimination, the Court said:

> ... juvenile proceedings to determine 'delinquency,' which may lead to commitment to a state institution, must be regarded as 'criminal' *for purpose of the privilege against self-incrimination . . . For this purpose, at least,* commitment is a deprivation of liberty.[42]

Of equal significance is the fact that the Court did not rest its various holdings on the need to prevent disparity of treatment between juveniles and adults.[43] The failure to rely on the Equal Protection Clause, combined with the Court's recognition of some unique features of juvenile court justice, indicates that the Court believes a state may rationally classify juvenile and adult offenders separately, even for procedural purposes. If this is true, it is another indication that the Supreme Court will permit the application in the juvenile courts of less than all procedural guarantees of adults accused of crime.

Finally, the Court also implicitly rejected Justice Harlan's suggested test, which is to

> ... determine what forms of procedural protection are necessary to guarantee the fundamental fairness of juvenile proceedings, and not which of the procedures now employed in criminal trials should be transplanted intact to proceedings in these specialized courts.[44]

It appears, therefore, that in *Gault* the Court embarked on the same course of selective incorporation of the guarantees of the Bill of Rights into the Fourteenth Amendment, in the context of state juvenile proceedings, that it has previously undertaken with respect to the

---

41. *Id.*

42. *Id.* at 49-50. (Emphasis supplied.)

43. The Court did take account of this factor. *Id.* at 29-30.

44. *Id.* at 74.

rights of adult defendants in criminal courts.[45] This course presents the difficulty of determining when and why a particular guarantee will be incorporated into the Fourteenth Amendment and imposed on the states. The nearest the Court has come to articulating a test is whether a right is "so fundamental and essential to a fair trial that it is incorporated in the Due Process Clause of the Fourteenth Amendment."[46]

Nevertheless, the selective incorporation technique has much to commend it, in view of the complex and fluid nature of juvenile justice. It provides a ready referent for the contours of procedural due process: the specific guarantees of the Bill of Rights.[47] It enables the Court to control the timing of the incorporation of particular guarantees. Most important, it gives the Court desirable flexibility in allowing the juvenile courts to preserve as much of their traditional non-adversary philosophy of dealing with juveniles as is consistent with

---

45. In a perceptive pre-Gault article on the Kent case, Professor Paulsen—while he apparently would have preferred the "fundamental fairness" test—urged the Court to utilize selective incorporation rather than to apply the Bill of Rights wholesale. He wrote:

"If the Court can selectively 'absorb' portions of the Bill of Rights in adult criminal cases it can do so for children's matters in juvenile court." Paulsen, Kent v. United States: The Constitutional Context of Juvenile Cases, 1966 SUPREME COURT REVIEW, 167, 186.

46. Washington v. Texas, 388 U.S. 14, 18 (1967), citing Gideon v. Wainwright, 372 U.S. 335, 342 (1963).

This approach may appear to differ little verbally from the "fundamental fairness" test but it could lead to drastically different results. In Gault "selective incorporation" led the Court to apply the rights of confrontation and cross-examination and the privilege against self-incrimination along with notice of charges and right to counsel, whereas Justice Harlan concurred on the notice and counsel points, dissented on confrontation, cross-examination, and the privilege against self-incrimination, and accepted the right to a transcript—an issue which the Court did not reach.

47. Justice Brennan said in the lecture which gave renewed impetus to the Court's use of selective incorporation:

"The Bill of Rights is the primary source of expressed information as to what is meant by constitutional liberty." Brennan, *The Bill of Rights and the States,* 36 N.Y.U. L. REV. 761, 776 (1961).

fair adjudication.[48] To the extent that the states can demonstrate that over-riding interests of the juvenile court system militate against adopting a particular guarantee, the Court is not committed to impose it on them.

In predicting the course of decision on particular problems, it is unlikely that the Court will impose a guarantee of the Bill of Rights in juvenile cases until it has first been applied in criminal trials.[49] This in itself preserves a wide range of choice, since all but a handful of the specifics of the Bill of Rights relating to criminal prosecutions have now been imposed on the states.[50] Indeed, assuming the process of incor-

---

48. The National Crime Commission has urged an accommodation of the "goal of procedural justice" with "the often competing goal of the child's welfare." It states:

"What is entailed is not abandonment of the unique qualities of the juvenile court or adoption of the precise model of the criminal trial in all its particulars." *Task Force,* p. 31. *See also* Resolution No. 2 of the National Council of Juvenile Court Judges, adopted June 29, 1967.

49. The Court's refusal to pass on two of the issues tendered by appellants in Gault—right to an appeal and right to a transcript—supports this conclusion, since neither has been held to be the constitutional right of criminal defendants. *See* 387 U.S. at 58. The cases invalidating denial of transcripts to indigent defendants have been based on the Equal Protection Clause, not on an absolute right to an appeal or a transcript. *See* Griffin v. Illinois, 351 U.S. 12 (1956); *cf.* Coppedge v. United States, 369 U.S. 438 (1962).

Justice Stewart pointed out that Gault—who was charged with a misdemeanor under Arizona law—was granted the right to appointed counsel, although the Court has not yet held that an adult misdemeanor defendant in a state court has such a right under Gideon. But the Court neatly finessed the point by stressing that the potential duration of Gault's commitment was six years. The court said:

"A proceeding where the issue is whether the child will be found to be 'delinquent' and subjected to the loss of his liberty for years is comparable in seriousness to a felony prosecution." 387 U.S. at 36.

50. The guarantees which have are:
Notice of charges—Cole v. Arkansas, 333 U.S. 196 (1948).
Public trial—In re Oliver, 333 U.S. 257 (1948).
Unreasonable search and seizure—Wolf v. Colorado, 338 U.S. 25 (1949); Mapp v. Ohio, 367 U.S. 643 (1961).
Cruel and unusual punishment—Robinson v. California, 370 U.S. 660 (1962).
Appointed counsel—Gideon v. Wainwright, 372 U.S. 335 (1963).
Privilege against self-incrimination—Malloy v. Hogan, 378 U.S. 1 (1964).
Confrontation and cross-examination—Pointer v. Texas, 380 U.S. 400 (1965).
Speedy trial—Klopfer v. North Carolina, 386 U.S. 213 (1967).
Compulsory process—Washington v. Texas, 388 U.S. 14 (1967).
An impartial jury—Parker v. Gladden, 385 U.S. 363 (1966).

poration continues at the present rate, virtually the entire Bill of Rights will soon be applicable to the States.

Even if an equivalent process takes place for the juvenile courts, its impact is almost certain to be cushioned by the new device the Court has fashioned as an adjunct to the incorporation process: prospective application of newly incorporated rights, whereby the states are bound to follow the new procedures in the future but adjudications prior to incorporation of a particular guarantee are left undisturbed. As we discuss in greater detail below,[51] although *Gault* itself is silent on the point, the same prospective application will probably be accorded to most, if not all, of the rights newly recognized in *Gault* and to those which may be applied in future cases.

IV. Gault as Applied to Particular Issues

We turn now to consider the application of *Gault* to some of the major legal issues likely to arise from the decision. In accordance with the Court's differentiation, the discussion will be divided into three parts: adjudicative, pre-judicial, and dispositional.

A. *The Adjudicative Stage*

Those procedural rights held applicable in *Gault* have manifold implications for existing practices in many juvenile courts and will require extensive further explication.

1. FAIR NOTICE

The Court's requirement of fair notice is deceptively simple, but it leads to elaborate consequences.[52] As the Court formulated the standard, due process requires "notice which would be deemed constitutionally adequate in a civil or criminal proceeding."[53]

Although the Court is unlikely to require pleading with the tech-

---

The guarantees which have not are:
Grand jury indictment
Double jeopardy
Trial by jury
Excessive bail

51. See pp. 28-31, *infra.*

52. In Gault the petition filed in the juvenile court recited only the conclusory allegation that Gault was "delinquent" and it was not served on the boy or his parents prior to the hearing.

53. 387 U.S. at 33.

nicality of a formal indictment,[54] it seems clear that a constitutionally sufficient petition will have to indicate both the factual and legal basis on which an adjudication of delinquency is sought. If the claim of delinquency rests on a law violation, the specific statute must be cited. No defendant in a civil or criminal case can adequately prepare a defense without knowing the rule of law invoked against him; this is especially true with respect to criminal violations, since the same conduct frequently may violate more than one statute.[55] The same principle should apply when the conduct charged may fall within one or more of the categories used to cover forms of delinquency not involving law violations, e.g., "truancy," incorrigibility," "beyond control."[56]

Another conclusion emerges from the requirement of fair notice: if a particular factual or legal basis for delinquency has not been indicated in a petition, an adjudication resting on it cannot stand, even though the evidence adduced at the hearing might be sufficient to support it. This proposition was established in *Cole* v. *Arkansas*,[57] in which it was held that a conviction on an indictment charging one section of a statute could not be supported on the theory that the evidence showed violation of another section. The Court said:

> To conform to due process of law, petitioners were entitled to have the validity of their convictions appraised on consideration of the case as it was tried and as the issues were determined in the trial court.[58]

---

54. Indictment by a grand jury has never been required by the Court in state criminal prosecutions. *See* Hurtado v. California, 110 U.S. 516 (1884). Of all the specifics of the Bill of Rights governing criminal prosecutions, it seems least likely to be incorporated into the Fourteenth Amendment. *See* Brennan, *supra* note 47, 36 N.Y.U. L. Rev. at 777.

55. The District of Columbia Court of Appeals, relying on Gault, has imposed this requirement on petitions in the Juvenile Court there. In the Matter of Wylie, 231 A.2d 81 (D.C. Ct. App. 1967). The Court found that factual allegations in the delinquency petition before it could be construed as charging a violation of the District statutes dealing with robbery, attempted robbery, assault, or all three.

56. *See* In the Matter of Elmore, *supra* n. 29.

57. 333 U.S. 196 (1948). The Court in Gault relied on Cole, 387 U.S. at 33.

58. 333 U.S. at 202. This principle provided another possible basis for reversal in Gault, which the Court found it unnecessary to decide: the juvenile court judge there testified that he found Gault delinquent partly under a section of the Arizona Juvenile Code defining a delinquent as one "habitually involved in immoral matters." This issue was never brought to the attention of the juvenile or his parents in any form, before or at the hearing which adjudicated him a delinquent. 387 U.S. at 34 n. 54.

It also follows from this analysis that it is essential to know what was actually decided in a delinquency proceeding in order to determine whether there was compliance with the requirement of fair notice. This will require the juvenile court judge to make known his factual findings and legal conclusions if he adjudicates delinquency without a jury and to delineate and separate the legal and factual issues if the case is tried to a jury.[59] Moreover, if there is a constitutional right to appeal or to obtain judicial review by some other method, an indication of what was actually decided in the juvenile court is indispensable to meaningful review.[60]

The constitutional concept of fair notice imported into juvenile court law by *Gault* has another far-reaching implication. The principle is not limited to notice of specific charges before adjudication,

---

59. In recognition of this principle, it has been held in a delinquency proceeding in the District of Columbia—where there is a statutorily recognized right to jury trial—that the court must instruct the jury on each specific issue in the case, and, if a possibility of violation of more than one statute is involved, must instruct them to return a separate verdict as to each such possible violation. In the Matter of Wylie, 231 A.2d 81 (D.C. Ct. App. 1967). The Court disapproved of the use of a general verdict of "involved" in such a situation as "too vague and indefinite to satisfy the requirement of due process;" it suggested that if the juvenile court did not wish to use the criminal form of verdict—*i.e.*, guilty or not guilty—because of the connotations of criminality, it should take a special verdict on each issue. *See also* In the Matter of Elmore, *supra* n. 29.

60. *See* pp. 27-28, *infra*.
The requirement of fair notice has an additional important function in the criminal law—to lay the basis for a claim of double jeopardy if there is a second prosecution on the same charges. The applicability of the double jeopardy prohibition to juvenile proceedings is another problem for the future. The Supreme Court has not yet held this clause applicable to the states, but its grant of certiorari in Cichos v. State of Indiana, 383 U.S. 966 (1966), (later dismissed as improvidently granted, 385 U.S. 76 (1966)), to consider this question indicates that it may soon do so. In any event, in view of the Court's rejection in Gault of the "civil" label as justification for dispensing with constitutional guarantees in juvenile cases, it is doubtful whether state courts can continue to reject applicability of the double jeopardy principle on the ground that delinquency proceedings do not put the juvenile in jeopardy. *See, e.g.,* Brooks v. Boles, W.Va.   , 153 S.E.2d 526 (1967). Several recent cases point toward holding the claim of double jeopardy available, at least when the delinquency charge is based on a violation of the criminal law. Garza v. State, 369 S.W.2d 36 (Tex. Crim. Apps. 1963); United States v. Dickerson, 168 F.Supp. 899 (D. D.C. 1958), *rev'd on other grounds*, 271 F.2d 487 (D.C. Cir. 1959); *cf.* In re Winburn, 32 Wisc.2d 152, 167, 145 N.W.2d 178, 185 (1966).

but also requires that the statute on which the charges are based give fair notice of the proscribed conduct. A criminal conviction cannot be based on a statutory standard too vague to be intelligible.[61]

This problem is acute in the juvenile courts because delinquency is often broadly defined to cover conduct or status which is imprecise, e.g., "truancy," "beyond control," "incorrigibility," and "habitually involved in immoral matters."[62] These categories invite a highly subjective judgment by the judge or jury, especially when there is added the vague concept of "involved," which is a common finding to support a delinquency adjudication. This feature permits the trier of fact to dispense with the need to find any specific act by the juvenile, even the degree of participation expressed in the criminal law concept of aiding and abetting.[63]

Provisions like these reflect the fact that juvenile courts have sought to regulate the behavior and morals of juveniles to a degree far beyond that of criminal codes. While such concern may denote laudable purposes, when it takes the form of a delinquency adjudication accompanied by threat of institutionalization, *Gault* plainly indicates that due process considerations, transcending juvenile court objectives, come into play.

It may be anticipated, therefore, that if states continue to apply the stigma of delinquency and the threat of commitment to juveniles engaged in non-criminal conduct—rather than resorting to the different approach summarized in the concept of "persons in need of supervision"[64]—their statutes may face comprehensive constitutional attack on grounds of vagueness.[65]

---

61. Lanzetta v. New Jersey, 306 U.S. 451 (1939). *See generally* Note, *The Void for Vagueness Doctrine in the Supreme Court,* 109 U. Pa. L. Rev. 67 (1960). (1960).

62. The latter was one of the statutory provisions involved in Gault.

63. *Cf.* In the Matter of Wylie, 231 A.2d 81 (D.C. Ct. App. 1967).

64. *See* pp. 7-8, *supra.*

65. The vagueness and apparent definitional arbitrariness of many juvenile court statutes have been the subject of much comment:

". . . statutes whose vagueness in some localities allow almost any child, given compromising circumstances, to be caught up in the jurisdictional net of the court, must be altered. . . . If disobedience, truancy and running away are retained as bases for juvenile court jurisdiction, statutes should be rigorously drawn to require a showing of their material relevance to serious law violations or a showing that other agencies have been incapable of contain-

2. RIGHT TO COUNSEL

Under *Gault* a juvenile is entitled to the assistance of counsel—appointed if necessary—at every point of the adjudicative phase of the proceeding.[66] The Court reiterated the principle of *Powell v. Alabama*[67] and stated that the juvenile "requires the guiding hand of counsel at every step in the proceedings against him."[68]

This should require that the juvenile be given the opportunity to be represented by counsel when he first appears before the court for an initial hearing, after a petition has been filed against him. Although *Gault* focused on the right to counsel at the hearing on the merits of the charges, it implies as much for the initial hearing, at least when the juvenile is called on then to admit or deny his involvement.[69]

This conclusion is consistent with the settled rule in criminal prosecution that a pretrial judicial proceeding at which a defendant is called upon to plead is a "critical stage" of the proceedings, he may be significantly prejudiced then, and he is therefore entitled to counsel at that point.[70] There is no doubt that the initial hearing is similarly a "critical stage" in the juvenile proceeding when the juvenile is called on to admit or deny involvement. Large numbers of juveniles have made admissions at the initial hearing when unrepresented by counsel.[71] The result, of course, is that the juvenile thereby foregoes his right to an adjudicative hearing on the merits. Because of the risk of

---

ing the problems." Lenert, *The Juvenile Court: Quest and Realties, Task Force,* Appendix D, pp. 99-100.

See also Note, *Rights and Rehabilitation in the Juvenile Courts,* 67 COLUM. L. REV. 281, 309-310 (1967); Report of the President's Commission on Crime in the District of Columbia, p. 729, (1966) [hereinafter "D.C. Crime Commission"].

66. 387 U.S. at 41. We discuss the implications of Gault for the right to counsel at the pre-judicial (*i.e.,* through intake) and dispositional phases at pp. 41-43, *infra,* respectively.

67. 287 U.S. 45, 69 (1932).

68. 387 U.S. at 36.

69. Gault's initial hearing was telescoped into a hearing on the merits of the charge, since, according to the judge who tried him, the juvenile made some admissions when he first appeared before the court, and the judge proceeded immediately to hear the merits that day and then again six days later.

70. White v. Maryland, 373 U.S. 59 (1963); *cf.* Hamilton v. Alabama, 368 U.S. 52 (1961).

71. *See* Note, *Juvenile Delinquents: The Police, State Courts, and Individualized Justice,* 79 HARV. L. REV. 775 (1966); D.C. Crime Commission, p. 646.

such prejudice, counsel will probably have to be provided at the initial hearing, and the right to counsel problem is therefore likely to shift to the pre-judicial stage—*i.e.,* whether counsel must be afforded at interrogation by police or juvenile court authorities—and to the dispositional stage.[72]

A problem still likely to arise at the adjudicative stage is that of waiver. Merely informing the juvenile and his parents at an initial hearing of their right to counsel is no guarantee that it will be exercised.[73] The question arises whether the right to counsel must be affirmatively asserted by the juvenile or whether counsel should be automatically provided, unless the juvenile affirmatively waives it. *Gault* does not resolve the issue explicitly either way, but it strongly suggests that counsel should be appointed automatically and the juvenile afforded the opportunity to talk to a lawyer before making a decision to plead involvement. The Court cited with apparent approval the National Crime Commission recommendation that in order to assure "procedural justice," it is necessary that "Counsel . . . be appointed as a matter of course wherever coercive action is a possibility, without requiring any affirmative choice by child or parent."[74]

In view of the Court's insistence in *Gault* that waiver is an " 'intentional 'relinquishment or abandonment' of a fully known right,"[75] it is a fair conclusion that, save in exceptional circumstances, there can be no valid waiver of the right to counsel by a juvenile in the adjudicative phase without the prior advice of counsel.[76]

---

72. *See* pp. 37-43, *infra.*

73. As noted by the Court in Gault, 85 to 90% of juveniles in the District of Columbia Juvenile Court at one time signed a form waiving their right to representation after being informed of it at an initial hearing. 387 U.S. at 41.

74. 387 U.S. at 38. (Emphasis supplied.) *But see* People v. Lara, 36 U.S.L.W. 2220 (Cal. Sup. Ct. Sept. 29, 1967), holding that there is no "blanket presumption" of a minor's incompetency to waive his constitutional rights to remain silent and to the assistance of counsel at custodial interrogation, although his immaturity will be considered when determining the voluntariness and intelligence of the waiver. As to the applicability of the *Miranda* guarantees at interrogation of juveniles, see pp. 37-41, *infra.*

75. 387 U.S. at 42.

76. If we are correct, this conclusion highlights the urgency of adequate provision by the states for representation by counsel competent to appear in juvenile proceedings. Whether the ultimate solution lies in a public defender system, a so-called "law guardian" system, state statutes modeled on the Federal Criminal Justice Act, enlargement of the segment of the private bar now regu-

3. RIGHT TO CONFRONTATION AND CROSS-EXAMINATION

The Court in *Gault* evidently contemplated that juvenile courts shall have somewhat greater leeway in admitting evidence than adult criminal courts. It cited as being "in general accord with our conclusions," the recommendations of the Children's Bureau of the U.S. Department of Health, Education and Welfare that "only competent material and relevant evidence under rules applicable to civil cases should be admitted in evidence."[77]

As a practical matter, this latitude should not be mistaken for a license to the juvenile courts to depart far from evidentiary principles applicable in criminal cases. The rules of evidence do not vary widely between civil and criminal cases.[78] Moreover, the Court recognized in *Gault* that some evidentiary rules—there, the hearsay rule—have a constitutional basis.[79]

Justice Jackson once wrote: [80]

> The hearsay evidence rule, with all its subtleties, anomalies and ramifications, will not be read into the Fourteenth Amendment.

That statement must be deemed abrogated as a result of recent cases dealing with the right of confrontation and cross-examination.[81] The trend culminated in *Gault,* which involved a compelling case for constitutional application of the hearsay rule: the complaining witness, the only person other than the accused juveniles who could offer evi-

---

larly appearing in juvenile courts, neighborhood legal services, increased participation by the entire private bar, or a combination of some or all of these is beyond the scope of this article. But to highlight the urgency of the problem and the exigency of the need is not.

77. 387 U.S. at 56-57. *See* HEW, Children's Bureau, "Standards for Juvenile and Family Courts," pp. 72-73 (1966) [hereinafter Standards].

78. A more significant criterion, relevant in both civil and criminal cases, is whether the trier of fact is judge or jury. Judges in both civil and criminal cases customarily exercise more leniency in admitting evidence when there is no jury present.

79. Another is the exclusionary rule for evidence obtained as a result of unlawful search and seizure. Mapp v. Ohio, 367 U.S. 643 (1961). We discuss Mapp's applicability in juvenile courts at pp. 31-33, *infra.*

80. Stein v. People, 346 U.S. 156, 196 (1953).

81. The other cases are Pointer v. Texas, 380 U.S. 400 (1965), and Douglas v. Alabama, 380 U.S. 415 (1965), establishing that the Sixth Amendment right of confrontation and cross-examination is applicable in state criminal trials.

The specific holding of Stein was overruled in Jackson v. Denno, 378 U.S. 368 (1964).

dence as to what acts were committed by the boys, never appeared before the trier of fact; the juvenile court judge relied for her version of the events entirely on the probation officer's account of a conversation with the complaining witness. A clearer case of the denial of confrontation and cross-examination can scarcely be imagined. Thus, while it may still be true that observance of all the nuances of the hearsay rule is not constitutionally required, the core of the rule certainly is.

Moreover, whatever leeway the juvenile courts may have in admitting evidence not ordinarily admissible in criminal cases must be considered in light of the Court's holding that a finding of delinquency, in the absence of a valid confession, can rest only on evidence given under oath by witnesses subject to confrontation and cross-examination. The Court thus appears to differentiate between evidence which may be received by the juvenile court and evidence which is sufficient to support a constitutionally acceptable delinquency adjudication; the latter is plainly controlled by requirements of confrontation and cross-examination.[82]

The decision to elevate the hearsay rule to a constitutional level,

---

82. Some states have statutorily drawn such a distinction. For example, California admits any evidence which is "relevant and material" but requires that findings of delinquency when a law violation is charged can rest only on evidence admissible in criminal cases. Calif. Welf. Instit. Code §701 (1966).

The Court carved out only one exception to the requirement that a delinquency finding rest on sworn testimony subject to the ordinary opportunity for cross-examination—a "valid confession" by the juvenile. 387 U.S. at 57. An interesting question, not dealt with by the Court, is whether such a confession, if made out of court by the juvenile and not reiterated there, must be corroborated by sufficient independent evidence, which has been subject to the opportunity for cross-examination, to establish the trustworthiness of the confession. Such is the rule in federal criminal trials under Smith v. United States, 348 U.S. 147 (1954), and Opper v. United States, 348 U.S. 84 (1954), although it is not clear whether it rests on constitutional grounds. In view of the Court's evident distrust of out-of-court juvenile confessions, which we discuss at pp. 37-41, *supra*, a requirement of independent corroborative evidence seems likely to be imposed. *Compare* Chief Judge Weintraub's concurring opinion in In the Interests of Carlo, 48 N.J. 224, 243, 225 A.2d 110, 121 (1966). This requirement has long been applicable in courts-martial, *see*, *e.g.*, United States v. Isenberg, 8 C.M.R. 149 (U.S.C.M.A. 1953), in evident recognition that confessions given by persons under military discipline, particularly to superior officers, are not so inherently reliable as to dispense with the need for independent evidence; the analogy to juvenile confessions leads to a similar conclusion there.

at least in some situations, has important implications for what is perhaps the most critical evidentiary problem in juvenile courts: reliance at the adjudicative stage on social reports and other investigative materials which may have been compiled on the juvenile. Such reports are hearsay, and to the extent that they contain statements and rumors passed on by other persons about the juvenile they are double and triple hearsay. Moreover, they may contain material relating to the juvenile's character and prior involvements with the law which could not be received in a criminal case, at least not unless a defendant put them in issue or made them relevant. A logical conclusion from *Gault* is that such materials cannot be considered by the trier of fact during the adjudicative stage and certainly cannot form the basis for a determination of delinquency based on a law violation.[83]

If such reports can be relied on by the trier of fact at the adjudicative stage despite the objections we have outlined, it seems clear that they must be disclosed to counsel for the juvenile. In *Gault* the juvenile court judge testified that in finding the juvenile to have been "habitually involved in immoral matters," he relied in part on an earlier "referral" to the juvenile court based on an incident in which Gault had allegedly stolen a baseball glove and lied to the police about it.[84] Not only was the charge of being "habitually involved in immoral matters" never disclosed to the juvenile or his parents before the hearing,[85] but there was no indication even at the hearing that this charge was in the

---

83. The Court in Gault cited the National Crime Commission recommendation that:

> "To minimize the danger that adjudication will be affected by inappropriate considerations, social investigation reports should not be made known to the judge in advance of adjudication." 387 U.S. at 57 n. 98.

See also Standards, supra note 77, pp. 66, 73; Vinter, *The Juvenile Court As An Institution, Task Force,* Appendix C, 88, 103.

The case may be otherwise in the instance of a delinquency adjudication based on a category such as habitual truancy, incorrigibility, or involvement in immoral matters, assuming they are not too vague to survive constitutional attack. Since they do not involve crimes if committed by adults, the Sixth Amendment right of confrontation and cross-examination in a criminal case arguably might be inapplicable. More important, since these amount to status offenses by juveniles, they involve by definition a continuing course of conduct by the juvenile and material in the social reports, including prior involvements with the court, is made relevant by law. *Cf.* Note, 67 COLUM. L. REV. *supra* note 65, at 337.

84. 387 U.S. at 9.

85. *Id.* at 34 n. 54.

case or that the judge was partly relying on it for the adjudication of delinquency. Although the Supreme Court found it unnecessary to reach this question, its earlier decision in *Kent* indicates that non-disclosure of material relied on for decision in the adjudicative stage is itself a denial of due process of law. The Court there held that in a waiver hearing in the juvenile court for trial as an adult, counsel for the juvenile had a right of access to the social file, since it entered into the juvenile court's determination. The Court said:

> With respect to access by the child's counsel to the social records of the child, we deem it obvious that since these are to be considered by the Juvenile Court in making its decision to waive, they must be made available to the child's counsel. . . . [The Juvenile Court judge] may not, for purposes of a decision on waiver, receive and rely upon secret information, whether emanating from his staff or otherwise.[86]

4. TRIER OF FACT AND STANDARD OF PROOF

Two related questions left undecided in *Gault* are whether there is a constitutional right to trial by jury and whether the commission of the act charged must be proved beyond a reasonable doubt.

a. *Trial by Jury*—The Sixth Amendment right to trial by jury has not yet been held to be fully incorporated into the Fourteenth Amendment and therefore applicable in state criminal trials.[87] We assume that until it is, it will not be constitutionally imposed on the state juvenile courts. Even then, under our analysis of *Gault,* the question will still be open whether a right of jury trial is essential to a fair trial in juvenile courts.

The rhetoric in favor of trial by jury is well known.[88] We submit that the reality supports the rhetoric, and that the considerations which have led to the establishment of trial by jury as the fundamental mode of trial in criminal cases throughout the United States and the rest of

---

86. 383 U.S. at 562-63. *See also* Vinter, *supra* note 83, at 101.

87. *See* pp. 12-13, *supra*. Parker v. Gladden, 385 U.S. 363 (1966), held that the Sixth Amendment guarantee of impartiality in a jury is incorporated, when the case is heard by a jury, but it did not pass on the precise question whether trial by jury itself is required in criminal cases in state courts. The Court is being asked this term to hold that jury trial is incorporated. Duncan v. State, No. 410, O.T. 1967.

88. III Blackstone, *Commentaries* 379; 2 Story, Constitution of the United States 527 (2d. ed. 1851).

the common-law world are equally applicable to the trial in juvenile courts of delinquency cases, at least those involving alleged violations of the criminal law. Recent studies attest to what trial lawyers have always believed—the efficacy of the jury as a fact-finding mechanism.[89] Juvenile court judges have no demonstrated superiority to juries in determining whether a law violation has been committed. Their expertise presumably lies in the selection among dispositional alternatives and the formulation of plans of individualized treatment.[90] The issues in the delinquency trial of a law violation are the same as in a criminal trial of the same offense. The jury function of weighing the evidence, evaluating credibility of witnesses, and finding the facts are no harder with respect to whether a juvenile committed a criminal act than whether an adult did. Other values of the jury system—as a bulwark against possible judicial arbitrariness, as an assurance that each case will receive individual attention and not become another item on the assembly line of an overworked judge, and as a means of filtering the enacted criminal law through current community standards of guilt— are as applicable for juvenile as for adult offenders.

Objections to the jury seem principally to turn on the fear that the jury would introduce undue formality and interfere with the rehabilitative objectives of the juvenile court by heightening the juvenile's sense of being an adversary of the court and society.[91] To this it may be answered that trial by jury is not a matter of form—like a judge's robe or gavel—but of substance, the product of long historical experience and expressing a profound judgment by our legal system about the means of adjudicating criminal behavior. If it thereby introduces an aura of formality or solemnity, it is formality desirable in a matter of such consequence. Further, we submit that such formality is more likely to infuse a juvenile with respect for the legal system than to heighten his feelings of alienation and in that sense may ultimately be therapeutic. To the suggestion sometimes made that the jury will intimidate a youthful defendant or that the jury represents public intrusion into the confidentiality of juvenile proceedings, the short answer

89. *See generally* Kalven and Zeisel, *The American Jury* (1966).

90. The Court noted in Gault that statistical studies show that a quarter of all juvenile court judges have no law school training, 387 U.S. at 14-15 n. 14.

91. *See* the discussion of the jury system in juvenile courts in *Task Force,* p. 38.

is that if an accused juvenile and his counsel do not want a jury trial, they do not have to have one.[92] Objections that stricter rules of evidence are usually enforced in a jury trial overlook the fact these rules ordinarily have their source in reason and experience; moreover, as we have shown, the *Gault* case looks in the direction of tightening the rules of evidence now in effect in many juvenile courts.

It should be emphasized that the right to jury trial as we contemplate it need not include every offense, however petty, that may give rise to an adjudication of delinquency. Petty offenses are not triable by jury as of right in the federal courts,[93] and there is no necessity for them to be in juvenile courts. Moreover, there is also no constitutional necessity to apply the right of jury trial to charges of delinquency not based on a violation of the criminal law. We are concerned primarily with the right in law violation cases, which present the factual

---

92. In the District of Columbia, where there is a statutorily recognized right to jury trial, there were three jury trials in juvenile delinquency cases in a two-year period from 1964 to 1966. D.C. Crime Commission, pp. 647, 1010 n. 41.

The question whether a public trial is now to be constitutionally required in juvenile cases is of course a different problem, but not a particularly difficult one. There is no constitutional reason why juvenile trials cannot continue to be conducted without admitting the public at large, subject to the choice of the juvenile and his counsel whether the public shall be admitted. Justice Black wrote in In re Oliver, 333 U.S. 257, 266 n. 12 (1948):

> Whatever may be the classification of juvenile court proceedings, they are often conducted without admitting all the public. But it has never been the practice wholly to exclude parents, relatives, and friends. . . .

The confidentiality of juvenile courts is for the benefit of the juvenile to hide youthful indiscretions from the public gaze. Similarly, the Sixth Amendment guarantee of a public trial is for the benefit of the accused to protect against secret inquisitorial practices. The Sixth Amendment is not for the benefit of the public at large, and neither it nor the First Amendment gives the public or the press an absolute right of entry to all judicial proceedings. *Id.* at 270 n. 25; Estes v. Texas, 381 U.S. 532, 539-40 (1965).

There is therefore no inherent conflict between the confidentiality of juvenile courts and the Sixth Amendment right to public trial; to the extent that they require accommodation in a particular case, it should be for the accused and his counsel to make. *Cf.* Calif. Welf. Instit. Code §676 (1966); Note, 67 COLUM. L. REV., *supra* note 65, at 330.

93. District of Columbia v. Clawans, 300 U.S. 617, 624 (1937); Frankfurter & Corcoran, *Petty Federal Offenses and the Constitutional Guarantee of Trial by Jury*, 39 HARV. L. REV. 917 (1926).

issues commonly tried by juries in criminal cases. On the other hand, categories such as habitual truancy and incorrigibility are not crimes at all but are essentially status offenses not well adapted to jury determination.[94] In these cases the juvenile court judge may have some special expertness making him the more appropriate fact-finder. There is no constitutional impediment to his exercising this function.[95]

b. *Standard of proof.* A similar analysis may help to determine the question whether the standard of proof of a law violation should be the criminal law standard of "beyond a reasonable doubt," the civil standard of "preponderance of the evidence,"[96] the test of "clear and convincing evidence,"[97] or some other formulation.

Although *Gault* does not pass on the question, its rejection of the "civil" label as a justification for differing procedures in the juvenile courts should be a red flag as to procedures imported from civil cases,

---

94. Analogous adult offenses, such as vagrancy, do not carry a right to jury trial under the Sixth Amendment. Bailey v. United States, 98 F.2d 306 (D.C. Cir. 1938).

95. Support for this resolution of the issue comes from In re Lambert, 203 F.2d 607 (D.C. Cir. 1953), in which the Court held there was no jury trial right in a dependency proceeding, although the District of Columbia juvenile court act appeared on its face to grant a jury trial in all cases. The Court held that the statute was intended to safeguard the Sixth Amendment jury trial right for juveniles, that it applied only to juveniles charged with a violation of the criminal law, and that other juvenile court proceedings which might affect the custody of a juvenile were equitable in nature and did not require a jury. *Id.* at 609-10.

This analysis recently was applied to uphold denial of a jury trial to a juvenile found truant and beyond control in In the Matter of Elmore, 222 A.2d 255 (D.C. Ct. App. 1966).

A recent state court decision held that Gault does not give juveniles the right to trial by jury even in a case alleging delinquency by reason of law violation. Commonwealth v. Johnson, 36 U.S.L.W. 2187 (Pa. Super. Ct. Sept. 15, 1967). *But see* Peyton v. Nord, 36 U.S.L.W. 2262 (N.M. Sup. Ct. Oct. 16, 1967), in which the court held that its juvenile court act should be interpreted to grant a right of jury trial to a juvenile charged with a law violation; the court observed that a different result might follow in the case of an alleged delinquent not charged with violation of a state criminal statute.

96. This is the standard in most states. Note, 79 HARV. L. REV., *supra* note 71, at 795.

97. This was the standard adopted by the Arizona Supreme Court in Gault, and urged as a compromise by the Children's Bureau of HEW, *Standards*, p. 72.

such as the preponderance of the evidence test.[98] This is true even though the Supreme Court has never held that the reasonable doubt standard is constitutionally required in state criminal cases.[99] While the antecedents and development of the concept are uncertain,[100] and it does not appear in the Bill of Rights, long usage in every jurisdiction has firmly implanted the standard as to proof of every element of a criminal offense. Moreover, there is much to be said in favor of the reasonable doubt standard over the preponderance of the evidence test, particularly if a jury is the trier of fact. The reasonable doubt standard impresses on the trier of fact the necessity of reaching a subjective state of certitude of the facts in issue; the preponderance test is susceptible to the misinterpretation that it calls on the trier of fact merely to per-

---

98. However, the District of Columbia Court of Appeals in its post-Gault opinion in In the Matter of Wylie, 231 A.2d 81 (D.C. Ct. App. 1967), adhered to its prior preponderance of the evidence rule. *See also* In the Matter of Elmore, 222 A.2d 255, 259 n. 6 (D.C. Ct. App. 1966); In re Bigesby, 202 A.2d 785, 786 (D.C. Ct. App. 1964).

The Supreme Court held this past Term that the standard of proof in a deportation proceeding is no less than proof by "clear, unequivocal, and convincing evidence." *Woodby v. Immigration and Naturalization Service,* 385 U.S. 276, 285-286 (1966). The Court said:

"To be sure a deportation proceeding is not a criminal proceeding. [Citation omitted.] But it does not syllogistically follow that a person may be banished from this country upon no higher degree of proof than applies in a negligence case." *Id.* at 285.

99. The closest the Court seems to have come in dealing with the point was its decision in Leland v. Oregon, 343 U.S. 790 (1952), in which it held that a state could constitutionally require a defendant raising the defense of insanity to prove it beyond a reasonable doubt. The only two dissenters were Justices Frankfurter and Black. Justice Frankfurter took an unusually activist view of the due process clause on this point:

"It is the duty of the Government to establish his guilt beyond a reasonable doubt. This notion—basic in our law and rightly one of the boasts of a free society—is a requirement and a safeguard of due process of law in the historic, procedural content of 'due process.'" 343 U.S. at 802-03.

100. According to Wigmore:

"This precise distinction seems to have had its origin no earlier than the end of the 1700s, and to have been applied at first only in capital cases, and by no means in a fixed phrase, but in various tentative forms." 9 Wigmore, *Evidence* §2497, at 317 (3d ed. 1940).

Interestingly, Wigmore then lists as earlier formulations, leading to what became the reasonable doubt test, such standards as "a clear impression," "upon clear grounds," and "satisfied"—none too different from the "clear and convincing" test adopted by the Arizona Supreme Court.

form an abstract weighing of the evidence in order to determine which side has produced the greater quantum, without regard to its effect in convincing his mind of the truth of the proposition asserted.[101] Finally, the reasonable doubt test is superior to all others in protecting against an unjust adjudication of guilt, and that is as much a concern of the juvenile court as of the criminal court. It is difficult to see how the distinctive objectives of the juvenile court give rise to a legitimate institutional interest in finding a juvenile to have committed a violation of the criminal law on less evidence than if he were an adult.

5. JUDICIAL REVIEW

Although the Court in *Gault* declined to pass on the contentions that due process requires a right of appeal from the juvenile court and a transcript of proceedings, it is apparent that the Court contemplates meaningful judicial review. It noted that failure to provide an appeal, to record the proceedings, or to state findings and conclusions supporting the adjudication of delinquency had the effect of burdening "the machinery for habeas corpus" and saddling "the reviewing process with the burden of attempting to reconstruct a record . . ."[102] While this does not necessarily connote a right to appeal, it implies that some mode of judicial review must be made available by the states. In view of the procedural rights recognized in *Gault,* the conclusion can hardly be otherwise. The Court could not have intended to create rights for which there was no enforcement remedy through meaningful review. The thrust of *Gault* is to convert the juvenile courts from "no law" areas,[103] with the attendant dangers of judicial arbitrariness, into tribunals functioning with procedural regularity. As the Court had said earlier in *Kent,* although a statute may confer on a juvenile court a

---

101. *See* James, *Civil Procedure* §7.6 (1965). The Supreme Court of New Jersey has recently imposed the "reasonable doubt" standard in delinquency cases involving a law violation. New Rule 6:9-1 (f) relating to juvenile court procedure, adopted Sept. 1, 1967, effective Sept. 11, 1967.

102. 387 U.S. at 58. *See* Ebersole v. State,   Idaho   , 428 P.2d 947 (1967), where the court, in granting habeas corpus relief to an adult petitioner, relied on Gault for its holding that the failure to make a transcript of the arraignment proceedings, at which he allegedly pleaded guilty and waived counsel, was a denial of fundamental fairness.

103. *See Task Force,* p. 4.

"substantial degree of discretion," it cannot grant "a license for arbitrary procedure."[104] Judicial review is the means of correcting such arbitrariness and preventing its recurrence.[105]

Once the availability of judicial review is recognized, it follows that for it to be meaningful, there must be some form of record of the proceedings, preferably a stenographic transcript or other verbatim recording,[106] and some indication by the juvenile court of what was decided and why. The latter point was virtually settled in *Kent,* where the Court said with respect to review of a juvenile court's waiver decision:

> Meaningful review requires that the reviewing court should review. It should not be remitted to assumptions. *It must have before it a statement of the reasons motivating the waiver.* . . .[107]

6. RETROACTIVITY OF GAULT

We have already remarked that a major problem is the extent to which, if at all, the rights recognized in *Gault* can be asserted by persons who were found delinquent prior to the decision. There is nothing in the *Gault* opinion on this subject one way or the other. Lower courts have begun to divide on the issue,[108] and it no doubt will ultimately be resolved by the Supreme Court.

---

104. 383 U.S. at 553.

105. From the standpoint of federalism, it is obviously preferable that the states should provide the machinery for judicial review in the first instance, rather than require litigants to resort to review in the United States Supreme Court or use federal habeas corpus as a means of vindicating the constitutional rights created by Gault. It is therefore both necessary and desirable that the states provide such review.

106. This is urged by the Children's Bureau, *Standards,* p. 76, and *Task Force,* p. 40.

107. 383 U.S. at 561 (Emphasis supplied). *See* In the Matter of Wylie, 231 A.2d 81 (D.C. Ct. App. 1967); In the Matter of Elmore, *supra* n. 29, both post-Gault decisions requiring specification of what was decided in a delinquency proceeding.

108. The Supreme Judicial Court of Massachusetts held *Gault* applicable to a 1965 adjudication of delinquency and set it aside for denial of the right to counsel, although acknowledging that "it, of course, would have been impossible for the judge in the Municipal Court in 1965 to have foreseen the Gault decision." Marsden v. Commonwealth, ___ Mass. ___, 227 N.E.2d 1 (1967). A lower Wisconsin Court in dictum has gone the other way on the counsel point, although setting aside the adjudication on other grounds. Rieck v. Hershman, 35 U.S.L.W. 2754 (Wis. Waukesha County Ct. June 1, 1967).

The notice requirements of Gault were held applicable only to cases tried

Much depends on the proper approach to retroactivity. If the question is one of the fundamental nature of a right, the issue would seem logically to have been determined by the holding that a right is "so fundamental and essential to a fair trial"[109] as to warrant incorporation in the Fourteenth Amendment. Any other course than retroactive application would seem to cast doubt on the Court's judgment as to the essentiality of the constitutional protection.

On the other hand, the trend in the Supreme Court seems to be running strongly in favor of prospective application of newly recognized constitutional procedural rights.[110] Most recently, the Court in *Stovall* v. *Denno,* holding the newly created right to counsel at a police lineup to be prospective only, emphasized the great weight to be given to "the reliance by law enforcement officials on the old standards."[111] It said that even procedural defects potentially affecting the reliability of the fact finding process at trial "must be weighed against the prior justified reliance upon the old standards and the impact of retroactivity on the administration of justice."[112] It further stressed that "Today's rulings were not foreshadowed in our cases . . . . Law enforcement authorities fairly relied on this virtually unanimous weight of authority, now no longer valid. . . ."[113]

Under the analysis of *Stovall,* the rights recognized in *Gault* are likely to be held prospective only. The decision could not be said to be foreshadowed in prior cases, with the possible exception of *Kent* on the right to counsel point only a year before. Reliance by the states

---

after Gault by the District of Columbia Court of Appeals in In the Matter of Wylie, 231 A.2d 81 (D.C. Ct. App. 1967).

There is also some indication of non-decisional retroactive application. In Pennsylvania, several lower courts have granted applications for rehearings for juveniles whose original hearings did not comport with the Gault standards. Letter to authors from David Rudovsky, Assistant Public Defender, Defenders Association, Philadelphia.

109. *See* Washington v. Texas, 388 U.S. 14, 17 (1967).

110. Only the right to counsel recognized in Gideon v. Wainwright, 372 U.S. 335 (1963), and the new rules for determining voluntariness of confessions laid down in Jackson v. Denno, 378 U.S. 368 (1964), have been held applicable to convictions which had become final before the date of the decisions. Pickelsimer v. Wainwright, 375 U.S. 2 (1963); Doughty v. Maxwell, 376 U.S. 202 (1965).

111. 388 U.S. 293, 297 (1967).

112. *Id.* at 298.

113. *Id.* at 299-300.

on the assumption that criminal safeguards did not apply as a constitutional matter in juvenile courts was almost total.[114] The effect in terms of necessity for retrials and potential release of persons from custody would be enormous.[115]

There is at least one right recognized by *Gault* as to which a different result should follow. This is the right to counsel, which after *Gideon* was held retroactive.[116] There are of course certain distinctions between the retroactivity problem arising from *Gault* and that arising from *Gideon*. The degree of reliance by the states on not having to furnish counsel in juvenile courts was vastly greater than it was in adult criminal cases prior to *Gideon*. Many states had anticipated *Gideon*, and under the "special circumstances" rule of *Betts* v. *Brady*,[117] a state could never be sure in any case that it would not be held on appeal that counsel should have been provided. The same is not true in the juvenile court area.[118]

---

114. The Court cited Judge Prettyman's Appendix in Pee v. United States, 274 F.2d 556 (D.C. Cir. 1959), listing authority in 51 jurisdictions to this effect. 387 U.S. at 17 n. 22.

115. The Court noted in Stovall that an impact in six states justified denial of retroactive application of a defendant's right to be free from comment on his failure to testify. Tehan v. United States ex rel Schott, 382 U.S. 406 (1966). *See* 388 U.S. at 300.

There is the added problem that in a number of states, although the juvenile court has authority to commit up to age 21, its authority to try stops at age 18. It therefore might be legally impossible to retry persons over 18 who win release if Gault is applied retroactively. *Cf.* Dillenburg v. Maxwell, 422 P.2d 783, 789 (Wash. Sup. Ct. 1967).

116. *See supra* note 110. Of the other constitutional rights recognized in Gault, one—the privilege against self-incrimination—has already been held prospective only in the case of adult criminal defendants, Tehan v. United States *ex rel.* Schott, 382 U.S. 406 (1966). As to the remaining rights—notice of charges and right to confrontation and cross-examination—the Supreme Court has not yet spoken on the retroactivity point in the case of adult criminal defendents.

117. 316 U.S. 455 (1942).

118. When the United States Court of Appeals for the District of Columbia Circuit held that there was a right to counsel in juvenile delinquency cases in the District—albeit purportedly only on statutory grounds—it made the right prospective only. Shioutakon v. District of Columbia, 236 F.2d 666 (1956). It did the same with respect to counsel at the waiver hearing in Black v. United States, 355 F.2d 104, 108 (1965).

There is a basis for treating juveniles under Gault differently from adults under Gideon, in view of the Court's apparent rejection of the equal protection rationale in Gault.

On the other hand, it seems paradoxical that the right to counsel, which was held to be so fundamental as to be retroactively applicable under *Gideon* in the case of an adult criminal defendant, should not be so fundamental in the case of a child who was incarcerated for delinquency. All the considerations which made the right to counsel fundamental in the case of an adult defendant apply with even greater force in the case of a child.[119]

B. *The Pre-Judicial Stage*

A wide range of problems may be expected to arise in the pre-judicial phase. Prevailing practices of arrest, detention and interrogation will come under increasing constitutional scrutiny. The question of the right to counsel at various points in the pre-judicial process is certain to confront the courts, as it has in so many criminal cases. We will concentrate on several of these problems, with the *caveat* that, in view of the Court's evident disposition to treat the pre-judicial and dispositional phases flexibly, few conclusions can be drawn with certainty at this time.

1. ARREST, SEARCH AND SEIZURE

The Court in *Gault* did not deal specifically with arrest and detention, except to note that Arizona did not follow the common law of

---

Two post-Gault decisions hold that even if Gault and Kent give juveniles a right to counsel at proceedings certifying them for trial as adult offenders, this ruling is in any event not retroactive. Cradle v. Peyton,   Va. 156 S.E.2d 874(1967); State v. Hance, 2 Crim L. Rptr. 2014 (Md. Ct. Spec. App. Sept. 29, 1967). Cradle v. Peyton, *supra,* along with State v. Acuna, 78 N.M. 119, 428 P.2d 658 (1967), seem incorrect in also holding that Gault and Kent do not give a juvenile the right to an attorney at certification proceedings. In view of the potential consequences to the juvenile of trial as an adult, certification is clearly a "critical stage" in the proceedings against him.

119. In addition, the problem of mass delivery of wrongdoers and of new trials for crimes dating back for many years is less serious in the case of juvenile offenders than of convicted adult criminals since juvenile court commitments terminate at the age of 21.

The broader question remains of course as to whether the approach taken by the Supreme Court in Stovall v. Denno and like cases represents a sound approach to the application of newly recognized constitutional rights. Cogent criticisms of the Court's recent predilection for prospective application have been made elsewhere, and need not be repeated here. *See, e.g.,* Mishkin, *Foreword: The High Court, The Great Writ, and the Due Process of Time and Law,* 79 Harv. L. Rev. 56 (1965); H. Schwartz, *Retroactivity, Reliability, and Due Process: A Reply to Professor Mishkin,* 33 U. Chi. L. Rev. 719 (1966).

arrest with respect to juveniles.[120] It is unlikely that the Court would regard as a constitutional question the applicability to juveniles of the common law of arrest—that is, the doctrines that arrests for misdemeanors may normally be made only on a warrant or for an offense committed in the officer's presence, and felony arrests may be made on probable cause.[121]

On the other hand, the Court will probably hold the Fourth Amendment guarantee of the right "of the people" to be free from unreasonable searches and seizures to be applicable to juveniles. The Fourth Amendment is not exclusively tied to the criminal law, so that the labeling of juvenile cases as either civil or criminal has no relevance. This Term, in *Camara* v. *Municipal Court*[122] and *See* v. *City of Seattle*,[123] the Court held that health and fire inspections— "civil" searches not directed at securing evidence of crime—are subject to the requirements of the Fourth Amendment. The Court stressed the Fourth Amendment as a bulwark of individual privacy against officialdom, however benevolent.

By parity of reasoning, the Fourth Amendment protects juveniles, as it does other citizens.[124] Whether it protects them in precisely the same way is another matter. With respect to arrests for law violations, there seems no reason to differentiate juveniles from adults with respect to the probable cause requirement of the Fourth Amendment. An arrest purely on suspicion of commission of a crime, or for no reason at all, is at least as objectionable for a juvenile as for an adult—and probably more so, for an adult ordinarily has the rights of prompt hearing to test the legality of his confinement and the right to bail,

---

120. 387 U.S. at 11 n. 7. The Court in Kent had reserved questions as to the constitutionality of the extraordinary arrest and detention powers asserted by many states over juveniles. 383 U.S. at 552.

121. Here again, the Court's rejection of the equal protection rationale opens the way to some permissible disparity in treatment of juveniles and adults. Moreover, the common law of arrest has been so altered by statutes, *e.g.,* authorizing arrest on probable cause for numerous misdemeanors, as to be almost unrecognizable.

122. 387 U.S. 523 (1967).

123. 387 U.S. 541 (1967).

124. The trend of recent authority is in this direction. *See e.g.,* Urbasek v. People, 222 N.E.2d 233, 238 (Ill. Ct. Apps. 1966); State v. Lowry, 95 N.J. Super. 307, 230 A.2d 907 (1967).

rights not accorded juveniles in many states.[125] But it must be recognized that juvenile courts have jurisdiction extending beyond law violations—to the categories previously mentioned, such as truancy, incorrigibility, neglect, dependency—to which the criminal "probable cause" standard is inappropriate. Here, too, the recent decisions in *Camara* and *See* point the way to a resolution of the problem. They deny officials the right to search (and, implicitly, to arrest and seize) for no reason at all, but allow the reasonable grounds required to be adapted to the requirements of particular situations.[126] Reason to believe that a juvenile is within a category of noncriminal juvenile court jurisdiction and that it is necessary for his own welfare to take him into custody should therefore be a tolerable constitutional standard.

The further question may be raised whether, assuming that the Fourth Amendment protects juveniles, the exclusionary rule applies to rule out evidence in a delinquency proceeding obtained by an unlawful arrest, search or seizure. Chief Judge Weintraub has argued for applying exclusionary rules in juvenile proceedings only against police "tactics" which are "palpably wrong."[127] He has written:

> With respect to crime, we suppress the truth even if it means the release of one who is plainly guilty, and this in the belief that the support thereby given a constitutional value outweighs the price tomorrow's victims may pay. I would suggest that it need not follow that the same course should be pursued with respect to juvenile delinquency, since as to it there is still another value to be weighed, to wit, the rehabilitation of the infant. To deny an infant the attention he needs because the police erred in obtaining evidence of that need may not be the parental thing to do.[128]

In answer, it must be recalled that the exclusionary rule is part of the Fourth Amendment, according to *Mapp* v. *Ohio*.[129] If its primary purpose is to deter conduct sought to be proscribed by the Fourth Amendment, the exclusionary rule should be as applicable in juvenile as in adult courts because juveniles as well as adults are protected against such conduct.[130]

125. *See* p. 34, *infra*.

126. 387 U.S. at 538-39, 387 U.S. at 545.

127. In the Interests of Carlo, 48 N.J. 224, 245-46, 225 A.2d 110, 122 (1966) (concurring opinion).

128. *Id*

129. 367 U.S. 643 (1961).

130. *Cf.* State v. Lowry, 95 N.J. Super. 307, 230 A.2d 907 (1967); Two Brothers and a Case of Liquor, Juv. Ct. D.C., Nos. 66-2652-J, 66-2653-J, December 28, 1966.

2. DETENTION

Problems arising from pre-hearing detention of juveniles are among the most troubling in the juvenile process.

The National Crime Commission has documented the abuses arising from the broad unregulated powers of detention over juveniles provided by many states.[131] The Commission found excessive reliance on detention in routine cases in which there was danger neither to the welfare of the juvenile nor community safety from releasing him; detention at times employed for shock effect on an alleged delinquent; a lack of articulated standards for determining when to detain; and overcrowding of detention facilities often leading to use of adult jails to confine juveniles.[132]

The denial to juveniles of such procedural rights as bail pending adjudicative hearing and prompt hearing on detention has generally been based on the traditional labeling of juvenile proceedings as noncriminal.[133] Denial of bail also receives support from a Supreme Court decision, holding that alien members of the Communist Party could be detained without bail pending deportation proceedings.[134] The Court reasoned that since deportation was not a criminal proceeding, the Eighth Amendment guarantee against excessive bail was inapplicable. It construed the Amendment as giving Congress power to define "the class of cases in which bail shall be allowed in this country" and stated that the very language of the Amendment fails to say all arrests must be bailable."[135]

---

131. For example, under the laws of Arizona, which are not atypical in this respect, a person over 18 charged with crime has the right to be taken before a magistrate without unnecessary delay, to a prompt preliminary hearing to determine the existence of probable cause for his continued detention, and to bail in all noncapital cases, Ariz. Rev. Stats. §§ 13-1417, 13-1420 (1956); Ariz. Rules of Crim. Proc. 16-37, 41 (1956). Gerald Gault, as a juvenile, was afforded none of these rights and could be detained without limits or standards defined by law.

132. *Task Force,* pp. 13, 19, 36-37. *See also* D.C. Crime Commission, pp. 665-670.

133. *See, e.g.,* Harling v. United States, 295 F.2d 161, 163 (D.C. Cir. 1961); Ex parte Cromwell, 232 Md. 305, 192 A.2d 775 (Md. Ct. App. 1963). *But see* the post-Gault decision of Smith v. McCravy, 1 Crim. L. Rptr. 2153 (Ky. Cir. Ct. May 25, 1967), in which the court interpreted the "broad and sweeping language" of Gault to give juveniles a right to bail under the Eighth and Fourteenth Amendments.

134. Carlson v. Landon, 342 U.S. 524 (1952).

135. 342 U.S. at 545, 546.

Nevertheless, the Court's rejection in *Gault* of the "civil" rationale as a basis for defining procedural rights of juveniles leaves the question of bail for juveniles very much alive, especially when the juvenile is charged with a violation of a criminal statute.[136] Several federal cases even before *Gault* have held bail to be a juvenile's constitutional right.[137] It is difficult to justify an absolute power to detain a juvenile without bail for any offense, however minor, without any showing of the necessity for detention to safeguard either the juvenile or the public safety. To view pre-hearing detention as part of the treatment process is unrealistic, in view of the limited amount which could be accomplished at such a time. Moreover, it assumes the very conclusion which it is the function of the adjudicative and dispositional hearings to arrive at

---

136. Justice Black's dissent in Carlson v. Landon foreshadows some of the reasoning in Gault and is apposite to the question of bail for juveniles:

"I reject the contention that this constitutional right to bail can be denied a man in jail by the simple device of providing a 'not criminal' label for the techniques used to incarcerate. Imprisonment awaiting determination of whether that imprisonment is justifiable has precisely the same evil consequences to an individual whatever legalistic label is used to describe his plight." 342 U.S. at 557.

See Stack v. Boyle, 342 U.S. 1, 4 (1952), in which the Court stated that since 1789:

"federal law has unequivocally provided that a person arrested for a non-capital offense *shall* be admitted to bail. This traditional right to freedom before conviction permits the unhampered preparation of a defense, and serves to prevent the infliction of punishment prior to conviction. . . . Unless this right to bail before trial is preserved, the presumption of innocence, secured only after centuries of struggle, would lose its meaning." [Emphasis in original]

137. *See, e.g.,* Trimble v. Stone, 178 F.Supp. 483, 485 (D. D.C. 1960), in which the Court said:

"the Juvenile Court Act is silent on the subject of bail. The higher law of the Constitution, however, prevails. The Eighth Amendment is self-executing and no statute is necessary to implement it. . . . A serious Constitutional question would arise if the statute expressly or by necessary implication denied the right to bail." *See also* ex parte Osborne, 127 Tex. Cr. R. 136, 75 S.W.2d 265 (Ct. Crim. Apps. 1934); State v. Franklin, 202 La. 439, 12 So.2d 211, 213 (1943).

The Eighth Amendment guarantee against excessive bail has not yet been held applicable to the states in criminal cases. In accordance with our previous analysis, we assume that its extension to adult criminal defendants is likely to precede its application to juveniles as a constitutional matter.

—whether the juvenile is delinquent and whether his treatment requires detention.

Recognition that the power to detain cannot constitutionally be absolute does not necessarily require admission to bail in the traditional form, *i.e.,* the posting of a monetary bond. The National Crime Commission expressed the view that bail "is one of those attributes of the criminal process that it is wise for the juvenile court to be free of."[138] What is vital is not a right to bail as such but a right to release for the juvenile, which may take different forms and be subject to various conditions.[139]

This right to release need not be absolute, any more than the power to detain can be permitted to be absolute. It is possible that sometimes the welfare of the juvenile may be better served by his detention in a juvenile facility than by releasing him back to his family, at least when no other supportive community facilities are immediately available.[140] When this can be shown, there should be no constitutional barrier to pre-hearing detention. Demonstrable serious danger to the community if the juvenile remains at large, equivalent to the occasions justifying pre-hearing detention where adults are involved, may also provide sufficient basis for such detention, although the constitutional difficulties inherent in preventive detention are formidable.[141]

As a concomitant to this right of release, it follows that there should be a right to a hearing on the necessity of pre-hearing detention. The decision to detain must ultimately be a judicial determination, based on defined standards as applied to the facts of the individual

---

138. *Task Force,* p. 36.

139. The Bail Reform Act of 1966, 18 U.S.C.A. §3146 (Supp. 1966), has sought to replace the money bond system in the federal courts with release on personal recognizance subject to conditions intended to assure appearance in court at the designated time. *Cf.* In re Castro, 243 Cal. App. 2d 402, 412, 52 Cal. Rptr. 469, 475 (1966).

140. Cases of neglected and dependent children are most likely to present this justification for temporary pre-hearing detention, but delinquency cases may as well.

141. The D. C. Crime Commission proposed preventive detention in certain cases, subject to carefully defined procedural safeguards, for felony defendants whose prior records or backgrounds indicated that their release would endanger the physical safety of the public. D. C. Crime Commission, pp. 527-528.

case. It is a matter of such consequence to the juvenile that due process should also afford him an opportunity to be heard meaningfully on the decision to detain.[142]

3. INTERROGATION

Gault leaves little doubt that the constitutional prohibition against involuntary confessions is fully applicable in juvenile delinquency proceedings. The Court cited approvingly recent state cases holding that involuntary confessions must be excluded in such proceedings.[143]

Indeed, the standard for admitting confessions challenged on involuntariness grounds in juvenile proceedings is likely to be stricter because of the Court's emphasis on the factors of age and immaturity and its statement that "authoritative opinion has cast formidable doubt upon the reliability and trustworthiness of 'confessions' by children."[144]

It also appears that *Miranda* v. *Arizona*[145] will be held applicable to custodial interrogation of juveniles in the pre-judicial stage, despite the Court's reservation of the question.[146] The reasons for this conclusion are several.

The Court chose deliberately to rest its holding of the applicability of the privilege against self-incrimination on broad grounds. Counsel for Gault stressed in their brief to the Supreme Court that the relationship between juvenile and adult criminal proceedings in Arizona

---

142. *Cf.* Kent v. United States, 383 U.S. 541 (1966); see *Task Force*, p. 37; D. C. Crime Commission, p. 670.

143. 387 U.S. at 46. In the Interests of Carlo, 48 N.J. 224, 225, A.2d 110 (1966); In the Matters of Gregory W. and Gerald S., 19 N.Y.2d 55, 277 N.Y.S.2d 675, 224 N.E.2d 102 (1966); *cf.* United States v. Morales, 233 F.Supp. 160 (D. Mont. 1964).

144. 387 U.S. at 52. In In the Interests of Carlo, 48 N.J. 224, 225 A.2d 110 (1966), questioning in a police station and denial to juveniles of access to their parents were considered virtually determinative of the voluntariness of their confessions. *See* 387 U.S. at 53-54.

145. 384 U.S. 436 (1966).

146. The admissions elicited from Gault at the hearings before the juvenile court judge followed a continuing process of extra-judicial interrogation by the juvenile court probation officers, who had the authority of peace officers under Arizona law and had the statutory responsibility to "make investigations and file petitions." The Court stated, however, that it could not consider the status of Gault's alleged admissions to the probation officers because the exact circumstances of the questioning and the admissions made under questioning did not appear in the record. 387 U.S. at 43 n. 74.

was such that at the time Gault was questioned by the judge at the hearings, he ran the risk of being waived to criminal court for trial as an adult charged with crime and therefore faced self-incrimination in the literal sense.[147] The Court, however, relied on this as merely one factor and held that the privilege applies in juvenile proceedings because of the possibility of commitment to a state institution.[148]

Moreover, once the Court decided that the privilege is applicable in juvenile proceedings, it could have stopped with the simple proposition that what occurred in Gault's hearing necessarily violated his privilege because he was required to testify in a court proceeding in which he was the defendant.[149] But the Court did not stop there—it proceeded to support its conclusion that the privilege was violated by citing a number of its leading confession cases, including *Miranda,* and by extensively discussing the dangers of juvenile confessions resulting from custodial interrogation. In other words, it construed the privilege in juvenile proceedings—as it had previously done in criminal cases in *Miranda*—as being broader than a testimonial privilege applicable in judicial proceedings and as being fully applicable in interrogation prior to appearance in court.[150] Thus the analytical framework for the application of the privilege in *Gault* is precisely the same as it was in *Miranda.*

Furthermore, despite its disclaimer that it was passing on the out-of-court admissions, the Court concluded its discussion of the privilege by stating that Gault's "confession" was first obtained by the probation officer out of the presence of his parents, without counsel and apparently without advising him of his right to silence. It stated "the process by which the 'admissions' were obtained and received

---

147. Brief for Appellants, pp. 50-57.

148. 387 U.S. at 50. It appears therefore that even if a state were to immunize a juvenile completely from treatment as an adult—by ruling out waiver to adult court and transfer to an adult penal institution—or were to grant complete immunity against the use of any evidence in adult proceedings obtained as a result of compelled statements in a juvenile proceeding, the privilege would still be applicable in the juvenile proceeding.

149. In a criminal case it abridges the privilege merely to call the defendant as a witness; he need not invoke the privilege specifically.

150. This provoked Justice Stewart to criticize the majority for confusing the constitutional prohibition against use of coerced confessions with the "testimonial privilege against self-incrimination," the same error, in his view, which the Court had committed in Miranda. 387 U.S. at 80-81 n.3.

must be characterized as lacking the certainty and order which are required of proceedings of such formidable consequences."[151] Thus the Court all but said that the *Miranda* requirements, including right to counsel, are applicable.[152]

Indeed, there is no tenable basis for holding *Miranda* inapplicable to custodial interrogation of juveniles. If the *Miranda* requirements, including the right to counsel, are necessary to prevent erosion of the privilege in the case of an adult, then the case of a juvenile is *a fortiori* because of considerations of age and immaturity. In addition, at the stage of custodial interrogation, particularly in a serious crime, there is the real possibility of waiver to criminal court for trial as an adult. The reasons for the *Miranda* requirements are therefore even stronger because the peril of self-incrimination, not merely as a juvenile delinquent, but as a criminal, is substantial.[153] When there is added the extraordinary detention powers over juveniles provided by the laws of many states, the risk that the privilege will in fact be eroded is so great that the case for the *Miranda* requirements becomes compelling.[154]

States continuing to believe that juvenile confessions serve legitimate rehabilitative purposes, which would be impeded by the *Miranda*

---

151. *Id.* at 56.

152. At another point, the Court stated that the "participation of counsel will, of course, assist the police . . . in administering the privilege." *Id.* at 55.

153. *See Standards,* p. 49:
". . . it cannot always be assumed that the police interview will lead only to a noncriminal proceeding. Therefore, in such situations all of the procedural safeguards in the criminal law should be followed."

154. Juveniles should have at least the same rights in this regard as members of the armed services, who have been held entitled to the benefits of Miranda under military interrogation. The Court of Military Appeals said this year:
"The time is long since past . . . when this court will lend an attentive ear to the argument that members of the armed services are, by reason of their status, ipso facto deprived of all protections of the Bill of Rights. Both the Supreme Court and this court are satisfied as to the application of constitutional safeguards to military trials, except insofar as they are made inapplicable either expressly or by necessary implication." United States v. Tempia, 16 U.S.C.M.A. 629, 37 C.M.R. 249 (1967).

requirements,[155] have a relatively simple solution at hand. That is to immunize the juvenile from the use of his statements, and any evidence obtained therefrom, in any subsequent proceedings to adjudicate him a delinquent. This would render the *Miranda* requirements inapplicable by removing the reason which generated them—the need to protect against compelled self-incrimination. This requires only an extension of the immunity principle already applied in many states— that statements of a juvenile elicited in the course of juvenile proceedings cannot be used against him in subsequent criminal proceedings if he is waived for trial as an adult.[156]

The use of statements and evidence resulting therefrom obtained without compliance with *Miranda* should be limited to informal adjustment and disposition of cases by juvenile authorities not involving an adjudication of delinquency with the possibility of commitment. This need not cripple or impede the juvenile process. As already noted, recent studies and enactments enhance the importance of informal

---

155. As Chief Judge Weintraub has put the point:
"The object of the juvenile process is to make men out of errant boys. In that process we build upon the truth. A juvenile should be led to believe the decent thing is to come clean, to face the music . . . an infant need not be warned that the truth will be used against him, for the very assumption of the juvenile process is that the truth will be used to help him." In the Interests of Carlo, 48 N.J. 224, 244, 225 A.2d 110, 121-122 (1966). Contrast Justice Fortas' conclusion:
". . . evidence is accumulating that confessions by juveniles do not aid in 'individualized treatment' . . . and that compelling the child to answer questions, without warning or advice as to his right to remain silent, does not serve this or any other good purpose." 387 U.S. at 51.

156. *See, e.g.,* Ariz. Rev. Stat. §8-228B (1956). The principal flaw in such statutes is the failure to provide complete immunity by preventing the use in adult court of evidence obtained as a result of the juvenile's statements in juvenile court and by prohibiting prosecution as an adult on any offense revealed by the statements. It is not sufficient merely to prohibit the use of the statements. *See* Counselman v. Hitchcock, 142 U.S. 547 (1892); Dendy v. Wilson, 142 Tex. 460, 179 S.W.2d 269 (1944).
The District of Columbia Circuit has carried the immunity principle one step farther by holding that statements obtained during custodial interrogation of a juvenile cannot be used against him in criminal court in the event of waiver. Harling v. United States, 295 F.2d 161 (D.C. Cir. 1961). *See also* Harrison v. United States, 359 F.2d 214 (D.C. Cir. 1965); Edwards v. United States, 330 F.2d 849 (D.C. Cir. 1964).

pre-judicial adjustment and disposition of juvenile cases.[157] To the extent that confession is good for the juvenile soul, it should still be possible to utilize it as a rehabilitative technique, while at the same time preserving the values and objectives of the constitutional privilege against self-incrimination.

4. COUNSEL AT INTAKE

The intake point in the juvenile court—when juveniles are customarily interviewed by the court staff—is a prolific source of juvenile admissions.[158] The preceding consideration of *Miranda* applies equally to questioning at the intake point. If the juvenile is to be encouraged to make admissions, despite the privilege against self-incrimination, he should be protected against the use of such admissions at ensuing delinquency proceedings.

Even if such insulation is provided, thus averting the *Miranda* self-incrimination problems, the need to afford counsel at the intake point is not thereby removed. There is increasing recognition of the importance of the intake process to the juvenile. The National Crime Commission has stated: "The need for counsel is not confined to the adjudicatory stages of the proceedings. Both at intake and at disposition, counsel is crucial."[159]

With the enhanced emphasis on informal pre-hearing adjustment and disposition, the importance of counsel at the intake point has grown:

> Clearly such a system would invite unfettered authoritarianism by non-judicial officials unless counsel were provided at the inception of informal proceedings involving coercion. This is particularly true with respect to the consent decree. In the juvenile no less than in the adult area, the presence of counsel representing the alleged offender is indispensable to a system of alternative tracks short of full use of the judicial proceedings.[160]

---

157. *See* pp. 5-6, *supra.* The Illinois and New York statutes providing for the use of informal pre-judicial conferences specify that statements made by the juvenile shall not be used against him in any delinquency proceedings which may ensue. N.Y. Family Court Act §735 (1962); Ill. Juvenile Court Act, Ill. Rev. Stat. ch. 37, §703-8(5) (1966). *See Task Force,* p. 38; Note, 67 COLUM. L. REV., *supra* note 65, at 306, 333-334.

158. *See* Note, 79 HARV. L. REV. *supra* note 71, at 789; Note, 67 COLUM. L. REV. *supra* note 65 at 332-333.

159. *Task Force,* p. 32.

160. *Id.* at p. 33. *See also* Paulsen, *Juvenile Courts, Family Courts and the Poor Man,* 54 CAL. L. REV. 694, 704 (1966).

Counsel can have a significant impact at the intake point in view of the range of alternative dispositions of the case potentially available at that time. Since one of those alternatives is the filing of a delinquency petition possibly leading to the juvenile's commitment, he may be prejudiced if he is not represented by counsel to contend against such a course of action. The intake stage is thus a critical stage of the proceedings for him, comparable to the decision whether to waive him for trial as an adult. The right of counsel seems to be the indispensable adjunct to a decision of such consequence.[161]

C. The Dispositional Stage

The dispositional stage presents problems both of a procedural nature and concerning the implementation of the principle of individualized treatment of juvenile offenders. It also offers opportunities to validate the rehabilitative assumptions underlying the juvenile court movement.

1. PROCEDURES

Once an adjudication of delinquency has been made, in accordance with the due process standards of *Gault,* the need for observance of procedures derived from the criminal law substantially evaporates. Due process surely applies to the dispositional stage,[162] as it does to the other phases, but its content can be shaped to the task at hand. The essence is a fair hearing, at which the juvenile is given an opportunity to be heard meaningfully on the appropriate disposition of his case. The range of alternatives open to the juvenile court is so vast[163] and

---

161. *Cf.* Kent v. United States, 383 U.S. 541 (1966). *See* D. C. Crime Commission, pp. 682-684; *Standards,* p. 113. New York's law guardian system provides counsel at the intake interview. New York Family Court Act, §241 (1962).

162. As Chief Justice Hughes said in Morgan v. United States, 304 U.S. 1, 18-20 (1938):

"Those who are brought into contest with the Government in quasi-judicial proceedings aimed at the control of their activities are entitled to be fairly advised of what the Government proposes and to be heard upon its proposals before it issues its final command . . . The requirements of fairness are not exhausted in the taking or consideration of evidence, but extend to the concluding part of the procedure as well as to the beginning and intermediate steps."

163. The juvenile court in Gault had 10 statutorily approved alternatives open to it, ranging all the way from committing the juvenile to the state industrial school, or to a variety of other institutions, or to the care of his parents subject to the supervision of the probation officer.

the result so crucial for the future development of the juvenile that a summary or *ex parte* proceeding would be intolerable. The hearing, while it need not be formal, "must measure up to the essentials of due process and fair treatment."[164]

The most important right of the juvenile which should be recognized at this hearing is the right to counsel. Informed commentary is virtually unanimous on this point. As the National Crime Commission study concludes:

> The outcome is critical for the life of the child and justice requires that he have the assistance of counsel in advancing his own interest before the court—by offering alternative plans, for example, or by calling attention to the factual and theoretical assumptions, the speculations, the degree of thoughtfulness and thoroughness of the probation officer's report. . . . The contribution of lawyers in choosing the most suitable dispositional alternative for the child, both at the pre-judicial intake stage and at the judicial disposition stage, cannot be overestimated, serving as it does both to protect the child and to advance the social interest in prevention of delinquency.[165]

As an adjunct to the right of counsel, a fair hearing at this stage should provide some measure of disclosure of the social reports and other investigative materials relied on by the court for disposition.[166] This is indispensable if counsel is to participate effectively in the dispositional decision and attempt to persuade the court that another form of treatment may be superior to that recommended by the juvenile court staff.

Although the Supreme Court has held in *Williams v. New York*[167] that there is no constitutional right to cross-examine witnesses who have supplied information in the pre-sentence report in a state criminal

---

164. *Cf.* Kent v. United States, 383 U.S. 541, 562 (1966).

165. *Task Force,* p. 33, *See also Standards,* p. 113; N.Y. Family Court Act, §241.

One empirical study of the role of attorneys in the juvenile court in California concluded:

". . . the major contribution of attorneys in the juvenile court lay in their ability to mitigate the severity of dispositions rather than disproving allegations of the petitions." Lenert, *The Juvenile Court, Quest and Realities, Task Force,* Appendix D, p. 103.

166. As we have previously discussed, pp. 20-22, *supra,* we believe that the dispositional phase, not the adjudicative hearing, is the appropriate place for judicial consideration of these materials when an alleged law violation is at issue.

167. 337 U.S. 241 (1949).

proceeding, this doctrine should not control the development of the dispositional phase of the juvenile proceeding. Last term the Court declined to extend *Williams* to a state proceeding in which a convicted sex offender could receive an indeterminate sentence up to life on a subsequent determination that he would be a threat to the public if at large or was a habitual offender and mentally ill.[168] Since new issues requiring new findings were presented in the commitment hearing, the Court deemed *Williams* inapplicable and held that the defendant must be accorded the rights of hearing, counsel, confrontation, and cross-examination, and the right to offer evidence of his own.

Where the juvenile statute requires further findings by the court to support confinement,[169] after an adjudication of delinquency, it follows that the court cannot rely on secret materials in making such findings and must accord the juvenile and his counsel the chance to meet them.[170] Even when additional findings are not a specific prerequisite to a particular disposition, the trend of authoritative opinion is in favor of disclosure of the basic information relied on in the disposition. For example, the Children's Bureau Standards state that "No judicial decision should be based upon an undisclosed fact."[171]

In view of the variety of dispositional alternatives and the difficulty of devising an adequate treatment plan for the juvenile, the need for full and accurate development of the facts about his personality, history, and family background, and about the community resources available, is greater than in the adult sentencing process, where the dispositional alternatives are more limited. Reliability in the process of factual determination leading to disposition is as important as it is in the adjudicative phase. Disclosure to the juvenile and his counsel of the information developed by the juvenile court staff studies is therefore of great importance in helping to assure development of a full picture. The interest in preserving the confidentiality of sources of

---

168. Specht v. Patterson, 386 U.S. 605 (1967).

169. *See, e.g.,* the Maryland statute involved in In the Matter of Cromwell, 232 Md. 409, 194 A.2d 88 (Md. Ct. App. 1963).

170. Kent v. United States, 383 U.S. 541 (1966).

171. *Standards*, p. 74. *See also* Paulsen, *supra* note 45, at 179-180.

The same trend is observable with respect to presentence reports in criminal cases despite Williams v. New York. The Supreme Court in 1966 promulgated new Federal Rule of Criminal Procedure 32 (a)(2) authorizing the federal courts in criminal sentencing to disclose all or part of the material in the presentence report and afford the defendant or his counsel an opportunity to comment.

information, which is the underlying basis of *Williams,* is legitimate and militates against automatic disclosure of everything, including confidential sources, in the juvenile court studies. But this interest can be accommodated by the courts with the need for disclosure.[172]

2. RIGHT TO TREATMENT

One of *Gault's* most provocative implications is that the courts may exercise a reviewing function in the area of treatment of adjudicated delinquents.

The Court commented at length on the doubt whether juveniles in fact receive the individualized rehabilitative treatment promised them.[173] It cited a number of cases in which "some courts have recently indicated that since treatment is the essential *quid pro quo,* a juvenile may challenge the validity of his custody on the ground that he is not in fact receiving any special treatment."[174]

---

172. *See, e.g.,* D. C. Crime Commission, p. 686; Paulsen, *supra* note 45, at 181. *See also* Matter of Blaine, 54 Misc. 2d 248 (Family Ct. 1967), in which Judge Dembitz established standards by which to regulate the admission and disclosure of psychiatric information in the dispositional phase of neglect proceedings.

173. 387 U.S. at 22-23 n. 30.

174. *Id.* In its post-Gault opinion in In the Matter of Elmore, *supra,* n. 29, the District of Columbia Circuit said:

"The Juvenile Court is armed with broad statutory powers to the end that the community's resources may be marshalled to provide individualized care and treatment. . . . Recognizing that full and imaginative use of these powers enables the Juvenile Court to fashion a dispositional decree tailored to meet the peculiar needs of a particular child, we [deem] that court obligated to conduct an 'appropriate inquiry' when presented with a 'substantial complaint' concerning commitment."

Accordingly, in the view of the D. C. Circuit, habeas corpus is available to a juvenile to test the juvenile court's compliance with this mandate to afford him treatment and to supervise the adequacy of the treatment given him.

Perhaps the most exigent case for such judicial intervention is presented by the extraordinary practice in some states of transferring juveniles committed as delinquents to adult penal institutions where they may be confined together with adult felons. Such a practice is wholly at variance with the juvenile court's professed objective of treatment, and it is difficult to see how it can be lawfully carried on without granting the juvenile all the constitutional guarantees of adults charged with crime. *See* In re Rich, 125 Vt. 373, 261 A.2d 266 (1966); White v. Reid, 126 F.Supp. 867 (D. D.C. 1954). *But see* Wilson v. Coughlin, 147 N.W.2d 175 (Iowa Sup. Ct. 1966).

Compare two recent cases recognizing a right to treatment for mental patients, Rouse v. Cameron, 373 F.2d 451 (D.C. Cir. 1966), *aff'd en banc on other grounds,* 36 U.S.L.W. 2177 (D.C. Cir. Sept. 1, 1967); Lake v. Cameron, 364 F.2d 657 (D.C. Cir. 1966). Note, *The Nascent Right to Treatment,* 53 Va. L. Rev. 1134 (1967).

Thus the judicial storm-signals are flying that the special handling of juveniles through the juvenile court process can be validated in the long run only if a concentrated assault is made on a major national problem: the poverty of community resources devoted to realization of rehabilitative goals. As the National Crime Commission stated:

> One reason for the failure of the juvenile courts has been the community's continued unwillingness to provide the resources—the people and facilities and concern—necessary to permit them to realize their potential. . . . The dispositional alternatives available even to the better endowed juvenile courts fall far short of the richness and the relevance to individual needs envisioned by the court's founders.[175]

The Supreme Court's concern with the quality of juvenile court justice is likely to be a long-term affair. And, as *Gault* manifests, the Court is impatient with the rhetoric and determined to confront the realities of the process. The real promise of the decision lies in the responsibilty and opportunity it affords all who are concerned with problems of the juvenile courts to do likewise.

------

175. *Task Force,* pp. 7-8. Despite all the emphasis which has been placed on the need of the juvenile courts to draw on the experience and learning of other disciplines, such as psychiatry and sociology, a National Crime Commission study of fulltime juvenile court judges reported that 83% had no psychiatrists or psychologists regularly available to their courts, and a third did not have regularly available probation officers or social workers. *Id.* at 6.

> "If . . . facilities are lacking at the treatment stage, then the major rationale for the withdrawal of some of the safeguards provided by the criminal court is also lacking . . . It is possible that the power of the courts may be used to release offenders from institutions in which treatment opportunities are not available, and in this way to compel improvement in treatment facilities and resources." Wheeler, Cottrell, and Romasco, *Juvenile Delinquency— Its Prevention and Control, Task Force,* pp. 421-422.

THE GAULT CASE

Justine Wise Polier

The Gault Case: Its Practical Impact on the Philosophy and Objectives of the Juvenile Court

HONORABLE JUSTINE WISE POLIER*

Now that the word has been spoken by the Supreme Court sixty-eight years after the creation of the first juvenile court, everyone agrees that juvenile delinquents, like adults, are entitled to a fair trial. To oppose the minimal requirements established by *Gault* would be very much like supporting sin. The first statement of the Counsel of Judges of the National Council on Crime and Delinquency hailed *Gault* as reaffirming the standards for juvenile and family courts developed over many years by it together with the National Council of Juvenile Court Judges and the United States Children's Bureau.

This statement acknowledged the obligation of all juvenile court judges to incorporate the mandates of *Gault* and noted that new legislation might be needed in many states to achieve such compliance.[2] A few weeks later at the national convention of the National Council of Juvenile Court Judges, a resolution was adopted by a majority of those present which included a *whereas* clause stating that "the decisions of the Supreme Court in those juvenile court cases which it has so far decided have left unresolved more questions than they have resolved."[3] However, in the substantive clauses of the same resolution, full acceptance was expressed of the actual findings in *Gault*, namely the right to notice, the right to counsel, the privilege against self-incrimination, and the right to confrontation of witnesses as contained in the

---

*Judge, New York State Family Court.

A new truth may be deprived of half its power by being mixed up with old formulas and venerable fallacies.[1]

1. Article published by Dr. Isaac Ray in 1870 on the Law of Insanity, quoted by Dr. Winfred Overholser in Introduction to Treatise on the Medical Jurisprudence of Insanity, Cambridge, Mass.: Harvard University Press, 1962.

2. Juvenile Court Digest, *The Gault Decision*, Vol. 1, No. 1, June, 1967.

3. *Thirtieth Annual Conference,* Fort Lauderdale, Florida, June 29, 1967.

Fifth and Sixth Amendments. The core of criticism was directed to two troubling questions discussed in but not decided by *Gault*.

First, how much further would or should safeguards established in criminal cases be extended to juvenile court proceedings? The resolution of the National Council reiterated that juvenile court proceedings were "civil" and not "criminal," and therefore need not conform with all the requirements of a criminal trial. Concerned by the threat of the imposition of procedures which would hobble the juvenile court by requiring strict adversary proceedings, a jury trial, and public hearings in juvenile cases, the framers of the resolution failed to evaluate what Professor Archibald Cox regarded as the most significant aspect of Kent. He saw this decision as evidence that the Supreme Court had moved from the traditional position that procedural rights should be determined on the basis of whether proceedings were designated as "civil" or "criminal" "toward reliance on a functional analysis that would focus on the consequences of the proceedings to the defendant, the role that the safeguard plays in assuring that the outcome of the proceedings is proper, and the cost to society of the safeguard."[4]

If Professor Cox is correct, and I believe he is, such an approach by the Supreme Court may augur well for social courts whose major concern is directed toward the welfare of the child and the protection of society. However, the restriction of the requirements of due process to the adjudicatory hearings in *Gault* and the narrow grounds on which *Kent* was decided still leave room for considerable doubt whether the Supreme Court is prepared to review questions of substantive as well as procedural rights under legislation aimed to help and rehabilitate children, the mentally ill, the narcotic addict, or those found guilty of other forms of deviant behavior for whom legislation mandates rehabilitative programs.

Judge Bazelon, who has challenged many old and outworn legal precedents in the light of current knowledge, has been one of the few appellate judges to question whether due process requirements do not become less than meaningful in the absence of substantive justice. Thus in *habeas corpus* proceeding by an old woman suffering from arterio sclerosis, lapses of memory, and confusion, who had been committed to an institution for the insane, he held, "Habeas corpus chal-

---

4. The Supreme Court 1965 Term, HARV. L. REV. Vol. 80, No. 1, Nov. 1966.

lenges not only the fact of confinement but also the place of confinement" and stated that it was the duty of the trial court to explore alternative places for appropriate care in such a case.[5] However, the strong dissent in this case reflects the traditional and prevailing view toward courts becoming involved in problems of substantive justice rather than in limiting their role to assuring adherence to procedural safeguards: "A United States court in our legal system is not set up to initiate inquiries and direct studies of social welfare facilities or other social problems."

The traditional refusal by appellate courts to consider the consequences of court proceedings for the individual lends weight to the skepticism of at least some juvenile court judges as to the benefits that will be derived from the present concentration on procedural rights at adjudicatory hearings.

Over fifteen years ago, Justice Douglas wrote, "Steadfast adherence to strict procedural safeguards is our main assurance that there will be equal justice under law."[6] The requirements of such safeguards, if extended in the future to dispositional hearings in the juvenile courts, may do much to prevent the continuation of discriminatory dispositions based on race, color, religion or national origin. Significant and necessary as is such progress, it must not be seen as fulfilling the ideal objective for a juvenile court. While equal justice is an essential ingredient in the work of all courts, the ideal of individualized justice demands more. It requires that the court shall make every effort to secure the care, the treatment, the remedy most appropriate to the needs of the individual child. This requirement may explain why the juvenile court has been denounced as a "socialistic" rather than a social court by some critics. While such critics have been dismissed as so benighted as not to know the difference in word-meaning, it may be that they sensed correctly that the juvenile court might become a vehicle for introducing the ideal of distributive justice,[7] a form of justice that should not only assure equality but that should seek to provide for each child in accordance with this need.

---

5. Lake v. Cameron, Supt. Saint Elizabeth: 331 F.2d, 771. Decided May 19, 1966.

6. Joint Anti Fascist Refugee Com. v. McGrath, 341 U.S. 123, 179 (1951).

7. See Henry H. Foster, *Social Work, The Law and Social Action,* Social Casework, Vol. XLV, No. 7, July, 1964.

The *second* and far more troubling question for juvenile court judges raised by *Gault* is how far the jurisdiction of the courts should be narrowed in the light of their actual capacity to secure the services needed for care, treatment and rehabilitation. The opinion in *Kent* raised the issue of how far the juvenile court could adequately perform its role of *parens patriae* in view of the lack of personnel, facilities and techniques to rehabilitate children, but the case was disposed of on narrower grounds. This was also true in *Gault* despite the extended review of the literature which raised the same issue. The dicta in both cases played upon the raw nerve of every juvenile court judge who must constantly struggle to find the best disposition among the limited ones available. For judges, who are deeply aware that the Supreme Court decisions have neither the power to obviate nor to repair the restrictions on resources that have persistently impaired the potential of the juvenile courts, the dicta have cast the longest shadows.

The resolution of the National Council of Judges expressed the viewpoint that the failure of the legislative and executive branches of government to provide the juvenile court with the means for regenerative treatment postulated by legislation "does not and should not vitiate such laws or render them unconstitutional." This reaction, rather than renewed insistence that the means to assure substantive justice must be made available, is unfortunate but understandable.

The value of the work of the juvenile courts had been questioned not only by the Supreme Court, by the President's Commission on Law Enforcement and Administration of Justice, by law professors, and by sociologists, but by those who equate efforts to treat and rehabilitate children with the "coddling of delinquents." Proposals had proliferated to whittle down the jurisdiction of the juvenile courts based on the assumption that local public and private child care agencies can now be entrusted with providing both preventive and treatement services. These proposals are linked with charges that juvenile court judges, by engaging in the administration or direction of services, have undertaken roles for which they are neither trained nor competent and which may engage them in positions of responsibility involving a conflict of interests.[8] Such charges are baffling to judges who have dis-

---

8. See William H. Sheridan, *New Directions for the Juvenile Court*, FED. PROB., June, 1967.

covered that they could only secure minimal services for children by presenting the need to their communities, by struggling to secure support, and by being ready to accept responsibility for the establishment of such services as shelters for neglected children, separate detention for delinquents, clinical services, foster home programs and youth camps. Their experience has made them skeptical of the current assumption, now in fashion, that the widespread inadequacy of services will suddenly be corrected by new community organizations supported by local, state and federal agencies.

While welcoming the new interest in recruiting and training personnel for services to children in the community, juvenile court judges are also aware of a comparable need for trained personnel in the public and private agencies who are given custody of children removed from their own homes. They know that the supply of such personnel will be short for many years, and that the assumption that children once placed in agencies will receive such care as their changing needs require, is unrealistic. They have seen the tragic procession of children lost to their families and the community once custody is granted to an agency whether by parents, welfare departments or courts. They have observed the selective intake policies that have excluded children who are not "good risks" and that have discriminated against children of minority groups. They have had to live with legislative mandates for services to ever larger numbers of children reduced to a hollow gesture by the withholding of necessary funds, personnel, and facilities.

The compelling needs of children unmet by specialists in schools, hospitals, social agencies, and the community have repeatedly compelled the juvenile court judge to become the generalist who must observe what is not being done, attempt to coordinate needed services, and find some practical way of filling the gap between compartmentalized services. If this be treason to the judicial image, perhaps it is time to examine whether the old judicial image needs to be modified so that substantive justice may replace blind-folded justice.

As the juvenile court judge reads the recent spate of writings by law professors and sociologists, the studies prepared for commissions, and the literature referred to in *Gault*, he notes the slight bow to the rationale for the growth of social as opposed to legalistic justice and the approval of efforts to bring the law into partnership with the emerging social and behavioral sciences. With a brief transition, the bow recedes and the conclusion is submitted that the first efforts to achieve this end through the juvenile court were greatly over-optimistic. A distinguished expert in the field of juvenile delinquency has taken the position that in order "to assure a program embodying the findings of the behavioral sciences, it should be under a person professionally trained in these sciences who has also demonstrated administrative ability."[9] Without gainsaying this goal or questioning how the rights of individuals would be protected, the juvenile court judge asks from what flock are such rare birds to be secured. The public welfare staffs generally untrained in the social sciences, the limited number of social workers prepared to work under pressure in crisis situations, the few clinical psychologists available, the rare psychiatrists concerned with community problems, do not offer the reserve from which they can be drawn. The sharp distinction between judicial responsibility and that of correctional or treatment personnel dealing with adult criminals, youthful offenders, alcoholics, narcotic addicts and sexual psychopaths does not give reason for confidence in such separation of responsibility.

Experience in the juvenile courts has alerted its judges to the fact that it is one thing to require procedural safeguards but that it is quite another to secure the services that demand far more from the community, its professional groups and the law. In states such as New York where the operative holdings of *Gault* have been in effect, judges are all too aware of how little adequate notice, the right to counsel, the privilege against self-incrimination, and the right to confront witnesses have affected what is done or left undone to meet the needs of children brought before the court.

The juvenile court judge is likely to welcome the increased interest in the economic and social influences that have burdened the lives of so many children brought before the court but also be troubled that the blueprints to correct basic conditions largely ignore the necessity for continuing work by the juvenile court, the probation officer, the correctional counselor or the psychiatrist. He knows that even if the pace of social change is greatly accelerated, it will not meet the problems of children and youth, now in being, whose personalities, character structure and mental health have been seriously impaired by their life experiences. The judge is properly concerned lest exclusive and belated emphasis on the broad social and economic conditions

---

9. Ibid. P. 17.

that call for change may be used to avoid facing the results of past failure to provide individualized care and treatment and the present responsibility for providing such care and treatment for those now in need. There is no question that the juvenile courts have been unable to stem the tide of family disorganization, to correct the environmental deprivations and injuries which increasingly oppress the children of the urban poor, to create compensatory services for children denied an adequate standard of living, health services, decent homes or good schooling. Nor have they been able to counter the denigration and hurts imposed on children through ongoing discrimination by reason of color or race. The work of juvenile courts, like that of criminal courts, mental hospitals, welfare agencies, and schools, has been restricted by community indifference, if not hostility, to those whose behavior is deviant, to those who are mentally ill and to those who are poor.

Recognition of the causes for the limited effectiveness of social institutions, including the juvenile court, requires that the juvenile court judge shall reexamine his practices and the results of his work in the light of whatever objective findings are available. He should welcome those procedural safeguards that will assure equal justice under law. But he must and can do more. He must be candid in presenting what the court can and cannot do. Aware of the inadequacy of preventive and treatment services in the community, whose absence has herded children into courts as a dumping ground, he can not only encourage the creation of needed services but present facts about the absence of such services and the consequences to children and the community. He should welcome constructive change which will harness the use of the behavioral sciences to schools, clinic, hospital, welfare services, while insisting that they also be integrated into court services for those children who cannot be helped in the community, and who frequently are most in need of intensive treatment.

Today the necessity for the enlargement of law to fulfill a role that not only expresses what the individual may not do, but what society must do to increase the welfare of more people, while protecting the rights and respecting the dignity of the individual, necessitates new concepts for courts and many other institutions created by law to meet social problems. It may well be that the juvenile court, whose ideal has not been reached, will move closer toward the ideal and stimulate a far more urgent search for social and distributive justice under law.

Equal justice through procedural safeguards that does not require substantive justice for each individual is not enough.

It has become increasingly clear that neither a factory model of efficiency in social agencies nor due process in the courts is adequate to meet the social problems that confront them. The times call for correcting the dehumanization of institutions and the depersonalization of treatment by all agencies of government including courts. "Humanization" of institutions was recently described as a short-cut word for creating concern for human beings and becoming more responsive to the people within the institutions and to the society from which they come. It is not impossible for a judicial system, which has moved during the past forty years away from control by general principles and precedents to an examination of specific facts in many areas of the law, to expand its concern for reality to include the specific problems of individuals and what can be done to help them most effectively.

This was exactly what pioneers of the juvenile court movement sought to do for children. The history of the juvenile court should not be read in terms of the faulty vision or over-optimism of its founders but in terms of the past under-achievement of the community. Today there is urgent need to reexamine the functioning of executive and judicial institutions so that methodological skills and procedures may be made increasingly relevant to the substantive goals for which they were created by the legislative branch of government. The history of the juvenile court presents excellent case material for a dialogue to achieve this goal. It provides one of many examples of the chasms between legislative goals and what the community is in fact ready and willing to do to fulfill the promise or pretensions of social legislation. The flimsy and narrow bridges that have provided escape passage for a few will have to be replaced by strong and humanized structures in order to meet the social problems that increasingly threaten the well-being of this country and many of its inhabitants.

THE DILEMMA OF THE
POST-GAULT JUVENILE COURT

Jerome G. Miller

The Dilemma of the Post-Gault Juvenile Court

JEROME G. MILLER*

The Gault decision has forced a reappraisal, not only of the operation of the juvenile court and its accompanying services (or lack thereof), but also a reexamination of the very structure of this form of court and of the social philosophy underlying the juvenile court itself. It was the original intent of the framers of the juvenile court to provide a non-punitive atmosphere within which to understand and deal with the young offender. This was in part a reaction to common law systems which allowed criminal trials for children over seven years of age – and in which children were uncritically and severely punished, ranging from long-term prison sentences to hanging.[1] In addition, the juvenile court was brought forth against a background of new-found optimism with reference to the understanding of anti-social behavior and the potential means available for personality change and social rehabilitation.

Few would quarrel with the motivation and need for the introduction of a humane approach to the juvenile offender at the time of the institution of the juvenile court. However, the implications of the decision to treat youths and children differently from adults were probably not thought through in detail. Indeed, the juvenile court strikes at the very underpinnings of the total criminal justice system. Roscoe Pound's famous statement[2] that the juvenile court represented one of the most significant advances in the administration of justice since the Magna Charta, is more than idle praise. It reflects an awareness of the profound issues forced upon the scene by the establishment of the juvenile court.

---

* The author has the Doctor's degree in Social Work and is an associate professor at Ohio State University.

1. Rubin and Shaffer, *Constitutional Protections for the Juvenile*, 44 DENVER L. J. 66, 66-67, 1967. Paulsen: *Kent v. United States: The Constitutional Context of Juvenile Cases*, 1966, SUPREME COURT REVIEW 167, 168-176.

2. Statement made by Dean Pound in address to annual meeting of the National Council of Juvenile Court Judges in 1950.

If the framers of the juvenile court system and the juvenile court judges were not aware of the deep and meaningful implications of their procedures, the organization of the criminal justice system reflected a latent concern. In looking at the organizational and administrative structure of courts, one can see that the "threat" (if it may be so termed) of the juvenile court to this structure has always been implicit—in the separate organization, the different sources of political power of juvenile court vs. other systems, etc. The juvenile court was rather quickly isolated as a different breed—an exception, an anomaly, an experiment, etc. One can often get the best glimpses of the relative standing of a philosophy or approach to problems by studying the organizational structures surrounding that approach. It is a contention of this paper that the juvenile court has represented to a degree, a basic threat to the organization and philosophy of the criminal justice system. This paper will, therefore, attempt to outline the sources of conflict arising from the establishment of the juvenile court, as they affect the court itself and more significantly, as they reflect conflicts within the larger society.

In an article written in 1918,[3] George H. Mead, the American social scientist, identified many of the sources of conflict arising from the establishment of the juvenile court system. His ideas have immediate relevance to the post-Gault juvenile court system.

It was Mead's view that the juvenile court offered the opportunity not only to assess and differentially handle juvenile offenders, but that the juvenile court forced a breach in the wall of the criminal justice system. Mead saw this system as an indicator of a society held together by hostile procedures directed at those who break the norms of that society. He viewed both the criminal and juvenile courts as systems of social control. However, he saw them as qualitatively different approaches to social control which betrayed basic attitudes within the larger society—attitudes so basic as to be among the very reasons for the cohesiveness of that society. Mead noted that the traditional criminal justice system is symptomatic of the social organization which arises from, and is dominated by, an attitude of hostility. In a provocative re-interpretation of the role of the criminal, he comments:

---

3. Mead, George H., *The Psychology of Punitive Justice* (reprinted from *The American Journal of Sociology*, XXIII [1918], 577-602), in *Theories of Society*, edited by Talcott Parsons et alii, Vol. II, pp. 876-886, Free Press of Glencoe, 1961.

Seemingly without the criminal the cohesiveness of society would disappear and the universal goods of the community would crumble into mutually repellent individual particles. The criminal does not seriously endanger the structure of society by his destructive activities and, on the other hand, he is responsible for a sense of solidarity, aroused among those whose attention would be otherwise centered upon interests quite divergent from those of each other. Thus, courts of criminal justice may be essential to the preservation of society even when we take account of the impotence of the criminal over against society, and the clumsy failure of criminal law in the repression and suppression of crime.

I am willing to admit that this statement is distorted, not, however, in its analysis of the procedure against the criminal, but in its failure to recognize the growing consciousness of the many common interests which is slowly changing our institutional conception of society, and its consequent exaggerated estimate upon the import of the criminal.[4]

Some would question whether this latter statement was overly optimistic, given the experience of the past 30 years. Having noted this, however Mead deals with the implications for a society in which solidarity is supported by mutually perceived hostility toward "outsiders"

But it is important that we should realize what the implications of this attitude of hostility are within our society. We should especially recognize the inevitable limitations which the attitude carries with it. Social organization which arises out of hostility at once emphasizes the character which is the basis of the opposition and tends to suppress all other characters in the members of the group. The cry of 'stop thief' unites us all as property owners against the robber. We all stand shoulder to shoulder as Americans against a possible invader. . . . as long as the social organization is dominated by the attitude of hostility, the individuals or groups who are the objectives of this organization will remain enemies. It is quite impossible psychologically to hate the sin and love the sinner. We are very much given to cheating ourselves in this regard. We assume that we can detect, pursue, indict, prosecute, and punish the criminal and still retain toward him the attitude of reinstating him in the community as soon as he indicates a change in social attitude himself, that we can at the same time overwhelm the offender, and comprehend the situation out of which the offense grows. But the two attitudes, that of control of crime by the hostile procedure of the law and that of control through comprehension of social and psychological conditions, cannot be combined. To understand is to forgive and the social procedure seems to deny the very responsibility which the law affirms, and on the other hand, the pursuit by criminal justice inevitably awakens the hostile attitude in the offender and renders the attitude of mutual comprehension practically impossible. The social worker in the court is the sentimentalist, and the

---

4. *Id.*, p. 882.

legalist in the social settlement in spite of his learned doctrine is the ignoramus.[5]

Mead comments that an attitude of hostility toward transgressors or external enemies gives a sense of solidarity which "arouses like a burning flame and which consumes the differences of individual interests" [6] He notes, however, that the price paid for this type of solidarity of feeling is very high, indeed, and may be disastrous.

It is at this juncture that Mead assesses the far-reaching and most basic implications arising out of the establishment of juvenile courts. Although he viewed the court as fulfilling therapeutic and rehabilitative needs for individuals it dealt with, he saw the juvenile court as a movement indicative of basic changes in the attitudes underlying social organization in our society.

> The juvenile court is but one instance of an institution in which the consideration of facts which had been regarded as irrelevant or exceptional has carried with it a radical change in the institution. But it is of particular interest because the court is the objective form of the attitude of hostility on the part of the community toward the one who transgresses its laws and customs and it is of further interest because it throws into relief the two types of emotional attitudes which answer to two types of social organization. Over against the emotional solidarity of the group opposing the enemy, we find the interests which spring up around the effort to meet and solve a social problem. These interests are at first in opposition to each other. The interest in the individual delinquent opposes the interest in property and the social order dependent upon it. The interest in the change of the conditions which foster the delinquent is opposed to that identified with our positions in society as now ordered, and the resentment at added responsibilities which had not been formerly recognized or accepted.[7]

This new kind of social organization brings with it a genuine effort to deal with problems. The engagement with these very real issues leads in turn to new interests, roles, norms and values. Mead felt that the concentration upon conditions which accompany and contribute toward delinquency, crime, unemployment, illness, etc., would lead to a new type of social organization focused upon growth, development, and constructive social change. He foresaw a unity and cohesiveness in society as its members joined together to combat human misery and build up human welfare. He saw this as ultimately more enhanc-

---

5. *Id.*, p. 882.
6. *Id.*, p. 882.
7. *Id.*, p. 884.

ing of man than social organization based upon hostility toward the norm breaker.

Mead, therefore, carries his discussion of the juvenile court far beyond the common characterization of its helping function for the individual child or youth. He sees the informal processes of the juvenile court as providing not only a rehabilitative function for the individual, but a change function for the larger society.

> If then we undertake to deal with the causes of crime in a fundamental way, and as dispassionately as we are dealing with the causes of disease, and if we wish to substitute negotiation and international adjudication for war in settling disputes between nations, it· is of some importance to consider what sort of emotional solidarity we can secure to replace that which the traditional procedures have supplied. It is in the juvenile court that we meet the undertaking to reach and understand the causes of social and individual breakdown, to mend if possible the defective situation and reinstate the individual at fault. This is not attended with any weakening of the sense of the values that are at stake. but a great part of the paraphernalia of hostile procedure is absent.[8]

He saw the juvenile court as bringing the beginnings of scientific technique into the criminal justice system. This would have far reaching implications if successfully implemented, since it would have its effect, not only upon procedures in the courtroom and the types of handling juveniles would receive by the court, but also upon the institutions to which juveniles would be sent. Ultimately, however, it appears that Mead foresaw the ideally successful juvenile court as affecting the basic structure of the criminal justice system by changing the focus from punishment of the offender, to the understanding of salient facts which contributed to the delinquency. Such a focus would immediately involve courts in coming to grips with such issues as family problems, quality of education, poverty, lack of job opportunities, etc. He saw the court as an agent in organizing society around these concerns with an emphasis upon the values of good family relationships, good schools, adequate job opportunities, etc. He saw all of these factors as entering the arena of the juvenile court.

This approach is contrasted with that of the adult criminal court where the central goal is "to determine by the application of fixed rules whether the man is a member of society in good and regular standing or is an outcast."[9] In this latter statement, Mead anticipates

8. *Id.*, p. 884.
9. *Id.*, p. 884.

the most current contemporary sociological theories of social deviance with focus upon (1) the processes whereby the deviant is defined, and (2) the relative power of the definers to make the definition stick, with "career" implications for the person so defined. The reader is referred to a number of writings in this regard.[10]

The fixed rules by which the adult criminal court effectively labels outcasts excludes material that does not come within strict legal definitions. Matters which bear upon such things as social problems, are not allowed to be considered directly in solving the problems presented in the courtroom. This is not the case in the ideally constructed juvenile court.

> In the juvenile court we have a striking instance of this material forcing its way into the institution of the court itself and compelling such a change in method that the material can be actually used.[11]

In reviewing the facts leading to the Gault decision, it is obvious that juvenile courts have failed to attain the social diagnostic and rehabilitative goals and procedures which Mead anticipated. In fact, few, if any, juvenile court systems approach the rehabilitative ideals of the founders of the system. With shortages of trained staff of high quality, inability to separate particular courts from political pressures, generally poor institutional settings, inadequate diagnostic procedures, etc., it has been relatively difficult to obtain a clear picture of the potential positive influence of the juvenile court system on individuals brought before it. However, the lack of true rehabilitative handling was a major prod to the Supreme Court's decision.

In this sense, the Gault decision demonstrates the recognition of the Supreme Court of the *de facto* punitive aspects of juvenile court proceedings. The objections of the Supreme Court are not unlike those of the Supreme Court of Michigan, which in 1908 held the constitutionality of the Detroit juvenile court to be invalid. They stated their objection in this way:

> The statute, it is true, declares that the proceedings shall not be taken to be criminal proceedings in any sense; and yet by Section 14 it is provided that if the child be adjudged a delinquent child, the court may place the

---

10. BECKER, HOWARD, OUTSIDERS, New York: The Free Press of Glencoe, 1963. BECKER, HOWARD, (editor), THE OTHER SIDE: PERSPECTIVE ON DEVIANCE, New York: The Free Press of Glencoe, 1964. E. RUBINGTON and M. WEINBERG (eds.), DEVIANCE: THE INTERACTIONIST PERSPECTIVE, New York: The MacMillan Company, 1968.

11. Mead, *infra*, p. 884.

case on trial, and impose a fine not to exceed $25.00 and costs, etc. This can have no other purpose than punishment for a delinquency, which means nothing less, or at least includes one who violates any law of this state or any city ordinance.

In the present case, however, this statute is a state law providing for a penalty. A complaint, an arrest, and trial are authorized, and, upon a determination, the imposition of a fine. It is difficult to conceive of any element of a criminal prosecution which may be said to be lacking. And, as Section 28 of Article 6 of the Constitution very plainly provides for a jury of twelve men in all courts of record in every criminal prosecution, the provisions for a jury of six for the trial of delinquents is in violation of this Section.[12]

One could hardly question whether sentencing to many, if not most of our contemporary "training schools" is less punishment than a fine of $25.00.

The Supreme Court, in the Gault decision, notes that the "highest motives and most enlightened impulses led to a peculiar system for juveniles, unknown to our law in any comparable context. The constitutional and theoretical basis for this peculiar system is, to say the least, debatable." This statement points to the basic source of the current conflict with reference to the place of the juvenile court. *Even if the juvenile court system had been totally effective in its substitution of "treatment" or "rehabilitation" for punishment—with a "clinical" rather than punitive approach, the constitutional and theoretical basis of such an approach would still be an open question.*

The Gault decision outlines the failure of juvenile courts to move from punitive to rehabilitative handling of juveniles—from punitive justice to treatment based upon consideration of all available salient facts. In fact, then, the juvenile court system by trying to have the "best" of both worlds (the punitive and the rehabilitative) has shied away from the constitutional confrontation which might have been created were it to be totally non-punitive—and in so doing has placed itself in a dilemma—reflecting in turn the dilemma of the larger society with reference to the handling of those defined as offenders. This is the issue to which Mead addresses himself.

Looking at the dilemmas created in the handling of juveniles in the juvenile court system, one sees that not only is there ambivalence in the *society* regarding "treatment" vs. punishment of the offender—there is ambivalence within the juvenile court system it-

---

12. Robinsons v. Wayne Circuit Judges, 151 Mich. 315, 115 N.W. 682, (1908).

self—and perhaps more significantly, there is ambivalence within the so-called helping professions—social work, psychology, and psychiatry which are distinguished by their supposed non-punitive approaches to persons.

In examining what actually happened to Gerald Gault, the court found the cumulative effect of the court procedures and the "treatment" to be punitive—even though the stated motivation of the court personnel may have been otherwise. Anyone well acquainted with juvenile court systems would not recognize the situation in the Gault case all that exceptional.

The failure to which the Supreme Court points is not only that of the juvenile court, but indirectly and perhaps more significantly, the failure of the helping professions which have been indirectly determining the diagnoses and "treatment" or "rehabilitative" procedures. To put this within another framework, one could state that the failure lies with those who have been determining the *labels* or definitions which allow the system to treat the labeled person in ways which it could not if it did not have the sanction provided by the label. If one looks at the handling (i.e., "treatment") of labeled persons, it is often difficult to see much difference in the approaches toward a person labeled as "possessed" or "sinful" vs. one labeled as "psychopathic," "sociopathic," "asocial," "genetically unsound," etc. This does not mean that criteria and planning were not different in these cases. It means, however, that the *actual handling* is difficult to distinguish aside from a difference in labels. The "prison" becomes a "reform school" becomes a "training school" becomes a "treatment center" with less substantive change than the name implies. Putting the deviant in a pit becomes "solitary" becomes "isolation" becomes "special care", (or more Kafkalike in an institution I recently visited, becomes the "freedom room"). Overt physical violence becomes semi-sophisticated psychological violence—nonetheless insidious if one takes the term to mean violation of an individual person's integrity.

In this basically dishonest situation, the helping professions have at times misinformed the judges and the public by implying that their methods were all that effective, or, indeed, in many cases, all that different from previous approaches to offenders. They have thus become unwitting agents of the ideology of punitive justice—the "psychojusters" of H. G. Wells. As a result of this, the potentially most important contribution of the juvenile court has been skirted—that factor which would deal with the basic contradictions between traditional criminal justice systems and juvenile court systems—the factor which ultimately confronts the problem of substituting a societal attitude toward the offender which is not based upon hostile retribution. Mead would argue that this contradiction is so basic that one cannot have it both ways. It is an "either-or" situation.

> But the two attitudes that of control of crime by the hostile procedure of the law and that of control through comprehension of social and psychological conditions, cannot be combined. To understand is to forgive and the social procedure seems to deny the very responsibility which the law affirms, and on the other hand the pursuit by criminal justice inevitably awakens the hostile attitude in the offender and renders the attitude of mutual comprehension practically impossible.[13]

One could point to many reasons for the failure of the juvenile courts to confront the essential issues surrounding punishment. Among these are the comparatively poorly trained professionals associated with the diagnostic and treatment programs of the courts. Clinical leadership roles in juvenile corrections are often held by the least competent professionals and least involved correctional staff. There is at times an inverse arrangement in court and correctional clinical services whereby the psychiatrist who would be at the lower rungs of the status-competency ladder among his peers in private practice or in non-correctional psychiatric settings is, by virtue of title and institutional need, placed in charge of correctional clinical and diagnostic programs for which he lacks competence. As a result of this recurring situation, creative and innovative approaches to diagnosis and treatment are difficult to find, and when found, are often the result of the efforts of other professions, e.g., education. In such structures, traditional approaches, wherein the clinician is a simple categorizing agent for the court system, become the rule rather than the exception.

Because of these contradictions within the system which have served to muddy the issues, the essential issues the juvenile court presents have not been effectively confronted. If the juvenile courts are to survive, it will be necessary for them to begin to make basic

---

13. Mead, op. cit. p. 882.

confrontations with reference to the enduring tendency on the part of our society to regress toward application of punitive justice as a means of maintaining its own cohesiveness.

Mead comments that it is difficult, if not impossible to "understand" a person's behavior and at the same time to maintain a retributive punitive attitude. He sees punitive justice as a function of a court system which systematically excludes significant facts and issues from the legal process—a process of legally selective inattention. He sees this process as leading to a hostile attitude toward the guilty person which serves the cohesiveness of the society. He interprets this process as leading to a hostile attitude toward the guilty person which serves the cohesiveness of the society. He interprets this process as one means of social control. He points to another means of social control which he views as more enduring and less destructive—one based upon constructive social activity rather than hostile retribution.

> The energy that expressed itself in burning witches as the causes of plagues expends itself at present in medical research and sanitary regulations and may still be called a fight with disease. In all these changes the interest shifts from the enemy to the reconstruction of social conditions. The self-assertion of the soldier and conqueror becomes that of the competitor in industry or business or politics, of the reformer, the administrator, of the physician or other social functionary. The test of success of this self lies in the change and construction of the social conditions which make the self possible, not in the conquest and elimination of other selves. His emotions are not those of mass consciousness dependent upon suppressed individualities, but arise out of the cumulative interest of varied undertakings converging upon a common problem of social reconstruction.[14]

Mead cautions that this form of social organization is more difficult to accomplish and is subject to more friction than "those which spring from war." Their emotional content may not be so vivid, but they are the only remedy for war, and they meet the challenge which the continued existence of war in human society has thrown down to human intelligence."[15]

This statement gives one some insight into the importance Mead attached to this need for a shift in motivations underlying social organization. He saw the juvenile court as providing an essential part

14. *Id.,* p. 886.
15. *Id.,* p. 886.

of the momentum if this change were to come about. This may appear at first glance to place exaggerated importance upon the court systems, and more specifically upon the juvenile courts. The reader might bear in mind that thoughtful men ranging from Durkheim to Churchill have noted that one of the best indicators of the level of civilization achieved by a particular society can be seen in that society's treatment of its criminals. In this sense, the courts provide fairly accurate barometers of social organization.

If the juvenile courts move toward confronting these very basic issues, one can expect an exacerbation of the traditional criticisms toward "bleeding heart" judges, "do-gooders," "coddling," etc. The only exit from this cul-de-sac is to involve the public in its responsibility for making decisions. This cannot be done, so long as the concern of the court is diverted by definitions which restrict information to factors surrounding the offense, shutting out other equally significant issues often confoundly "distant" from the offense — social class, race, education, etc. A retreat to legalism would be a betrayal of the original aims of the court just as surely as a punitive approach under the guise of "understanding" betrays the same ideals. The courts must, therefore, renew their educative functions for the community. To the degree that they withdraw from the community under the guise of factors such as confidentially, ability to handle cases informally, etc. — to that degree they invite an ultimate return to retributive punitive justice for that juvenile.

The Supreme Court Gault decision is an appropriate and reasonable reaction to the inability of the juvenile courts and associated professions to meet the primary responsibility underlying the development of the juvenile court system — the responsibility of significantly affecting the basic structure of the total criminal justice system. Only in this basic way can the criminal justice system be taken off the horns of the dilemma of hostility and impulsive aggression versus reasoned consideration and handling leading to successful re-entry of the "offender" into society.

Ultimately, it is only in this way that effective rehabilitation of the youthful offender can be, in fact, begun.

CHILDREN AND YOUTH
Social Problems and Social Policy

An Arno Press Collection

Abt, Henry Edward. **The Care, Cure and Education of the Crippled Child.** 1924

Addams, Jane. **My Friend, Julia Lathrop.** 1935

American Academy of Pediatrics. **Child Health Services and Pediatric Education:** Report of the Committee for the Study of Child Health Services. 1949

American Association for the Study and Prevention of Infant Mortality. **Transactions of the First Annual Meeting of the American Association for the Study and Prevention of Infant Mortality.** 1910

Baker, S. Josephine. **Fighting For Life.** 1939

Bell, Howard M. **Youth Tell Their Story:** A Study of the Conditions and Attitudes of Young People in Maryland Between the Ages of 16 and 24. 1938

Bossard, James H. S. and Eleanor S. Boll, editors. **Adolescents in Wartime.** 1944

Bossard, James H. S., editor. **Children in a Depression Decade.** 1940

Brunner, Edmund DeS. **Working With Rural Youth.** 1942

Care of Dependent Children in the Late Nineteenth and Early Twentieth Centuries. Introduction by Robert H. Bremner. 1974

Care of Handicapped Children. Introduction by Robert H. Bremner. 1974

[Chenery, William L. and Ella A. Merritt, editors]. **Standards of Child Welfare:** A Report of the Children's Bureau Conferences, May and June, 1919. 1919

The Child Labor Bulletin, 1912, 1913. 1974

Children In Confinement. Introduction by Robert M. Mennel. 1974

Children's Bureau Studies. Introduction by William M. Schmidt. 1974

Clopper, Edward N. **Child Labor in City Streets.** 1912

David, Paul T. **Barriers To Youth Employment.** 1942

Deutsch, Albert. **Our Rejected Children.** 1950

Drucker, Saul and Maurice Beck Hexter. **Children Astray.** 1923

Duffus, R[obert] L[uther] and L. Emmett Holt, Jr. **L. Emmett Holt: Pioneer of a Children's Century.** 1940

Fuller, Raymond G. **Child Labor and the Constitution.** 1923

Holland, Kenneth and Frank Ernest Hill. **Youth in the CCC.** 1942

Jacoby, George Paul. **Catholic Child Care in Nineteenth Century New York:** With a Correlated Summary of Public and Protestant Child Welfare. 1941

Johnson, Palmer O. and Oswald L. Harvey. **The National Youth Administration.** 1938

The Juvenile Court. Introduction by Robert M. Mennel. 1974

Klein, Earl E. **Work Accidents to Minors in Illinois.** 1938

Lane, Francis E. **American Charities and the Child of the Immigrant:** A Study of Typical Child Caring Institutions in New York and Massachusetts Between the Years 1845 and 1880. 1932

The Legal Rights of Children. Introduction by Sanford N. Katz. 1974

Letchworth, William P[ryor]. **Homes of Homeless Children:** A Report on Orphan Asylums and Other Institutions for the Care of Children. [1903]